Ward Smathers

A GUIDE FOR THE PRIMARY CARE PHYSICIAN

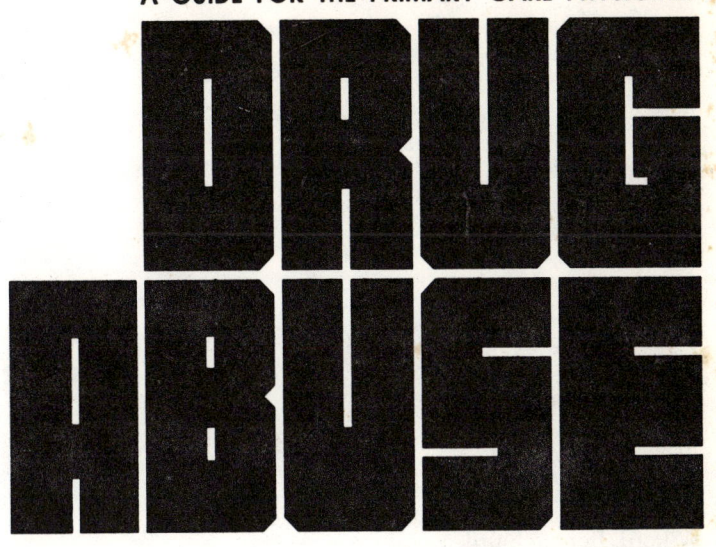

DRUG ABUSE

Bonnie Baird Wilford
Assistant Director
Department of Mental Health
American Medical Association

American Medical Association
Chicago, Illinois
1981

Library of Congress Cataloging in Publication Data
Wilford, Bonnie Baird.
　　Drug abuse, a guide for the primary care physician.

　　Includes index.
　　1. Drug abuse. 2. Family medicine. I. Title.
(DNLM: 1. Drug abuse. 2. Primary health care.
WM 270 W677d)
RC564.W54　　616.86　　80-26234
ISBN 0-89970-088-8

First Edition 1981
© Copyright 1981

American Medical Association
535 North Dearborn Street
Chicago, Illinois 60610

All Rights Reserved

Additional copies may
be purchased from:

Order Department OP-323
American Medical Association
P.O. Box 821
Monroe, WI 53566

IAF: 80-1083 OP-323: 4/81: 2M

CONTENTS

Tables in this Volume v
Preface vii

Section I: Defining the Problem

1. **Definition and Etiology of Drug Abuse** 3
   Definition of Drug Abuse 3
   Etiology of Drug Abuse 8

2. **Major Drugs of Abuse** 21
   Classification of Drugs of Abuse 22
   Nomenclature of Drugs of Abuse 23
   Opioids 23
   Depressants 33
   Stimulants 40
   Hallucinogens 47
   Phencyclidines 58
   Cannabinoids 64
   Inhalants 73

3. **Trends in Drug Abuse** 85
   Historical Preferences in Drugs 85
   Contemporary Preferences in Drugs 86

4. **Physician Attitudes Toward Drug Abuse** 103
   Sources of Attitudinal Barriers to Care 103
   Overcoming Attitudinal Barriers to Care 105

Section II: Clinical Problems and Procedures

5. **Screening for Drug Abuse in a General Patient Population** ... 113
   The Patient History 114
   The Physical Examination 116
   Confrontation and Counseling 119

6. **Care of Acute Drug Reactions** 123
   Acute Management 125
   Establishing a Differential Diagnosis 129
   Sub-Acute Management 131
   Special Problems 167

7. **Clinical Complications of Drug Abuse** 177
   Physiological Disorders 177
   Medical Problems Unrelated to, but Complicated by, Drug Abuse .. 191
   Surgical Problems 191
   Maternal and Neonatal Complications 193
   Sexual Dysfunction 197
   Psychiatric Disorders 198

8. Post-Acute Care and Rehabilitation of Drug Abusers 203
  Origins of Modern Treatment Methods 203
  Contemporary Approaches to Treatment 207
  Assessing Patient Needs 228
  Developing a Treatment Plan 231
  Providing Long-Term Follow-up 243

Section III: Legal and Social Issues

9. Legal Considerations in Treating Drug Abusers 251
  Restrictions on the Treatment of Drug Abusers 254
  Confidentiality Issues in the Treatment of Drug Abusers 257

10. Prescribing Practices and Drug Abuse 263
  Guidelines for Prescribing Psychoactive Drugs 266
  Restrictions on Prescribing Psychoactive Drugs 269
  Indications for Prescribing Psychoactive Drugs 272
  Improving Patient Compliance 279
  Identifying the "Patient Hustler" 280
  A Theoretical Framework for Rational Prescribing 282

11. The Drug-Abusing Physician 285
  State Medical Society Programs 286
  Hospital-Based Programs 288
  State Medical Board Programs 289
  Confronting the Drug-Abusing Physician 289
  Treating the Drug-Abusing Physician 291
  Opportunities for Prevention 294

12. Approaches to Drug Abuse Prevention and Early Intervention 299
  The Physician's Role in Prevention and Early Intervention 300
  Drug Abuse Programs in the Schools 305
  Drug Abuse Programs in the Workplace 306
  Sources of Additional Information 310

Index 317

TABLES IN THIS VOLUME

Table Number	Page Number
1. Localization and Possible Function of Opiate Receptors	16
2. Drug Classification Used in this Text	22
3. Opioids: Nomenclature	27
4. Opioids: Characteristics and Effects	31
5. Depressants: Nomenclature	35
6. Depressants: Characteristics and Effects	39
7. Stimulants: Nomenclature	42
8. Stimulants: Characteristics and Effects	46
9. Psychoactive Substances Used in Herbal Preparations	50
10. Hallucinogens: Nomenclature	53
11. Hallucinogens: Characteristics and Effects	57
12. Phencyclidines: Nomenclature	60
13. Phencyclidines: Characteristics and Effects	63
14. Cannabinoids: Nomenclature	67
15. Cannabinoids: Characteristics and Effects	71
16. Inhalants: Nomenclature	75
17. Inhalants: Characteristics and Effects	79
18. Chronology of Non-Medical Substance Use in the United States	86
19. Estimated Prevalence of Non-Medical Drug Use, 1979	88
20. Drugs Most Frequently Associated with Emergency Room Visits and Deaths, January-December 1979	89
21. Opioids/Analgesics: Changes in Non-Medical Use, by Age Group	90
22. Depressants: Changes in Non-Medical Use, by Age Group	91
23. Stimulants: Changes in Non-Medical Use, by Age Group	92
24. Hallucinogens: Changes in Non-Medical Use, by Age Group	94
25. Phencyclidines: Changes in Non-Medical Use, by Age Group	94
26. Marijuana: Changes in Non-Medical Use, by Age Group	95
27. Inhalants: Changes in Non-Medical Use, by Age Group	96
28. Spectrum of Physician Attitudes	107
29. Cutaneous Signs of Drug Abuse	118
30. Tests to Confirm Suspected Drug Use, by Class of Drug	120
31. Most Common Acute Drug Reactions, by Class of Drug	124
32. Clinical Manifestations of Acute Drug Reactions, by Class of Drug	132
33. Potential Elements of a Drug Treatment Plan	209
34. Phenobarbital Withdrawal Equivalents for Common Sedative/Hypnotic Drugs	217
35. Phases of Drug Abuse Treatment	234
36. Sources of Information on Drug Abuse Treatment Programs: State Agencies	239
37. Abbreviated Schedule of Controlled Substances: Federal Classification	271

PREFACE

This book is for the primary care physician, not only as a medical practitioner, but as a citizen of his or her community. It is a product of the American Medical Association's long-standing concern for problems associated with misuse and abuse of mood-altering substances, and reflects the increasing involvement of physicians in treating the physical and psychological concomitants of drug abuse, and in attempting to reduce its prevalence.

Over the years, the AMA has sponsored several conferences on drug abuse and dependence, and has issued frequent statements and reports on various aspects of this issue. *Drug Dependence: A Guide for Physicians,* published by the AMA in 1970, summarized much of that activity, as well as the research available at the time.

Since then, the volume of research on the etiology, pharmacology and sociology of drug abuse has expanded at a rapid rate. Unfortunately, so has the proportion of the population—youth and adult—that is experimenting with, or engaging in regular use of, illicit drugs. Physicians are seeing a growing number of patients whose medical and psychological problems are caused or exacerbated by drug abuse, at the same time that the relevant literature has become so rich and diverse as to require exhaustive and time-consuming study.

Recognizing this dilemma, the AMA Department of Mental Health determined that physicians might welcome a concise text that attempted to incorporate the latest research on and clinical experience with drug abuse: its causes, incidence, diagnosis, treatment and prevention.

Of course, such an ambitious project carries with it certain limitations. First is the limitation of size: no single volume can adequately reflect all of the research now available on a topic so complex as drug abuse. For more detailed information, the interested reader is directed to the numerous excellent publications available from private and governmental sources, many of which are cited in the reference lists at the end of each chapter.

Second, there must be a limitation of scope. This is most obvious in the omission of any detailed discussion of alcohol abuse. Dependence on alcohol is a problem of such magnitude as to warrant special attention in and of itself. The reader interested in this topic is referred to the AMA *Manual on Alcoholism* and other authoritative texts.

Finally, there are limits imposed by the lack of unanimity among respected researchers on many topics involved in drug abuse. Nowhere is this more apparent than in discussions of etiology. Where the research reflects multiple theories, we have attempted to present an overview of the best current thinking; omission of a particular theory, however, does not imply a negative judgment as to its validity.

Within these constraints, our goal has been to present a comprehensive view of drug abuse in a form that will be useful to primary care physicians, for it is these practitioners who frequently are called upon to diagnose, treat and counsel drug abusers, and to provide an authoritative voice in communities grown increasingly concerned and confused about how to deal with drug abuse.

To the extent that this book attains such a goal, it reflects the contributions of a great many people. Chief among these contributors are three members of the Panel on Drug Abuse of the AMA Council on Scientific Affairs: Sidney Cohen, M.D., Clinical Professor of Psychiatry at the Neuropsychiatric Institute, UCLA; Joseph H. Skom, M.D., past President of the Illinois State Medical Society and Chairman of the Panel; and David E. Smith, M.D., founder and Medical Director of the Haight-Ashbury Free Medical Clinic, San Francisco.

Richard B. Seymour, M.A., Director of the Haight-Ashbury Training and Education Projects, provided valuable suggestions and constant encouragement. Edward C. Senay, M.D., Executive Director of Substance Abuse Services and Professor of Psychiatry at the University of Chicago School of Medicine, contributed critical insights. James F. Callahan, Deputy Chief of the Manpower and Training Branch, National Institute on Drug Abuse, and John N. Chappel, M.D., Professor of Psychiatry at the University of Nevada School of Medicine, generously offered materials that were of inestimable value in preparing this text. Donald R. Bennett, M.D., Ph.D., and John R. Lewis, Ph.D., of the AMA Division of Drugs, gave freely of their time and expertise in reviewing the manuscript.

Emanuel M. Steindler, Director of the AMA Department of Mental Health, conceived the project and provided consistently helpful advice and encouragement in bringing it to fruition. Also within the Department of Mental Health, Rose Roach patiently researched the literature and offered expert guidance on sources of information that might otherwise have been overlooked. Finally, Jean Owens worked tirelessly on all the details so essential in transforming a raw manuscript into a finished work.

To all of these individuals, and to the extraordinary group of physicians and scholars whose work has enlarged our knowledge of drug abuse, we owe a debt of gratitude.

B.B.W.

Section I
Defining the Problem

CHAPTER 1
DEFINITION AND ETIOLOGY OF DRUG ABUSE

Drug abuse has become a major public health problem over the past 30 years, with the level of concern increasing in direct proportion to the size of the drug-taking population. In the 1950's, for example, drug abuse meant primarily heroin abuse, and the population involved was about 100,000 persons in the deprived areas of large cities. By 1980, on the other hand, the drug-taking population could be counted in the tens of millions. This multitude is no longer a fairly homogeneous group at the low end of the socioeconomic structure; rather, it includes a broad spectrum of social and economic strata and life stages: adolescents, young adults, the middle-aged and the elderly.

The use of drugs to alter man's perception of himself and his condition is not a recent phenomenon. Since the dawn of civilization, humans have used an almost endless variety of spirits, herbs and potions to relieve their feelings of sadness, loneliness, tension and boredom. This use for the most part has been sanctioned as acceptable behavior so long as the drugs were taken in moderation, by members of the prevailing culture, for legitimate social, religious and medicinal purposes. Drugs used immoderately or by a non-conforming counter-culture often have been made illegal and their users condemned as sinners, criminals, social deviates or emotional cripples. Thus, a particular segment of society might consider the recreational use of a drug acceptable, while the majority considers it illegal and dangerous.

The degree of hazard associated with drug use can be assessed in terms of (1) the immediate psychic and physical effects of the drug on the individual and (2) the consequences of continued drug use for society as a whole. (Based on these considerations, alcohol is far more hazardous than any other drug. As Gay and Way[1] observe, "in terms of incidence of use, complications from acute overdose, long-term effects on the physical and mental state of an individual, and ultimate consequences for society, there is no close second to alcohol.")

DEFINITION OF DRUG ABUSE

In the common parlance, the distinction between drug use and abuse is largely subjective. The person who takes drugs may define his behavior as natural and non-abusive, whereas society at large probably holds quite a different point of view. Even societal attitudes vary widely from culture to culture, and also from time to time within the same culture. For example, in Western society, chronic intoxication with alcohol usually is considered drug abuse, whereas occasional intoxication with alcohol is not. Similarly, the use of medically prescribed barbiturates to induce sleep is considered acceptable, but the use of the same amount of barbiturates, self-administered to create euphoria, is not. In most Western societies, the use of cocaine in any amount, at any time, to modify mood is considered drug abuse, but in the Andes the practice of chewing coca leaves is indulged in by 90% of the adult male population.[2]

Such cultural variations also are seen with respect to the use of opioids. In the United States, the use of medically prescribed opioid analgesics for the relief of physical pain is acceptable, but self-administration of the same drug in the same dosage to escape psychic pain is not. By contrast, the smoking of opium was, until recently, a socially acceptable practice in many Oriental cultures.

In Western society, the meaning of the term "drug abuser" has been stretched to include, at one end of the spectrum, anyone who experiments with a drug such as marijuana and, at the other extreme, one who has developed a strong physical and psychological dependence on heroin.

The breadth and imprecision of this definition are tolerable only insofar as drug abuse constitutes a social problem rather than a medical one. When drug use leads to or complicates the diagnosis and treatment of physical and psychiatric disorders (that is to say, becomes a medical problem), the relevant vocabulary must be defined more precisely. Thus, experts in the field have suggested the following general definitions.

DRUG EXPERIMENTATION: Drug "experimenters" or "experience-seekers" probably constitute the largest group of young people who take drugs. As Jaffe[2] explains, experimentation is "largely a matter of availability, curiosity, the attitude and drug-using behavior of one's friends, the social acceptability of a given form of drug use, the risks believed to be associated with experimental use, and the tendency of the individual to respect social norms."

Once drug experimenters have satisfied their curiosity, many either use drugs infrequently or discontinue their drug use altogether. For example, a 1978 survey of 17,800 seniors in 131 high schools across the United States[3] found that, while 64% of the students said they had used illicit drugs at some time in their lives, the number who were currently using such drugs was 11%. The figures for illicit drugs other than marijuana were even lower: less than one percent of the students reported current daily use of such drugs, although 37% said they had used them at least once.

DRUG USE: Drug "users" can be divided into two general categories. Those in the first group take drugs occasionally, influenced largely by the social circumstances of the moment. They can and do control their drug intake because they are aware of the effects of high and low doses. "Responsible" drinking of alcohol is a good example of this form of self-discipline.

Persons in the second category use drugs fairly regularly but are not physically or psychologically dependent on them. For example, individuals who take sleeping pills for months rather than occasionally are considered regular users. Some persons who take narcotic drugs also fall into this "regular user" category.

The fact that many users of psychoactive drugs, including heroin, cannot be cast in the traditional role of the "junkie" is underscored by a 1976 report of the Drug Abuse Council.[4] This report cited suggestive evidence in three different studies that (1) there are many more heroin users than had previously been supposed, (2) many people who use heroin are not addicts, and (3) most non-addicted heroin users may not actually require treatment.

Extensive studies of this non-addicted drug-using population have only recently been undertaken. Zinberg[5] believes such reticence probably reflects (1) the concern of the scientific community that the mere recognition of such use might encourage the unsophisticated to experiment with drugs, (2) the difficulty of achieving any reasonable quantitative estimates of such use, and (3) the imprecision of the terminology used to describe drug-taking styles.

A fourth concern may be related to the fact that almost all drug dependent persons studied report that they began their drug-taking as occasional users and, at least initially, believed they could maintain this level of use indefinitely without developing physical or psychological dependence.

In defining drug use as opposed to abuse, it becomes crucial to consider not only the nature and amount of the drug used, but also the situation in which the drug is used, the personality, experience and expectations of the person using it, and the prevailing attitudes of society.[1]

DRUG ABUSE: Scientifically speaking, "excessive drug intake" would be a more accurate and precise term than "drug abuse." After all, people abuse themselves, not drugs. "Drug abuse," however, is accepted terminology throughout the world in both professional and lay circles; for that reason, it is the term used throughout this text.

There are numerous definitions of drug abuse, some so broad that they tend to blur the boundaries of the subject, others so narrow that they exclude a wide range of relevant experience.

At one extreme, excessive intake of any substance is termed drug abuse. Under this rubric would fall the 10-cup-a-day coffee drinker, the two-pack-a-day cigaret smoker, and the four-in-one-gulp aspirin taker.

At the other extreme, only chronic ingestion that leads to a state of physical and psychological dependence is termed drug abuse. This definition rejects intermittent use, which accounts for perhaps 75% of all psychoactive drug-taking.

Between these extremes, other definitions incorporate one or more of the following criteria for drug abuse:

- Excessive taking of any psychoactive substance, as distinguished from a drug that does not act primarily on the central nervous system.
- Self-administration of a drug for non-therapeutic purposes or without the advice or direction of a physician.
- "Over-prescription" or "over-administration" of drugs (especially barbiturates, tranquilizers and amphetamines) under the direction of a physician.
- Drug-taking that causes or exacerbates any physical or mental illness or impairment.
- Drug-taking that leads to anti-social behavior.

For medical purposes, which of these concepts is useful?

Excessive (as opposed to moderate or minimal) *intake* effectively removes from concern those persons who are not likely to require general medical or psychiatric intervention as a consequence of their drug use.

Self-administration is a useful concept, if it is qualified to include amounts and frequencies beyond those prescribed or otherwise indicated for therapy.

Over-prescription and *over-administration* under the direction of a physician, on the other hand, are not useful concepts because these activities only contribute to drug abuse; they do not constitute drug abuse in and of themselves. Such practices are better described as drug "misuse."

Injury to one's physical or mental self is a useful concept, because it represents drug use as a personal health hazard.

Anti-social behavior associated with drug-taking, although limited to certain psychoactive substances, is of medical interest because of the psychiatric implications of such behavior and because of possible injury to others through acts of aggression, accidental injury or the spread of disease by those under the influence of drugs.

Drug abuse therefore can be defined as *the ingestion of a psychoactive substance that is capable of producing physical or psychological dependence, in an amount and at a frequency likely to result in overt intoxication or to lead to physical or psychological problems or anti-social behavior.* Said another way, when the continued use of a mood-altering substance means more to an individual than the problems associated with such use, that individual can be described as abusing drugs.

DRUG DEPENDENCE: Most persons in the world today are drug dependent, according to Seevers,[6] in the sense that they have a psychological reliance on mild stimulants such as caffeine and nicotine or on potent agents that they use therapeutically in a controlled way. Such dependence has little social import because its behavioral concomitants are minimal. Of major concern is the dependence that develops in certain susceptible individuals following the continual use of more potent psychoactive substances.

"Drug dependence" is now an accepted term in the medical literature, replacing and incorporating two other terms, "addiction" and "habituation," as recommended by the World Health Organization. WHO defines drug dependence as *a state, psychic or also sometimes physical, resulting from the interaction between a living organism and a drug, and characterized by behavioral and other responses that always include a compulsive desire or need to use the drug on a continuous basis in order to experience its effects and/or avoid the discomfort of its absence.*[7]

Physical dependence develops when body cells have adapted to a new biochemical environment that contains the addicting drug (or metabolite of the drug) to an extent that a new steady-state equilibrium has evolved. The drug then is an essential constituent whose presence has become necessary to cellular functioning.[1]

If *tolerance* develops, increasing quantities of the drug must be administered to produce the same pharmacological effects. (Tolerance also can develop to the effects of certain drugs that do not cause physical dependence, such as amphetamines.) Development of tolerance to one drug in a class usually indicates *cross-tolerance* to other drugs in the same class.

Psychological dependence is characterized by the compulsive use of a drug and overwhelming involvement in drug-seeking and drug-taking. The intensity of such dependence may range from a mild desire to a strong compulsion to use a drug.[2] In a state of psychological dependence, the craving for a particular drug is not necessarily related to any physical need for the substance, but rather to the individual's seeking a type of reward that is psychodynamically satisfying for him. When physical dependence becomes established following chronic use, however, it serves as a powerful secondary reinforcer of psychological dependence.

Psychological dependence often persists for extended periods beyond the disappearance of physical dependence, as demonstrated chiefly by relapse to drug abuse.[2] It is questionable whether an individual ever returns to his pre-drug state, either physically or psychologically, following recovery from drug dependence.

There is abundant evidence that dependence on one drug or class of drugs can lead to dependence on other types of drugs. The ability of one drug to suppress the symptoms of physical dependence produced by another drug and to maintain a physically dependent state is termed *cross-dependence*. Jaffe[2] observes that cross-dependence may be partial or complete and that the degree of cross-dependence is more closely related to pharmacological effects than to chemical similarities.

In this volume, the term "drug abuse" is used to describe a high level of involvement in the non-medical use of drugs and other substances, *with or without* the presence of clinically significant physical and psychological dependence. It should be noted, however, that the ICD-9* and the DSM-III** define drug abuse as all illicit use up to, but *not* including, the development of dependence.

ETIOLOGY OF DRUG ABUSE

Just as definitions of drug abuse vary, so do explanations of its etiology. Many variables enter the question: who the individual is, physically, psychologically and socially; what substance he is taking; why he is taking it; how much he takes and how often he takes it; where and with whom he takes it. Even the person who abuses drugs may harbor a broad range of attitudes toward his own actions: he may or may not approve of his behavior, may or may not be comfortable with the goals and consequences of his drug abuse.

Nurco[8] suggests that, although the desire to use drugs generally is a voluntary one, the motivation to select a particular drug—or, for that matter, to use any drug at all—may arise from powerful physical, psychological, social and economic needs.

---

*International Classification of Disease, 9th revision (World Health Organization, Geneva, 1979)

**Diagnostic and Statistical Manual, 3rd edition (American Psychiatric Association, Washington, D.C. 1980)

Huba et al[9] propose that drug-taking behavior is caused by several large constellations of forces within and outside the individual. They suggest that these factors interact to modify each other, thus determining the presence or absence of a variety of behaviors, including drug abuse. They group these "domains of influence" approximately as follows:

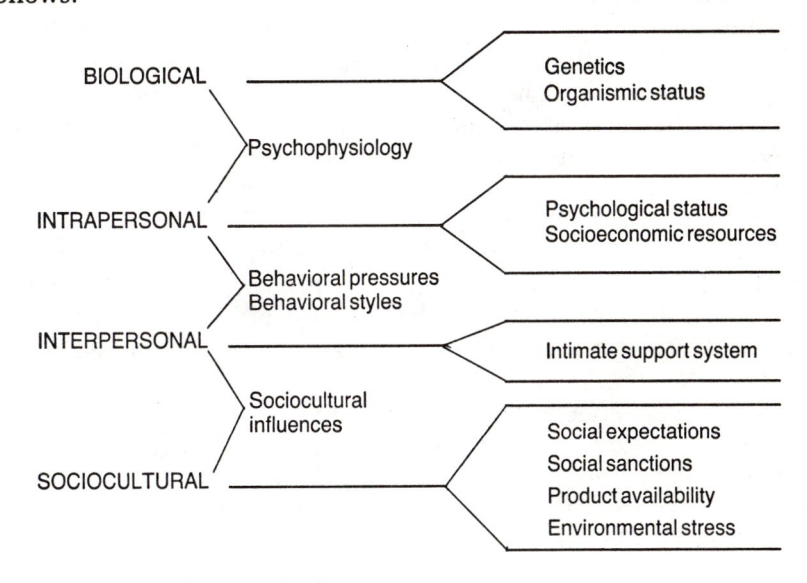

Domain	Via	Factors
BIOLOGICAL	Psychophysiology	Genetics; Organismic status
INTRAPERSONAL	Behavioral pressures; Behavioral styles	Psychological status; Socioeconomic resources
INTERPERSONAL	Sociocultural influences	Intimate support system
SOCIOCULTURAL		Social expectations; Social sanctions; Product availability; Environmental stress

Solomon,[10] while acknowledging that there are mixed types, identifies three major categories of drug abuse, each with its own dominant etiology. The first, "social drug-taking," he sees as arising from identity-seeking; the second, "neurotic drug-taking," as a means to obtain relief from anxiety; and the third, "psychotic drug-taking," as an escape from deep-seated problems.

Blachly[11] believed that certain high-risk individuals can be identified early, and asserted that "this predictability may be dramatized by considering how we might maliciously and deliberately set about in childhood to grow a person to be a high risk.... The fundamental rule is to structure the environment so the child is unable to make any long-range allegiances or predictions; particularly, make it impossible for him to predict the consequences of his own behavior."

In attempting to identify predictors of drug abuse at an individual level, Nurco[8] and others have found that "the most potent [predictors] are those that establish a pattern of deviance at an early age, often beginning in elementary school. Moreover, it appears that the earlier the onset of the deviant behaviors, the more malignant the process involved and the more ominous the prognosis." Robins[12] suggests that, while occasional or *moderate* drug use seems not to reflect an antisocial personality, the correlates of *serious* drug abuse are very similar to those of antisocial personality.

Other studies show that young people who come from intact families that emphasize traditional values seem to be at a markedly lower risk of drug abuse than youth who come from single-parent families that have less rigid convictions and more opportunistic lifestyles.[8]

These explanations, of course, deal only in a general way with causative factors and predictors. To delve deeper into the etiology of drug abuse, we must consider some of the relevant psychological, sociological and physiological factors separately, although they are almost always intertwined in actual experience.

PSYCHOLOGICAL FACTORS: Many psychological factors have been found to be operative in some cases of drug abuse, but to say that any of them are common to all cases would be purely speculative. For example, attempts have been made to construct a model of the drug-dependent personality as one with diminished self-esteem and capacity for affection, low frustration tolerance, excessive attachment to mother or a mother-substitute, and feelings of hostility toward father or a father-figure. Such a formulation might adequately describe an appreciable number of drug-dependent persons but, even if it did, it would not necessarily represent a cause-and-effect relationship.

Even less valid are depictions of all drug abusers as "sick-minded" or "unhealthy personalities." A psychological inventory of 148 college students[13] showed that those who used marijuana were socially poised, open to experience and concerned about the feelings of others, even though they also tended to be impulsive, pleasure-seeking and rebellious. Non-users were characterized in this study as generally responsible and rule-abiding, but also as inflexible, conventional and relatively narrow in their interests.

As increasing numbers of adolescents have begun to experiment with and regularly use psychoactive substances at progressively earlier ages, numerous psychological and demographic profiles of drug abusers in this age group have been constructed. Adolescents who use drugs heavily have been described both clinically and in survey investigations as manifesting more psychopathology than non-users. Described symptoms include depression, feelings of inadequacy, frustration and helplessness, as well as immaturity, self-alienation, poor object relations, and major deficiencies in ego structure and functioning. Green[14] notes that "a relative lack of social inhibitions, when coupled with psychic turmoil, leads some individuals to engage in a wider range of deviant behaviors, including drug use, than are manifested in their more stable, less impulsive counterparts."

Finally, Pittel[15] theorizes that some individuals who appear to have a reasonable degree of personality organization may become dependent on drugs when they are subjected to unusually severe situational stress, chronic pain or anxiety. He believes this is especially prevalent among young adolescents who experience unusual stresses in addition to "the normal social and biological burdens of puberty. The normal child undergoes massive personality reorganization at this time, so the preadolescent ego is particularly vulnerable to any additional assaults. The early adolescent who finds that drugs can compensate for temporary ego weakness might well become drug dependent without ever testing his own resources. Just as the superego is said to dissolve in alcohol, it is likely that other personality structures are weakened by a continual reliance on chemical rather than psychological means of dealing with anxiety."

To explain why some individuals become dependent on drugs, while other users can stop short of physical or psychological dependence, Nurco[8] offers six factors, operating singly or in combination: (1) a need to suppress frustration and aggressive impulses, (2) inability to defer gratification, (3) lack of adequate sexual identification, (4) insufficient means to achieve socially acceptable goals, (5) use of risk-taking behavior to demonstrate personal adequacy, and (6) suppression of boredom.

Obviously, the subjective euphoric effects of drug-taking are a precursor to repeated drug abuse and to the development of psychological dependence. The dysphoria that accompanies abstinence in a physically dependent individual also may be seen as directly promoting subsequent drug-seeking behavior.

Other possible influences of a psychogenic nature are not so obvious or clear-cut. We are on firm ground, however, when we say that psychological factors do play a role in the causation and development of drug abuse. Examples abound in the literature and in the daily office practice of many physicians.

SOCIOLOGICAL FACTORS: Sociological factors operate largely through the psychological make-up of each individual: seldom can they be isolated and said to motivate behavior directly. Responses to such influences thus are properly termed "psychosocial" to reflect the fact that each individual perceives social phenomena in terms of his own experiences and psychological make-up and reacts to them in relatively unique ways.

The exceptions to this generalization are those sociological elements that do not depend on personal motivation. For example, the actual and perceived availability of drugs on a city street, at a suburban school or in a hospital pharmacy is a necessary precondition for—and, some investigators[16] would argue, a factor motivating toward—drug abuse. Drug availability may be related to levels of morbidity and mortality among drug users in the same way the Ledermann (log-normal) curve[17] depicts alcohol availability as positively correlated to levels of alcohol-related morbidity and mortality. Analysis of recent government data on the perceived familiarity and proximity of illicit drugs in various population groups, as compared with the actual levels of use of the same drugs in those groups, suggests that *opportunity* may be the variable that bridges the gap between community factors and individual response in predicting drug-using behavior.[16,18]

As noted earlier, many researchers point to *family relationships* as a factor in the development of drug abuse and dependence, and it is in the family that the interplay of social and psychological factors is most evident. Feelings of love and hostility, of dominance and dependence, of rejection and acceptance—all are evoked in the intensely personal interaction that takes place in the home. Researchers[8] have found that families in which drug abuse is absent or infrequent are characterized by adherence to traditional values, including perceived love between parents and offspring; by parents whose influence is stronger than that of the peer group; by a tendency to downplay frustrations and deny negative feelings; by considerable religious involvement and avowed love of country; by emphasis on self-control and discipline; and by adherence to traditional sex roles.

Parallel studies[8] have shown that families in which drug abuse is a frequent behavior often are characterized by a dominant, overprotective mother and a detached, uninvolved or absent father; by a tendency for males to continue living arrangements with their mothers or other female relatives long past the usual age; and by parental acceptance of, or involvement with, alcohol and drugs.

Peer pressure to conform emerges as a factor in drug abuse as the child approaches adolescence. Ungerleider and Bowen[19] have observed that "in some schools, 'turning on' is a puberty rite for entry into the adolescent world." The child or adolescent not only may be introduced to the world of drugs by his companions, he might well be sustained and supported in this activity through a drug subculture or mini-society that includes drug-taking as an expected behavior. In fact, as Wikler [20] suggests, "the rituals and argots constantly associated with use of particular drugs may come, in time, to elicit effects similar to those produced by the drug itself ... and thus facilitate renewed participation in the cult, including drug use."

Such specialized cults or "in groups" have their own objectives, taboos and sanctions, the last ranging from reprimands to ostracism to corporal punishment. Even when the dangers of drug abuse are comprehended by individual members of the group, those dangers might seem to be outweighed by the penalties involved in not going along with the rest of the group, especially when one of those penalties is social isolation.

There seems little doubt that peer pressure is overwhelmingly important in the initiation into drug use and abuse.[18] Brown and others[21] found that the influence of friends and/or relatives was the major reason for first use of heroin in more than half of the cases surveyed, and that peer influence was especially strong among female and juvenile heroin users. Zinberg[22] maintains that "the social setting, with its formal and informal controls, its capacity to develop new informal social sanctions and rituals, and its transmission of information in numerous informal ways, is a crucial factor in the controlled use of any intoxicant."

The *community*—both the immediate environment and the world beyond—also can be influential in numerous ways. Community pressures generally are regarded as positive influences that help individuals conform to society's norms. It has been suggested, however, that "addiction, at least in certain urban environments, may be less a response designed to meet the pathology of the individual than a response designed to meet the pathology of the community."[21] Indeed, drug use—especially heroin use—long has been regarded as a "symbol of belonging" in the ghetto, and the heroin-dependent person allegedly is reinforced by the drug culture that exists there. Moreover, Espada[23] believes that "there is a sharply qualitative difference in opiate abuse in the minority communities. Opiate abuse affecting one-half of one percent of the white adult male population may be (and often is) viewed as a . . . significant form of deviancy. However, when a similar problem affects . . . five percent of the young adult males in the minority communities, another situation develops. Involvement with or addiction to opiates then becomes a significant way of life, pervading a community; a competing and often destructive lifestyle. It becomes a condition the community lives with at all times, rather than an event galvanizing people into action."

Another facet of environmental linkage is the role of unemployment in drug abuse and ghetto life. Although comparatively few data are available on the employment status of individuals prior to their development of drug dependence, O'Donnell[24] noted that less than half the persons he studied showed a pattern of steady employment prior to the start of their drug-taking behavior. In similar studies, Nurco and Lerner[25] found an unemployment rate of 47.5%. Of course, unemployment is a daily fact of life in the ghetto, with as much as half of all poverty area residents unemployed at any given time.[8] As Ward[26] has observed, joblessness deprives individuals of the status attached to a trade or profession. Nurco[8] adds that this lack of status, coupled with the absence of "formalized and long-term family arrangements, ... leads to a type of extended adolescence, at least with respect to steady or long-term employment. In such a situation, status is acquired through illicit activities."

If the degradation and despair of the ghetto induce members of disadvantaged groups to use drugs, the detachment and isolation of high-rise apartment dwelling may be equally powerful influences on the more privileged classes. In many cultures, frequent use of hallucinogens is associated with some form of social deprivation; perhaps the "privilege" of upper-class isolation should be regarded as a form of deprivation in American culture today.[27]

The fear, anxiety and feelings of hopelessness occasioned by actual and threatened national and international crises unquestionably have some influence on patterns of drug abuse, although their role can be exaggerated. Nonetheless, many social commentators have observed that contemporary American society is marked by a growing demand for the institutional management of physical and psychic pain, replacing the traditional emphasis on competence in dealing with suffering. Illich[28] suggests that "by becoming unnecessary, pain has become unbearable," making it culturally preferable to flee pain rather than face it, even at the cost of addiction.

Institutions such as schools, places of employment and churches can be strong forces directed against drug abuse. However, to the degree that they are seen by the young as sources of confinement and unreasonable regimentation, they serve as citadels of the Establishment, against which drug abuse—as a weapon of rebellion—can be directed. In this sense, institutionalized living can lay the groundwork for drug abuse by prompting vague desires to "break out." Increasingly, institutions such as schools and workplaces also are serving as marketplaces for illicit drugs and thus enhancing their availability.

PHYSIOLOGICAL FACTORS: What role does physiology play in drug abuse? The factors cited above and those identified by other researchers traditionally have been classified as social and environmental variables. They clearly imply that drug abuse is determined by an individual's environment, and there is little doubt that environmental factors play a crucial role. However, physiological factors also are important. For example, Jaffe[2] suggests that one person may experience a more intense response to a drug than another person taking the same drug at the same dose. He speculates that such heightened reactions might be the result of differences in sensitivity to drug effects and that "constitutional and genetic factors . . . might be responsible . . . for unusually positive or negative responses to drug use or drug withdrawal." Schuckit[29] points to a small but growing body of evidence that genetic factors may have a significant role in alcoholism and in certain forms of deviant and anti-social behavior, including drug abuse. Dole[8] has predicted that a specific biochemical abnormality will be discovered among alcohol- and drug-dependent persons.

Whatever part physiology may play in the development of a drug-dependent state, there is ample evidence that physiological factors are involved in the perpetuation of drug abuse. For example, Snyder[30] hypothesizes that administration of exogenous opiates stimulates the neurons that produce enkephalins, overloads the receptor sites and halts further production of endogenous opiates. When the supply of exogenous opiates is cut off (as during withdrawal), the neuron receptor sites—lacking the supply of endogenous opiates that normally bathe them—become exposed, leading to the CNS symptoms associated with opiate withdrawal.

The presence of analgesic receptor sites that interact with various chemical compounds to produce analgesia was proposed many years ago, but it is only within the past decade that researchers[30,31,32,33] have identified specific binding sites as receptors and determined their anatomical distribution.

The density of opiate binding sites varies markedly in different regions of the central nervous system. These sites are heavily concentrated in anatomical areas associated with physiological functions that are altered by opioid drugs, suggesting a correlation between site of action and drug effect. Snyder[30] has suggested linkages between the location of the various receptors and the functions they may perform, as shown in Table 1, below.

Neurochemical evidence suggests that the receptors are associated with synapses of the brain and that they function as sites for a natural neurotransmitter substance.[34,35] Endogenous polypeptides, which bind to opiate binding sites and mimic some of the actions of opioid drugs, have been found in brain tissue and identified as naturally occurring fragments of lipotropin with opiate activity (β-endorphin, γ-endorphin, α-endorphin) and as naturally occurring endogenous opioid peptides that appear to arise biosynthetically from precursors other than lipotropin (α-neo-endorphin, leucine enkephalin, β-neo-endorphin, methionine enkephalin).[30]

Several types of receptors have been postulated to explain the different actions of the various opioids. These have been designated υ, κ and σ. The υ-receptor probably mediates morphine-like analgesia

TABLE 1

Localization and Possible Function of Opiate Receptors

Location	Functions Influenced by Opiates
Spinal cord	
Laminae I and II	Pain perception in body
Brainstem	
Substantia gelatinosa of spinal tract of caudal trigeminal	Pain perception in body
Nucleus of solitary tract, nucleus commissuralis, nucleus ambiguus	Vagal reflexes, respiratory depression, cough suppression, orthostatic hypotension, inhibition of gastric secretion
Area postrema	Nausea and vomiting
Locus coeruleus	Euphoria
Habenula-interpeduncular nucleus-fasciculus retroflexus	Limbic, emotional effects, euphoria
Pretectal area (medial and lateral optic nuclei)	Miosis
Superior colliculus	Miosis
Ventral nucleus of lateral geniculate	Miosis
Dorsal, lateral, medial terminal nuclei of accessory optic pathway	Endocrine effects through light modulation
Dorsal cochlear nucleus	Unknown
Parabrachial nucleus	Euphoria in a link to locus coeruleus
Diencephalon	
Infundibulum	ADH secretion
Lateral part of medial thalamic nucleus, internal and external thalamic laminae, intralaminar (centromedian) nuclei, periventricular nucleus of thalamus	Pain perception
Telencephalon	
Amygdala	Emotional effects
Caudate, putamen, globus pallidus, nucleus accumbens	Motor rigidity
Subfornical organ	Hormonal effects
Interstitial nucleus of stria terminalis	Emotional effects

Source: Snyder, S. H. The opiate receptor and morphine-like peptides in the brain *American Journal of Psychiatry* 135(6):648 (June 1978) Copyright 1978, American Psychiatric Association. Reprinted by permission.

and euphoria. The κ-receptor probably mediates pentazocine-like analgesia, sedation and miosis. The σ-receptor mediates dysphoria and hallucinations produced by pentazocine and other drugs with antagonist activity.[34,35,36]

The relative analgesic potency of the various opioid drugs seems to parallel their affinity for specific binding sites. Morphine, for example, has a greater affinity for opiate binding sites than does codeine.[34] Similarly, the benzodiazepines of higher potency bind to their receptors more firmly than do those of lower potency.[37] As Cohen[38] notes, when benzodiazepines are ranked according to their clinical potency, the ranking generally corresponds to their affinity for the identified receptors.

Although the discovery of the opiate receptors and naturally occurring opioids has led to a greater understanding of the physiological actions of all dependence-producing substances, additional studies are needed to explain the mechanism of action more fully. More detailed discussions of this subject are presented in many reviews in the literature.[30-41]

CONCLUSIONS

Because etiology is multi-dimensional, it is not always possible to identify even the principal factors leading to drug abuse by a given individual. Yet, it is important that an attempt be made to do so in every case, so that long-term treatment and rehabilitation can be individualized. Physicians and other treatment personnel should keep in mind that psychological, sociological and physiological elements invariably are interwoven and that, to be successful, therapeutic plans must take all three components into consideration.

REFERENCES

1. Gay, G. R. and Way, E. L. Pharmacology of the opiate narcotics *in* D. E. Smith and G. R. Gay (eds.) *It's So Good, Don't Even Try It Once* (Prentice-Hall, Englewood Cliffs, N.J., 1972)
2. Jaffe, J. H. Drug addiction and drug abuse *in* A. G. Gilman, L. S. Goodman and A. Gilman (eds.) *The Pharmacological Basis of Therapeutics* (Macmillan, New York City, 1980)
3. Johnston, L. D., Bachman, J. G. and O'Malley, P. M. *Drugs and The Class of '78: Behaviors, Attitudes and Recent National Trends* (National Institute on Drug Abuse, Rockville, Md., 1979)
4. Drug Abuse Council, *The Heroin Epidemics: A Study of Heroin Use in the United States, 1965-1975* (Spectrum Publications, New York City, 1976)
5. Zinberg, N. E. Nonaddictive opiate use *in* R. I. DuPont, A. Goldstein and J. O'Donnell (eds.) *Handbook on Drug Abuse* (National Institute on Drug Abuse, Rockville, Md., 1979)
6. Seevers, M. H. Psychopharmacological elements of drug dependence JAMA 206:1263 (November 4, 1968)
7. *WHO Expert Committee on Addiction-Producing Drugs, 13th Report* publication 273, World Health Organization Technical Report Series, Geneva (1964)

8. Nurco, D. N. Etiological aspects of drug abuse in R. I. DuPont, A. Goldstein and J. O'Donnell (eds.) *Handbook on Drug Abuse* (National Institute on Drug Abuse, Rockville, Md., 1979)
9. Huba, G. J., Wingard, J. A. and Bentler, P. M. Framework for an interactive theory of drug use in D. J. Lettieri, M. Sayers and H. W. Pearson (eds.) *Theories on Drug Abuse: Selected Contemporary Perspectives* Research Monograph 30 (National Institute on Drug Abuse, Rockville Md., 1980)
10. Solomon, P. Medical management of drug dependence *JAMA* 206(7):1521 (November 11, 1968)
11. Blachly, P. H. The seductive threshold as a concept for prophylaxis in P. H. Blachly (ed.) *Drug Abuse: Data and Debate* (Chas. C. Thomas, Springfield, Ill., 1970)
12. Robins, L. N. The natural history of drug abuse in D. J. Lettieri, M. Sayers and H. W. Pearson (eds.) *Theories on Drug Abuse: Selected Contemporary Perspectives* Research Monograph 30 (National Institute on Drug Abuse, Rockville, Md., 1980)
13. Hogan, R. et al. Personality correlates of undergraduate marijuana use *J. Consulting and Clinical Psychology* 35(1):58 (1970)
14. Green, J. Overview of adolescent drug use in G. M. Beschner and A. S. Friedman (eds.) *Youth Drug Abuse* (D. C. Heath & Company, Lexington, Mass., 1979)
15. Pittel, S. M. Psychological aspects of heroin and other drug dependence in D. E. Smith and G. R. Gay (eds.) *It's So Good, Don't Even Try It Once* (Prentice-Hall, Englewood Cliffs, N.J., 1972)
16. Rittenhouse, J. D. *Social Psychological Aspects of Drug Abuse* (Paper presented at the annual meeting of the American Psychological Association, New York City, August 1979)
17. Hyman, M. H. The Ledermann curve: comments on a symposium *Journal of Studies on Alcohol* 40(3):339 (1979)
18. Winick, C. A theory of drug dependence based on role, access to, and attitudes toward drugs in D. J. Lettieri, M. Sayers and H. W. Pearson (eds.) *Theories on Drug Abuse: Selected Contemporary Perspectives* Research Monograph 30 (National Institute on Drug Abuse, Rockville, Md., 1980)
19. Ungerleider, J. T. and Bowen, H. L. Drug abuse and the schools *American Journal of Psychiatry* 125(12) (June 1969)
20. Wikler, A. Some implications of conditioning therapy for problems of drug abuse in P. H. Blachly (ed.) *Drug Abuse: Data and Debate* (Chas. C. Thomas, Springfield, Ill., 1970)
21. Brown, B. S., Gauvney, S. K., Meyers, M. B. and Stark, S. D. In their own words: addicts' reasons for initiating and withdrawing from heroin *International Journal of the Addictions* 6(4):635 (1971)
22. Zinberg, N. E. The social setting as a control mechanism in intoxicant use in D. J. Lettieri, M. Sayers and H. W. Pearson (eds.) *Theories on Drug Abuse: Selected Contemporary Perspectives* Research Monograph 30 (National Institute on Drug Abuse, Rockville, Md., 1980)
23. Espada, F. The drug abuse industry and the "minority" communities: time for change in R. I. Dupont, A. Goldstein and J. O'Donnell (eds.)

Handbook on Drug Abuse (National Institute on Drug Abuse, Rockville, Md., 1979)

24. O'Donnell, J. A. *Narcotic Addicts in Kentucky* (National Institute on Mental Health, Rockville, Md., 1969)
25. Nurco, D. N. and Lerner, M. Occupational skills and lifestyles of narcotics addicts in C. Winick (ed.) *Sociological Aspects of Drug Dependence* (CRC Press, Cleveland, Ohio, 1974)
26. Ward, H. *Employment and Addiction: Overview of Issues* (Drug Abuse Council, Washington, D.C., 1973)
27. Johnson, B. D. Toward a theory of drug subcultures in D. J. Lettieri, M. Sayers and H. W. Pearson (eds.) *Theories on Drug Abuse: Selected Contemporary Perspectives* Research Monograph 30 (National Institute on Drug Abuse, Rockville, Md., 1980)
28. Illich, I. Medical nemesis *Lancet* 918 (May 11, 1974)
29. Schuckit, M. A. A theory of alcohol and drug abuse: a genetic approach in D. J. Lettieri, M. Sayers and H. W. Pearson (eds.) *Theories on Drug Abuse: Selected Contemporary Perspectives* Research Monograph 30 (National Institute on Drug Abuse, Rockville, Md., 1980)
30. Snyder, S. H. The opiate receptor and morphine-like peptides in the brain *American Journal of Psychiatry* 135(6):648 (June 1978)
31. Smyth, D. G. Opioid peptides: a new understanding of pain; 1. The endogenous opiate peptides *British Pharmaceutical Journal* 356 (October 6, 1979)
32. Snyder, Scott. The opiates, opioid peptides (endorphins), and the opiate receptor *Texas Medicine* 75:41 (September 1979)
33. Goldstein, A. Recent advances in basic research relevant to drug abuse in R. I. DuPont, A. Goldstein and J. O'Donnell (eds.) *Handbook on Drug Abuse* (National Institute on Drug Abuse, Rockville, Md., 1979)
34. *AMA Drug Evaluations, Fourth Edition* (American Medical Association, Chicago, Ill., 1980)
35. Hollt, V. and Wuster, M. The opiate receptors in A. Herz (ed.) *Developments in Opiate Research* (Marcel Dekker, Inc., New York City, 1978)
36. Bunney, W. E. Jr. (moderator). Basic and clinical studies of endorphins *Annals of Internal Medicine* 91:239 (August 1979)
37. Paul, S. M., Marangos, P. J., Skolnick, P. and Goodwin, F. K. Brain-specific benzodiazepine receptors and putative endogenous "benzodiazepine-like" compounds *Psychopharmacology Bulletin* 16(1):9 (1980)
38. Cohen, S. Benzodiazepine receptors in the brain *Drug Abuse & Alcoholism Newsletter* 8(9):1 (November 1979)
39. Cleghorn, R. A. Endorphins — morphine-like peptides of the brain *Canadian Journal of Psychiatry* 25:182 (March 1980)
40. Adler, M. W. Minireview: opioid peptides *Life Sciences* 26(7):497 (1980)
41. DiPalma, J. R. Analgesic polypeptides: the endorphins *American Family Practice* 21(3):155 (March 1980)

CHAPTER 2
MAJOR DRUGS OF ABUSE

Why are certain drugs abused? Which of their effects are so desirable that users are willing to risk social and legal sanctions, heavy economic costs, and the possibility of serious illness or even death? Why do different persons select different drugs of abuse? What kinds of emotional experiences do they seek?

All drugs of abuse alter the user's mood and either raise or lower consciousness. The changes in awareness induced by drugs range from a complete obliteration of consciousness, as effected by large doses of central nervous system depressants, to a vast intensification of awareness, as experienced in the LSD state. However, some drugs that markedly alter awareness are rarely or never abused. The avoidance of such drugs may be partially due to their unpleasant side effects, although some drugs that produce equally unpleasant side effects are widely abused.

The best explanation for the selection of one drug over another probably relates to the feeling tone called euphoria, or "high." Cohen[1] describes this sensation as "perenially sought after. This sense of physical and emotional well-being has been searched for since the ascent of man and woman. Almost every society has its culturally acceptable euphoriant. We even have accumulating evidence that other animal species are inclined to use agents that will intoxicate them."

However, the classical interpretation of euphoria as "a feeling of well-being or elation"[2] is difficult to reconcile with the effects of some drugs that are widely abused. Cowen et al[3] suggest that drugs such as heroin may be used to relieve persistent feelings of defeat, not by producing an opposite feeling (such as success), but by allowing the user to suppress the negative feeling. As Cohen[1] explains, the "search for euphoria is, for many, really a flight from dysphoria, or from what is more painful, aphoria."

In addition to the capacity to produce euphoria, drugs have other characteristics that help determine which substances become popular as drugs of abuse. These characteristics — which are common to many, but not all, abused drugs — include the ability to produce tolerance in the user and the appearance of a withdrawal syndrome if the drug is discontinued after a period of regular use.[4]

Another factor in the selection process probably is the speed with which a given drug takes effect. For example, cocaine acts more rapidly than amphetamines, and secobarbital more rapidly than phenobarbital. The drug with the more rapid action usually is the drug more widely abused.[1]

An additional explanation is that the choice of a drug of abuse — and even the extent of that abuse — may be related to the nature and extent of an individual's ego impairment. Pittel[5] suggests that persons with few or minor ego impairments are likely to prefer specific drugs, while persons with many or relatively severe ego impairments are likely to show a pattern of multiple drug use or to become truly dependent on a particular drug. He cites as an example moderate users of psychedelic drugs, who appear to have certain well-developed ego capacities and to get along well without their preferred drug, as contrasted with heroin addicts who, he says, show little ability to deal with stress or frustration.

CLASSIFICATION OF DRUGS OF ABUSE

Drugs of abuse can be classified in several ways, some of which are best for research and others of which are more pharmacologically accurate. They are classified in this text according to their most prominent effects on the central nervous system, because this method seems most useful to the practicing clinician. The various classes, with examples of the most frequently abused drugs in each class, are presented in Table 2 and explained below.

TABLE 2

Drug Classification Used In This Text	
Class	Examples
Opioids	Heroin, morphine, methadone
Depressants	Barbiturates, methaqualone
Stimulants	Amphetamines, cocaine
Hallucinogens	LSD, mescaline
Phencyclidines	PCP, ketamine
Cannabinoids	Marijuana, hashish
Inhalants	Acetone, benzene, ethyl acetate, nitrous oxide

OPIOIDS: Also called "narcotic analgesics," these drugs are used clinically to decrease pain. This class includes morphine and other alkaloids of opium, as well as synthetic morphine-like substances and semisynthetic opium derivatives.[6]

DEPRESSANTS: These drugs depress excitable tissues at all levels of the brain.[4] The central nervous system depressants include almost all antianxiety drugs (such as diazepam) and sleeping aids (such as chloral hydrate).

STIMULANTS: The most prominent effect of these drugs is their ability to stimulate the central nervous system.[6] Aside from caffeine, the stimulants most commonly encountered in clinical situations are the amphetamines and cocaine.

HALLUCINOGENS: These substances produce hallucinations, usually of a visual nature,[6] but sometimes also auditory or olefactory. The hallucinogens, which have no accepted medical use, include LSD and mescaline.

PHENCYCLIDINES: Phencyclidine and phencyclidine analogs are pharmacologically related to the hallucinogens and produce somewhat similar effects. However, several researchers believe that these drugs constitute a separate class because they yield different symptoms of tolerance and withdrawal.[7]

CANNABINOIDS: Marijuana and hashish, as well as their principal active ingredient, delta-9-tetrahydrocannabinol (THC), produce an intoxicated state marked by altered time sense, euphoria and — at high doses — hallucinations.[9]

INHALANTS: This class includes solvents that are widely used in cleaning compounds, aerosol sprays, fuels and glues. As drugs of abuse, inhalants are used to induce altered states of consciousness, primarily lightheadedness and confusion.[4,6]

NOMENCLATURE OF DRUGS OF ABUSE

The nomenclature of almost all drugs in use today includes a chemical or nonproprietary (generic) name and one or more trade names. With drugs of abuse, the clinician also will encounter a variety of "street names" applied by users. This part of the nomenclature changes rapidly and varies from one geographic area to another, so that, for example, heroin may be called "horse" in one part of the country and "estuffa" in another. Despite the transitory nature of these street names, they are a significant aspect of the drug culture. Street language becomes important to the clinician because many drug users, especially the recently initiated, know the drugs they use only by these terms. Therefore, tables listing the chemical, trade and most common street names for major drugs of abuse have been included in this text.

OPIOIDS

The term *opioid* describes any natural or synthetic drug whose pharmacological actions resemble morphine. (In the literature, *opioid* is used interchangeably with the term *narcotic analgesic*.) The principal medical use of the opioids is for the relief of pain.[7,8]

DRUGS IN THE OPIOID CLASS

The major opioids include *natural* substances (such as opium, morphine and codeine), *semisynthetic* drugs produced through minor chemical alterations of the basic poppy product (such as heroin), and *synthetic* analgesics (such as meperidine and propoxyphene).[6] Effects similar to the opioids are produced by certain opiate *antagonists* (such as nalorphine).[9]

NATURALLY OCCURRING OPIOIDS: The poppy *Papaver somniferum* is the main source of opium and its two types of natural alkaloids: the benzylisoquinoline series (papaverine and noscapine), which have neither euphoriant nor analgesic properties, and the phenanthrane alkaloids (morphine, codeine and thebaine), from which the major natural narcotics are derived.[9]

Opium is obtained from the milky exudate of the incised unripe capsules of the poppy plant. The milky juice of the poppy, when air-dried, forms a brownish, gummy mass. This is further dried to make powdered opium.[8,9]

A small amount of opium is used in the manufacture of antidiarrheal preparations such as paregoric, but most of the opium legally imported into the United States is refined to produce its alkaloid constituents, principally morphine and codeine.[9]

Morphine, which constitutes 4% to 21% of raw opium, is the prototype of the strong analgesics.[7] Marketed in the form of white crystals, hypodermic tablets and injectable preparations, morphine is odorless, tastes bitter and darkens with age. It can be injected subcutaneously, intramuscularly or intravenously (the last method being the one most preferred by illicit users). Tolerance and dependence develop rapidly in the regular user.[9]

Only a small part of the morphine obtained from opium is used medically, primarily in hospitals. Most licit morphine is converted to codeine and hydromorphone.[9]

Codeine is found in raw opium in concentrations ranging from 0.7% to 2.5%, but most codeine for medical use is converted from morphine. It is widely distributed in tablet form (alone or combined with aspirin or acetaminophen) for the relief of moderate pain, and in liquid form as an antitussive. Codeine is the natural opioid most widely used in medical treatment.[7,9]

Thebaine, a minor constitutent of opium that is chemically similar to morphine, can be converted into a number of medically useful compounds, including codeine, hydrocodone, oxycodone, oxymorphone, nalbuphine and naloxone.[9]

SEMISYNTHETIC OPIOIDS: The semisynthetic derivatives of opium and morphine can be made through relatively simple modifications of the morphine or thebaine molecule.[8] These semisynthetic opioids include heroin, hydromorphone, oxycodone and etorphine.

Heroin (diacetylmorphine) has an addictive potential greater than that of any other drug, due to its marked euphoriant properties and rapid onset of action.[10] Pure heroin is a white powder with a bitter taste, while street samples of heroin vary in color from white to dark brown because of impurities residual to the manufacturing process or because ingredients such as food coloring, cocoa or brown sugar have been added to create volume.[9] A currently popular form of Iranian heroin called Persian Brown is a dark reddish-brown granular powder.[11]

Analysis of street samples of heroin shows that most purchases contain only 2% to 4% pure heroin, with the rest of the powder composed of fillers such as sugars, starch, powdered milk and quinine.[9,11] An exception to this general rule is Persian Brown, samples of which contain at least 92% heroin, making it the most potent form of the drug available on illicit markets.[11]

Hydromorphone (Dilaudid) is the second oldest narcotic analgesic. Available in both tablet and injectable form, hydromorphone is shorter-acting, about eight times more potent, and has more sedative properties than morphine.[9]

Oxycodone (Percodan) is synthesized from thebaine. Although similar to codeine and useful medically for the relief of pain, oxycodone is more potent than codeine and has a higher dependence potential. In the United States, it is available only in combination products. Illicit users generally ingest oxycodone orally or dissolve the tablets in water, filter out the insoluble material and inject the remaining solution.[9]

Etorphine, which is manufactured from thebaine, is much more potent than morphine as an analgesic, sedative and respiratory depressant. Its potency is a disadvantage in humans because of the danger of an overdose, but etorphine hydrochloride (M99) is used by veterinarians to immobilize large animals.[9]

SYNTHETIC OPIOIDS: The synthetic opioids are those drugs which, although structurally unrelated to morphine, apparently act by the same mechanism, have analgesic properties, are cross-tolerant to morphine, and are effective in relieving the symptoms of morphine withdrawal.[8] The most widely available synthetic opioids are meperidine, methadone and propoxyphene.

Meperidine (pethidine, Demerol) was the first synthetic opioid. Although chemically distinct from morphine, meperidine resembles it in analgesic activity and hypotensive effects. It is the opioid most widely used for the relief of pain. Available in pure form and in combination with other ingredients, meperidine is administered either orally or by injection (the latter method being preferred by illicit users). Meperidine tolerance and dependence develop with chronic use, and large doses can produce convulsions.[7,9]

Methadone (Dolophine) is chemically distinct from morphine, but produces similar effects.[7] Methadone differs from morphine in its longer duration of action and the greater relative effectiveness of oral to injected doses. Long-term use of methadone produces tolerance and dependence states similar to morphine and withdrawal symptoms that are less severe but more prolonged.[9]

Methadone has found wide use in detoxification and maintenance treatment programs for heroin addicts, but also has emerged in some areas as a major cause of overdose deaths.[9]

Propoxyphene (Darvon), which is closely related to methadone, is used medically to relieve mild to moderate pain.[7] Although less likely to produce dependence than the more potent opioids, propoxyphene also is less effective as an analgesic.[9] In recent years, it has become the object of widespread abuse.

Fentanyl (Fentanyl Citrate), a synthetic opioid related to the phenylpiperidines, is estimated to be 50 to 100 times more potent an analgesic than morphine. High doses of fentanyl produce marked muscular rigidity and almost instant respiratory arrest. Although fentanyl is used medically only as an anesthetic, a methyl analog of fentanyl produced in clandestine laboratories is being sold on the West Coast as a "super heroin."[7,8]

OPIOID ANTAGONISTS: The search for an effective analgesic that does not produce dependence has led to the development of a class of drugs called *mixed agonist-antagonists* or *partial agonists*. These drugs, which have analgesic properties but also tend to block and reverse the effects of opioids, include nalorphine and pentazocine. Others, including naloxone and naltrexone, have antagonist activities, but lack analgesic effects.[9]

Nalorphine is a mixed agonist-antagonist: in a drug-free individual, nalorphine produces morphine-like effects, but in a person under the influence of opioid drugs, it counteracts those effects.[7,9] Its side effects prevent its use as an analgesic.

Pentazocine (Talwin) is an analgesic and a weak opioid antagonist.

Clinical studies show that pentazocine is about one-fourth to one-sixth as potent as morphine. It is effective in relieving moderate pain, but less effective than morphine in relieving severe pain. Because of its mixed agonist and antagonist properties, pentazocine has less

TABLE 3

Opioids: Nomenclature		
Drug Names	**Trade and Generic Names**	**Street Names**
Codeine	Codeine (methylmorphine) Empirin with codeine Phenergan with codeine Robitussin A-C and other cough compounds Tylenol with codeine	
Heroin	Diacetylmorphine	Big H, Boy, Brown, Brown Sugar, Caballo, Chiva, Crap, Do-Jee, Estuffa, H, Heroina, Hombre, Horse, Jive, Junk, Material, Mexican Mud, Mud, Polvo, Product, Scag, Smack, Stofa, Stuff, Thing ALSO, FOR IRANIAN HEROIN: Dava, Rufus, Persian, Persian Brown
Methadone	Dolophine (methadone hydrochloride)	
Morphine and related opioids	Demerol, Pethadol (meperidine) Dilaudid (hydromorphone) Numorphan (oxymorphone) Percodan (oxycodone)	Cube First Line Goma Morf, Morfina, Morpho, Morphy, Mud
Opium	Paregoric Parepectolin Tincture of Opium	Op Poppy
Other Opioids	Darvon (propoxyphene) Fentanyl Citrate (fentanyl) Leritine (anileridine) Levo-Dromoran (levorphanol) Lomotil (diphenoxylate + atropine) Nisentil (alphaprodine) Talwin (pentazocine)	China White

Sources: Controlled Substances: Uses and Effects *Drug Enforcement* 6(2):20 (July 1979)
Palmer, D. Northeast Metropolitan Narcotics and Dangerous Drug Enforcement Group (private communication) Elmhurst, Illinois (December 1979)

dependence liability than more conventional opioids; nevertheless, abuse and dependence have been reported.[7]

Naloxone (Narcan) is a relatively pure antagonist: it has no morphine-like effects and is useful as an antidote to opioid overdose.[9]

Naltrexone is a long-lasting pure antagonist that is effective when administered orally. It is currently under investigation as a useful agent in maintaining withdrawn abusers in a drug-free state.[9]

PREVALENCE AND PATTERNS OF OPIOID ABUSE

Two basic patterns of opioid use and dependence have been identified. The first involves initiation into opioid use in the course of legitimate medical treatment. This group constitutes a very small portion of the opioid abusing population. The second pattern begins with experimentation, then progresses to more intensive involvement. This pattern is most common among adolescents and young adults.[10,13]

Most heroin users are initiated into drug use by other users. After the first experience (which frequently is quite unpleasant), many persons never use opioid drugs again, some defer the next use for weeks or months, and a small percentage make a conscious decision to continue using the drugs as often as their finances permit. Where group values encourage use of drugs such as heroin, a high percentage of casual users go on to become dependent on opioids, despite the associated health risks and legal sanctions.[13,14]

The use of heroin increased significantly in the United States in the late 1960's, possibly as a reflection of changed societal attitudes toward drug use, wider availability of illicit drugs and the sharply increased size of the adolescent population. This upsurge was followed by a slight downward trend in the 1970's.[12]

Heroin use remains most prominent in the lowest socioeconomic strata, but has become increasingly common in more affluent groups. Contemporary estimates of the number of persons who abuse heroin and other opioids are not totally reliable because they generally include both episodic users ("experimenters") and chronic, compulsive users.[6,10,13]

PHARMACOLOGICAL ACTIONS OF THE OPIOIDS

Pharmacologically, an opioid is a substance that combines the actions of an analgesic (it relieves pain), a hypnotic (it produces sleep) and a euphoriant (it produces feelings of well-being or loss of care).[10]

The various opioid drugs are metabolized by the body in similar ways. Heroin is rapidly converted by the body into morphine, with detoxification occurring primarily in the liver. The resulting metabolites are excreted through the urine and bile. Over 90% of a dose of an opioid drug (with the exception of a few long-acting substances such as methadone) is excreted within the first 24 hours, although metabolites can be identified for 48 hours or more.[6] The duration of action of heroin and morphine generally is three to five hours.[4]

Because the opioids directly stimulate the chemoreceptor trigger zones of the brain, they result in nausea and vomiting. They also stimulate the release of an antidiuretic hormone, which decreases urine output. These drugs have a marked constricting effect on the pupils of the eye: "pinpoint" pupils are a characteristic sign of opioid use. Opioid drugs also cause constipation by decreasing gastrointestinal motility and propulsive contraction force.[4,5]

Sex hormone levels are depressed in individuals who use morphine and morphine derivatives over long periods of time. This may account for the observed decrease in libido and alterations of menstrual cycles in heroin addicts.[4,7]

Administration of morphine or heroin triggers the release of histamine from body stores. Wheals or hives at the injection site may result, along with generalized itching and a slightly decreased blood pressure secondary to the vasodilatory effect of the histamine.[4]

Administration of opioids also causes a generalized depression of the central nervous system. This includes suppression of the cough reflex, drowsiness, respiratory depression, and—in high doses—coma. Unlike barbiturates, this depression is not accompanied by anticonvulsant activity.[4,7]

TOLERANCE, TOXICITY AND DEPENDENCE ON THE OPIOIDS

A striking degree of tolerance develops to the respiratory depressant, analgesic, sedative, emetic and euphorogenic effects of the opioids, but the rate at which this tolerance develops depends on the pattern of use. With episodic use, it is possible to achieve the desired analgesic and sedative effects from therapeutic doses for an indefinite period of time. Continuous use of doses in excess of the therapeutic level, however, quickly leads to the development of significant tolerance, although such tolerance does not develop evenly or at the same rate to all of the opioid's effects. (Chronic users of opioids may develop tolerance to all but the respiratory depressant effects of these drugs.)[6,13,14]

It has been amply demonstrated that an individual who is tolerant to one opioid drug will be tolerant to all other opioids, even if they are chemically disimilar. Tolerance diminishes rapidly as withdrawal is completed.[6,13]

The nature and severity of withdrawal symptoms depend on the particular opioid involved, the total daily dose, the duration of use and the health and personality structure of the user. With heroin and morphine, withdrawal symptoms appear just prior to the time of the next scheduled dose, increase in intensity for the next 36 to 72 hours, then gradually decline. Without treatment, the gross physiological signs of withdrawal disappear between seven and 10 days, but the duration of psychological symptoms is less predictable. Administration of appropriate amounts of an opioid drug will immediately and completely suppress withdrawal symptoms at any point in this process.[6,8,13]

Abrupt withdrawal from semisynthetic and synthetic opioids produces symptoms that are qualitatively similar to those of morphine withdrawal. Drugs with shorter durations of action generally produce shorter, more intense withdrawal syndromes than drugs that are longer acting.[6,13,14]

EFFECTS FOR WHICH OPIOIDS ARE ABUSED

Although heroin can be administered orally, nasally ("snorting") or subcutaneously ("skin-popping"), most users prefer intravenous injection ("mainlining"). Rapid intravenous injection of heroin (and most other opioids) produces "a warm flushing of the skin and sensations in the lower abdomen described by addicts as similar in intensity and quality to sexual orgasm, and known as a 'rush,' 'kick,' or 'thrill'."[13]

To "mainline" heroin, the user places one or two "caps" or "envelopes" of heroin in a spoon or bottle cap with some water. The receptacle then is heated with a match to dissolve the heroin. The user draws the resulting solution into a syringe through a small ball of cotton to filter out the filler substances that will not dissolve with the heroin. Finally, the user places a tourniquet above the site of injection and inserts the hypodermic needle into a vein. The superficial veins of the forearm are preferred sites because they are relatively easy to reach and the injection scars ("tracks") can be covered by long-sleeved garments.[14]

The first sensation experienced after injecting the heroin is the "rush." This sensation affects the entire body and is described by users as the most intense pleasure that can be experienced. In addition to the physical sensation, varying degrees of euphoria, emotional well-being and fulfillment are experienced.[14]

After a period of minutes, the "rush" fades and the user lapses into a state of mental and physical relaxation called a "nod," which may last for several hours. In this state, mental awareness and motor

TABLE 4

Opioids: Characteristics and Effects

Effects for which drug is used: Euphoria, escape, reduction of aggressive or sexual drives
Other possible effects: Drowsiness, respiratory depression, constricted pupils, nausea

Drug Name	Usual Route of Adminis.	Duration of Effects (in hours)	Potential for Physical Dependence	Potential for Psychological Dependence	Potential for Tolerance
Codeine	Oral (liquid or tablets) Injection	3-6	Moderate	Moderate	Yes
Heroin	Injection in muscle or vein Inhalation	3-6	Very high	Very high	Yes
Methadone	Oral (liquid) Injection	12-24	High	High	Yes
Morphine	Injection Oral (liquid or tablets)	4	High	High	Yes
Opium	Oral (smoking)	4	High	High	Yes
Other Opioids:					
Darvon	Oral (tablets)	4	Moderate	Moderate	Yes
Lomotil	Oral (liquid)	4	Low	Low	Yes
Dilaudid	Injection	4	High	High	Yes
Demerol	Injection	4	High	High	Yes
Cough syrup	Oral (liquid)	4	Moderate	Moderate	Yes

Sources: Controlled Substances: Uses and Effects *Drug Enforcement* 6(2):20 (July 1979)
Schuckit, M. A. *Drug and Alcohol Abuse: A Clinical Guide to Diagnosis and Treatment* (Plenum Medical Book Co., New York City, 1979)
Gay, G. R. and Way, E. L. Pharmacology of the opiate narcotics *in* D. E. Smith and G. R. Gay (eds.) *It's So Good, Don't Even Try It Once* (Prentice-Hall, Englewood Cliffs, N.J., 1972)

coordination are reduced and all drives are decreased. This state is followed in six to 12 hours by the early signs of withdrawal, which can be alleviated by repeating the ritual.

The effects described here are most common in the second (regular use) stage of heroin abuse. In the first (novice) stage, the experience is more likely to be somewhat unpleasant, with the new user experiencing nausea and vomiting, followed by a mild "high." By the time the second stage is reached, the user is ingesting heroin regularly, developing a physical dependence on it, and beginning to experience withdrawal symptoms when use is interrupted. As the user's tolerance increases over a period of months, greater quantities of heroin are required to experience the "rush." Finally, in the third stage, the user's intake of heroin does not allow him a significant feeling of euphoria, but simply prevents the withdrawal syndrome.[14]

Heroin and the other opioid drugs all produce several distinct physiological changes in the user:

ANALGESIA: Opioids relieve the subjective feeling of pain and reduce the perception of pain by raising the pain threshold.

DROWSINESS: Some sedative effect is noticed with therapeutic doses of opioids; in fact, such doses occasionally modify EEG tracings toward normal patterns of sleep.

MOOD CHANGES: Mood changes in response to opioids are highly variable: some persons report no mood changes, while others report varying degrees of depression (euphoria is rare among new users).

MENTAL CLOUDING: A somewhat dreamy, mentally slow feeling is frequently reported.[10,14]

Jaffe and Martin[8] have observed that when a moderate dose (5 to 10 mg) of morphine is given to patients with pain, worry, tension or other discomfort, the patients report that the pain is entirely gone or less intense, or that they are less distressed by it. At this dose level, drowsiness occurs, the extremities feel heavy and the body warm, the face and nose may itch, and the mouth becomes dry. Sleep may ensue.

As the dose size is increased, the subjective effects become more pronounced. Jaffe and Martin[8] found that, at higher doses, "there is increased drowsiness that leads to sleep, . . . the euphoric effect is accentuated, [and] patients with severe pain . . . are usually relieved."

The opioids also are highly effective tranquilizers. Gay and Way[10] note that, "in those who are feeling fatigue, worry, tension or anxiety, the euphoriant effects afford considerable relief and may allow the individual to feel 'larger than life.' . . . Anxiety disappears, as do feelings of inferiority. Since the user no longer cares about life's problems in general, everything looks rosy, until the pleasurable drug effects wear off, at which time he needs a pharmacologic restoration of this euphoria with another dose."

DEPRESSANTS

The category of depressants includes a variety of drugs that differ markedly in their physical and chemical properties, but share the common characteristic of causing generalized depression of the central nervous system. Sedative/hypnotic drugs and antianxiety agents are the most widely prescribed drugs in the United States.[15]

DRUGS IN THE DEPRESSANT CLASS

The depressant drugs include the *barbiturates, barbiturate-like* substances, *benzodiazepines, carbamates, chloral hydrate* and *paraldehyde*. These agents differ in their pharmacologic actions and in the onset and duration of their effects, but they all exhibit some degree of cross-tolerance and cross-dependence.[4] Depressant drugs also are cross-tolerant to alcohol, although concomitant use of alcohol and another CNS depressant may potentiate the effects of both.[6]

BARBITURATES: Simple manipulation of barbituric acid yields a number of active central nervous system depressant drugs. The addition of side groups of higher lipid solubility to the basic barbituric nucleus produces depressant drugs of shorter duration but increased intensity of action.[4,7]

Small therapeutic doses of barbiturates are used to calm nervous conditions, while large doses induce sleep within 20 to 60 minutes of oral administration. At high doses, the effects of barbiturates progress through sedation, sleep, and coma, to death from respiratory arrest and cardiovascular complications.[7,9]

Barbiturates are classified as ultrashort, intermediate and long-acting.

The ultrashort-acting barbiturates (hexobarbital, methohexital, thiamylal, thiopental) produce anesthesia within one minute of intravenous administration. Their rapid onset and brief duration of action make them undesirable as drugs of abuse.[4]

The short- and intermediate-acting barbiturates include amobarbital (Amytal), pentobarbital (Nembutal) and secobarbital (Seconal), which are three of the most widely abused depressants. With oral administration, the onset of action for these drugs is 20 to 40 minutes and the duration of effects is four to six hours. These barbiturates are used medically to induce sedation or sleep.[4,7,9]

Long-acting barbiturates have onset times of up to one hour and durations of action of up to 16 hours. They are medically useful as sedatives, hypnotics and anticonvulsants. These drugs are infrequently abused because of their slow onset of action, and usually appear on illicit drug markets only as counterfeits of the more popular compounds. The long-acting barbiturates include phenobarbital (Luminal), barbital (Veronal), mephobarbital (Mebaral) and metharbital (Gemonil).[7,9]

BARBITURATE-LIKE DRUGS: The barbiturate-like drugs were developed in an attempt to avoid some of the common side effects associated with the barbiturates, including morning-after "hangover," residual sleepiness, drug-induced disturbances in sleep patterns, and the highly lethal overdose potential of barbiturates. However, most of these barbiturate substitutes (especially glutethimide, ethchlorvynol and methaqualone) share the dangers and abuse potential of the barbiturates.[4,7,9]

Glutethimide (Doriden) was introduced in 1954 as a barbiturate substitute without a dependence potential. However, it has been found to have no advantages over the barbiturates and several important disadvantages, chiefly the long duration of its effects (which begin about 30 minutes after oral administration and last for four to eight hours) and the fact that it is difficult to dialyze out of the system. Thus, it is exceptionally difficult to reverse overdoses of glutethimide, which frequently result in death.[9]

Ethchlorvynol (Placidyl) also is especially dangerous in overdoses because it is highly fat-soluble and resistant to excretion.[4] Like glutethimide and methaqualone, it has very limited antianxiety action and is marketed only as a hypnotic.[7]

Methaqualone (Quaalude, Sopor) is a synthetic sedative that is chemically unrelated to the barbiturates. It has been widely abused since its introduction as a barbiturate substitute. Large doses cause coma, which may be accompanied by thrashing movements or convulsions, and chronic use can lead to tolerance and dependence. (Counterfeit Quaalude tablets, which do not necessarily contain methaqualone, are common on the illicit drug market.)[7,9]

BENZODIAZEPINES: The benzodiazepine drugs relieve anxiety, tension and muscle spasms, produce sedation and prevent convulsions. These substances are marketed as minor tranquilizers, sedatives, hypnotics or anticonvulsants.[9] Although their margin of safety is greater than that of the other CNS depressants, they also can produce physical and psychological dependence and withdrawal symptoms after prolonged use.[15] Among the benzodiazepines marketed in the United States, chlordiazepoxide (Librium), diazepam (Valium) and flurazepam (Dalmane) are by far the most widely prescribed.[15] Other drugs in this group include clonazepam (Clonopin), clorazepate (Tranxene, Azene), lorazepam (Ativan), oxazepam (Serax) and prazepam (Verstran).[7,9]

TABLE 5

Depressants: Nomenclature		
Drug Names	**Trade and Generic Names**	**Street Names**
Barbiturates	Amytal (amobarbital)	Bluebirds, Blue Devils, Blue Heavens, Blues
	Butisol (butabarbital)	—
	Luminal (phenobarbital)	Purple Hearts
	Nembutal (pentobarbital)	Nebbies, Nimbies, Yellow Jackets, Yellows
	Seconal (secobarbital)	Reds, Redbirds, Red Devils
	Tuinal (Amytal + Seconal)	Christmas Trees, Rainbows, Tooies, Trees
		ALSO: Barbs, Beans, Blockbusters, Downers, Foolpills, Goofballs, Green Dragons, Mexican Reds, Pajao Rojo, Pink Ladies, Pinks, Reds & Blues, Sleeping Pills, Stumblers
Barbiturate-like substances	Doriden (glutethimide)	—
	Noludar (methyprylon)	—
	Placidyl (ethchlorvynol)	—
	Quaalude, Sopor (methaqualone)	Ludes, Quads, Quas Soapers, Sopes
	Valmid (ethinamate)	—
Benzodiazepines	Ativan (lorazepam)	
	Azene, Tranxene (clorazepate)	
	Clonopin (clonazepam)	
	Dalmane (flurazepam)	
	Librium (chlordiazepoxide)	
	Serax (oxazepam)	
	Valium (diazepam)	
	Verstran (prazepam)	
Carbamates	Equanil, Miltown (meprobamate)	
	Salacen, Tybatran (tybamate)	
Other depressants	Noctec, Somnos (chloral hydrate)	
	Paraldehyde	

Sources: Controlled Substances: Uses and Effects *Drug Enforcement* 6(2):20 (July 1979)
Palmer, D. Northeast Metropolitan Narcotics and Dangerous Drug Enforcement Group (private communication) Elmhurst, Illinois (December 1979)
Schuckit, M. A. *Drug and Alcohol Abuse: A Clinical Guide to Diagnosis and Treatment* (Plenum Medical Book Co., New York City, 1979)
Handbook of Psychoactive Drug Prescribing Information (Physicians Postgraduate Press, Memphis, Tenn., 1979)

CARBAMATES: The carbamates (meprobamate and tybamate), like the benzodiazepines, have been widely prescribed for the relief of anxiety, tension and muscle spasms. Meprobamate (Miltown, Equanil) ushered in the era of the "minor" tranquilizers when it was introduced in 1950, and today more than 200 tons of the drug are distributed each year. Although the onset and duration of action of meprobamate resemble the short-acting barbiturates, it differs from them in that it is a muscle relaxant, does not produce sleep in therapeutic doses and is relatively less toxic. Excessive use can produce physical and psychological dependence.[4,7,9]

CHLORAL HYDRATE: A clinically effective sedative and hypnotic, chloral hydrate (Noctec, Somnos) is the oldest of the hypnotic drugs. Although its popularity declined after the introduction of the barbiturates, chloral hydrate still is widely used. Its rapid onset of action and short half-life make the drug especially useful in treating insomnia, but it is not effective as an antianxiety agent. Chloral hydrate, though not a popular drug of abuse among younger people, occasionally is misused by older adults.[7,9]

PARALDEHYDE: Formerly prescribed to treat insomnia, paraldehyde today is used occasionally to treat selected cases of alcohol withdrawal.[9]

PREVALENCE AND PATTERNS OF DEPRESSANT ABUSE

The extent to which depressant drugs are abused cannot be measured with precision, but such abuse is believed to far exceed the abuse of opioids.[12]

Illicit traffic in depressant drugs diverted from legal markets or manufactured in clandestine laboratories is common. A less common but still operative source of supply is licit prescriptions obtained from medical practitioners.[14,15]

Four basic patterns of depressant abuse have been identified. The first pattern involves persons who use depressants for their sedative effects during episodes of emotional distress, then accelerate their use to obtain more constant and more profound levels of sedation. In a second group, depressants are used to achieve a paradoxical stimulant effect. Such excitation occurs when tolerance to the sedative effects has developed, in response to an idiosyncracy of body chemistry, or as a result of the depressants' ability to supress various inhibitory mechanisms. A third pattern involves persons who use depressants to counteract the effects of various stimulant drugs, particularly the amphetamines. Simultaneous dependence on both stimulants and depressants is not uncommon in this group. In a fourth category are persons who abuse multiple drugs — usually including alcohol, other CNS depressants and opioids — in an effort to achieve more intense effects than are produced by any of these agents alone.[6,15]

PHARMACOLOGICAL ACTIONS OF THE DEPRESSANTS

The specific pharmacologic mechanisms by which the CNS depressants exert their effects are not completely understood but, in general, these drugs produce a reversible depression of the activity of all excitable tissues — especially in the central nervous system — with the greatest effects on the synaptic junctures between nerve cells.[6]

Both acute and chronic intoxication with the CNS depressants produce general sluggishness, difficulty in thinking, slowness of speech and comprehension, poor memory, faulty judgment, narrowed range of attention, emotional lability and exaggeration of basic personality traits. Irritability, quarrelsomeness and moroseness also are common. There may be episodes of laughing or crying without provocation, untidiness in personal habits, hostile and paranoid ideas, and suicidal tendencies.[13,15,16,17]

Occasionally the hypnotics and antianxiety drugs cause extreme excitement rather than sedation (paradoxical effect) in children and the elderly, as well as in patients in pain.[6,16]

Unlike the opioids, the CNS depressants are ineffective analgesics. While they produce general depression of excitable tissues in the CNS, the skeletal and smooth muscles are only mildly depressed, even at high doses.

Although the barbiturates were used as sleep-inducing agents for many years, it is now recognized that the sleep they induce does not follow normal sleep patterns. For example, hypnotic doses of the barbiturates and most other depressants appear to depress the rapid eye movement (REM) part of the normal sleep cycle, so the user does not feel rested upon awakening. When the use of these drugs is discontinued, prolonged REM sleep, characterized by unrestful sleep and increased nightmares, may persist for several months (rebound effect).[4]

The major toxic effect of the barbiturates and other CNS depressants is on respiration. These drugs depress the medullary centers of the brain responsible for respiratory drive and rhythm. Ultimately, coma, respiratory arrest and circulatory collapse result from overdoses of barbiturates.[4,6,16]

TOLERANCE, TOXICITY AND DEPENDENCE ON THE DEPRESSANTS

Chronic intoxication with short-acting barbiturates and related depressants results in both increased metabolism of the drug after its administration (metabolic tolerance) and apparent adaptation of the central nervous system to the presence of the drug (pharmacodynamic tolerance).[6,13] This tolerance has an upper limit that gives chronic intoxication with depressants a distinctive clinical picture. For example, an individual tolerant to 1.2 gm of pentobarbital may show little evidence of intoxication at that dose, but an increase of 0.1 gm per day can produce prolonged intoxication. Another distinctive characteristic of depressants as a class is that, while users may develop considerable tolerance to their sedative and intoxicating effects, the dose that will produce death from respiratory depression is not much larger for chronic users than for non-users.[13]

The dose level required to produce physical dependence can be as small as 0.4 gm of barbiturates per day for several months, but more commonly is at the level of 1.0 to 2.0 gm of barbiturates daily for a similar period. The non-barbiturate depressants produce a similar degree of dependence, but usually require higher dose levels and/or longer periods of regular use to do so.[13,14]

The withdrawal syndrome associated with the depressants is marked by symptoms ranging from paroxysmal EEG irregularities through tremulousness, anxiety, weakness and insomnia, to postural hypotension, fever, grand mal seizures and delirium. With the short-acting barbiturates, withdrawal symptoms begin about 12 hours after the missed dose and peak at 24 hours, then decline and gradually disappear about the eighth day. With the longer-acting barbiturates and benzodiazepines, withdrawal symptoms generally peak more slowly and last slightly longer. Once a state of delirium develops, the withdrawal syndrome cannot be immediately reversed, even by administering large doses of barbiturates.[13,14,15]

EFFECTS FOR WHICH DEPRESSANTS ARE ABUSED

Most regular users of CNS depressants ingest the drugs orally, but some dissolve the capsules in water and inject the resulting solution intravenously to achieve the "rush" effect—a warm, drowsy feeling experienced immediately after injection.[13,15]

Intoxication with barbiturates and other CNS depressants is qualitatively similar to intoxication with alcohol. Depending on the drug, the dose and the individual, the mood changes induced range from exhiliration to unhappiness or irritability. Feelings of elation or excitation are principally the result of depressed judgment and inhibitions, with accompanying release from anxiety and corresponding good feeling.[14,15]

TABLE 6

Depressants: Characteristics and Effects

Effects for which drug is used: Euphoria, escape, reduction of aggressive or sexual drives

Other possible effects: Drowsiness, respiratory depression, constricted pupils, nausea

Drug Names	Usual Route of Adminis.	Duration of Effects (in hours)	Potential for Physical Dependence	Potential for Psychological Dependence	Potential for Tolerance
Barbiturates	Oral (pills or capsules) Injected	4	High to moderate	High to moderate	Yes
Barbiturate-like substances	Oral (pills or capsules)	4	High	High	Yes
Benzodiazepines	Oral (pills or capsules)	4-6	Low	Low	Yes
Carbamates	Oral (pills or capsules)	4	Moderate	Moderate	Yes
Other depressants: Chloral hydrate Paraldehyde	Oral (pills or capsules)	4	Moderate	Moderate	Possible

Sources: Controlled Substances: Uses and Effects *Drug Enforcement* 6(2):20 (July 1979)
Fort, Joel *The Pleasure Seekers* (Bobbs-Merrill Co., Indianapolis, Ind., 1969)
Schuckit, M. A. *Drug and Alcohol Abuse: A Clinical Guide to Diagnosis and Treatment* (Plenum Medical Book Co., New York City, 1979)

The desired effect of barbiturate intoxication generally is "disinhibition euphoria," a state in which mood is elevated; self-criticism, anxiety and guilt are reduced; and feelings of energy and self-confidence are increased.[15]

The barbiturate-like substances produce a similar euphoric state, but the individual's mood may be quite labile, shifting rapidly from euphoria to sadness, irritability, anxiety, agitation and hypochondriacal concerns.[15] Within the drug culture, the barbiturate-like substance methaqualone is believed to produce a dissociative "high" without the drowsiness that characterizes barbiturate use. Certain aphrodisiac properties also have been imputed to this drug. These unsubstantiated beliefs undoubtedly contribute to the widespread popularity of methaqualone as a drug of abuse.[15,16]

Combined use of amphetamines and barbiturates produces greater elevation of mood than use of either drug alone. This phenomenon may be responsible for the frequent simultaneous abuse of amphetamines and barbiturates.[13]

The use of barbiturates or glutethimide to augment the effects of weak heroin is quite common, with the result that many heroin users also are physically dependent on a CNS depressant.[13]

STIMULANTS

Stimulants have been used for thousands of years by the majority of mankind. The two most prevalent stimulants are the nicotine in tobacco products and caffeine, the active ingredient in coffee, tea and some cola beverages. The juices of coca leaves traditionally have been used as a stimulant by the Andean Indians, while the leaves of the Khat plant are chewed in East Africa and the Near East for similar purposes. Cocaine, the most potent stimulant of natural origin, is extracted from the leaves of the coca plant (*Erythroxylon coca*), which has been cultivated in the Andean highlands of South America since prehistoric times.[6,7,9]

Among the synthetic stimulants, amphetamine was first prepared in 1887 by Edeleano and methamphetamine in 1919 by Ogata, but it was not until 1927 that the psychopharmacological effects of amphetamine were first described by Alles.[7,9]

DRUGS IN THE STIMULANT CLASS

All of the natural and synthetic compounds in this class have the ability to stimulate the central nervous system at multiple levels.[6] The stimulant drugs most often abused are *cocaine* and the *ampheta-*

mines. Other, less frequently abused stimulants are *methylphenidate* and *phenmetrazine*.[4,9]

COCAINE: Pure cocaine was first isolated in the 1880's for use as a local anesthetic. It became particularly useful in nose and throat surgery because, in addition to blocking nerve conduction, cocaine's vasoconstrictor properties tended to limit bleeding. However, cocaine is not metabolized as fast as many of the synthetic local anesthetics, so it is more toxic after subcutaneous administration than many of its substitutes.[6,9]

Illicit cocaine is distributed as a while crystalline powder, often adulterated to about half its original potency with a variety of ingredients, most commonly sugars such as lactose and local anesthetics such as lidocaine.[9]

AMPHETAMINE: Amphetamine became a drug of abuse as early as 1935, when it was readily available in nasal decongestant inhalers and other over-the-counter preparations.[9] Subsequent recognition of its limited therapeutic value and high abuse potential has led to a marked reduction in the medical use of amphetamine.[6,7]

Amphetamine sulfate (Benzedrine), dextroamphetamine (Dexedrine) and methamphetamine (Methedrine) are so similar in their actions and effects that they can be differentiated only by laboratory analysis.[7,9]

METHYLPHENIDATE and PHENMETRAZINE: The patterns of abuse and adverse effects of methylphenidate (Ritalin) and phenmetrazine (Preludin) are almost identical to those of the other stimulants.[9,18] Abuse of methylphenidate involves injection of the tablet form dissolved in water, while abuse of phenmetrazine involves both oral and intravenous administration. Medical complications of such abuse are common, because the tablet forms of both drugs contain insoluble materials such as talc which, when injected, can block small blood vessels, especially in the lungs and retina of the eye.[9,19]

OTHER STIMULANT DRUGS: Several drugs developed in recent years to replace amphetamines as appetite suppressants have slight abuse potential. These anorectic agents include benzphetamine (Didrex), chlorphentermine (Pre-Sate), clortermine (Voranil), diethylpropion (Tenuate), mazindol (Sanorex) and phentermine (Adipex).[9,19]

PREVALENCE AND PATTERNS OF STIMULANT ABUSE

Non-medical use of stimulant drugs fluctuates widely over time in response to cycles of popularity. During the early 1960's, a high rate of amphetamine abuse was identified in both the civilian and military populations. In the 1970's, the use of amphetamines declined, but the level of cocaine use rose dramatically.[13,14,20]

TABLE 7

Stimulants: Nomenclature		
Drug Names	**Trade and Generic Names**	**Street Names**
Amphetamines	Benzedrine (amphetamine sulfate)	Bennies, Peaches, Splash
	Desbutal (methamphetamine + pentobarbital)	—
	Dexedrine (dextroamphetamine)	Copilots, Dexies, Oranges, Footballs
	Diphentamine, Biphetamine (dextroamphetamine + amphetamine)	—
	Eskatrol (dextroamphetamine + prochlorperazine)	—
	Methedrine, Desoxyn (methamphetamine)	Crystal, Crank, Meth, Speed, Water ALSO: Beans, Black Beauties, Black Cadillacs, Black Mollies, Brown & Clears, Crosses, Crossroads, Double Cross, Hearts, Minibennies, Pep Pills, Rosas, Roses, Thrusters, Truck Drivers, Uppers, Wake-ups, Whites
Cocaine	Cocaine hydrochloride Cocaine, N.F.	Blow, C, Coca, Coke, Cola, Flake, Girl, Heaven Dust, Lady, Line, Mujer, Nose Candy, Paradise, Perico, Peruvian Flake, Pharmaceutical Powder, Polvo Blanco, Rocks, Snow, Toot, White ALSO, FOR COCAINE SULPHATE: Freebase
Methylphenidate	Ritalin	
Phenmetrazine	Preludin	
Other Stimulants	Adipex Ionamin Tenuate Bacarate Plegine Tepanil Cylert Pre-Sate Voranil Didrex Sanorex	

Sources: Controlled Substances: Uses and Effects *Drug Enforcement* 6(2):20 (July 1979)
Palmer, D. Northeast Metropolitan Narcotics and Dangerous Drug Enforcement Group (private communication) Elmhurst, Illinois (December 1979)

A common pattern of abuse with the amphetamines involves persons who first obtain prescriptions for these drugs from a physician in the course of treatment for obesity or depression, then gradually become habituated. More often, however, individuals seek out amphetamines and cocaine specifically for their euphoric effects.[13,20,21]

PHARMACOLOGICAL ACTIONS OF THE STIMULANTS

The most obvious actions of the stimulant drugs are on the central nervous system, the peripheral nervous system and the cardiovascular system.[6] Most of the stimulant drugs have effects similar to amphetamine, although methamphetamine (Methedrine) has milder cardiac effects, especially at low doses, while methylphenidate (Ritalin) and phenmetrazine (Preludin) have lower levels of potency. Cocaine, which is quite potent, has effects similar to intravenously injected amphetamine.[6]

Clinically, all of the stimulant drugs produce euphoria, decreased fatigue and need for sleep, increased feelings of sexuality, interference with normal sleep patterns, decreased appetite and increased energy. Physically, they all produce tremor of the hands, restlessness and a rapid heart rate.[6,7]

Amphetamines and cocaine produce markedly similar psychological effects, including excitability, progressively severe anxiety and confusion, and ultimately paranoia and toxic psychosis.[4,19,22,23] The fully developed amphetamine psychosis is characterized by vivid visual, auditory and olfactory hallucinations, delusions of persecution, body-image changes, and sometimes picking and excoriating of the skin. Dyskinetic and dystonic reactions also have been reported. In chronic amphetamine users, this psychosis may be very difficult to distinguish from a schizophrenic reaction, especially where the physical signs are not clear.[13,21]

Once such a psychosis is manifested, certain symptoms such as delusions may persist. The individual has a lower threshold for precipitation of psychosis with subsequent amphetamine use, even after long periods of abstinence.[13,21]

TOLERANCE, TOXICITY AND DEPENDENCE ON THE STIMULANTS

Tolerance to the central effects of amphetamines develops rather rapidly with regular use. It may be that, since amphetamine's appetite-suppressant effects foster ketosis and amphetamines are excreted much more rapidly in acidic urine, some of this apparent tolerance is simply due to rapid elimination of the drug.[13,21]

Whether cocaine produces tolerance is open to question. Given the known ability of the liver to detoxify cocaine rapidly, even the high doses ingested by chronic abusers do not necessarily demonstrate the development of tolerance.[13,20]

Researchers have demonstrated cross-tolerance among the amphetamine-like sympathomimetics, but cross-tolerance between cocaine and the amphetamine-like compounds has not been reported.[13]

Amphetamine toxicity is manifested in signs and symptoms consistent with overstimulation of the central nervous system. At high doses, headaches, flushed skin, chest pain with palpitations, circulatory collapse, cerebral hemorrhages and coma may occur. (These effects, as well as respiratory depression and direct cardiac toxicity, also can be produced by cocaine, but are seen less often with that drug because cocaine is metabolized more rapidly.)[4,9,19,20,24] Physical exercise can exacerbate these symptoms by taxing the already-impaired cardiovascular and temperature-regulating mechanisms. Fatalities in response to extreme exertion have been reported among athletes who have taken stimulant drugs in moderate amounts.[9]

Physical dependence like that encountered with the opioids does not develop with the amphetamines, but the prolonged sleep, lassitude, fatigue, hyperphagia and occasional profound depression that follow abrupt discontinuation of these drugs is difficult to attribute solely to the preceding loss of sleep and weight. Consequently, most observers now recognize these symptoms as indicators of an amphetamine withdrawal syndrome.[13,18,23]

EFFECTS FOR WHICH STIMULANTS ARE ABUSED

Stimulants are used in two ways to achieve euphoria. The most common pattern involves intermittent use of oral agents (such as ingestion of amphetamine capsules or inhalation of cocaine). At times, these agents may be used in combination with marijuana, depressants or hallucinogenic drugs.[14]

When used alone, stimulants produce increased alertness and a feeling of well-being. In larger doses, they evoke a temporary sense of exhiliration, super-abundant energy, hyperactivity, extended wakefulness and loss of appetite.[9,14] At this dose level, the user also may experience vertigo, tremor, confusion, headaches, flushing or sweating, nausea or chest pain, and the sensation of a racing heart.[14]

So long as stimulant use remains intermittent, tolerance does not develop and there is no need to increase dose size to achieve the desired effects. This pattern of use is common among persons who obtain stimulants through legal prescriptions.[6,14,20,23]

The other pattern of stimulant use involves intravenous injections, most commonly of methamphetamine ("speed"). This pattern generally develops after a period of oral ingestion (swallowing, smoking or inhaling amphetamines or cocaine).[14,23] After a 10 mg intravenous dose of amphetamine (which is customarily repeated at one- to two-hour intervals), users report an initial "flash" or "rush" — a sudden, intense, generalized sensation that many liken to a sudden splash of cold water or a total body orgasm. Immediately, total euphoria occurs and feelings of boredom or depression are lost. Users also may believe they have markedly enhanced physical strength and mental capacity.[13,14] (It is possible that other substances contribute to this effect, inasmuch as different "batches" of amphetamine have different effects, and because the pure, commercially manufactured product apparently does not produce as intense an initial euphoria or "flash.")[14]

With intravenous use, tolerance develops rapidly, and the user must inject 100 to 200 mg to achieve the desired effect. As the dose level increases, the user may develop paranoid feelings similar to psychotic paranoia or become transfixed ("hung-up") with endless, compulsive work at a nonsensical task.[4,6]

Desire to reexperience the "flash," combined with aversion to loss of the stimulant's effects and the onset of withdrawal symptoms, leads some chronic users to engage in "speed runs" — days of continuous amphetamine use during which as much as 1 gm of the dissolved crystals is injected at one- to two-hour intervals.[4,6]

After experiencing the "flash," most users remain under the influence of the drug for several hours. At this point, the typical user desires group activity and wants to talk incessantly. As the "run" continues, the individual loses his ability to perform complex actions. Exaggeration of personal characteristics — especially compulsive traits — occurs, and persecutive fantasies and other illusions may appear.[14]

The user eventually becomes exhausted, disorganized and tense, and stops taking the drug ("crashes"). At this point, he may sleep for 24 to 48 hours, often with the aid of barbiturates or heroin. He awakens with a voracious appetite, but may feel lethargic for several days to several weeks. During the phase when he is not using the drug, the chronic user is prone to panic reactions, depression and a tendency toward irritable, assaultive and suicidal behavior.[4,6,14,23]

Cocaine users describe the euphoric effects of their drug in terms that are almost identical to those employed by amphetamine users. Like amphetamines, cocaine produces intense feelings of well-being, animation and power. However, the effects of inhaled, smoked or

TABLE 8

Stimulants: Characteristics and Effects

Effects for which drug is used: Euphoria, stimulation, relief of fatigue, suppression of appetite

Other possible effects: Excitation, increased pulse rate and blood pressure, insomnia

Drug Names	Usual Route of Adminis.	Duration of Effects (in hours)	Potential for Physical Dependence	Potential for Psychological Dependence	Potential for Tolerance
Amphetamines	Oral (pills or capsules) Injection	4	Possible	High	Yes
Cocaine	Inhalation Oral (capsules or smoking)	2	Possible	High	Possible
Methylphenidate	Oral (tablets)	4-6	Possible	High	Yes
Phenmetrazine	Oral (tablets)	4-6	Possible	High	Yes
Other stimulants	Varies	2-4	Possible	High	Yes

Sources: Controlled Substances: Uses and Effects *Drug Enforcement* 6(2):20 (July 1979)
Fort, Joel *The Pleasure Seekers* (Bobbs-Merrill Co., Indianapolis, Ind., 1969)
Schuckit, M. A. *Drug and Alcohol Abuse: A Clinical Guide to Diagnosis and Treatment* (Plenum Medical Book Co., New York City, 1979)

swallowed cocaine are of much briefer duration than those of amphetamines: the effects of cocaine may last only a few minutes, whereas those of the amphetamines may persist for several hours.[13,20]

The common practice of breathing cocaine crystals into the nostrils ("snorting") tends to limit the available dose, since cocaine is a potent vasoconstrictor that slows absorption in the nose even as it is being ingested. Maximum blood levels of the active ingredients thus reach a peak only after 20 minutes to an hour following inhalation or swallowing. After the brief cocaine "rush," the user quickly starts to "crash," so that within 10 to 15 minutes, feelings of depression emerge and the user requires another dose to maintain equilibrium.[14,23]

In the newer practice of smoking cocaine sulphate or "base" ("freebase"), the vasoconstrictive effect of the drug does not slow absorption, so maximum blood levels are reached within two to five minutes. The greater frequency of toxic effects with this mode of ingestion appears related to the speed with which the active ingredients enter the bloodstream. These toxic effects can include paranoia, depression, extreme agitation and dramatic increases in heart rate and blood pressure. Some users have suffered persistent psychotic episodes that required psychiatric hospitalization. Recent research shows that cocaine smokers suffer a far higher incidence of toxic effects than those who inhale or swallow the drug.[22]

Regardless of the route of administration, the subjective effects and toxic syndromes of all the stimulants are similar and, when one of these substances is unavailable for illicit use, another frequently is substituted.[13,20,23]

HALLUCINOGENS

Hallucinogens are substances that distort the user's perception of objective reality. In large doses, they produce a variety of effects that users term the "psychedelic experience."[4,9]

Although the commonly abused hallucinogens are derived from a variety of sources, most are structurally similar and many resemble the amphetamines. In fact, under certain conditions or at toxic doses, several classes of drugs (amphetamines, anticholinergics, antimalarials, bromides, cocaine, corticosteroids and opioid antagonists) can induce hallucinations, delusions and illusions. What distinguishes the substances classed here as hallucinogens is their ability to reliably induce states of altered perception, thought and feeling that are not (or cannot be) experienced otherwise except in dreams or at times of religious exultation.[4,13]

DRUGS IN THE HALLUCINOGEN CLASS

The major hallucinogens include natural substances (mescaline, psilocybin, nutmeg, morning glory seed) and synthetic compounds (the amphetamine variants). As with any scheme of classification, the inclusion or exclusion of drugs in this class is somewhat arbitrary. Many of the drugs classed as hallucinogens are related to the *indolealkylamines* (LSD, psilocybin, DET, DMT), to the *phenylethylamines* (mescaline), or to the *phenylisopropylamines* (DOM, DOE, MMDA). Other, chemically unrelated substances (anti-Parkinson drugs and herbal preparations such as mandrake and nutmeg) are included in this class because of the effects for which they are abused. The cannabinoids and phencyclidines produce psychological effects that are closely related to those of the drugs classified here as hallucinogens, but they also exhibit sufficient differences to justify separate classifications.[4,6,13]

INDOLEALKYLAMINES: Of the drugs in this class, *LSD* (d-lysergic acid diethylamide) is the most commonly abused. First synthesized in 1938, lysergic acid is produced from the ergot fungus that grows in the heads of rye and wheat, or from morning glory seeds.[9,14] It is a highly potent drug that produces frank hallucinations at doses as low as 20 to 25 micrograms.[6,9,14]

LSD is a colorless, tasteless substance that usually is sold in the form of capsules or pills, as a white powder, in thin squares of gelatin ("windowpanes") or impregnated in paper ("blotter acid"). Some users inject the drug subcutaneously or intravenously, but oral ingestion is much more common.[6,9]

Psilocyn (psilocybin) is derived from the mushroom *Psilocybe*, which has been used for centuries in Indian ceremonies. Psilocyn and psilocybin, which are the active ingredients in the mushrooms, are chemically related to LSD. Although these drugs now can be manufactured synthetically, much of what is sold illicitly actually consists of other chemical compounds.[6,9]

DET (diethyltryptamine) and *DMT* (dimethyltryptamine), although generally regarded as interchangeable with LSD, have markedly different potencies, durations of action and somatic side effects. They are relatively inactive when ingested as capsules and must be inhaled or smoked to produce hallucinogenic effects.[13]

PHENYLETHYLAMINES: The principal agents of abuse in this group are *peyote* and *mescaline*, derived from the *Peyote* cactus. Also produced synthetically, mescaline originally was manufactured from the fleshy "buttons" of peyote plants, which the Indians of Northern Mexico have used in religious rites from the earliest recorded time.[6,9]

PHENYLISOPROPYLAMINES: The drugs in this group are synthetic hallucinogens that bear a chemical resemblance to both mescaline and the amphetamines, and produce effects similar to LSD.[6] The most popular phenylisopropylamine compound is DOM (4-methyl-2, 5-dimethoxyamphetamine), first synthesized in 1963. DOM was quickly renamed "STP" in the drug culture, initially after a commercial motor oil additive and later as an acronym for "Serenity-Tranquility-Peace."[9,13]

Related chemicals include DOB (4-bromo-2, 5-dimethoxyamphetamine), DOE (2, 5-dimethoxy-4-ethylamphetamine), MDA (methylenedioxyamphetamine) and MMDA (3-methoxy-4, 5-methylenedioxyamphetamine). These drugs differ markedly in rapidity of onset, duration of effects and capacity to modify mood. Also, because they are produced in clandestine laboratories, they are seldom pure and the dose in a single capsule or on a square of impregnated paper can vary widely.[9,13]

OTHER HALLUCINOGENS: Hallucinogenic effects have been imputed to a variety of substances by members of the drug culture. While clinical studies have failed to confirm some of these allegations, other substances have been found to produce "psychedelic" episodes under certain conditions and at sufficiently large doses.

Artane (trihexyphenidyl) and *Cogentin* (benzotropine mesylate) typify the diversion of medically useful drugs to illicit use. These anti-Parkinsonian agents are synthetic anticholinergics that are prescribed to control extra-pyramidal symptoms of Parkinsonism and the phenothiazine derivatives. They are used in the drug culture to achieve a "high" that is likened to the combined effects of LSD and amphetamines.[25]

Mappine (bufotenine) is a dimethyl-serotonin that can be extracted from the skin of the toad *Bufo marinus*, the toadstool *Amanita mappa*, or the South American shrub *Piptadenia peregrina*. Used by the Vikings as well as in Siberia and the Caribbean (where it is called "cohaba snuff"), intravenously injected mappine produces altered perceptions of time and space.[26]

Herbal preparations in the form of teas, cigarets, smoking mixtures and capsules are widely available in health food stores and by direct mail order from importers and suppliers. Some of these preparations include non-psychoactive ingredients (such as rosemary, thyme and spearmint), while others contain plants with verified psychoactive effects (see Table 9, below). Non-medical use of herbal intoxicants has gained popularity as a legal alternative to the illicit hallucinogens. Many of these herbal preparations are advertised and used for their ability to evoke euphoric and hallucinogenic effects.[27]

TABLE 9

Psychoactive Substances Used in Herbal Preparations

Labeled Ingredient	Botanical Source	Pharmacologic Principle	Suggested Use	Reported Effects
African Yohimbe Bark; Yohimbe	*Corynanthe yohimbe*	Yohimbe	Smoke or tea as stimulant	Mild hallucinogen
Broom; Scotch Broom	*Cytisus spp*	Cytisine	Smoke for relaxation	Strong sedative/hypnotic
California Poppy	*Eschscholtzia californica*	Alkaloids & glucosides	Smoke as marijuana substitute	Mild euphoriant
Catnip	*Nepeta cataria*	Nepetalactone	Smoke or tea as marijuana substitute	Mild hallucinogen
Cinnamon	*Cinnamomum camphora*	?	Smoke with marijuana	Mild stimulant
Damiana	*Turnera diffusa*	?	Smoke as marijuana substitute	Mild stimulant
Hops	*Humulus lupulus*	Lupuline	Smoke or tea as sedative and marijuana substitute	None
Hydrangea	*Hydrangea paniculata*	Hydrangin, saponin, cyanogenes	Smoke as marijuana substitute	Stimulant
Juniper	*Juniper macropoda*	?	Smoke as hallucinogen	Strong hallucinogen
Kavakava	*Piper methysticum*	Yangonin, pyrones	Smoke or tea as marijuana substitute	Mild hallucinogen
Kola Nut; Gotu Kola	*Cola spp*	Caffeine, theobromine, kolanin	Smoke, tea, or capsules as stimulant	Stimulant
Lobelia	*Lobelia inflata*	Lobeline	Smoke or tea as marijuana substitute	Mild euphoriant
Mandrake	*Mandragora officinarum*	Scopolamine, hyoscyamine	Tea as hallucinogen	Hallucinogen

TABLE 9 (continued)

Labeled Ingredient	Botanical Source	Pharmacologic Principle	Suggested Use	Reported Effects
Mate	*Ilex paraguayensis*	Caffeine	Tea as stimulant	Stimulant
Mormon Tea	*Ephedra nevadensis*	Ephedrine	Tea as stimulant	Stimulant
Nutmeg	*Myristica fragrans*	Myristicin	Tea as hallucinogen	Hallucinogen
Passion Flower	*Passiflora incarnata*	Harmine alkaloids	Smoke, tea, or capsules as marijuana substitute	Mild stimulant
Periwinkle	*Catharanthus roseus*	Indole alkaloids	Smoke or tea as euphoriant	Hallucinogen
Prickly Poppy	*Argemone mexicana*	Protopine, bergerine, isoquinilines	Smoke as euphoriant	Narcotic analgesic
Snakeroot	*Rauwolfia serpentina*	Reserpine	Smoke or tea as tobacco substitute	Tranquilizer
Thorn Apple	*Datura stramonium*	Atropine, scopolamine	Smoke or tea as tobacco substitute or hallucinogen	Strong hallucinogen
Tobacco	*Nicotiana spp*	Nicotine	Smoke as tobacco	Strong stimulant
Valerian	*Valeriana officinalis*	Chatinine, velerine alkaloids	Tea or capsules as tranquilizer	Tranquilizer
Wild Lettuce	*Lactuca sativa*	Lactucarine	Smoke as opium substitute	Mild narcotic analgesic
Wormwood	*Artemisia absinthium*	Absinthine	Smoke or tea as relaxant	Narcotic analgesic

Source: Siegel, R. K. Herbal intoxication: psychoactive effects from herbal cigarettes, tea, and capsules *JAMA* 236(5):473 (August 2, 1976)

Ibogaine is a complex 20-carbon compound with an indole nucleus that is derived from the African shrub *Tabernanthe iboga*. Derivatives of this plant reportedly have been used by African tribal hunters because ibogaine's ability to distort time perception allows them to remain motionless for protracted periods while stalking game. Now commercially available, ibogaine is abused for its hallucinogenic potential.[27]

Morning glory seeds, when pulverized and ingested in large amounts (the equivalent of 200 to 300 seeds per dose) are hallucinogenic. Although they produce an LSD-like effect, morning glory seeds are not a preferred hallucinogenic compound because they contain toxins that produce extremely unpleasant side effects (nausea, vomiting, diarrhea).[26]

Nutmeg (Myristica) is a minor hallucinogen that generally is used only when more potent agents are not available. Oral ingestion of the equivalent of two grated nutmegs produces euphoria and hallucinations, but the onset of action is delayed for two to five hours. Failure to use fresh nutmeg can result in side effects such as nausea, vomiting, cramps and vertigo.[26]

PREVALENCE AND PATTERNS OF HALLUCINOGEN ABUSE

Use of LSD and related hallucinogens reached a peak of popularity in the United States during the mid-1960's, gradually declined in the late 1960's and early 1970's, then showed some resurgence of popularity in the late 1970's.[12]

Used more by college students, the affluent and the creative community than by the poor or the sociopathic, hallucinogens commonly are employed to achieve an occasional "trip," followed by weeks or months during which marijuana is used with variable frequency. Chronic use of hallucinogens is quite uncommon and rarely involves taking such drugs more than once a week. Most abusers of hallucinogens are not involved in repetitive use over long periods of time.[4,9,13]

PHARMACOLOGICAL ACTIONS OF THE HALLUCINOGENS

The physiological effects of acute intoxication with LSD and other hallucinogens are distinctive. They include pupillary dilation, increased blood pressure and body temperature, tachycardia, hyperreflexia, piloerection, muscle weakness and tremor, and elevation of free fatty acids in the blood.[4,13,28]

Oral doses of 100 to 250 micrograms of LSD produce, within a few minutes, dizziness, weakness, drowsiness, nausea and paresthesias, sometimes followed by feelings of inner tension that are relieved by

TABLE 10

Hallucinogens: Nomenclature		
Drug Types	**Trade and Generic Names**	**Street Names**
Indolealkylamines	Delysid (d-lysergic acid diethylamide) LSD	Acid, Barrels, Blotter Acid, Blue Cap, Blue Dragon, California Sunshine, Camel, Candles, Cupcake, Four-Way, Green Dragon, Haze, King Tut, Microdots, Mr. Natural, Orange Sunshine, Paper Acid, Purple Haze, Red Dragon, Sunshine, The Force, Wedges, White Lightning, Windowpanes, Zig-Zag Man
	Psilocyn (psilocybin)	Magic Mexican Mushroom, Mushroom, Silly Putty
	DET (diethyltryptamine)	—
	DMT (dimethyltryptamine)	Businessman's Special
Phenylethylamines	Mescaline (peyote)	Big Chief, Buttons, Cactus, Mesc, Mescal
Phenylisopropylamines	DOB (4-bromo-2, 5-dimethoxy-amphetamine)	—
	DOE (2, 5-dimethoxy-4-ethyl-amphetamine)	—
	DOM (2, 5-dimethoxy-4-methyl-amphetamine)	STP (Serenity-Tranquility-Peace Pill)
	MDA (methylenedioxyamphetamine)	Love Pill
	MMDA (3-methoxy-4, 5-methylene-dioxyamphetamine)	—
Other Hallucinogens	Artane (trihexyphenidyl) Cogentin (benzotropine mesylate) Mappine (bufotenine) Herbal preparations Ibogaine Morning glory seeds Nutmeg (myristica)	

Sources: Controlled Substances: Uses and Effects *Drug Enforcement* 6(2):20 (July 1979)
Schuckit, M. A. *Drug and Alcohol Abuse: A Clinical Guide to Diagnosis and Treatment* (Plenum Medical Book Co., New York City, 1979)
Inaba, D., Way, E. L., Blum, K. and Scholl, S. H. *Pharmacological and Toxicological Perspectives on Commonly Abused Drugs* Medical Monograph Series, Vol. I, No. 5 (January 1978)

laughing or crying. After one or two hours, visual illusions, wavelike recurrences of perceptual changes and affective symptoms may occur. At this point, the user may be hypervigilant or withdrawn, or alternate between those states. Many users also experience fears of fragmentation or disintegration of the self. After-images are prolonged, with overlaping of present and past perceptions, and some users elaborate this confluence into hallucinations.[13,14]

Perceptions of time are profoundly altered, so that clock time seems to pass extremely slowly. Thoughts and memories can become quite vivid, to the point of being distressing. Mood may be labile, shifting from depression to happiness, from euphoria to fear. After four to five hours, the user may experience a sense of detachment and a feeling of utter control. The entire syndrome begins to clear after about 12 hours. All of the psychological and physical effects increase in intensity in direct proportion to the size of the dose ingested.[13,14]

Acute anxiety and panic reactions (terror, confusion, dissociation, fear of losing control) are the most common adverse psychological effects of the hallucinogens. These reactions usually are temporary, lasting no more than 24 hours with LSD. They can persist for two days or more, however, and occasionally progress into a long-lasting toxic psychosis.[4,14]

The most common prolonged adverse reaction is post-LSD depression. Although this usually is a short-lived state, it has been known to last as long as eight months.[14]

The phenomenon of the flashback reaction ("free trip") is not completely understood. Users describe it as a transient, spontaneous recurrence of certain aspects of a previous hallucinogenic experience following a period of apparent normalcy. The effects experienced in flashback reactions usually are unpleasant, often involving visual distortions and altered self-perception. Flashback reactions appear to be most common among users who have ingested LSD or other hallucinogens on multiple occasions, who have combined the hallucinogens with other psychoactive drugs (such as chlorpromazine), or who are undergoing psychological stress. This phenomenon can occur sporadically or several times a day, can last from minutes to hours, and can persist for as long as a year after drug use is discontinued.[4,14]

The psychological and physical effects produced by the other hallucinogens generally are similar to those produced by LSD; yet, there are significant differences in potency, rates of absorption, metabolism and duration of action. For example, LSD is 100 times more potent than psilocybin and 4,000 times more potent than mescaline in producing altered states of consciousness. Some differences in the frequency of somatic effects also have been found, so that, for instance, vomiting is more frequent with mescaline than with LSD.[13]

All of these reactions are altered by adulteration of hallucinogens with other drugs, which is a common practice in the drug culture. For example, street samples of hallucinogens frequently contain large amounts of strychnine or amphetamines, which shorten the onset time, prolong the duration and increase the intensity of the psychedelic experience (amphetamines also increase the level of anxiety accompanying the experience). Analyses of drugs purchased illicitly have shown that, while 87% of LSD samples were pure, up to 95% of the drugs sold as mescaline or psilocybin actually contained phencyclidines, DOM or LSD, usually combined with amphetamines. Thus, it is difficult to predict the precise effects of any street drug based on the compound the user thinks he has ingested.[6,14]

TOLERANCE, TOXICITY AND DEPENDENCE ON THE HALLUCINOGENS

A high degree of tolerance to the behavioral effects of LSD emerges after three or four daily doses, but sensitivity returns after a comparable drug-free interval. Considerable cross-tolerance has been observed among LSD, mescaline and psilocybin, but none is evident between LSD and the amphetamines. No withdrawal symptoms are precipitated by abrupt discontinuation of these drugs.[6,12]

No deaths directly attributable to ingestion of LSD have been reported, although deaths from accidents or suicide while intoxicated with hallucinogens are not unknown. Research on teratogenic effects and chromosomal aberrations related to use of hallucinogens—particularly LSD—still is inconclusive, but suggests that the chromosomal damage inflicted by LSD may be no greater than that caused by many more common drugs.[13,14]

The psychological hazards associated with use of hallucinogens have been amply documented. The most common adverse effect is the panic reaction ("bad trip"), which cannot be reliably prevented and has been known to occur even in users who have had many previous "good trips." Recurrence of drug effects without the use of drugs (flashback reactions or "free trips") also are frequently associated with hallucinogen use. Both effects can be treated by reassurance in a supportive environment, use of antianxiety agents or phenothiazines, or barbiturates sufficient to induce sleep. Serious depressions, paranoid behavior and psychotic episodes have developed concurrently with use of hallucinogens, but a cause-and-effect relationship has not been firmly established.[4,13,14]

EFFECTS FOR WHICH HALLUCINOGENS ARE ABUSED

The subjective effects of LSD and the other hallucinogens depends on several psychological factors (including the user's personality structure, emotions and attitude at the time of the drug experience, as well as the environment in which the drug experience takes place), and on physical factors such as whether the user is fed or hungry, rested or tired, warm or cold. Familiarity with other psychoactive drugs also seems relevant, in that users who have extensive experience with such drugs seem better able to cope with the LSD experience.[14]

The psychologically effective dose of LSD is 100 to 250 micrograms, which produces an experience that lasts 8 to 12 hours. Effects usually begin within an hour after ingestion and peak at two to three hours.[14]

First use of LSD usually produces effects that are atypical, albeit more vivid, startling and dramatic than those of later use. Changes in visual perception often are the most dramatic for first-time users, with alterations in auditory perception, thought and mood more prominent during subsequent use. In general, perception of all sensory input is affected in the psychedelic state: awareness of colors, sound and textures is heightened, imagery fills the visual field (often in the form of a fine lacework of pattern over everything viewed), and contours of objects appear distorted (buildings may appear to be leaning over and furniture may seem to swell and shrink as though breathing).[14] Overflow from one sensory modality to another (synesthesias), in which the user "hears" colors and "sees" sounds, may occur at this point. As the user's thought processes are altered, he may develop a shortened concentration span, interposed thoughts and mind-wandering or, conversely, become enthralled with a mundane object and concentrate on it for hours.[13,14]

Mescaline doses of 300 to 500 mg produce psychological effects that are essentially identical to those of LSD. These effects appear one to two hours after ingestion and last 8 to 12 hours. They include altered sensations of sight, smell, touch and hearing, but with less mental reorganization than is caused by LSD. Mescaline also brings on kinesthetic sensations, such as a feeling of floating or separation of body parts.[14]

With psilocybin, a dose of 20 to 60 mg produces effects that are similar to those of LSD and mescaline, but which last only five to six hours.[14]

Small doses of DOM produce subjective feelings of enhanced self-awareness and euphoria, apparently without hallucinations or intellectual impairment. Higher doses (in the range of 5 mg) result in hallucinogenic reactions that can last up to 72 hours and physiological effects similar to those of LSD.[14]

TABLE 11

Hallucinogens: Characteristics and Effects

Effects for which drug is used: Euphoria, altered perception of visual and auditory stimuli

Other possible effects: Illusions and hallucinations, poor judgment, impaired perception of time and distance

Drug Names	Usual Route of Adminis.	Duration of Effects (in hours)	Potential for Physical Dependence	Potential for Psychological Dependence	Potential for Tolerance
Indolealkylamines LSD	Oral (liquid capsule, pill or sugar cube)	12	None	Degree unknown	Yes
Psilocyn	Oral (liquid, capsule, pill or sugar cube)	6	None	Degree unknown	Possible
DET, DMT	Oral (inhaled or smoked)	Up to days	Unknown	Degree unknown	Yes
Phenylethylamines Mescaline	Oral	4	None	Degree unknown	Yes
Phenylisopropylamines DOB, DOE, DOM, MDA, MMDA	Oral (pills or capsules)	Up to days	Unknown	Degree unknown	Yes
Other Hallucinogens Herbal preparations	Oral (capsules, tea, cigarets)	2	None	Degree unknown	Possible
Nutmeg	Oral	2	None	Degree unknown	Possible

Sources: Controlled Substances: Uses and Effects *Drug Enforcement* 6(2):20 (July 1979)
Fort, J. *The Pleasure Seekers* (Bobbs-Merrill Co., Indianapolis, Ind., 1969)
Schuckit, M. A. *Drug and Alcohol Abuse: A Clinical Guide to Diagnosis and Treatment* (Plenum Medical Book Co., New York City, 1979)
Siegel, R. K. Herbal intoxication: psychoactive effects from cigarettes, tea, and capsules *JAMA* 236(4):473 (August 2, 1976)

DMT also produces psychological effects approximating those of LSD, but lasting only one hour. Ineffective when swallowed, DMT usually is mixed with tobacco or marijuana and smoked, or inhaled as snuff. With these modes of ingestion, onset time generally is less than five minutes.[13,14]

MDA causes an inwardly focused experience. At doses of 60 to 120 mg, the user believes he has heightened self-insight and esthetic appreciation. These effects begin about one hour after ingestion, peak at one and a half to two hours, and usually last about eight hours.[14]

Herbal preparations and nutmeg produce a variety of effects, depending on the plant species and the amount ingested. Users have reported hallucinations, visual distortions, dizziness, giddiness, confusion, poor motor coordination and incoherent speech.[14,27]

PHENCYCLIDINES

Phencyclidines, because of their widely varied effects at different dose levels, cannot be accurately placed in the established categories of stimulants, hallucinogens or depressants.[29] Depending on dose size, phencyclidines act as excitants or cataleptoid anesthetics. They frequently are labeled cataleptoid or sympathomimetic anesthetics.[30]

DRUGS IN THE PHENCYCLIDINE CLASS

Phencyclidine (1-[1-phenylcyclohexyl] piperidine HCL) is a stable solid that is readily soluble in water or ethanol.[29] When it was developed in the late 1950's, initial interest focused on phencyclidine's potential as a "dissociative" anesthetic. In clinical trials, surgical patients anesthetized with phencyclidine felt dissociated from their environment, with analgesia and some amnesia, but without significant respiratory or cardiovascular depression.[30,31] However, emergence from the anesthetic state often was marked by psychological symptoms ranging from mild to profound disorientation, agitation, manic excitation, delirium and hallucinations. As a result, the manufacturer discontinued human trials in 1965.[6,29,31]

In 1967, phencyclidine became available for veterinary use under several trade names (Sernyl, Sernylan, Synalar); however, the veterinary product has since been withdrawn from the market.[6,29]

More than 30 *phencyclidine analogs* have been developed through minor modifications of the manufacturing process. The most popular analogs on illicit markets are ketamine, PCE (N-ethyl-1-phenylcyclohexylamine), PCPy and PHP (1-[1-phenylcyclohexyl] pyrrolidine), and TCP or TPCP (1-[1-(2-thienyl)-cyclohexyl] piperidine).[9,31,32]

Some of these analogs are capable of producing the same physiological and psychological effects as phencyclidine, and most are sold as that drug on illicit markets.[9,32]

Identification of phencyclidine and its analogs is complicated by the great variation in appearance of these drugs. In its pharmaceutically pure form, phencyclidine is a white, crystalline powder. However, the makeshift manufacture of most phencyclidine available on illicit markets results in the inclusion of a high level of contaminants (including potassium cyanide) that can cause the color to range from tan to brown and the consistency to vary from powder to a gummy mass.[9,31] PCP also is sold as a liquid and in tablet form, the latter in a variety of colors.[32]

A further difficulty in identifying phencyclidine is that it frequently is combined with other abused drugs, such as barbiturates, heroin, cocaine, amphetamines, methaqualone, LSD, mescaline, marijuana and procaine.[31,32]

Powdered phencyclidine often is sprinkled on parsley, mint, oregano or other leafy material and rolled into cigarets.[6,31,32] When phencyclidine is sold as powder (most commonly under the street name "Angel Dust"), its purity usually is in the range of 50% to 100%. When it is sold under other names or as other drugs, or as a liquid, tablets or one-gram "rock" crystals, the purity drops to 10% to 30%, with the leafy mixtures containing even less.[32]

When misrepresented, phencyclidine most often is sold as THC (the principal psychoactive ingredient in marijuana), cannabinol (another marijuana constituent), mescaline, psilocybin, LSD and even amphetamine or cocaine.[31]

PREVALENCE AND PATTERNS OF PHENCYCLIDINE ABUSE

The incidence and patterns of use associated with the phencyclidines do not correspond with the known incidence and use patterns of other commonly abused drugs. Many sources report that phencyclidine appeared briefly on the illicit drug market in Los Angeles in 1965, but did not attract any considerable attention. It appeared in San Francisco in 1967 as the "PeaCe Pill" and in New York City in 1968 as "hog."[31] The drug developed a poor reputation among street users at each of these locales and, for the next four or five years, was sold mainly as a counterfeit of more popular drugs such as THC, mescaline and psilocybin.[6,29,31]

A paradox not yet fully explained is the recent increase in phencyclidine use despite its poor "street" reputation. For example, Siegel's study[33] found that 319 adult users of phencyclidine reported mixed

TABLE 12

Phencyclidines: Nomenclature

Drug Names	Trade and Generic Names	Street Names
Phencyclidine	Sernyl* Sernylan* (1-[1-phenylcyclohexyl] Synalar* piperdine HCL)	Angel Dust, Crystal, Cyclone, DOA, Dead on Arrival, Dummy Dust, Dust of Angels, Embalming Fluid, Goon, Hog, Killer Weed, Krystal, Mintweed, Monkey Dust, Ozone, Peace, PeaCe Pill, PCP, Scuffle, Sherman, Supergrass, Surfer, T, Tic Tac, Tranq
Phencyclidine analogs	Ketamine PCE (N-ethyl-1-phenylcyclo- hexylamine) PCPy, PHP (1-[1-phenylcyclo- hexyl] pyrrolidine) TCP, TPCP (1-[1-(2-thienyl)- cyclohexyl] piperidine)	PCE PCPy, PHP TCP, TPCP ALSO: Rocket Fuel

*No longer manufactured for clinical (veterinary) use.

Sources: Controlled Substances: Uses and Effects *Drug Enforcement* 6(2):20 (July 1979)
STASH notes: phencyclidine (PCP) *STASH Capsules* 5(2):1 (April 1973)
Pittel, S. M. and Oppedahl, M. C. The enigma of PCP *in* R. I. DuPont, A. Goldstein and J. O'Donnell (eds.) *Handbook on Drug Abuse* (National Institute on Drug Abuse, Rockville, Md., 1979)
Petersen, R. C. and Stillman, R. C. Phencyclidine abuse *Drug Enforcement* 5:19 (July 1978)

negative and positive effects on many occasions on which the drug was used. Phencyclidine's growing popularity despite a relatively high rate of undesirable effects may simply reflect its low cost and ease of manufacture[32] or, as Mello[34] speculates, it may be related to the reinforcement value of mood alteration, even if that alteration is not marked by positive aspects in the usual sense. Petersen and Stillman[32] suggest that the unpredictability of phencyclidine's subjective effects may even contribute to its popularity: "the excitement of not knowing just how the experience will turn out and the ability to later boast of the risks taken may convey a certain amount of status, especially in drug-using peer groups." For whatever reason, it is clear that the incidence of phencyclidine use is rising. Surveys conducted by the National Institute on Drug Abuse[32] found that one in eight persons in the 18 to 25 year old survey group and one in 20 persons in the 12 to 17 year old group had used the drug at least once. Further, the National Youth Polydrug Study[35] of 2,750 persons under the age of 19 in drug treatment centers found that, of all individuals exposed to the drug, approximately 23% became chronic users.

Ethnographic studies confirm that phencyclidine is most popular among young adolescents, although James and Andresen[36] also found older, socially marginal groups using the drug for its powerful mood-altering capacity, and Cleckner[37] has reported on a group of users she characterizes as "an upper-class, highly educated collection of drug experimenters who seek excellence."

Novice users frequently are introduced to phencyclidine openly or covertly by smoking 1 to 100 mg sprinkled on marijuana, tobacco or parsley leaves in a cigaret. Chronic users may ingest 100 mg to one gram in a 24-hour period.[29,31,32]

Although it can be orally ingested by swallowing tablets or inhaling ("snorting") the powder, phencyclidine is most often smoked because that method allows maximum control over the dose ingested. Overdoses appear to be more common with the tablet form because of the slower onset of action and greater concentration of active ingredients. Intravenous injection, although relatively rare, has been reported.[29,31]

Drug effects are similar for all methods of ingestion and generally last four to six hours with moderate doses.[29,31]

PHARMACOLOGICAL ACTIONS OF THE PHENCYCLIDINES

The major physiological effects of the phencyclidines are sympathomimetic and include increases in blood pressure, heart rate, respiration and reflexes (the latter resulting in muscle rigidity). The drug also has cholinergic effects that include sweating, flushing, drooling and pupillary constriction. Cerebellar effects include dizziness, lack of coordination, slurred speech and nystagmus.[6,29]

The range of CNS effects induced by phencyclidine appear to vary with the size of the dose administered. Doses of 2 to 5 mg typically produce a mild depression, followed by stimulation. Approximately 10 mg produces the sensory-deprived state desired by most users, while doses of 20 mg or more can result in catatonia, coma and convulsions. Large doses also may produce seizures, respiratory depression and cardiac instability.[4,29,32]

Psychological effects of the phencyclidines, although dependent on a number of pharmacological, physical and sociocultural variables, have been grouped by Smith et al[38] into four distinct and often successive stages:

STAGE 1: Acute toxicity, marked by combativeness, visual illusions and occasional auditory hallucinations.

STAGE 2: Toxic psychosis, marked by impaired judgment and paranoid delusions, with agitation and both auditory and visual hallucinations. In this stage, users can become destructive to themselves or others. (Stage 2 apparently is not related to toxic blood levels of phencyclidine and does not inevitably follow Stage 1.)

STAGE 3: Psychotic episodes, sometimes lasting a month or more, that bear a strong clinical resemblance to schizophrenia. Symptoms include autistic and delusional thinking involving global paranoia, delusions of superhuman strength and invulnerability, blunted affect and unpredictable behavior.

STAGE 4: Depression, attended by a high risk of suicide or use of other psychoactive drugs to achieve symptomatic relief (Stage 4 may follow any of the previous stages and can last from one day to several months.)

Peterson and Stillman[32] caution that phencyclidine psychosis can constitute a psychiatric emergency, if the patient is dangerous to himself because of delusions, depression and suicidal ideation, or dangerous to others because of paranoia and strong tendencies toward violence.

TOLERANCE, TOXICITY AND DEPENDENCE ON THE PHENCYCLIDINES

User accounts suggest that phencyclidine use leads to some degree of tolerance. Uninterrupted use of the drug to achieve a continuous state of intoxication (a "run") creates a need for progressively larger doses to achieve the desired effects.[32]

The relatively low ratio between the amount of phencyclidine needed to induce the desired level of intoxication and the amount that will cause a toxic reaction makes it difficult to distinguish between a toxic state and the sought-after drug effects. Physically, a toxic reaction is typified by sympathetic and cholinergic hyperactivity, which can occur at doses as low as 5 mg. Other symptoms of toxicity include vertigo, skin flushing, nausea and vomiting, enhanced reflexes, tremor, pupillary constriction, nystagmus and double vision, bilateral ptosis or drooping eyelids, increased blood pressure, dry mouth or drooling.[6,29,32]

Toxic reactions to large doses (15 mg or more) can include decreased respiration, epileptic seizures, body rigidity, coma and—

TABLE 13

Phencyclidines: Characteristics and Effects

Effects for which drug is used: Detachment from surroundings, decreased sensory awareness, illusions of superhuman strength and invulnerability

Other possible effects: Anxiety, impaired coordination, psychotic episodes

Drug Names	Usual Route of Adminis.	Duration of Effects (in hours)	Potential for Physical Dependence	Potential for Psychological Dependence	Potential for Tolerance
Phencyclidine	Oral (smoked, tablets or liquid) Injection	4-6 hours up to days	Degree unknown	High	Yes
Phencyclidine Analogs	Oral (smoked, tablets or liquid) Injection	Varies	Degree unknown	High	Yes

Sources: Controlled Substances: Uses and Effects *Drug Enforcement* 6(2):20 (July 1979)
Schuckit, M. A. *Drug and Alcohol Abuse: A Clinical Guide to Diagnosis and Treatment* (Plenum Medical Book Co., New York City, 1979)
Petersen, R. C. and Stillman, R. C. Phencyclidine: an overview *in* R. C. Petersen and R. C. Stillman (eds.) *Phencyclidine (PCP) Abuse: An Appraisal*, Research Monograph 21 (National Institute on Drug Abuse, Rockville, Md., 1978)

rarely—death. (Schuckit[6] notes that the combination of a coma-like state, open eyes, decreased pain perception, temporary periods of excitation and body rigidity is particularly indicative of a phencyclidine reaction.) Some authorities cite hypertensive crisis as the leading cause of death with phencyclidine,[4] while others suggest that severe overdoses of the drug act as central nervous system depressants, leading to death from respiratory arrest.[6,29,32]

The psychological manifestations of a toxic reaction include detachment and lack of response to external stimuli, occasionally punctuated by outbursts of excitement and hostility.[6,35]

The chemical structure of phencyclidine suggests that a withdrawal syndrome may occur after chronic use.[6] Several studies indicate that psychological, if not physical, dependence develops in some users.[29,31]

EFFECTS FOR WHICH PHENCYCLIDINES ARE ABUSED

Although phencyclidines often are classed as hallucinogens, they do not produce the type of visual hallucinations associated with LSD or mescaline. Instead, most users experience visual illusions and distorted perceptions of reality.[38,39]

At moderate doses, depersonalization and distortions of body image are the effects most frequently reported. Users describe a sense of distance and estrangement from their surroundings. Time seems to expand and body movements seem slowed. A sense of increased physical strength frequently occurs, and sensations of touch and pain are dulled. Speech usually is sparse, purposeless or completely blocked.[29,32]

At higher doses, auditory and visual hallucinations may occur, as well as intermittent feelings of severe anxiety, doom or impending death. Bizarre behavior, such as nudity in public places, occasionally occurs.[29,32]

Users report that feelings of immobility, numbness and detachment are among the desired effects of the drug. Other sought-after effects include feelings of strength, power and invulnerability, coexisting with a dream-like estrangement from reality and a comical lack of coordination. As with the hallucinogens, some users claim that, under the influence of phencyclidines, they see their lives freshly and with a new sense of unity.[29,32]

CANNABINOIDS

Cannabis (marijuana) is obtained from the flowering tops, leaves and stems of the hemp plant *(Cannabis sativa* or *Cannabis indica)*, an herbaceous annual that grows throughout most of the tropic and temperate zones of the world.[9] The two main types of hemp plant are distinguished by the concentration of the principal psychoactive substance (delta-9-tetrahydrocannabinol) they contain: fiber-type hemp generally contains less than 1.0% Δ-9-THC, while drug-type hemp contains concentrations of up to 5.0% Δ-9-THC. Although the concentration of Δ-9-THC in a plant depends on genetic and environmental factors,[40] selective breeding now yields marijuana with a much higher concentration than was available 10 year ago.[41]

It is uncertain whether Δ-9-THC alone is responsible for marijuana's psychoactive effects. Other cannabinoids, such as cannabidiol and tetrahydrocannabidiolic acid (which are extremely heat labile), are decarboxylated and isomerized to THC in the process of smoking marijuana cigarets, contributing to their psychoactivity. Other pyrolytic compounds also may exist.[41]

DRUGS IN THE CANNABINOID CLASS

Marijuana and hashish are the principal drug-type products of the hemp plant. However, biochemists have isolated and identified more than 400 compounds from the plant resin, of which 61 are known cannabinoids. A group of non-nitrogenous compounds sometimes erroneously referred to as alkaloids, cannabinoids are the agents responsible for producing the hallucinogenic and other biological effects of marijuana.[41]

Marijuana is composed of the cut and dried stems, leaves and tops of the hemp plant. It usually is rolled in paper and smoked like a tobacco cigaret. The average marijuana cigaret weighs 0.5 to 1.0 gm and contains 5 to 20 mg of Δ-9-THC.[13,40]

Most marijuana produced in the United States is considered inferior because it contains a low concentration of Δ-9-THC (usually less than 0.5%). Jamaican, Colombian and Mexican varieties contain Δ-9-THC in concentrations ranging from 0.5% to 4.0%. The most potent product is reputed to be *Sinsemilla*, prepared from unpollenated female hemp plants from Thai, Nepalese and Indian stock. Samples of Sinsemilla have been found to contain up to 6.0% Δ-9-THC.[9]

Hashish is a concentrated preparation of the resinous secretions of the hemp plant, which are collected, dried and compressed into balls, cakes or cookie-like sheets. In the United States, hashish varies in potency, with the Δ-9-THC content ranging from trace amounts up to 10%. The average concentration in samples purchased from illicit vendors is about 1.8%.[9,40]

Hashish oil is produced through repeated extraction of hemp plant materials to yield a dark, viscous liquid, current samples of which contain about 20% Δ-9-THC. One or two drops of this liquid on a tobacco cigaret produces a psychoactive effect equal to one marijuana cigaret.[9]

THC (the dextro isomer of Δ-9-THC) is the principal active ingredient of cannabis and usually constitutes 2.0% to 4.0% of the pure resin by weight.[41] Although THC is widely sought on illicit markets for its supposed purity and potency, many of the substances sold as THC actually are other psychoactive drugs, such as lysergic acid (LSD) or phencyclidine (PCP).[6,42]

Other common names for products of the hemp plant include charas, bhang and ganja. *Charas* is the name used in the Far East for the resinous exudate known in Europe and the United States as hashish. The dried leaves and flowering shoots of the hemp plant are called *bhang* and the resinous mass from the small leaves and brackets of inflorescence is called *ganja*.[13]

PREVALENCE AND PATTERNS OF CANNABINOID ABUSE

Marijuana use has increased dramatically in the United States and Europe over the past decade.[13] It now often begins at a much earlier age than it did in 1970, and is more likely to be frequent rather than experimental use.[43] The 1979 National Survey on Drug Abuse[12] found that, among persons who reported current marijuana use, slightly more than two-thirds of the young adults and one-half of the youth and older adults said they had used marijuana five days or more in the month preceding the survey.[12]

The perspective that emerges from this and other surveys is that, as Jessor[42] observes, some experience with marijuana has become "statistically normative among older adolescents and young adults." Many researchers suggest that actual use of marijuana may even exceed the survey results, since household surveys do not capture persons who do not live in households and school surveys do not capture drop-outs. In both cases, Jessor[42] notes, "the groups that are missed probably have higher rates of marijuana use than those who are included, and the survey findings are, to some degree, likely to be underestimates of population prevalence."

PHARMACOLOGICAL ACTIONS OF THE CANNABINOIDS

Despite the popular opinion that, whereas opioids are "hard drugs," marijuana is a "soft drug," recent research shows that cannabinoids contain psychoactive substances of high potency and rapid onset. The widespread effects of marijuana, which involve cerebral, cardiovascular, pulmonary and neuro-regulatory systems, can be seen on in-

TABLE 14

Cannabinoids: Nomenclature		
Drug Names	**Trade and Generic Names**	**Street Names**
Hashish	Cannabis sativa Cannabis indica	Goma de Mota Hash Soles
Hashish Oil	Cannabis sativa	Hash Oil
Marijuana	Cannabis sativa Cannabis indica	Bang, Bhang, Bo, Boo, Charas, Cannabis, Colombian, Ganja, Gold, Grass, Griffa, Hay, Hemp, Herb, Hawaiian, J, Jamaican, Jay, Mary Jane, Mota, Mutah, Pot, Sativa, Sinsemilla, Tea, Weed, Yerba ALSO: *Marijuana cigaret* Ace, Joint, Number, Reefer, Roach, Smoke, Stick *Grades of marijuana* Acapulco Gold, Berkeley Boo, Panama Red *Tobacco & marijuana mix* Kiff *Acetone extract of cannabis* Smash
THC	Δ-9-Tetrahydrocannabinol	THC

Sources: Controlled Substances: Uses and Effects *Drug Enforcement* 6(2):20 (July 1979)
Palmer, D. Northeast Metropolitan Narcotics and Dangerous Drug Enforcement Group (private communication) Elmhurst, Illinois (December 1979)

halation of burned material, on swallowing, and after intravenous administration of purified extracts and synthetic analogs.[44]

Nahas[40] explains that Δ-9-THC (which is four times more potent when inhaled than when swallowed) undergoes a complex transformation in the body. Because Δ-9-THC is fat-soluble, it leaves the bloodstream very rapidly. It is stored in body fats, where it has a half-life of eight days. Thus, repeated administration of cannabinoids at intervals of less than eight to 10 days results in the accumulation of Δ-9-THC and its metabolites in body tissues.

The target organ for marijuana is the brain, where it acts to produce euphoria and detachment. Heath and other researchers[45] have observed structural changes in the brain tissue of primates exposed to marijuana, as well as persistent changes in the patterns of brain waves originating in the limbic area. Heath[46] explains that the Δ-9-THC molecule interacts with nerve cells by being absorbed into the cell membrane. It does not act like opioids by substituting itself for a normal body chemical; rather, it acts like a foreign body in the brain. Nor is it readily broken down; instead, it accumulates in the brain. This, says Heath, is why cannabinoids are potentially more destructive to brain tissue than are opioids.

Acute marijuana intoxication impairs learning, memory, thinking, comprehension and general intellectual performance. Even at "moderate" levels of social use, psychomotor performance (such as driving skill) is impaired.[47]

Clinical studies have demonstrated other effects of marijuana:

RESPIRATORY SYSTEM: Marijuana smoke contains larger amounts of carcinogenic hydrocarbons than tobacco smoke.[47] Tennant[48] has shown serious pathological conditions ("hashish bronchitis" and "bronchitis-emphysema") in a group of American soldiers who used hashish preparations for six to 12 months. Tashkin[49] has reported that smoking an average of five marijuana cigarets a day for two to three months reduces pulmonary function through obstruction of the large and small airways. Mendelsohn[50] noted similar losses of respiratory capacity in male volunteers after several weeks of heavy smoking. In animal studies that were calibrated to simulate the average daily intake of human marijuana smokers, Rosenkrantz[51] found that lesions of lung tissue appeared after three months' exposure. Longer exposure led to (1) an intensive inflammatory response, (2) tissue damage and breakdown of air sacs in the lung and (3) the formation of cholesterol deposits in the lung.

CARDIOVASCULAR SYSTEM: The most consistent effects of marijuana on the cardiovascular system are a marked reddening of the conjuctivae and an increase in heart rate. The increase in heart rate is dose-related, and its onset and duration correlate well with blood concentrations of Δ-9-THC. Increases of 20 to 40 beats per minute are usual, but a tachycardia of 140 beats per minute is not uncommon.[13]

REPRODUCTIVE SYSTEM: Chronic use of marijuana has been associated with disruption of the menstrual cycle and at least temporary infertility. For example, Smith[52] has found that exposure to Δ-9-THC during the latter part of rhesus monkeys' 28-day menstrual cycle rendered the monkeys infertile during the following cycle by inhibiting ovulation. This effect was attributed to suppressed production by the pituitary gland of two hormones that control the menstrual cycle and the normal process of ovulation. Bauman[53] studied the menstrual cycles of 26 human volunteers (aged 18 to 30) who had used marijuana an average of four days per week for at least six months, as well as a control group. She found that 38% of the marijuana users had defective menstrual cycles, including several who failed to ovulate, whereas only 12.5% of the control group had defective cycles, with only one anovulatory cycle.

Sassenrath[54] found that rhesus monkeys given Δ-9-THC during pregnancy had a 44% incidence of reproductive failures (spontaneous abortion, stillbirths, etc.), as compared to an 8% incidence in a control group. She suggests that this may represent either direct toxicity of Δ-9-THC to the developing fetus or impairment of the maternal support system.

In studies of male reproductive processes, Zimmerman[55] found that mice exposed to Δ-9-THC presented a higher incidence of abnormal sperm than did a control group, as well as abnormal chromosomes in the germ cells from which spermatozoa are produced. Fujimoto,[56] Harclerode[57] and Huang[58] reported that mice and rats treated with marijuana smoke, marijuana extract or Δ-9-THC demonstrated atrophy of the testis, seminal vesicles and prostate gland. In human studies, Hembree[59] found that 16 males who smoked marijuana heavily for one month in a controlled hospital setting showed (1) reduced sperm count, (2) decreased sperm motility and (3) sperm of abnormal appearance.

PSYCHOLOGICAL FUNCTIONING: Many clinicians believe that regular marijuana use may seriously interfere with psychological functioning, personality development, and emotional growth and learning, especially in childhood and adolescence.[47] Numerous studies show that enduring psychological impairment may result from heavy use. Large doses of Δ-9-THC can induce frank hallucinations, delusions and paranoid feelings. Thinking becomes confused and disoriented, while depersonalization and altered time sense are accentuated. Euphoria may give way to anxiety reaching panic proportions. With sufficiently large doses, the clinical picture is that of a toxic psychosis, with hallucinations, depersonalization and loss of insight.[13]

At moderate doses, there is less agreement on psychological effects. Grinspoon[60] and others maintain that, compared to other psychoactive drugs, moderate doses of marijuana are relatively safe. They base this assertion partially on the 1975 "Jamaica study," which found no evidence of "amotivational syndrome" among field workers in Jamaica who smoked marijuana daily. On the other hand, several researchers have suggested that results among uneducated manual laborers in a rural, agrarian society have little application to typical marijuana users in the United States. Further, Brill[60] notes that, even in Jamaica, "where the effects of cannabis had been thought to be relatively benign, among the middle class it is now found to be associated with school drop-outs, transient psychoses, panic states, and adolescent behavior disorders."

THERAPEUTIC VALUE: Several therapeutic uses—including the treatment of asthma, glaucoma and nausea arising from chemotherapy—have been suggested for various components of the hemp plant. In a 1980 report to the U.S. Congress,[43] the Secretary of Health, Education and Welfare summarized current research on therapeutic applications of marijuana, THC and related drugs and concluded that, while these substances have shown "definite promise" in treating the nausea and vomiting that often accompany cancer chemotherapy, they have not proved invariably superior to other medications. Similarly, trials of oral Δ-9-THC to reduce intraocular pressure in open-angle glaucoma produced varied results, which were most favorable when the Δ-9-THC was used in combination with standard drugs. Cautioning that "much work remains to be done," the Secretary noted that any therapeutic pharmaceuticals developed through these trials will be "chemically related, but not identical" to the natural material.[43]

TOLERANCE, TOXICITY AND DEPENDENCE ON THE CANNABINOIDS

Animal studies have demonstrated tolerance developing to the hypothermic and certain behavioral effects of the cannabinoids. Although some species develop high levels of tolerance to Δ-9-THC, this tolerance does not develop uniformly to all effects of the drug. The duration of tolerance after the drug is discontinued is related to the dose, frequency of administration and species studied.[13]

Reports from other countries indicate that many regular users of hashish consume Δ-9-THC in amounts that would produce toxic effects in most Western users. Mendelsohn and others[50] have found that human subjects tend to increase their intake of marijuana cigarets or synthetic cannabinoids as an experiment progresses and to show decreased drug effects; however, if the total dose is low, subjects continue to experience a "high" after the first cigaret of the day. Some degree of cross-tolerance between Δ-9-THC and alcohol has been reported, but there is no cross-tolerance between the cannabinoids and the hallucinogens.[13]

Physical and psychological dependence on cannabinoids are suggested but not documented in numerous reports. For example, researchers have observed irritability, restlessness, nervousness and insomnia in subjects who abruptly discontinue chronic heavy use of

TABLE 15

Cannabinoids: Characteristics and Effects

Effects for which drug is used: Europhia, relaxation of inhibitions, heightened sexual arousal

Other possible effects: Increased appetite, disorientation, impaired judgment and coordination

Drug Names	Usual Route of Adminis.	Duration of Effects (in hours)	Potential for Physical Dependence	Potential for Psychological Dependence	Potential for Tolerance
Hashish	Oral (smoked)	2-4	Degree unknown	Moderate	Yes
Hashish Oil	Oral (smoked or swallowed)	2-4	Degree unknown	Moderate	Yes
Marijuana	Oral (smoked or swallowed)	4	Degree unknown	Moderate	Yes
THC	Oral Injection	2-4	Degree unknown	Moderate	Yes

Sources: Controlled Substances: Uses and Effects *Drug Enforcement* 6(2):20 (July 1979)
Fort, J. *The Pleasure Seekers* (Bobbs-Merrill Co., Indianapolis, Ind., 1969)
Schuckit, M. A. *Drug and Alcohol Abuse: A Clinical Guide to Diagnosis and Treatment* (Plenum Medical Book Co., New York City, 1979)

marijuana, but no generally recognized or sharply defined cannabinoid withdrawal syndrome has been demonstrated.[13]

EFFECTS FOR WHICH CANNABINOIDS ARE ABUSED

Marijuana frequently is classified as a hallucinogen, but at the doses most commonly taken, the predominant effects are euphoria and a change in the level of consciousness without frank hallucinations. The changes in mood that occur with cannabinoids depend not only on the dose and frequency of administration, but also on the setting and the user's expectations.[6]

In addition to euphoria, users report feelings of relaxation and heightened sexual arousal,[6] vivid visual imagery and a keen sense of hearing.[13] Subtle visual and auditory stimuli previously ignored may take on a novel quality, and the senses of taste, touch and smell may seem to be enhanced. Altered time perception, in which time seems to pass more slowly, is a consistent effect of cannabinoids.[13]

Many users report that they did not achieve a feeling of euphoria or "high" the first time they smoked marijuana, but subsequently "learned to get high." This involves learning to identify the desired euphoric effects, as well as the proper technique for inhaling the smoke, which is drawn into the lungs with enough air to fill the lungs to their vital capacity, then held in the expanded lungs as long as possible before exhaling.[14]

Because of the rapid onset of effects when marijuana is smoked (usually peaking within 10 to 30 minutes), and the relatively low Δ-9-THC content of marijuana produced in the United States (averaging 2.5 to 5.0 mg per cigaret), most users are able to regulate their intake so as to avoid the more serious unpleasant effects of marijuana use. For the same reasons, psychiatric emergencies as a result of smoking marijuana are uncommon.[13] However, even with moderate doses (the equivalent of two marijuana cigarets), some users experience mild levels of suspiciousness or paranoia, and intoxication during a period of high stress can lead to an elevated level of aggressiveness, although the usual effect of marijuana is to produce a reduction in this attribute.[6]

The psychological effects of mild intoxication can include fine shakes or tremors, a slight decrease in body temperature, a decrease in muscle strength and balance, impaired motor coordination, dry mouth and bloodshot eyes. Some individuals experience nausea, headache, nystagmus and slightly lowered blood pressure. Δ-9-THC also can precipitate seizures in epileptics.[6]

INHALANTS

One method of introducing mood-altering chemicals into the body is through inhalation of volatile substances, which are chemicals that vaporize to a gaseous form at normal room temperatures.[61] When inhaled, these substances can intoxicate quickly, because the large surface area of the lungs provides easy access and ensures a rapid onset of sensation.[62]

Aviado[63] suggests that the chemicals most likely to be abused by inhalation have four characteristics in common: (1) they are present in consumer products that are available to the public, (2) the product is voluntarily inhaled so that the intoxicating chemicals can be absorbed in the respiratory tract, (3) the chemical substance absorbed is a stimulant or depressant, or exerts both actions on the central nervous system and (4) abuse of the inhalant is potentially fatal.

SUBSTANCES IN THE INHALANT CLASS

Jaffe[13] describes the catalog of inhalants that have been used to achieve subjective changes as "impressive" and notes that "each generation not only adds a few new substances, but seems impelled to reevaluate the old." Classification of these substances is difficult, as Cohen[64] explains, because household and commercial products may have unknown formulations (which need not be chemically pure) or contain ingredients that are more toxic than the chemical for which the product is inhaled (as with the lead content of gasoline).

With the exception of the anesthetics, the commonly inhaled volatile substances are complex chemical compounds. Their contents generally belong to chemical groups variously consisting of alcohols, aliphatic hydrocarbons, aliphatic nitrites, aromatic hydrocarbons, fluorinated hydrocarbons, dichlorinated and trichlorinated hydrocarbons, esters and ketones.[61]

In the *anesthetic* group, nitrous oxide has been abused since the 19th century, when demonstrations of "laughing gas" and "ether frolics" were common parlor games among the upper classes. Today, *nitrous oxide* has a number of commercial uses, including that of general anesthetic (particularly in dental offices), as a propellant for whipped cream, in rocket fuel and as a leak detector. As a propellant, nitrous oxide is available in small metal cylinders for use with a dispensing machine. These cylinders, popularly called "Whippets," are sold in drug paraphernalia shops, as are balloons for inhaling gas and pipes ("buzz bombs") for smoking it.[61]

Amyl nitrite has a similar history of appropriation from medical use to abuse. When amyl nitrite became available as an over-the-counter drug in 1960, it also became popular as a drug of abuse. The mesh-covered glass vials or ampules of amyl nitrite (called "poppers") were crushed and inhaled for a quick "high."[61]

When amyl nitrite was reclassified as a prescription drug in 1969, *butyl nitrite* replaced it in the drug culture. Sold as a "room odorizer" or "liquid incense" under a variety of names that are suggestive of its odor ("Banapple Gas," "Locker Room," "Rush," "Jac Aroma," "Satan's Scent," "Locker Popper"), butyl nitrite is widely (and legally) available in novelty stores and drug paraphernalia shops.[61]

The list of inhalable substances found in abused commercial preparations is too extensive to enumerate here. While the known toxic chemicals and their most common commercial applications are listed in Table 16, there are dozens of other chemicals in abused products about which little is known, especially the combined chemical compounds.[61]

PREVALENCE AND PATTERNS OF INHALANT ABUSE

Despite the world-wide extent of inhalant abuse, Hecht[65] observes, it has only been in the past 30 years that social scientists have studied this phenomenon in the United States. The earliest reported episodes involved sniffing gasoline in the 1950's and model airplane cement in the 1960's. Other commercial inhalants commonly abused at the time included the vapors of contact cements, paints, lacquers, drycleaning fluids, transmission fluids, liquid waxes, shoe polish, lighter fluids, nail polish remover, degreasers and refrigerants.[65]

Abuse of aerosol sprays gained popularity in the 1960's, beginning with glass chillers and nonstick vegetable pan coatings. Hecht[65] notes that every type of aerosol has been abused, including cold weather car starters, air sanitizers, window cleaners, furniture polishes, insecticides, disinfectants, spray medications, deodorants, hair sprays, antiperspirants, clear lacquers and gold and bronze spray paints.

The 1970's were marked by an upsurge in the abuse of nitrous oxide, as well as amyl and butyl nitrite, often packaged as "room odorants."

In discussing patterns of abuse, Cohen[66] identifies three degrees of inhalant use. The first (and largest) group of users are the experimenters, who sample an inhalant a few times and then discontinue the practice, either because the experience was unpleasant or not sufficiently reinforcing to lead them to continue their use. The second group Cohen identifies are the occasional or "social" users. The members of this group, he says, "use infrequently, perhaps once a month, when the situation is conducive, but do not make a career of

TABLE 16

Inhalants: Nomenclature		
Chemical Class	**Chemical Name**	**Ingredient in:**
Alcohols	Ethanol	Aerosol sprays, model cement, paint thinner
	Isopropanol	Aerosol sprays, anti-freeze, degreasers, model cement, paint thinner, spray shoe polish
	Methanol	Anti-freeze, paint thinner, windshield washing fluids
Aliphatic hydrocarbons	n-Heptane	Adhesives, rubber cement, gasoline, paint thinner
	n-Hexane	Adhesives, rubber cement, gasoline, model cement
Aliphatic nitrite	Butyl nitrite	Room odorants
Anesthetics	Freon	Aerosol sprays
	Methylene chloride	Degreasers, paint thinner
	Nitrous oxide	Foam dispensers
	Tetrachloroethylene	Degreasers
	Trichloroethylene	Degreasers
Aromatic hydrocarbons	Benzene	Adhesives, rubber cement, degreasers, gasoline
	Naphthalene	Adhesives, rubber cement, gasoline, paint thinner
	Styrene	Adhesives, rubber cement, model cement
	Toluene	Adhesives, rubber cement, aerosol sprays, degreasers, gasoline, model cement, paint thinners, spray shoe polish
	Xylene	Adhesives, rubber cement, aerosol sprays, degreasers, gasoline, model cement, paint thinner
Esters	Ethyl acetate	Paint thinner
	n-Butyl acetate	Degreasers
	n-Propyl acetate	Paint thinner
Ketones	Acetone	Model cement, paint thinner
	Methyl butyl ketone	Paint thinner
	Methyl ethyl ketone	Degreasers, paint thinner

Source: *Inhalants: The Deliberate Inhalation of Volatile Substances* Report Series 30, No. 2 (National Institute on Drug Abuse, Rockville, Md., 1978)

the practice." Cohen describes members of the third group as "heads," who use inhalants daily and who are at the greatest risk of sustaining physical and psychological damage as a result of their use.

While the most widespread use of inhalants traditionally has been among young adolescents, recent surveys have found marked increases in use among young adults and older adults. Hecht[65] also records this upward shift in the mean age of inhalant abusers and cites studies showing that, as they grow older, many inhalant abusers start to use other drugs, but only reduce (rather than discontinue) their inhalant use. She maintains that current use of nitrous oxide and butyl nitrite among college students also contradicts the prevailing view that inhalant abuse is largely confined to early adolescents who are poor, urban dwellers and frequently Hispanic.

PHARMACOLOGICAL ACTIONS OF THE INHALANTS

Inhalants gain access to the systemic circulation through the respiratory tract, says Cohen,[66] with the bulk of the chemicals transported across the alveolar-pulmonary capillary membrane. Thus, the effects of sniffing are felt almost immediately.[61]

Tissues with high lipid levels receive increased amounts of inhaled solvents because of the affinity of solvents for lipids. The brain and spinal cord probably preferentially receive higher concentrations than other organs.[66] The lipid solubility of the volatile solvents presumably causes CNS depression by impairing membrane permeability and neural transmission.[61]

At high doses, inhalants can cause rapid loss of control and consciousness, leading to potential overdose and death from respiratory arrest, or irreversible damage to brain and body tissue. Another cause of death during acute exposure is suffocation, as when a user loses consciousness and falls on a cloth containing evaporating material or asphyxiates after exhausting the oxygen in a plastic bag placed over the head or entire body to concentrate the vapors.[66]

Acute hazards associated with aerosols include possible laryngospasm or airway freezing as a result of rapid vaporization, as well as obstruction of oxygen passage across the alveolar-capillary membrane when Freon mechanically prevents oxygen diffusion. Death also may result from the ingestion of toxic ingredients along with the aerosol substance.[66]

The effects of chronic ingestion of lower doses are less well documented, although recent studies in which young animals have been exposed to intermittent doses are designed to mimic use patterns in humans. Current animal research and reports of toxic reactions in humans, Cohen[66] says, suggest the following effects:

BENZENE: Sufficient exposure to benzene results first in leucocytosis and anemia and eventually in pancytopenia, myeloid leukemia or aplastic anemia. Other toxic effects identified include fatty degeneration, necrosis and ultimately yellow atrophy of the liver. Gastrointestinal effects include gastric pain, anorexia, dyspepsia and chronic gastritis. CNS effects may include headache, drowsiness and irritability.

TOLUENE: Chronic toxic effects of toluene are reported to include gastrointestinal reactions (nausea, epigastric discomfort, anorexia, jaundice and hepatomegaly), urinary dysfunctions (pyuria, hematuria, proteinuria and renal tubular necrosis), hematopoietic abnormalities (reversible anemia) and neurological reactions (mental dulling, tremors, emotional lability, nystagmus, cerebellar ataxia, polyneuropathies and permanent encephalopathies).

HEXANE: Chronic exposure to hexane has been associated with anemia and sensorimotor polyneuropathy, involving muscle weakness, hypoesthesias, paresthesias, muscle atrophy and slowed nerve conduction times.

XYLENE: Mucous membrane irritation and lead poisoning have been noted with chronic exposure to xylene.

GASOLINE: In addition to the toxic reactions caused by gasoline additives (such as benzene), gasoline sniffing has been associated with neurological effects (confusion, tremor, ataxia, paresthesias, neuritis and paralysis of peripheral and cranial nerves), gastrointestinal disturbances (nausea, vomiting, anorexia, abdominal pain and weight loss), and such general effects as anemia, weight loss and fatigue.

CARBON TETRACHLORIDE: A highly toxic solvent, carbon tetrachloride use can lead to renal and hepatic failure, accompanied by anemia and convulsions. Gastrointestinal symptoms include nausea, vomiting, anorexia, abdominal pain and weight loss. Deaths have occurred following exposure to modest amounts of carbon tetrachloride in an unventilated space.

TRICHLORETHYLENE: Liver cell dysfunction in the form of centrilobular necrosis has been associated with inhalation of trichlorethylene, as have the possibility of optic and other cranial nerve damage and renal tubular necrosis.

KETONES: Cases of peripheral neuropathies with demonstrable neural pathology have occurred with inhalation of ketones.

COMBINED MIXTURES: Any two or more solvents that are of lesser toxicological potential when inhaled separately can produce unexpected tissue damage when taken together.

TOLERANCE, TOXICITY AND DEPENDENCE ON THE INHALANTS

Tolerance does develop to the intoxicating effects of inhalants. Cohen[66] states that large daily doses will induce tolerance within a week, while lesser amounts induce tolerance after longer exposure. For example, tolerance was observed in one subject who inhaled model airplane cement once a week for three months. The degree of tolerance established also is impressive, says Cohen, citing one user who experienced fewer effects from eight tubes of plastic cement than he had obtained from a single tube three years earlier.

Toxic effects of inhalant abuse generally are transient in nature, and include dizziness, loss of memory, inability to concentrate, confusion and unsteady gait.[61] However, more serious reactions are not uncommon, including cardiac arrest and depression of myocardial contractility.[63] The most prominent hazard associated with inhalant abuse is Sudden Sniffing Death (SSD), a syndrome related to inhalation of the fluorocarbons contained in aerosols. In cases of SSD, the fluorocarbons (particularly trichlorofluoromethane) sensitize the heart to the stimulant effects of epinephrine, leading to wildly erratic heartbeat, increased pulse rates and, ultimately, cardiac arrest.[61,63]

Physical dependence on the inhalants has not been clinically established, although there are reports of tremulousness, irritability, loss of appetite and insomnia following abrupt cessation of inhalant use. Cohen[66] notes that these reactions could represent either minor abstinence symptoms or nonspecific resurgent anxiety effects.

Psychological dependence, on the other hand, has been widely documented, and is evidenced by repeated relapse to solvent inhalation despite evident physical damage to the user, repeated incarceration and the threat of further punishment. Several studies show that this dependence develops to the state of intoxication, rather than to any specific chemical.[66]

EFFECTS FOR WHICH INHALANTS ARE ABUSED

Adolescents bent on getting "high" choose inhalants for a number of reasons, says Hecht:[65] the intoxicating effect is immediate (though not long-lasting), the products inhaled are inexpensive, legal and readily available in the home or workplace, and the compact packaging of items such as glue or nail polish remover makes these items easy to carry in a pocket or purse.

Several methods of ingesting inhalants have been reported, according to Cohen.[66] Solvents most often are poured or sprayed onto a cloth, which is placed on the mouth or around the nose so that the vapors can be inhaled. Plastic or paper bags sometimes are used to contain solvents for inhalation, and balloons have been used to capture the spray from an aerosol can. Some users warm the solvents (especially from aerosols) before inhaling so they will not chill the

TABLE 17

Inhalants: Characteristics and Effects

Effects for which drug is used: Euphoria, excitement, relaxation of inhibitions

Other possible effects: Excitation, hallucinations, slurred speech, ataxia, drowsiness, headache, nausea, amnesia, respiratory depression, cardiac arrest

Drug Names	Duration of Effects	Potential for Physical Dependence	Potential for Psychological Dependence	Potential for Tolerance
Alcohols	5-45 minutes	Possible	Degree unknown	Yes
Aliphatic hydrocarbons	Up to 2 hours	Possible	Degree unknown	Yes
Aliphatic nitrites	5-30 minutes	None	Degree unknown	Yes
Anesthetics	Up to 2 hours	Possible	Degree unknown	Yes
Aromatic hydrocarbons	Up to 2 hours	Possible	Degree unknown	Yes
Esters	5-45 minutes	None	Degree unknown	Yes
Ketones	About 1 hour	Possible	Degree unknown	Yes

Source: *Inhalants: The Deliberate Inhalation of Volatile Substances* Report Series 30, No. 2 (National Institute on Drug Abuse, Rockville, Md., 1978)

respiratory tract, while other users spray aerosols directly into the mouth. A particularly dangerous practice is the placing of a plastic bag over the head or entire body to increase the concentration of vapors.

Users describe the sensations evoked by inhalants as euphoria and excitement, accompanied by a feeling that "something wonderful is about to happen." Immediate and transient effects range from somnolence and dizziness to delusions of unusual strength or the ability to fly. Visual and auditory hallucinations are reported at high doses. Slurred speech, ataxia, impaired judgment and feelings of giddiness and drunkenness are reported by almost all users, even on the occasion of first use. These feelings are accompanied by a sense of reckless abandon and omnipotence, often leading to impulsive or destructive behavior. Other users have described feelings of numbness or of floating in space. Distortions of visual perception are not uncommon.[61]

REFERENCES

1. Cohen, S. Pharmacology of drugs of abuse *Drug Abuse & Alcoholism Newsletter* 5(6):1 (July 1976)
2. *Webster's New Collegiate Dictionary* (G. & C. Merriam Co., Springfield, Mass., 1979)
3. Cowan, J. D., Kay, D. C., Neidert, G. L., Ross, F. E. and Belmore, S. Drug abusers: defeated and joyless *in* L. S. Harris (ed.) *Problems of Drug Dependence, 1979* Research Monograph No. 27 (National Institute on Drug Abuse, Rockville, Md., 1980)
4. Inaba, D., Way, E. L., Blum, K. and Schnoll, S. H. *Pharmacological and Toxicological Perspectives on Commonly Abused Drugs* Medical Monograph Series, Vol. I, No. 5 (January 1978)
5. Pittel, S. M. Psychological aspects of heroin and other drug dependence *in* D. E. Smith and G. R. Gay (eds.) *It's So Good, Don't Even Try It Once* (Prentice-Hall, Englewood Cliffs, N.J., 1972)
6. Schuckit, M. A. *Drug and Alcohol Abuse: A Clinical Guide to Diagnosis and Treatment* (Plenum Medical Book Co., New York City, 1979)
7. *AMA Drug Evaluations, Fourth Edition* (American Medical Association, Chicago, Ill., 1980)
8. Jaffe, J. H. and Martin, W. R. Opioid analgesics and antagonists *in* A. G. Gilman, L. S. Goodman and A. Gilman (eds.) *The Pharmacological Basis of Therapeutics* (Macmillan, New York City, 1980)
9. Drugs of abuse *Drug Enforcement* 6(2):10 (July 1979)
10. Gay, G. R. and Way, E. L. Pharmacology of the opiate narcotics *in* D. E. Smith and G. R. Gay (eds.) *It's So Good, Don't Even Try It Once* (Prentice-Hall, Englewood Cliffs, N.J., 1972)

11. Inaba, D. S., Johnson, G., Smith, D. E. and Newmeyer, J. A. Persian heroin in the San Francisco Bay area, 1977-1980: the new wave? *Newsletter from the California Society for the Treatment of Alcoholism and Other Drug Dependencies* 7(2):1 (April 1980)
12. *The National Survey on Drug Abuse: Main Findings 1979* (National Institute on Drug Abuse, Rockville, Md., 1980)
13. Jaffe, J. H. Drug addiction and drug abuse *in* A. G. Gilman, L. S. Goodman and A. Gilman (eds.) *The Pharmacological Basis of Therapeutics* (Macmillan, New York City, 1980)
14. Hennessee, J., Mulry, J., Wehrspann, B. and Holzaepfel, J. *Drug Information Syllabus* Student American Medical Association Local Issues Conference on Drug Abuse (American Medical Association, Chicago, Ill., 1970)
15. Smith, D. E., Wesson, D. R. and Seymour, R. B. The abuse of barbiturates and other sedative-hypnotics *in* R. I. DuPont, A. Goldstein and J. O'Donnell (eds.) *Handbook on Drug Abuse* (National Institute on Drug Abuse, Rockville, Md., 1979)
16. Harvey, S. C. Hypnotics and sedatives *in* A. G. Gilman, L. S. Goodman and A. Gilman (eds.) *The Pharmacological Basis of Therapeutics* (Macmillan, New York City, 1980)
17. Cohen, S. Benzodiazepine receptors in the brain *Drug Abuse & Alcoholism Newsletter* 8(9):1 (November 1979)
18. Weiner, N. Norepinephrine, epinephrine, and the sympathomimetic amines *in* A. G. Gilman, L. S. Goodman and A. Gilman (eds.) *The Pharmacological Basis of Therapeutics* (Macmillan, New York City, 1980)
19. Franz, D. N. Central nervous system stimulants *in* A. G. Gilman, L. S. Goodman and A. Gilman (eds.) *The Pharmacological Basis of Therapeutics* (Macmillan, New York City, 1980)
20. Petersen, R. C. and Stillman, R. C. *Cocaine: 1977* Research Monograph 13 (National Institute on Drug Abuse, Rockville, Md., 1977)
21. Ellinwood, E. H. Jr. Amphetamines/anorectics *in* R. I. DuPont, A. Goldstein and J. O'Donnell (eds.) *Handbook on Drug Abuse* (National Institute on Drug Abuse, Rockville, Md., 1979)
22. Smoking cocaine: a dangerous switch *Science News* 116(22):373 (December 1, 1979)
23. Smith, D. E., Wesson, D. R., Buxton, M. E. and Seymour, R. B. (eds.) Stimulant use, misuse and abuse: a ten year follow-up *Journal of Psychedelic Drugs* 10(4) (October-December 1978)
24. Ritchie, J. M. and Greene, N. M. Local anesthetics *in* A. G. Gilman, L. S. Goodman and A. Gilman (eds.) *The Pharmacological Basis of Therapeutics* (Macmillan, New York City, 1980)
25. Anti-Parkinsonian drugs: a new high for the abuser *Emergency Medicine* 11(10):176 (October 15, 1979)
26. Kelley, J. *Current Non-Medical Drug Use Guide* (TUATARA, Dallas, Tex., n.d.)

27. Siegel, R. K. Herbal intoxication: psychoactive effects from herbal cigarettes, tea, and capsules *JAMA* 236(5):473 (August 2, 1976)
28. Baldessarini, R. J. Drugs and the treatment of psychiatric disorders *in* A. G. Gilman, L. S. Goodman and A. Gilman (eds.) *The Pharmacological Basis of Therapeutics* (Macmillan, New York City, 1980)
29. Grinspoon L. and Bakalar, J. B. *Psychedelic Drugs Reconsidered* (Basic Books, Inc., New York City, 1979)
30. Domino, E. F. Neurobiology of phencyclidine—an update *in* R. C. Petersen and R. C. Stillman (eds.) *Phencyclidine (PCP) Abuse: An Appraisal* Research Monograph 21 (National Institute on Drug Abuse, Rockville, Md., 1978)
31. Pittel, S. M. and Oppedahl, M. C. The enigma of PCP *in* R. I. DuPont, A. Goldstein and J. O'Donnell (eds.) *Handbook on Drug Abuse* (National Institute on Drug Abuse, Rockville, Md., 1979)
32. Petersen, R. C. and Stillman, R. C. Phencyclidine: an overview *in* R. C. Petersen and R. C. Stillman (eds.) *Phencyclidine (PCP) Abuse: An Appraisal* Research Monograph 21 (National Institute on Drug Abuse, Rockville, Md., 1978)
33. Siegel, R. K. Phencyclidine and ketamine intoxication: a study of four populations of recreational users *in* R. C. Petersen and R. C. Stillman (eds.) *Phencyclidine (PCP) Abuse: An Appraisal* Research Monograph 21 (National Institute on Drug Abuse, Rockville, Md., 1978)
34. Mello, N. K. Control of drug self-administration: the role of aversive consequences *in* R. C. Petersen and R. C. Stillman (eds.) *Phencyclidine (PCP) Abuse: An Appraisal* Research Monograph 21 (National Institute on Drug Abuse, Rockville, Md., 1978)
35. Lerner, S. E. and Burns, R. S. Phencyclidine use among youth: history, epidemiology, and acute and chronic intoxication *in* R. C. Petersen and R. C. Stillman (eds.) *Phencyclidine (PCP) Abuse: An Appraisal* Research Monograph 21 (National Institute on Drug Abuse, Rockville, Md., 1978)
36. James, J. and Andresen, E. Sea-Tac and PCP *in* H. W. Feldman, M. H. Agar and G. M. Beschner (eds.) *Angel Dust: An Ethnographic Study of PCP Users* (Lexington Books, Lexington, Mass., 1979)
37. Cleckner, P. J. Freaks and cognescenti: PCP use in Miami *in* H. W. Feldman, M. H. Agar and G. M. Beschner (eds.) *Angel Dust: An Ethnographic Study of PCP Users* (Lexington Books, Lexington, Mass., 1979)
38. Smith, D. E., Wesson, D. R., Buxton, M. E., Seymour, R. B. and Kramer, H. M. The diagnosis and treatment of the PCP abuse syndrome *in* R. C. Petersen and R. C. Stillman (eds.) *Phencyclidine (PCP) Abuse: An Appraisal* Research Monograph 21 (National Institute on Drug Abuse, Rockville, Md., 1978)
39. Johnson, K. M. Neurochemical pharmacology of phencyclidine *in* R. C. Petersen and R. C. Stillman (eds.) *Phencyclidine (PCP) Abuse: An Appraisal* Research Monograph 21 (National Institute on Drug Abuse, Rockville, Md., 1978)

40. Nahas, G. Symposium on marijuana: Rheims, France, 22-23 July 1978 *Bulletin on Narcotics* 30(3):23 (July-September 1978)
41. Maher, J. T. Cannabis *Drug Enforcement* 7(1):22 (March 1980)
42. Jessor, R. Marijuana: a review of recent psychosocial research *in* R. I. DuPont, A. Goldstein and J. O'Donnell (eds.) *Handbook on Drug Abuse* (National Institute on Drug Abuse, Rockville, Md., 1979)
43. *Marijuana and Health: Eighth Annual Report to the U.S. Congress from the Secretary of Health, Education and Welfare* (National Institute on Drug Abuse, Rockville, Md., 1980)
44. Fink, M. Effects of acute and chronic inhalation of hashish, marijuana and Δ-9-tetrahydrocannabinol on brain electrical activity in man: evidence for tissue tolerance *in* R. Dornbush, A. Freedman and M. Fink (eds.) *Chronic Cannabis Use* (Annals of the New York Academy of Sciences, New York City, 1976)
45. Heath, R. G. *Marijuana and the Brain* (Second Annual Conference on Marijuana at New York University Post-Graduate Medical School, American Council on Marijuana and Other Psychoactive Drugs, June 28-29, 1979, unpublished transcripts)
46. Heath, R. G. *Testimony at Hearings on Marijuana Usage Before the Subcommittee on Criminal Justice of the Committee on the Judiciary* (United States Senate, January 16-17, 1980)
47. Pollin, W. *Testimony at Hearings on Marijuana Usage Before the Subcommittee on Criminal Justice of the Committee on the Judiciary* (United States Senate, January 16-17, 1980)
48. Tennant, F. S. Jr., et al. Medical manifestations associated with hashish *JAMA* 216:1965 (1971)
49. Tashkin, D. P., et al. Subacute effects of heavy marihuana smoking on pulmonary function in healthy men *New England Journal of Medicine* 294:125 (1976)
50. Mendelsohn, J. H., et al. Behavioral and biologic aspects of marijuana use *in* R. Dornbush, A. Freedman and M. Fink (eds.) *Chronic Cannabis Use* (Annals of the New York Academy of Sciences, New York City, 1976)
51. Rosenkrantz, H. and Fleischman, R. W. Effects of cannabis on lungs *in* G. Nahas and W. Paton (eds.) *Marihuana: Biological Effects* (Pergamon Press, New York City, 1979)
52. Smith, C. G., et al. Effect of delta-9-THC on female reproductive function *in* G. Nahas and W. Paton (eds.) *Marihuana: Biological Effects* (Pergamon Press, New York City, 1979)
53. Bauman, J. *Effects of Chronic Marijuana Use on Endocrine Function of the Human Female* (Second Annual Conference on Marijuana at New York University Post-Graduate Medical School, American Council on Marijuana and Other Psychoactive Drugs, June 28-29, 1979, unpublished transcripts)
54. Sassenrath, E. N., et al. Reproduction in rhesus monkeys chronically exposed to delta-9-THC *in* G. Nahas and W. Paton (eds.) *Marihuana: Biological Effects* (Pergamon Press, New York City, 1979)

55. Zimmerman, A. M., et al. Effects of cannabinoids on spermatogenesis in mice *in* G. Nahas and W. Paton (eds.) *Marihuana: Biological Effects* (Pergamon Press, New York City, 1979)
56. Fujimoto, G. I., et al. Effects of cannabinoids on reproductive organs in the female Fischer rat *in* G. Nahas and W. Paton (eds.) *Marihuana: Biological Effects* (Pergamon Press, New York City, 1979)
57. Harclerode, J., et al. Effects of cannabis on sex hormones and testicular enzymes of the rodent *in* G. Nahas and W. Paton (eds.) *Marihuana: Biological Effects* (Pergamon Press, New York City, 1979)
58. Huang, H. F. S., et al. Effects of marijuana smoke on spermatogenesis in mice *in* G. Nahas and W. Paton (eds.) *Marihuana: Biological Effects* (Pergamon Press, New York City, 1979)
59. Hembree, W. C. III, et al. Changes in human spermatozoa associated with high dose marijuana smoking *in* G. Nahas and W. Paton (eds.) *Marihuana: Biological Effects* (Pergamon Press, New York City, 1979)
60. Senate Judiciary Committee to vote on marijuana decriminalization; Senator Mathias holds hearings on effects of marijuana *Newsletter of the American Council on Marijuana and Other Psychoactive Drugs* 2(1):2 (Winter 1980)
61. *Inhalants: The Deliberate Inhalation of Volatile Substances* Report Series 30, No. 2 (National Institute on Drug Abuse, Rockville, Md., 1978)
62. Watson, J. M. Solvent abuse by children and young adults: a review *British Journal of Addiction* 75:27 (1980)
63. Aviado, D. M. Pharmacology of abused inhalants *in* C. W. Sharp and L. T. Carroll (eds.) *Voluntary Inhalation of Industrial Solvents* (National Institute on Drug Abuse, Rockville, Md., 1978)
64. Cohen, S. Glue sniffing *JAMA* 231(6):653 (February 10, 1975)
65. Hecht, A. Inhalants: quick route to danger *FDA Consumer* 14(4):19 (May 1980)
66. Cohen, S. Inhalants and solvents *in* G. M. Beschner and A. S. Friedman (eds.) *Youth Drug Abuse* (Lexington Books, Lexington, Mass., 1979)

CHAPTER 3
TRENDS IN DRUG ABUSE

Preferences for particular drugs of abuse are shaped by multiple factors and tend to vary across time and place. A primary determinant, of course, is the availability of specific drugs. Where multiple drugs are available, however, more subtle factors influence the selection of a particular psychoactive agent. These factors may include *economics* (the cost of one drug or mode of administration as opposed to another), *personal values* (such as the perception that smoked substances are less dangerous or more "licit" than injected drugs), *peer group preferences*, and even felt needs to *self-medicate* physical and psychic ills.

Prevailing societal mores also play a role in determining which drugs will be abused and the extent of that abuse. Social custom determines the prevailing distinctions between levels of drug use that are acceptable and those that are unacceptable and therefore defined as "abuse." These social dicta have varied over time as widely as have the types of drugs adopted for non-medical use.

HISTORICAL PREFERENCES IN DRUGS

With the exception of alcohol—the oldest drug of abuse—significant problems with drug abuse did not appear until the 16th century A.D. Opium was used medicinally from the 15th century B.C. in Egypt and cannabis from the second century B.C. in Asia, but dependence on or abuse of these substances was not recorded until the early 17th century.

Beginning in the 16th century, psychoactive substance abuse began to rise in response to three developments. First, major sociocultural changes during this period made the Western world more receptive to the adoption of innovative drug use. Life was becoming increasingly urbanized, facilitating the rapid spread of drug-using behaviors throughout large populations. Traditional social and religious controls over behavior were loosened at the end of the Middle Ages as a more secular, modern society developed.

Second, increased exploration and colonization efforts brought contact with new peoples who used new substances. Western explorers, in turn, carried their use of both old and new substances to the rest of the world.

Third, technological developments in distillation made it possible to increase the alcohol content of distilled beverages from about 14%

to 50% or more. When cheap spirits became widely available for the first time during a period of social dislocation and stress, the results were widespread problems with alcohol abuse.

In short, the 16th century saw newer and more potent substances become available at a time when general sociocultural conditions were making men more receptive to innovative drug use. The social problems posed by substance abuse conseqently assumed greater importance than in any previous period. Thus, this period represents a critical turning point in the history of substance abuse.[1,2,3]

TABLE 18

Chronology of Non-Medical Substance Use in the United States

Substance	1700	1800	1900
ALCOHOL	—	████████	████████
OPIATES		███████	████████
COCAINE		███████	████████
CANNABIS			████████
ETHER			███████
AMPHETAMINES			████
BARBITURATES			████
HALLUCINOGENS			███

Source: Austin, G. A. *Perspectives on the History of Psychoactive Substance Use* (National Institute on Drug Abuse, Rockville, Md., 1978)

CONTEMPORARY PREFERENCES IN DRUGS

Projections of future trends in drug abuse — and, in some instances, reports of current activities — are beset by semantic and statistical difficulties. As a result, numerical representations and interpretations of drug survey data often are the subject of considerable controversy among authorities in the field. For example, in years past the most commonly used indicators of drug use trends were visits to hospital emergency departments and applications for admission to drug treatment programs. The federal Drug Abuse Warning Network (DAWN) is typical of this type of monitoring, in that it collects data on drug-related visits for emergency medical care. Reports based on these indicators have been widely criticized, however, for overemphasizing the portion of the drug-using population that experiences serious medical problems and ignoring persons who engage in drug use without severe health consequences, as well as for relying heavily on self-reporting of the nature, quantity and sources of abused substances.

Conversely, reports based on interviews with broad population samples have been criticized for focusing on lifetime prevalence of drug use (thus failing to distinguish between occasional and regular use), as well as for excluding significant portions of the drug-using population. The federal National Surveys on Drug Abuse, for example, are based on personal interviews with more than 7,000 persons living in households, but exclude transients and persons living in college dormitories, on military bases and in prisons, where drug use rates are thought to be higher than in the general population. Thus, these survey data probably underestimate the true prevalence of chronic drug use in the United States.

If accurate statistics are so difficult to derive, why are data on drug use trends important? One answer, according to Richards,[4] is that "numbers never stand completely alone . . . they are always numbers *of* something." For instance, data from the National Surveys on Drug Abuse describe the phenomenon of illicit drug use as a social problem whose dimensions are only crudely reflected in the cases that come to the attention of treatment personnel. On the other hand, reports from DAWN and other monitoring systems complement the survey data by highlighting the health consequences of drug abuse. A further refinement of data collection techniques is evident in recent efforts to include data on current use of illicit drugs, in addition to figures on lifetime prevalence.[4]

Because they reflect (however imperfectly) contemporary preferences in, levels of involvement with, and medical complications of non-medical drug use, survey and monitoring data are useful in raising health professionals' awareness that illicit drug use may be a factor in the physical and psychological problems for which patients seek medical care.

CURRENT SURVEY FINDINGS

Recent national surveys show that the number of Americans who have used illicit drugs increased dramatically in the 1960's and 1970's. A retrospective study[5] by the National Institute on Drug Abuse found that, since 1962, the percentage of Americans 18 to 25 years old who have used marijuana has increased from 4% to 68%, while the percentage who have tried other drugs (including cocaine, heroin, hallucinogens and inhalants) has increased from 3% to 33%.

TABLE 19

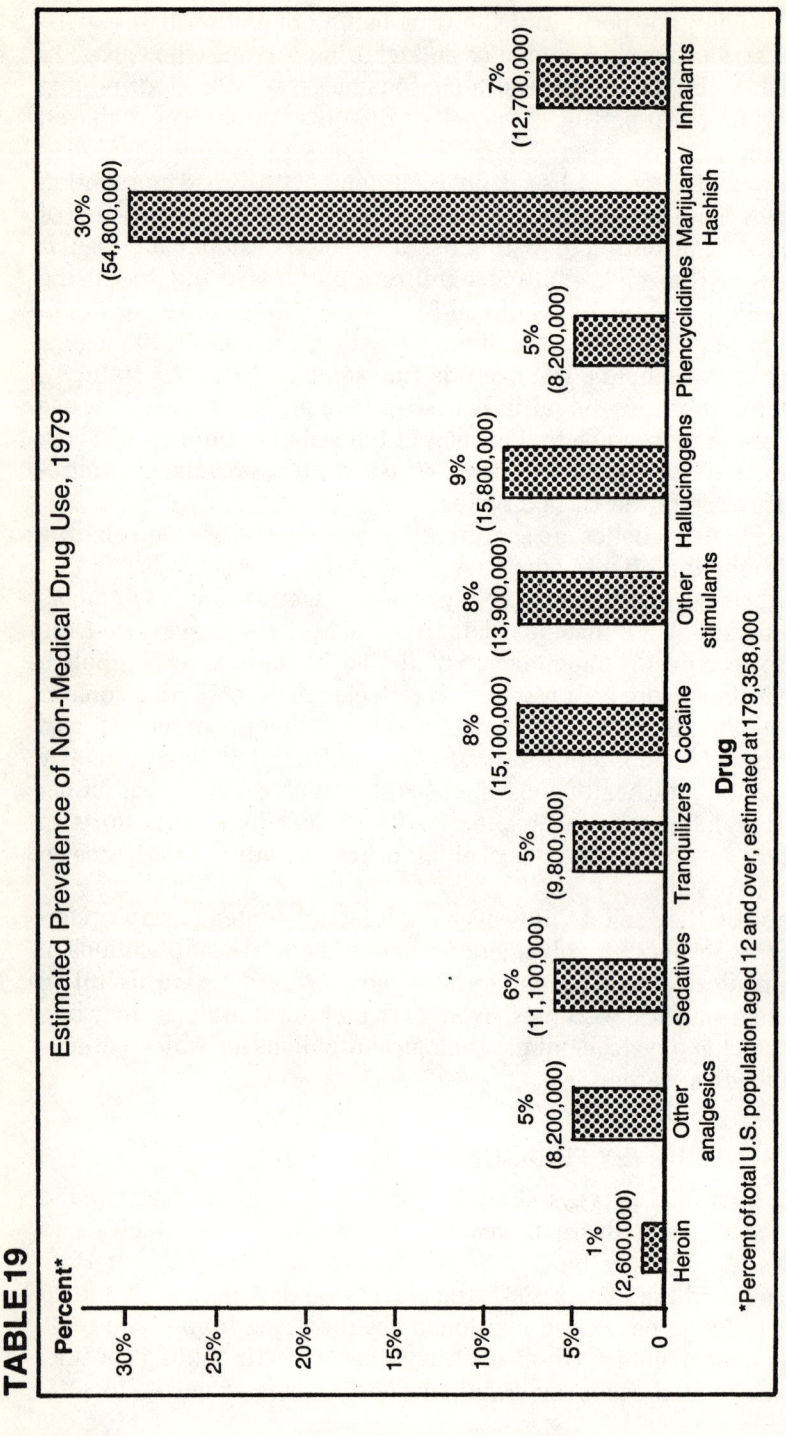

Estimated Prevalence of Non-Medical Drug Use, 1979

Drug	Percent*	Number
Heroin	1%	2,600,000
Other analgesics	5%	8,200,000
Sedatives	6%	11,100,000
Tranquilizers	5%	9,800,000
Cocaine	8%	15,100,000
Other stimulants	8%	13,900,000
Hallucinogens	9%	15,800,000
Phencyclidines	5%	8,200,000
Marijuana/Hashish	30%	54,800,000
Inhalants	7%	12,700,000

*Percent of total U.S. population aged 12 and over, estimated at 179,358,000

Source: *National Survey on Drug Abuse: Main Findings, 1979* (National Institute on Drug Abuse, Rockville, MD., 1980)

In younger (12 to 17 years) and older (than 26 years) age groups, experience with marijuana and cocaine doubled between 1972 and 1979.[6] The figures shown in Table 19, at left, are government estimates of the number and percent of United States residents over age 12 who have used drugs for non-medical purposes.

DAWN surveys show that heroin, plus alcohol in combination with another drug, account for one-third of all drug-related deaths seen in hospital emergency departments. The drugs most frequently encountered by emergency department personnel and medical examiners, as reported to the DAWN system, are listed in Table 20.

TABLE 20

Drugs Most Frequently Associated with Emergency Room Visits and Deaths, January-December 1979

Ranking by Estimated Number of Emergency Visits	Drug	Ranking by Medical Examiners' Reports
1	Alcohol in combination with another drug	1
2	Diazepam — Valium	6
3	Heroin/morphine	2
4	Aspirin	14
5	PCP/PCP Combination	15
6	Flurazepam — Dalmane	17.5
7	Marijuana	—
8	d-Propoxyphene Darvon	4
9	Amitriptyline — Elavil	3
10	Acetaminophen — Tylenol	17.5
11	Methaqualone — Quaalude	19
12	Chlordiazepoxide — Librium	—
13	Cocaine	13
14	Phenobarbital	9
15	Secobarbital/Amobarbital	10
16	Hydantoin	—
17	Methadone	5
18	Over-the-counter sleep aids	—
19	Chlorpromazine — Chlorazine	—
20	Amphetamine	—
—	Secobarbital	7
—	Codeine	8
—	Pentobarbital	11
—	Ethchlorvynol — Placidyl	12
—	Amobarbital — Amytal	16
—	Thioridazine — Mellaril	20

Source: DAWN reports, 1979 (Drug Enforcement Administration, Washington, D.C. and National Institute on Drug Abuse, Rockville, Md., 1980)

Reports of recent experience in individual hospital emergency departments support the national averages developed through the DAWN network.[8,9,10] It should be remembered, however, that there are wide local and regional variations in the types of drugs abused and that abuse patterns change rapidly.

OPIOIDS/ANALGESICS

Current data on the use of opioids and other analgesics show mixed trends. The number of heroin addicts and heroin-related deaths declined gradually in the 1970's,[11,12] while the non-medical use of propoxyphene and other analgesics increased[5,6] (see Table 21, below).

TABLE 21

Opioids/Analgesics: Changes in Non-Medical Use, by Age Group			
	1972 Ever Used (percent)	1979 Ever Used (percent)	1979 Used in Past Month (percent)
HEROIN			
12 to 17 years old	0.6	0.5	less than 0.5
18 to 25 years old	4.6	3.5	less than 0.5
26 years or older	less than 0.5	1.0	less than 0.5
PROPOXYPHENE			
12 to 17 years old	n.a.*	1.4	less than 0.5
18 to 25 years old	n.a.	8.8	less than 0.5
26 years or older	n.a.	2.2	less than 0.5
OTHER ANALGESICS			
12 to 17 years old	n.a.	2.7	0.6
18 to 25 years old	n.a.	7.6	0.6
26 years or older	n.a.	1.2	less than 0.5
*not available			

Sources: *National Survey on Drug Abuse: Main Findings, 1979* (National Institute on Drug Abuse, Rockville, Md., 1980)
A Drug Retrospective: 1962 to 1980 (National Institute on Drug Abuse, Rockville, Md., 1980)

Data for 1979 show that the trend toward declining use of heroin appears to be ending. Recent large harvests of opium poppies in the "Golden Crescent" (Afghanistan, Iran, Libya, Pakistan and Turkey) and "Golden Triangle" (Cambodia, Laos and Thailand) have increased street supplies and reduced prices in major U.S. cities.[9,13,14] Given the high potency and relatively low price of current heroin supplies, many authorities[10,15,16,17] believe that heroin use will increase. (The practice of smoking high-potency heroin is bringing heroin use to an affluent population that previously may have only experimented with cocaine inhalation. This population mistakenly sees its heroin habit as non-addictive because the substance is smoked rather than injected.) Other observers[18] contend that inflation is increasing heroin prices sufficiently to lead many users to adopt less expensive alternatives, such as prescription analgesics and methaqualone. In fact, both trends may be developing simultaneously in different strata of the drug-using population, with individual financial resources the principal determinant of preferred drugs and modes of administration.

DEPRESSANTS

The most significant change in use of tranquilizers and sedatives during the 1970's occurred in the 18 to 25 year old age group, whose experience with these drugs doubled between 1972 and 1979[5,6] (see Table 22, below). Little change was observable in younger and older age groups surveyed. During the last quarter of 1979 and the first nine months of 1980, an appreciable increase in methaqualone mentions in hospital emergency departments was noted by the DAWN system.

TABLE 22

Depressants: Changes in Non-Medical Use, by Age Group			
	1972 Ever Used (percent)	1979 Ever Used (percent)	1979 Used in Past Month (percent)
INTERMEDIATE/LONG-ACTING BARBITURATES			
12 to 17 years old		1.1	less than 0.5
18 to 25 years old		3.8	less than 0.5
26 years or older		0.9	less than 0.5
SHORT-ACTING BARBITURATES			
12 to 17 years old	3.0*	1.3	less than 0.5
18 to 25 years old	10.0*	8.2	0.5
26 years or older	2.0*	1.7	less than 0.5
OTHER SEDATIVES			
12 to 17 years old		2.0	0.5
18 to 25 years old		13.4	2.1
26 years or older		3.1	less than 0.5
BENZODIAZEPINES			
12 to 17 years old	3.0**	3.7	0.6
18 to 25 years old	7.0**	15.1	2.0
26 years or older	5.0**	2.7	less than 0.5

*all sedatives
**all tranquilizers

Sources: *National Survey on Drug Abuse: Main Findings, 1979* (National Institute on Drug Abuse, Rockville, Md., 1980)
A Drug Retrospective: 1962 to 1980 (National Institute on Drug Abuse, Rockville, Md., 1980)

Another development has been the sharp reduction in prescriptions written for all tranquilizer and sedative drugs during the past five years. The National Prescription Audit, a private survey conducted for U.S. drug manufacturers, found that most of this decrease was concentrated in prescriptions for Valium, which declined from 57 million in 1975 to 38 million in 1979.[19] The reduced number of prescriptions written for depressant drugs is significant because it reflects a corresponding reduction in opportunities for diversion of these drugs from licit medical channels to illicit use. It also signifies a greater degree of caution in physicians' prescribing practices.

STIMULANTS

For stimulants, as for opioids and depressants, illicit use is significantly greater among young adults than among youth and older adults. However, experience with cocaine tripled between 1972 and 1979 in all age groups, while experience with other stimulant drugs increased by 50%[5,6,20] (see Table 23, below).

TABLE 23

Stimulants: Changes in Non-Medical Use, by Age Group			
	1972 Ever Used (percent)	1979 Ever Used (percent)	1979 Used in Past Month (percent)
COCAINE			
12 to 17 years old	1.5	5.4	1.4
18 to 25 years old	9.1	27.5	9.3
26 years or older	1.6	4.3	0.9
AMPHETAMINES			
12 to 17 years old	n.a.*	2.6	0.8
18 to 25 years old	n.a.	15.3	2.6
26 years or older	n.a.	4.7	0.5
NON-AMPHETAMINE ANORECTICS			
12 to 17 years old	n.a.	1.4	0.5
18 to 25 years old	n.a.	6.2	0.8
26 years or older	n.a.	1.6	less than 0.5
*not available			

Sources: *National Survey on Drug Abuse: Main Findings, 1979* (National Institute on Drug Abuse, Rockville, Md., 1980)
 A Drug Retrospective: 1962 to 1980 (National Institute on Drug Abuse, Rockville, Md., 1980)

The stimulant abuse pattern of greatest recent concern is the practice of smoking cocaine.[21,22,23] This practice, called "freebasing," was first identified on the West Coast in the past five years and is believed to have spread to major metropolitan areas across the country. The National Institute on Drug Abuse estimates that there are more than one million regular users of freebase cocaine in the United States.[21,23]

Until recently, cocaine smoking did not present a significant problem because cocaine in its "street" form (cocaine hydrochloride) is not effective when smoked. In the mid-1970's, however, North American drug users adopted a method similar to the South American practice of smoking coca paste (base), a potent extract of coca leaves. Users "free" cocaine hydrochloride of its salts and adulterants and convert it to cocaine sulphate through a hazardous chemical process that involves heating flammable solvents such as petroleum ether. The potent cocaine base that results usually is smoked in a water pipe or sprinkled on a tobacco or marijuana cigaret to produce a rapid, intense euphoric state.[21,23]

Drug paraphernalia shops (and, in some areas, liquor stores) sell prepackaged freebase conversion kits legally, except in the few states that have enacted antiparaphernalia laws.[21] Recent government reports estimate that sales of cocaine paraphernalia — scales, spoons and mirrors, as well as freebase kits — rose 50% at some 20,000 retail outlets between 1977 and 1978. The dollar volume of such sales is believed to be $50 million to $3 billion annually.[23]

Observers of the freebase trend believe the single factor that may limit its spread is cost. Cocaine sells on the street for $75 to $125 per gram, so a week-long freebase "binge" could cost $2,000 to $12,000.[21,23]

A very recent development in stimulant abuse is the appearance on illicit markets of pills, made to resemble classic amphetamines, that contain large concentrations of caffeine as their only active ingredient. The popularity and effects of these concoctions (which are not illegal because they contain no restricted substances) have yet to be determined.

HALLUCINOGENS

Hallucinogen use increased most dramatically in the late 1960's and early 1970's, especially among young adults. In the 18 to 25 year old age group, hallucinogen use appeared about 1960, increased gradually through 1967, then grew rapidly until 1972. After 1972, use of these substances declined slightly, but entered another sharp rise in popularity after 1977. Use patterns in younger and older age groups followed approximately the same fluctuations, but at lower levels of use[5,6] (see Table 24, below).

These fluctuations in hallucinogen use appear to reflect the variety of substances included in this drug class. Use of hallucinogens was

TABLE 24

Hallucinogens: Changes in Non-Medical Use, by Age Group			
	1974 Ever Used (percent)	1979 Ever Used (percent)	1979 Used in Past Month (percent)
12 to 17 years old	6.0	7.1	2.2
18 to 25 years old	16.6	25.1	4.4
26 years or older	1.3	4.5	less than 0.5

Sources: *National Survey on Drug Abuse: Main Findings, 1979* (National Institute on Drug Abuse, Rockville, Md., 1980)
A Drug Retrospective: 1962 to 1980 (National Institute on Drug Abuse, Rockville, Md., 1980)

more prevalent than use of cocaine during the early 1970's but, by 1979, about the same number of young adults reported experience with each substance.[24]

PHENCYCLIDINES

In the past decade, use of phencyclidines (PCP, Angel Dust) increased in all age groups, but most sharply among young adults.[5,6] One recent study estimated that 7 million Americans have tried PCP.[25,26] Of even greater concern are recent data showing that the number of PCP-related emergency department admissions and deaths doubled between 1977 and 1978, and that more injuries are attributable to PCP than to any other drug.[25] Trend data on PCP use in all age groups are presented in Table 25, below.

TABLE 25

Phencyclidines: Changes in Non-Medical Use, by Age Group		
	1976 Ever Used (percent)	1979 Ever Used (percent)
12 to 17 years old	3.0	3.9
18 to 25 years old	9.5	14.5
26 years or older	0.7	2.2

Sources: *National Survey on Drug Abuse: Main Findings, 1979* (National Institute on Drug Abuse, Rockville, Md., 1980)
A Drug Retrospective: 1962 to 1980 (National Institute on Drug Abuse, Rockville, Md., 1980)

One recent report from the West Coast describes the growing popularity of the phencyclidine analog, PHP (phenocyclohexylpyrrolidine).[27] PHP is similar to PCP chemically and pharmacologically and produces the same subjective effects. It is as easy and inexpensive to manufacture as PCP; however, the chemicals used in its manufacture are not legally restricted and thus are easier to obtain. PHP is not detected by most laboratory tests for PCP, thus reducing the user's risk of identification.

CANNABINOIDS

Marijuana is the third most frequently used drug in the United States, after alcohol and cigarets.[6] As compared to a decade ago, marijuana use now often begins at a much earlier age and is more likely to be frequent rather than experimental use. Between 1971 and 1979, for example, experience with marijuana use more than doubled in the 12 to 17 year old age group and increased significantly among adults[5] (see Table 26, below). Despite these increases in use, however, a majority of persons in all age groups continue to disapprove of regular marijuana use and to advocate its continued prohibition.[6,28,29]

TABLE 26

Marijuana: Changes in Non-Medical Use, by Age Group			
	1971 Ever Used (percent)	1979 Ever Used (percent)	1979 Used in Past Month (percent)
12 to 17 years old	14.0	30.9	16.7
18 to 25 years old	39.3	68.2	35.4
26 years or older	9.2	19.6	6.0

Sources: *National Survey on Drug Abuse: Main Findings, 1979* (National Institute on Drug Abuse, Rockville, Md., 1980)
A Drug Retrospective: 1962 to 1980 (National Institute on Drug Abuse, Rockville, Md., 1980)

"Street" marijuana has increased markedly in potency over the past five years. Samples of the drug confiscated by law enforcement agencies in 1975 rarely exceeded one percent Δ-9-tetrahydrocannabinol (THC), whereas concentrations of 5% THC were not uncommon in 1979. "Hash oil," a marijuana extract that was unavailable until less than 10 years ago, typically has a THC content of 15% to 20%.[28] Sinsemilla, a type of marijuana now widely available on the West Coast, has a similarly high concentration of THC. Street grades of hashish have THC concentrations in the range of 10%.[30]

Finally, the practice of combining marijuana and alcohol use is becoming more common, and poses a hazard of more widespread and severe reactions to the combined effects of these drugs.[30]

INHALANTS

Hundreds of intoxicating volatile solvents are available in the home and in the marketplace. These substances are more available to young people than alcohol and can be found in remote areas where alcoholic beverages cannot be obtained.[31] Thus, it is not surprising that current use of inhalable solvents is highest among youth 12 to 17 years of age, even though lifetime experience with inhalants is greatest in the 18 to 25 year old age group[6] (see Table 27, below).

TABLE 27

Inhalants: Changes in Non-Medical Use, by Age Group			
	1974 Ever Used (percent)	1979 Ever Used (percent)	1979 Used in Past Month (percent)
12 to 17 years old	8.5	9.8	2.0
18 to 25 years old	9.2	16.5	1.2
26 years or older	1.2	3.9	0.5

Sources: *National Survey on Drug Abuse: Main Findings, 1979* (National Institute on Drug Abuse, Rockville, Md., 1980)
A Drug Retrospective: 1962 to 1980 (National Institute on Drug Abuse, Rockville, Md., 1980)

Earlier studies depicted solvents as the intoxicants of the very young—predominantly young males. However, this pattern is changing as more persons over 21 years of age and more women engage in inhalant abuse.[31]

Within the broad category of inhalable solvents, changing preferences for certain products are apparent. For example, model airplane cement was supplanted in popularity by spray paints (including metallic paints containing copper), gasoline, vegetable oil pan coating sprays, transmission fluid, liquid shoe polish and paint thinners. Gaining wide popularity in all age groups are locker room odorizers that contain amyl or butyl nitrite. These substances, sold in drug paraphernalia and pornography shops, are used to obtain a subjective sense of time prolongation at the moment of sexual orgasm and to briefly alter the user's level of consciousness. Some users inhale the substances at short intervals throughout their waking hours.[31] The

1979 National Survey on Drug Abuse found that 3.1% of youth, 5.1% of young adults and 0.6% of older adults had used locker room odorizers.[6]

OVER-THE-COUNTER DRUGS

A variety of nonprescription medications have been overused or abused to achieve mood elevations or altered states of consciousness. These drugs are, of course, simple to obtain and generally less expensive than the substances sold by "street" vendors. Although precise figures on this pattern of drug abuse are unavailable, the types of compounds most often subject to such abuse have been identified.

SLEEP AIDS: Many nonprescription medications to induce sleep contain scopolamine, an atropine-related alkaloid. Above the recommended dose level, these products can produce anticholinergic toxicity marked by dilated, fixed pupils; dry mouth; flushed, dry skin; rapid pulse; and a florid delirium. An atropine-like psychosis also can result when one of these compounds is used concurrently with an anticholinergic drug prescribed for Parkinsonism, gastric distress, depression or other emotional disorders.[32] Some sleep aids contain an antihistamine in addition to scopolamine.

ANTIHISTAMINES: Antihistamines are found in nonprescription cold remedies, cough syrups, sleep aids, allergy medications, anti-motion sickness compounds and analgesics. Large amounts of antihistamine compounds can produce an intoxication resembling the barbiturates, except that antihistamine toxicity is marked by fixed, dilated pupils.[32]

CODEINE: Codeine cough syrups are widely abused by youths and by heroin addicts who cannot obtain their drug of choice. A four-ounce bottle of codeine cough syrup contains 240 mg of codeine and is equivalent to 20 or 25 mg of oral morphine. Thus, codeine cough syrups can initiate or sustain an opioid-type dependence. Although some states require a prescription for these compounds, they are available without prescription in most areas.[32]

STIMULANTS: Some nasal sprays, anti-asthmatics, weight-reducing drugs, cough syrups and cold remedies contain ephedrine, phenylephrine, naphazoline, phenylpropanolamine and other mild stimulants. When large quantities of these compounds are ingested, an amphetamine-type psychosis can result. Ephedrine and phenylpropanolamine also have been identified as adulterants in street samples of cocaine and amphetamine. Combinations of ephedrine, phenylpropanolamine and procaine are sold in many drug paraphernalia shops as a "poor man's cocaine" under trade names such as "Pseudococaine," "Coco Snow," "Real Caine" and "Rock Crystal."[32]

SALICYLATES: High-dose, chronic use of salicylates (aspirin, salicylamide) can result in a toxic psychosis marked by delirium, acneform skin rash, cerebellar signs, metabolic acidosis leading to hyperventilation, and tinnitus with hearing loss. Acute salicylate poisoning is one of the most common causes of accidental death due to drug use, and a dose as small as 10 gm of aspirin may be fatal to small children.[32]

ACETAMINOPHEN: Higher than recommended doses of acetaminophen (Tylenol, Vanquish, etc.) can produce serious to fatal liver necrosis, particularly in persons who combine use of acetaminophen with alcohol.[32]

BROMIDES: Chronic overuse of preparations containing bromide salts results in a toxic psychosis marked by acneform rash and delirium. Bromide abuse has declined considerably in the past 25 years, but has not yet disappeared entirely.[32]

Physical dependence on over-the-counter medications is uncommon, but not unheard of. These substances provide poor quality "highs" and intoxicated states, but their disadvantages are offset for many persons by the wide availability, relatively low cost and lack of restrictions on nonprescription drugs.

MULTI-DRUG ABUSE

The true extent of multiple drug abuse is not known, but it appears to be a fairly common practice among chronic drug abusers. Evidence of its prevalence is found in recent data showing that 90% of young adults have used alcohol,[33] 68% have used marijuana, 27% have used cocaine, and 25% have used hallucinogens.[6]

Common patterns of multi-drug abuse involve:

- Persons who are dependent on one drug and use other drugs only when they are readily available.
- Persons who are dependent on one drug and use other drugs only when their preferred substance is not available.
- Persons who prefer one drug, but use a second drug to diminish the side effects of the primary substance.
- Persons who abuse any drug and also consume large amounts of alcohol.
- Persons who abuse different drugs at different times of the day, perhaps using stimulants in the morning, tranquilizers during the day and hypnotics at night.
- Persons who have no drug preference, but take any drug that is available.[33,34]

Ages of first use and abuse and patterns of drug intake vary considerably among individuals and groups. Young people in the United States typically initiate their use of drugs with coffee, tobacco and alcohol. If they go on to use other substances, the next drug is likely to be marijuana, followed (in order of frequency) by hallucinogens, depressants or stimulants. Those who graduate to heavier drug use may adopt intravenous modes of administration and/or progress to opioids.[33]

This pattern of abuse is viewed by some researchers as a "stepping-stone" sequence, in which individuals move along a continuum from drug non-use to use of beer or wine, then to cigarets or hard liquor, to marijuana, and finally to the use of other drugs. Other researchers argue that the pattern really represents clusters of age-related behaviors that are only incidentally sequential.[33] There *is* widespread acceptance of the notion that, once an individual has violated legal and social prohibitions to use one drug, it becomes easier to go on to use a second and third drug.[33,34]

INTERNATIONAL TRENDS

Collection of data on international trends in drug abuse has been given increasing emphasis in the past five years, as the linkages between drug supplies in one part of the world and drug use in another have become more apparent. The World Health Organization (WHO), the United Nations Division of Narcotic Drugs, the United Nations Educational, Cultural, and Scientific Organization (UNESCO), the United Nations Defense Research Unit, and the International Council on Alcohol and Addictions all collect and interpret epidemiological information on drug abuse.[35]

A recent report by the U.N. Commission on Narcotic Drugs says that illicit drug smuggling and sales have reached "pandemic proportions" and that the illegal drug business has "generated sums [of money] of such staggering size that the economic and political stability of some countries is threatened."[36] Other findings presented in the Commission's report are as follows:

- The quantity of heroin being distributed today is far less than that of other drugs (including marijuana and some psychotropic substances), but "in potency and as a source of death," heroin has no equal.
- Opium poppy cultivation appears to be uncontrolled in Iran. Drug abuse is spreading in Iran and that country "continues to serve as an important transit area for the international drug traffic."

- Afghanistan is one of the largest producers of opium for illegal markets. Only 10% to 15% of Afghanistan's opium crop in 1979 was used by Afghans, with most of the remainder going to Western Europe.
- The Middle East is a growing supplier of drugs to the United States and Canada, as well as Western Europe. Despite intensive control efforts, the European problem with "illicit traffic, drug abuse and drug-related deaths remains serious and is deteriorating."
- Mexico's strong commitment to drug control has led to a decline in the proportion of Mexican heroin used in the United States.[36]

REFERENCES

1. Austin, G. A. *Perspectives on the History of Psychoactive Substance Use* (National Institute on Drug Abuse, Rockville, Md., 1978)
2. Musto, D. F. Historical highlights of American drug use (1800-1940) *in* C. Kryder and S. P. Strickland (eds.) *Americans and Drug Abuse: Report from the Aspen Conference* (Aspen Institute for Humanistic Studies, Aspen, Col., 1977)
3. Bryant, T. E. Recent history of drug use and abuse *in* C. Kryder and S. P. Strickland (eds.) *Americans and Drug Abuse: Report from the Aspen Conference* (Aspen Institute for Humanistic Studies, Aspen, Col., 1977)
4. Richards, L. G. Introduction *in* L. G. Richards and L. B. Blevens (eds.) *The Epidemiology of Drug Abuse: Current Issues* Research Monograph 10 (National Institute on Drug Abuse, Rockville, Md., 1977)
5. *A Drug Retrospective: 1962 to 1980* (National Institute on Drug Abuse, Rockville, Md., 1980)
6. *National Survey on Drug Abuse: Main Findings, 1979* (National Institute on Drug Abuse, Rockville, Md., 1980)
7. Drug-related deaths tallied *Focus on Alcohol and Drug Issues* 2(1):22 (January-February 1979)
8. Ficarra, B. J. Toxicologic states treated in an emergency department *Clinical Toxicology* 17(1):1 (1980)
9. The early stages of a massive heroin crisis *Addiction and Substance Abuse Report* 11(10):1 (October 1980)
10. Southwest Asian heroin hits four U.S. cities *ADAMHA News* 6(17):3 (August 22, 1980)
11. *Heroin Indicators Trend Report—An Update, 1976-1978* (National Institute on Drug Abuse, Rockville, Md., 1979)
12. Addict population decline reported *ADAMHA News* 6(6):1 (March 21, 1980)
13. Heroin—1980 *Addiction and Substance Abuse Report* 11(9):1 (September 1980)

14. S. W. Asian heroin now dominates market, White House tells Congress; hints possibility of more money *Washington Drug Review* 5(8):1 (August 31, 1980)
15. Heroin: another epidemic? *Focus on Alcohol and Drug Issues* 2(1):19 (January-February 1979)
16. Boin, J. K. U.S. faces another heroin challenge *U.S. Journal of Drug and Alcohol Dependence* 3(10):7 (November 1979)
17. Asian heroin hits northeast cities *U.S. Journal of Drug and Alcohol Dependence* 4(7) (September 1980)
18. Inflation changes street drug habits *U.S. Journal of Drug and Alcohol Dependence* 3(12) (January 1980)
19. Rx's for psychoactive drugs plummet *ADAMHA News* 6(22):5 (October 31, 1980)
20. Seidler, G. Cocaine rising in popularity *Focus on Alcohol and Drug Issues* 2(1):15 (January-February 1979)
21. Freebase cocaine: hazardous and costly habit *ADAMHA News* 6(19):3 (September 19, 1980)
22. Allport, S. Epidemic of cocaine smoking seen *Medical Tribune* 21(3) (January 16, 1980)
23. The sale of cocaine paraphernalia (News Notes) *Washington Drug Review* 5(4):13 (April 1980)
24. Miller, J. D. and Cisin, I. H. *Highlights from the National Survey on Drug Abuse: 1979* (National Institute on Drug Abuse, Rockville, Md., 1980)
25. Phencyclidine *Registrant Facts* 6(1):8 (1980)
26. Aniline, O., Allen, R. E., Pitts, F. N. Jr., Yago, L. S. and Pitts, A. F. The urban epidemic of phencyclidine use: laboratory evidence from a public psychiatric hospital inpatient service *Biological Psychiatry* 15(5):813 (1980)
27. Budd, R. D. PHP, a new drug of abuse (Letter) *New England Journal of Medicine* 588 (September 4, 1980)
28. *Marijuana and Health, Eighth Annual Report to the U.S. Congress from the Secretary of Health, Education and Welfare, 1980* (National Institute on Drug Abuse, Rockville, Md., 1980)
29. A survey: young people consider marijuana *Addiction and Substance Abuse Report* 10(11):1 (November 1979)
30. *Health Aspects of Marijuana Use*, Report of the Council on Scientific Affairs (American Medical Association, Chicago, Ill., December 6, 1977)
31. Cohen, S. Inhalants *in* R. I. DuPont, A. Goldstein and J. O'Donnell (eds.) *Handbook on Drug Abuse* (National Institute on Drug Abuse, Rockville, Md., 1979)
32. Cohen, S. Over-the-counter medicines: psychophysiologic reactions *Drug Abuse and Alcoholism Newsletter* 9(7):1 (September 1980)
33. Schuckit, M. A. *Drug and Alcohol Abuse: A Clinical Guide to Diagnosis and Treatment* (Plenum Medical Book Company, New York City, 1979)

34. Carroll, J. F. X., Malloy, T. E. and Kendrick, F. M. Multiple substance abuse: a review of the literature *in* S. E. Gardner (ed.) *National Drug/Alcohol Collaborative Project: Issues in Multiple Substance Abuse* (National Institute on Drug Abuse, Rockville, Md., 1980)
35. Hughes, P. H. International issues—epidemiology *in* R. I. DuPont, A. Goldstein and J. O'Donnell (eds.) *Handbook on Drug Abuse* (National Institute on Drug Abuse, Rockville, Md., 1979)
36. United Nations Commission on Narcotic Drugs holds special session *Division of Narcotic Drugs Information Letter* 4-6:1 (April-June 1980)

CHAPTER 4
PHYSICIAN ATTITUDES TOWARD DRUG ABUSE

A physician's patient management decisions depend not only on medical knowledge, but also on his or her self-image, personal values and attitudes. In fact, physician attitudes have a crucial influence on the quality and quantity of care patients receive. However, research[1-5] has shown that many physicians have negative attitudes toward patients who abuse mood-altering drugs.

The effects of these negative attitudes are evident at many levels:

DIAGNOSIS: Diagnoses may be missed or delayed. Studies of diagnostic practice indicate that most physicians have a high index of suspicion when they develop a diagnosis, *except* in cases involving drug or alcohol abuse. Then, physicians seem reluctant to diagnose abuse or dependence until clear signs of intoxication or withdrawal are present.[1]

ACCESS TO TREATMENT: Negative attitudes are a factor in excluding drug-dependent persons from the health care system. Alcohol-dependent persons have been discriminated against in hospital admissions,[6,7] and Chappel[1] believes the same phenomenon exists for persons who are dependent on drugs.

REFERRALS: Referral for treatment is similarly affected by physician attitudes. In fact, a study by Chafetz et al[8] showed a strong correlation between the effectiveness of referrals and the emotional tone conveyed in the referring physician's voice.

TREATMENT: The place of treatment selected for chemically-dependent persons is influenced by physician attitudes,[1] as demonstrated in studies by Mendelson[9] and Knox.[10] Goldstein[11] has even shown that physician pessimism about treatment outcome has the effect of self-fulfilling prophecy.

SOURCES OF ATTITUDINAL BARRIERS TO CARE

HISTORICAL BARRIERS: Physicians have had a prominent role in the history of interactions between men and drugs.[5] Early recognition of the dangers of unsupervised drug use led to the designation of physicians as "gatekeepers" for many drugs.[12] The Harrison Narcotic Act of 1914, originally designed to control the distribution and sale of opiates, later was used to close medical treatment facilities for heroin addicts and to harrass physicians who attempted to treat narcotic addicts with opiates.

In response to these changed societal and legal attitudes, medical societies advised physicians not to treat narcotic addiction and, for decades, medical schools avoided the problems of addiction. Information on narcotics abuse often was taught in a way that encouraged a phobic response in student physicians. The failure of legal sanctions to stem human drug use did not deter the development of medical opinion that abstinence was the treatment of choice for drug dependence. Freedman[13] has described the early leaders in psychiatry as "fervent prohibitionists." As Chappel[5] observes, "unfortunately, this attitude often led to the prohibition of the drug-dependent individual as a medical patient when he failed to achieve and maintain an abstinent state."

BARRIERS WITHIN THE PATIENT: Drug-dependent persons often exhibit a strong resistance to treatment, Chappel[5] notes. Many project their problems onto various aspects of the environment to avoid treatment. When such defenses fail, they may take the simplistic view that drug use is their only problem.

The relationships drug abusers form with physicians and other treatment personnel often are transient: they tend to make contact, become disappointed or frustrated, withdraw from the relationship and then look elsewhere for help. Some patients seem frightened by the possibility of success: they develop some rapport with a physician, begin to respond, then move away. The self-destructive aspects of this behavior can be a source of despair for physicians who are concerned about the well-being of their patients.

The behavior of drug abusers also poses problems for the physician-patient relationship. Compulsive drug-seeking may lead such persons to lie, steal, forge prescriptions, attempt to manipulate the physician, and make excessive and/or inappropriate demands. Despite the physician's best attempts to manage withdrawal, drug-dependent patients often seek only some form of drug replacement, rather than treatment that starts with a cessation of drug use.

The values of many drug abusers add another barrier to involvement with physicians. Such persons may reject traditional values, as well as authority figures. On the street, they may form subcultures that provide a sense of identity and pseudointimacy with other persons who use the same drugs; in hospitals, they may form anti-therapeutic groups that serve the dual purpose of perpetuating drug culture values and avoiding effective treatment. Drug abusers who have had jail experience are particularly adept at this form of resistance.

BARRIERS WITHIN THE PHYSICIAN: The psychopathology, behavior and values of drug-dependent persons have provided many physicians with unpleasant experiences. Such patients may leave the hospital against medical advice, refuse to cooperate with treatment recommendations, and—most frustrating of all—fail to get better, occasionally even dying. The physician is left disappointed, depressed and bitter. He may even conclude that effective treatment is impossible.

The physician's dilemma is complicated by his lack of preparation in developing skills to manage drug dependence problems. Drug-dependent patients rarely find their way into teaching hospitals, even though an increasing number of medical schools are incorporating comprehensive instruction in substance abuse into their curricula.

Physicians often find that their authority is challenged by drug-dependent patients. The medical model is based on a patient voluntarily seeking help and cooperating with the physician in his own treatment. Ideally, such a patient gives accurate information, allows the physician to conduct various tests and procedures, listens carefully and follows instructions accurately. The drug abuser, on the other hand, rarely fits this model: he is compliant rather than cooperative and covertly or overtly challenges the physician's authority. To the physician, he is an undesirable patient.

Physician pride may pose another barrier, according to Chappel.[5] A physician's pride in his knowledge and competence is challenged by the drug-abusing patient. In using drugs, this patient has been prescribing for his own ills and, in effect, acting as his own physician. In the area of illicit drugs, such a patient may even know more than the physician does. This is an uncomfortable situation for physicians. Cohen[14] poses the question, "How does one move unflinchingly into an arena where he is made to feel unwanted, incompetent, and even malevolent?"

OVERCOMING ATTITUDINAL BARRIERS TO CARE

Medical societies can play an important role in helping physicians overcome their negative feelings, Chappel[5] suggests. The support of organized medicine, he says, is needed in the development and evaluation of adequate drug treatment programs within the existing health care system. Medical schools should be encouraged to institute effective teaching programs on the management of chemical dependence (including alcoholism) at the undergraduate and postgraduate levels. The American Medical Association developed guidelines for such programs in 1972.[12]

Chappel[5] cites three areas of activity that can increase the effectiveness of physicians' efforts to treat drug dependence:

DEVELOPMENT OF EFFECTIVE CHEMOTHERAPEUTIC SUPPORTS: The substitution of legal drugs for dependence-producing substances, under medical supervision, can facilitate the treatment process. Chappel describes substitutes like methadone as a kind of "treatment glue" that keeps the drug-dependent person coming back to the treatment setting and to the interpersonal aspects of treatment that are designed to achieve long-term behavioral change.

DEVELOPMENT OF DRUG-DETECTION TECHNOLOGY: Treatment of drug dependence on an outpatient basis requires methods of detecting illicit drug use that are rapid, efficient and objective. Tools like thin-layer chromatography and breathalizer results help both the physician and the patient examine objective evidence of drug dependence and explore the patient's behavior as a first step to better understanding and increased self-control.

DEVELOPMENT OF FORMER DRUG USERS AS PARAPROFESSIONAL MENTAL HEALTH WORKERS: Paraprofessionals who formerly abused drugs are sources of (1) identification and hope for the drug abuser who considers himself hopeless and beyond help, (2) communication, without the need to cross socioeconomic, racial, cultural and other attitudinal barriers and (3) behavioral control. In some cases, these workers may even act as liaison or interpreter between patient and physician.

To help physicians overcome barriers that can prevent early access to appropriate medical care, Chappel[1] has devised attitudinal goals for continuing medical education, as shown in Table 28.

CONCLUSIONS

Although relatively few physicians will choose to become directly involved in the long-term treatment of drug dependence, primary care physicians have an important role in making a diagnosis and referring patients. Physicians can prepare the patient for treatment, communicate hope, and provide the kind of emotional and chemotherapeutic support that can be a critical step in getting the patient into a treatment program. Physicians also will be called on to manage drug overdoses, severe withdrawal states and drug-related emergencies. Drug-dependent persons will continue to get pregnant, have accidents and suffer the full spectrum of human ills. Physicians can help all of these patients gain full access to the health care system.

The pressure on physicians and other medical resources to become involved with drug-abusing patients is likely to increase as the use of psychoactive drugs becomes more widespread.[4] Thus, whether or not a physician treats drug dependence, he is almost certain to treat patients with drug dependence problems.[5] As Chappel[1] observes, "every physician who sees patients will encounter substance abusers. Even if he does not wish to treat these patients, he has a minimum responsibility for diagnosis and referral. The earlier this can be done, the better the chance each patient has to regain normal function and escape or avoid the bondage of substance dependence...."

TABLE 28

Spectrum of Physician Attitudes

TOWARD DRUGS

Dysfunctional Attitudes	Functional Attitudes
Narcotics are dangerous and create addicts.	Narcotics have a potential for producing dependence. Patients should be informed and seen often.
Physicians are very familiar with barbiturates, tranquilizers and amphetamines. Their danger has been exaggerated.	Barbiturates and other CNS depressants have abuse potential. Patients should be informed and seen often to prevent dependence.
Street drugs are very dangerous. They are all unknowns, illegal, and are taken only by those who are fools or suicidal.	Physicians should be curious about the functions street drugs serve and the dangers they represent for patients.

TOWARD DRUG-ABUSING PATIENTS

Dysfunctional Attitudes	Functional Attitudes
Drug-dependent persons are the dregs of society.	How can drug-dependent persons be helped to find a more effective way to live?
An addict should be called an addict.	Addict is a negative label and should not be applied first by me. What is the problem? How can it be described?
Drug abuse is a social or legal problem, not a medical one.	Drug abuse represents problems that require medical as well as other treatment.
Drug addicts are unmotivated and impulsive, rarely show normal feelings, and usually cannot be helped.	Drug abusers are very defensive, make a great effort to avoid treatment, and require persistent, structured effort.
Drug abuse is bad, sinful and ignorant.	There is a reason this person behaves in self- or socially-destructive ways. What purpose could this behavior serve?
The drug addict deserves whatever he gets.	The world probably has punished this person enough. What will help change his behavior?

TABLE 28 (Cont'd.)

TOWARD THE TREATMENT OF DRUG-ABUSING PATIENTS

Dysfunctional Attitudes	Functional Attitudes
The hospital is the only place to treat a drug addict.	Hospitalization serves a brief, supportive role in long-term treatment, but it encourages dependence.
The physician's only role in treatment is in managing overdose, withdrawal or medical complications.	Medical skills are an important support for drug-dependent patients and should be available during their long-term treatment.
Every patient must be detoxified first, before any other treatment can take place.	Withdrawal is a part of treatment that may need to follow other forms of management.
Drug addicts cannot be treated as outpatients.	Long-term outpatient treatment in a community is necessary if the drug abuser ever is to live normally.
Providing chemical substitutes, antagonists or symptom relievers is the only role a physician can play in treatment.	As important as chemotherapy is, attempting to understand the patient's problems and giving support to the other kinds of treatment needed is equally important.
Chemotherapy is best provided by a physician specializing in the field.	Specialists in the field can serve as consultants, but there never will be enough specialists to treat all drug-dependent patients.
Prescribing medication only perpetuates the problem for persons who already have demonstrated that they cannot control their intake of drugs.	Abstinence may be the ultimate goal, but normal functioning is the immediate goal. If chemotherapy helps a patient function better, it should be used.
Angry confrontation by a physician is necessary to break through defenses and help motivate the patient to accept treatment.	Realistic, non-hostile confrontation by a physician may need to be repeated many times to break through defenses and help to motivate the patient to accept treatment.

Source: Chappel, J. N. Physician attitudes and the treatment of alcohol and drug-dependent patients *Journal of Psychedelic Drugs* 10(1):27 (January-March 1978) Copyright 1978, *Journal of Psychedelic Drugs*. Reprinted by permission.

REFERENCES

1. Chappel, J. N. Physician attitudes and the treatment of alcohol and drug dependent patients *Journal of Psychedelic Drugs* 10(1):27 (January-March 1978)
2. Chappel, J. N., Smith, D. E. and Buxton, M. Training techniques for physicians in the diagnosis and treatment of amphetamine abuse *Journal of Psychedelic Drugs* 10(4):393 (October-December 1978)
3. Chappel, J. N., Jordan, R. D., Treadway, B. J. and Miller, P. R. Substance abuse attitude changes in medical students *American Journal of Psychiatry* 13(4):379 (April 1977)
4. *The National Survey on Drug Abuse: Main Findings 1979* (National Institute on Drug Abuse, Rockville, Md., 1980)
5. Chappel, J. N. Attitudinal barriers to physician involvement with drug abusers *JAMA* 224(7):1011 (May 14, 1973)
6. Jellinek, E. M. *The Disease Concept of Alcoholism* (Hillhouse Press, New Haven, Conn., 1960)
7. Mayfield, D. and Fowler, D. R. Diagnoses and undersigned alcoholism *Southern Medical Journal* 63:593 (1970)
8. Chafetz, M. E., Blane, H. T. and Hill, M. J. The doctor's voice: post-dictor of successful referral of alcoholic patients in *Frontiers of Alcoholism* (Science House, New York City, 1970)
9. Mendelson, J. H., Wexler, D., Kubzansky, P. E., Harrison, R., Leiderman, G. and Solomon, P. Physicians' attitudes toward alcoholic patients *Archives of General Psychiatry* 11:392 (1964)
10. Knox, W. J. Attitudes of psychiatrists and psychologists toward alcoholism *American Journal of Psychiatry* 127:1675 (1971)
11. Goldstein, A. P. *Therapist-Patient Expectancies in Psychotherapy* (Macmillan, New York City, 1962)
12. American Medical Association Council on Mental Health: medical school education on abuse of alcohol and other psychoactive drugs *JAMA* 219:1746 (1972)
13. Freedman, D. X. Implications for research: conference on drug abuse *JAMA* 206:1280 (1968)
14. Cohen, C. P., White, E. H. and Schoolar, J. C. Interpersonal patterns of personality for drug-abusing patients and their therapeutic implications *Archives of General Psychiatry* 24:353 (1971)

Section II
Clinical Problems and Procedures

CHAPTER 5
SCREENING FOR DRUG ABUSE IN A GENERAL PATIENT POPULATION

The prevalence of drug abuse among general medical patients in the United States has received little attention, although epidemiological data at least suggest the dimensions of the problem. For example, Tennant et al[1] report that when 150 consecutive, first-visit, general medical patients were screened for drug and alcohol abuse by questionnaire, personal inquiry and physical examination, 11.3% were found to be engaged in current abuse of psychoactive drugs (excluding alcohol). As Tennant et al observe, this figure exceeds the proportion of disease usually detected by more common screening techniques such as chest x-ray, tuberculin skin test, occult blood, urine culture, blood glucose and Pap smear. Yet many physicians do not routinely screen their patients for substance abuse problems, and some even seem reluctant to diagnose drug dependence until presented with irrefutable evidence in the form of an acute toxic drug reaction or withdrawal syndrome.

However, the widespread use of illicit drugs, coupled with the frequency with which patients misuse prescription drugs, makes it increasingly likely that primary care physicians will encounter a variety of drug-related problems among their patients. Therefore, every physician confronts the problem of identifying drug-abusing patients and trying to achieve some form of treatment or referral.[2]

Such identification often requires a certain amount of guesswork. The physician's suspicions may be aroused by requests for frequent prescription refills, excuses involving lost prescriptions, requests for more powerful drugs or frequently missed office appointments. Certain symptom complexes (such as nervousness, insomnia, chronic headache, backache or abdominal pain) also are frequently associated with drug dependence.[2] A careful history and interview may elicit a voluntary admission that the patient is abusing psychoactive drugs. Or the physician may be approached by parents who know or suspect that their children are using drugs, or by adolescents seeking information and/or guidance[3] (see Chapter 12).

Regardless of how the suggestion of drug abuse is raised, it is essential that physicians be aware of the various indicators of drug abuse in a patient's history, physical examination and laboratory results, so that an appropriate diagnosis can be made.[4]

THE PATIENT HISTORY

Many physicians ask every patient to complete a brief medical history form at the time of the initial visit. This form can be expanded to include questions specifically designed to elicit information about drug and alcohol abuse. In their study of 150 general medical patients, Tennant et al[1] found that 82% of the patients who abused psychoactive drugs either checked "drug abuse" as a problem on the history form or entered the names of the psychoactive drugs they used. The pertinent section of the form used in that study is reproduced below.

Questionnaire Section of Medical History Form Used to Screen for Drug and Alcohol Abuse

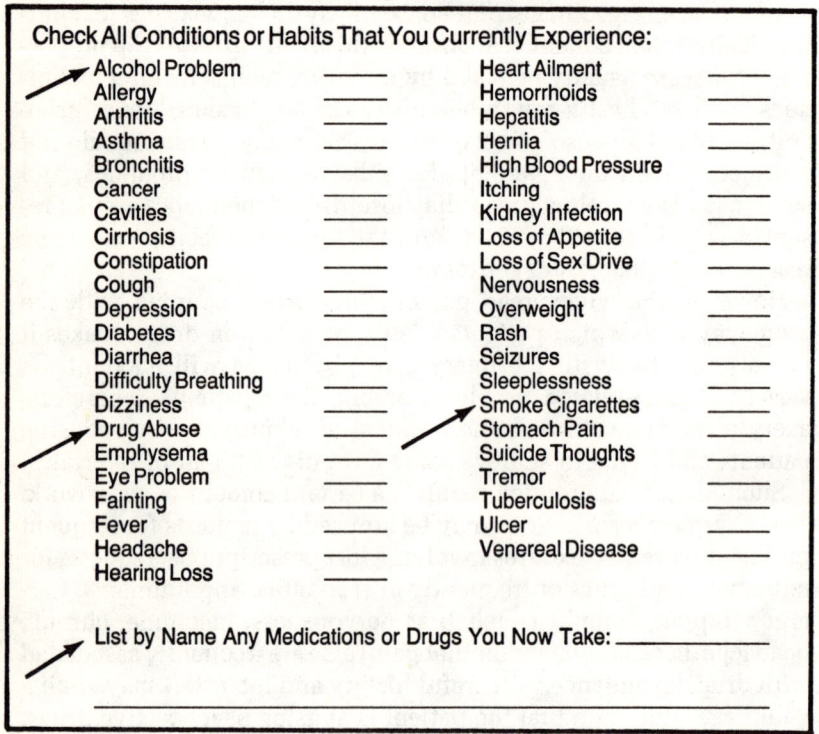

Check All Conditions or Habits That You Currently Experience:

Alcohol Problem	___	Heart Ailment	___
Allergy	___	Hemorrhoids	___
Arthritis	___	Hepatitis	___
Asthma	___	Hernia	___
Bronchitis	___	High Blood Pressure	___
Cancer	___	Itching	___
Cavities	___	Kidney Infection	___
Cirrhosis	___	Loss of Appetite	___
Constipation	___	Loss of Sex Drive	___
Cough	___	Nervousness	___
Depression	___	Overweight	___
Diabetes	___	Rash	___
Diarrhea	___	Seizures	___
Difficulty Breathing	___	Sleeplessness	___
Dizziness	___	Smoke Cigarettes	___
Drug Abuse	___	Stomach Pain	___
Emphysema	___	Suicide Thoughts	___
Eye Problem	___	Tremor	___
Fainting	___	Tuberculosis	___
Fever	___	Ulcer	___
Headache	___	Venereal Disease	___
Hearing Loss	___		

List by Name Any Medications or Drugs You Now Take: _____

Source: Tennant, F. S. Jr., Day, C. M. and Ungerleider, J. T. Screening for drug and alcohol abuse in a general medical population *JAMA* 242(6):533 (August 10, 1979)

MEDICAL HISTORY

The medical history form and personal interview should cover drug and alcohol use as part of the individual and family history and review of systems. In questioning patients about drug and alcohol history, it is essential that the physician approach these topics with sensitivity and discretion. Before asking direct questions about drug and alcohol abuse, the physician might first inquire about the frequency with which coffee and cigarets are used, then about the use of any prescription drugs (including sedative/hypnotics, tranquilizers, antidepressants, etc.), then about the use of wine, beer and liquor, and finally about the use of illegally obtained drugs. Inquiring about which drugs are used, why they are used and the effects achieved often yields useful information.[2]

The history of drug and alcohol use is especially important when the physician is dealing with a patient who tries to manipulate him to obtain drugs. Such a patient often will invent or exaggerate a medical problem (and even simulate its symptoms) in an effort to persuade the physician of the need for chemical relief.[2] (See the discussion of how to identify "patient hustlers," Chapter 10.)

On the other hand, a patient who is abusing drugs may be unaware that he has a problem. The chronic user of amphetamines, sedative/hypnotics, anxiolytics or analgesics may have developed considerable tolerance to the effects of those substances—and, in fact, be physically or psychologically dependent on them—but be aware only that he does not feel well when his use of the drug is interrupted.[2]

In reviewing the patient's history of drug and alcohol use, the physician should remember that persons who have had an alcohol abuse problem in the past are at greater risk of developing dependence on drugs than those who have had no problems with chemical dependence. The converse also is true: persons who have been drug abusers in the past are at greater than average risk of developing dependence on alcohol or another drug.[2]

The physician may suspect past or current drug abuse if certain physical problems appear repeatedly or in combination. These conditions include:

- A history of trauma (including burns and broken bones) at a greater frequency than would normally be expected, given the patient's occupation and activities

- Bizarre infections, including malaria and tetanus (70% of the tetanus cases in the United States are related to drug abuse)

- Hepatitis

- Subacute bacterial endocarditis or fungal infection of the heart valves

- Seizures, especially those that first appear between the ages of 10 and 30

- Pulmonary problems (cigaret smoking may merely mask the irritating effects of Persian heroin or cocaine freebase)
- General debilitation.

SOCIAL HISTORY

Assessments of social functioning provide essential information about the severity of the present illness and an important baseline for evaluating treatment outcome. Thus, the patient history should include information about educational background, employment history, family life and social activities.[2]

Items in the social history suggestive of drug (or alcohol) abuse would include repeated automobile accidents and/or drunk driving arrests, difficulty with employment, child abuse or other severe family problems.[4]

PSYCHOLOGICAL HISTORY

Drug abuse often is associated with psychiatric problems. Although the non-psychiatrist physician need not make a precise diagnosis of mental illness, he or she should be able to ascertain whether psychiatric problems exist. Interview questions should probe for mood disturbances, suicidal thoughts, lack of impulse control, thought disorders and sexual dysfunction.[2]

In conducting an interview with a suspected drug abuser, the physician should be aware that the patient may be giving false information. This is typical of the "conning" behavior so important to survival in the drug culture. To overcome this problem, the physician should attempt to verify key information by asking the same question several times in different ways during the interview. Verification by outside sources (always respecting the patient's privacy) also may be necessary.[2]

CURRENT BEHAVIOR

The patient's behavior during the interview may lead the physician to suspect drug abuse. Patients whose behavior is manipulative, seductive, evasive or otherwise suspicious, or who try to direct the interview, may be attempting to conceal a drug problem or to obtain drugs from the physician.[2]

THE PHYSICAL EXAMINATION

During the physical examination, the physician should be aware of some of the more common signs and symptoms of drug abuse. For example, debilitation that does not arise from the medical problems the patient overtly presents should raise the suspicion of substance abuse. So should any physical findings that are seriously out of proportion to the patient's complaints. Other suggestive findings include unsteady gait, slurred speech, inappropriate pupil dilation, nystagmus, unexplained sweating or chills, and inappropriate lapses in conversation.[2]

The physician also should be alert to the cutaneous signs of drug abuse, which can be readily divided into direct and indirect sequelae.[2,4]

DIRECT SEQUELAE of drug abuse include:
- Skin tracks and related scars on the neck, axilla, forearm, wrist, hand, foot, ankle, under the tongue, and on the dorsal vein of the penis. Such marks usually are multiple, hyperpigmented and linear. New lesions may be inflamed.
- Needle puncture marks located over veins
- "Pop" scars from subcutaneous injections on the arm (especially in the deltoid or gluteal areas), abdomen, thigh and shoulder. These scars are permanently circumscribed depressions in the skin similar to pock marks.
- Abscesses, infections or ulcerations on the arm, thigh, shoulder, abdomen, chest, hand or finger. These may be infective or chemical reactions to injections.
- Gangrene of the skin (sphaceloderma)
- Edema of the hand or irreducible finger flexion (camptodactylia) occurs when drugs are injected into veins of the finger or hand
- Thrombophlebitis at possible injection sites
- Accidental tattoos at possible injection sites result from carbon produced by flaming needles in an attempt to sterilize them.
- Toxic dermatitis at possible injection sites may be "fixed drug eruption"
- Purpura, urticaria or pruritus sometimes represent allergic reactions
- Ulceration or perforation of the nasal septum can result when inhaled heroin or cocaine irritates or infects the nasal mucosa.

INDIRECT SEQUELAE of drug abuse include:
- Acne excoriee or self-induced excoriations from itching
- Tattoos of figures, characters or words related to drug abuse, possibly placed to disguise skin tracks

TABLE 29

Cutaneous Signs Of Drug Abuse		
DIRECT SEQUELAE	**Local**	Abscesses Bullae Edema of the hand Infections Perforated septum "Pop" scars Shooting tattoos Skin tracks Sphaceloderma Thrombophlebitis Ulcerations
	Systemic	Edema of the eyelids Fixed drug eruption Pruritis Purpura Urticaria
INDIRECT SEQUELAE	**Other stigmata**	Acne excoriee Excoriations Self-induced tattoos Tourniquet pigmentation Wrist scars
	Medical problems	Bullous impetigo (staphylococcal) Cheilitis Contact dermatitis Dental disorders Jaundice Pigmentary problems Piloerection Pseudo acanthosis nigricans Skin infections/infestations Trench mouth

Source: Cohen, S. and Gallant, D. M. *Diagnosis of Drug and Alcohol Abusers* Medical Monograph Series, Vol. II, No. 2 (National Institute on Drug Abuse, Rockville, Md., 1980)

- Tourniquet pigmentation, which is a poorly defined linear mark that appears above the antecubital space from the repeated use of tourniquets for intravenous injections
- Hypopigmentation or hyperpigmentation of areas around possible injection sites
- Pseudo acanthosis nigricans of the axillae
- Bullous impetigo (staphylococcal)

- Cracked skin at the corners of the mouth (cheilitis)
- Contact dermatitis at possible injection sites or around the nose, mouth and hands (in those who inhale volatile substances, this is call "glue sniffer's rash")
- Dental disorders, including trench mouth
- Skin infections and infestations caused by scabies, lice, fungi or bacteria
- Piloerection (gooseflesh) on the trunk and arms (a common sign of opioid withdrawal)
- Jaundice as a sign of hepatitis from contaminated equipment
- Wrist scars resulting from suicide attempts, which are relatively frequent among substance abusers.

USEFUL DIAGNOSTIC TESTS

The diagnostic studies most often employed to detect drug use are toxicologic screens of the urine (to determine *if* a drug has been ingested within the preceding one to seven days) and the blood (to determine *how much* of a substance is in the blood).

Other tests used to confirm the presence, and assess the degree, of drug use include cultures of wounds or drainage, hepatic enzyme studies, chest x-rays, tubercular skin tests and specialized procedures such as planograms, arteriograms and intravenous pyelograms.[2]

The studies most commonly used to confirm suspected use of various classes of drugs are shown in Table 30, below.

CONFRONTATION AND COUNSELING

Once drug dependence has been diagnosed, direct confrontation of the patient is imperative.[6] In this situation, the physician should avoid showing antagonism or a judgmental attitude. Interest and a non-threatening concern are the keys to helping the patient acknowledge his problem.[7]

A variety of confrontation approaches may be used:
- Address the problem directly ("Mrs. Smith, I am concerned that the sleeping pills you are taking aren't working anymore, and I think we should talk about helping you stop"[7] or "Mr. Jones, my records show that you've been calling in early for refill prescriptions, and it's important for me to know why"[8])
- Begin by discussing some of the patient's known problem areas—family, career, health, etc.—and then present a concern that drug use may be playing a part in those problems.[7] ("Mrs. Brown, the number

TABLE 30

Tests to Confirm Suspected Drug Use, By Class Of Drugs

Suspected problem		Test
OPIOIDS	Intoxication	Blood or urine levels of opioids
	Withdrawal	Urine test for opioids or quinine, which may be present for 24 to 48 hours after the last dose
DEPRESSANTS	Intoxication	Blood or urine levels of depressant EEG-nonspecific depressant effect
	Withdrawal	EEG showing bursts of spiked high amplitude slow waves in non-epileptics
STIMULANTS	Intoxication	Blood or urine levels of amphetamine or cocaine
	Withdrawal	Abnormal sleep EEGs Urine screen for amphetamine or cocaine Depression scales
HALLUCINOGENS	Intoxication	None widely available (some laboratories can assay urine and blood levels)
	Withdrawal	
PHENCYCLIDINE	Intoxication	Blood or urine levels of phencyclidine. Either GC apparatus with a nitrogen detector or GC-MS is required for detection in the low nanogram range; otherwise, a false negative may confuse the diagnosis. The test may be positive up to 7 days after the last dose.
	Withdrawal	

Source: Cohen, S. and Gallant, D. M. *Diagnosis of Drug and Alcohol Abusers* Medical Monograph Series, Vol. II, No. 2 (National Institute on Drug Abuse, Rockville, Md., 1980)

of tranquilizers you've been taking may be one reason you have so little energy" or "Miss Black, recent scientific studies show that regular use of marijuana can change the pattern of menstrual cycles")

- Ask the patient if he believes he has a problem with a drug[7] ("Mr. Adams, how do you feel about using pain medications so long after your broken leg has healed?")

When confronted gently but directly, some patients will express relief that the topic has been approached. Others will vehemently deny that they have a problem. Such denial often arises out of the social stigma attached to the "addict" stereotype. Especially in the case of prescription drug abuse, the patient may view his use of drugs as legitimate and thus "incongruous with addiction, which by social definition is not legitimate."[9] Families and even physicians sometimes reinforce the patient's denial for the same reason: the patient obviously is not a criminal and is, or was, medically ill.

Still other patients will admit to use of drugs, but fail to recognize that such use is responsible for, or is exacerbating, their medical problems. These patients need help in understanding the relationship between abuse of drugs and their deteriorating health.[2]

Overcoming denial requires firmness and persistence on the part of the physician. In the course of one or more confrontation sessions, the physician should explain the problems associated with drug dependence (including any relevant special considerations, such as the potentiating effect of alcohol in combination with certain drugs) and indicate a willingness to continue the dialog.[2]

Some physicians avoid confronting patients about drug problems because they fear those patients may withdraw completely from medical care or seek out a less observant or more compliant source of care. Physicians experienced in the field, however, maintain that this reaction is largely confined to situations in which the physician's approach is incorrect or misconstrued, or where the patient is intent on continuing the abuse and wants to avoid treatment for it.[7,8]

Assuming that the confrontation leads the patient to acknowledge his problem, he may ask the physician for guidance in the next step. For most patients, including those with an element of physical dependence, the principal therapeutic challenge is to reduce the psychological dependence on drugs, identify the causes and consequences of that dependence, and design a treatment plan that deals with each of these areas. Since the causes and consequences of drug dependence are multiple and complex, the therapeutic strategies also are multiple and must be tailored to meet each patient's needs.[8]

Few primary care physicians have the time or expertise required to personally conduct the full range of support services that may be required. Psychiatric care or referral to a specialized drug treatment program may be required. However, the various treatment modalities may be coordinated by the family physician, who thus maintains a continuing supportive relationship with the patient.[8]

The essential point for the physician to remember in counseling the patient is that drug dependence can be a chronic problem. Long-term management may require behavioral changes such as avoiding certain psychoactive drugs, substituting certain other drugs or altering the patient's lifestyle.[6] As with any chronic disease, relapses and exacerbations will occur. Thus, any recurrence of drug abuse should be regarded as part of the disease process, rather than as a treatment failure.[7]

REFERENCES

1. Tennant, F. S. Jr., Day, C. M. and Ungerleider, J. T. Screening for drug and alcohol abuse in a general medical population *JAMA* 242(6):533 (August 10, 1979)
2. Cohen, S. and Gallant, D. M. *Diagnosis of Drug and Alcohol Abusers* Medical Monograph Series, Vol. II, No. 2 (National Institute on Drug Abuse, Rockville, Md., 1980)
3. Senay, E. C. and Lewis, D. *The Primary Physician's Guide to Drug & Alcohol Abuse Treatment* Medical Monograph Series, Vol. I, No. 6 (National Institute on Drug Abuse, Rockville, Md., 1980)
4. Smith, D. E. *Identifying the Drug User: The History and Physical* (Workshop on the Ethics & Practice of Prescribing Psychoactive Drugs, Haight Ashbury Training and Education Project, San Francisco, June 18, 1980)
5. Schuckit, M. A. *Drug and Alcohol Abuse: A Clinical Guide to Diagnosis and Treatment* (Plenum Medical Book Company, New York City, 1979)
6. Moessner, H. The use and abuse of drugs *Journal of the Iowa Medical Society* 64
7. Kramer, J., Manoguerra, A. and Schnoll, S. H. When drug abuse enters the differential *Patient Care* 110 (December 1, 1976)
8. Jacob, M. S. and Sellers, E. M. Use of drugs with dependence liability *Canadian Medical Association Journal* 121:717 (September 22, 1979)
9. Walker, L. Iatrogenic addiction and its treatment *International Journal of the Addictions* 13(3):461 (1978)

CHAPTER 6
CARE OF ACUTE DRUG REACTIONS

Any primary care physician may be called upon to care for a patient who is experiencing an acute drug reaction. Such an emergency may involve central nervous system depression, organ malfunction, behavioral disturbance, exacerbation of preexisting illness, or any combination of the above. The situation may be complicated by concurrent illness or injury, which may either augment the drug effect or fail to show the usual symptoms because of the drug effect.[1] Some patients suffering acute drug reactions are deeply comatose or unresponsive, while others are wildly agitated, delirious or combative.[2]

The following are the most frequently encountered types of acute drug reactions:

ACUTE INTOXICATION/OVERDOSE: Acute intoxication or overdose occurs when an individual ingests a drug dose large enough to interfere with the proper functioning of body support systems.[1,3]

WITHDRAWAL: The withdrawal or abstinence syndrome is characterized by the development of physical and psychological signs and symptoms in response to the abrupt discontinuation of a dependence-producing drug.[1,4]

FLASHBACK REACTIONS: A flashback reaction is the unwanted recurrence of drug effects in the absence of current drug use.[1,3]

PANIC REACTIONS: A panic reaction is characterized by the onset of severe agitation shortly after ingestion of a drug (usually by a novice) and the emergence of drug effects. Typically, the user develops acute anxiety over losing control or sanity, and fears that he has done physical harm to himself by taking the drug.[3]

PSYCHOTIC REACTIONS: Drug psychoses can occur, with the development of hallucinations or delusions. In such a state, the drug user loses contact with reality and may present with physical symptoms such as rapid pulse or elevated blood pressure.[1,3]

ORGANIC BRAIN SYNDROME: An organic brain syndrome is characterized by confusion, disorientation and decreased intellectual functioning. It may be accompanied by high levels of fear or irritability and, occasionally, by hallucinations.[3]

The most frequently encountered emergency reactions for each major class of drugs are shown in Table 31, below.

TABLE 31

Most Common Acute Drug Reactions, by Class of Drug

	Opioids	Depressants	Stimulants	Hallucinogens	Phencyclidines	Cannabinoids	Inhalants
Acute intoxication/ overdose	X	X	X	X	X	X	X
Withdrawal	X	X	X				
Flashback reaction				X	X	X	
Panic reaction			X	X	X	X	
Psychotic reaction		X	X	X	X		
Organic brain syndrome	X	X	X	X	X	X	X

Source: Bourne, P. G. (ed.) *A Treatment Manual for Acute Drug Abuse Emergencies* (National Institute on Drug Abuse, Rockville, Md., 1974) Senay, E. C., Becker, C. E. and Schnoll, S. H. *Emergency Treatment of the Drug-Abusing Patient for Treatment Staff Physicians* Medical Monograph Series, Vol. I, No. 4 (National Institute on Drug Abuse, Rockville, Md., 1977) Schuckit, M. A. *Drug and Alcohol Abuse: A Clinical Guide to Diagnosis and Treatment* (Plenum Medical Book Company, New York City, 1979)

ACUTE MANAGEMENT

Crisis intervention is, by definition, short-term; it involves instituting life-sustaining measures and alleviating the patient's pain and confusion.[4]

The *conscious* patient often is experiencing severe emotional stress. In such cases, the physician should use good communication skills to build a short-term working relationship that will reduce the patient's level of anxiety and produce a clearer understanding of the patient's problem. Senay and Lewis[5] suggest several techniques to achieve this goal:

PROVIDE A REALITY BASE: The physician should identify himself and his position, use the patient's name, and anticipate concerns of the patient, his family and friends.

PROVIDE APPROPRIATE NON-VERBAL SUPPORT: The physician should maintain eye contact with the patient and a relaxed body posture, touching the patient if that seems appropriate.

ENCOURAGE COMMUNICATION: In communicating with the patient, the physician should ask clear, simple, open-ended questions and show tolerance for repetition of questions and answers.

FOSTER CONFIDENCE: The physician should project a calm, assured, nonjudgmental attitude. He should listen carefully and respond to the patient's feelings, identifying and reinforcing progress wherever possible.

The *unconscious* patient presents a different set of treatment problems. The patient's level of anxiety is not a concern (although that of family or friends may be), but the patient also cannot volunteer any information for the physician to use in shaping the diagnosis or the treatment plan.

In addressing the life-threatening problems that may be associated with acute drug reactions, the major priorities are to establish an adequate airway, support circulation, control hemorrhaging, and then deal with any destructive behavior.[1,3,4] Schuckit[3] and Senay and Lewis[5] suggest the following steps in the management of drug emergencies:

STEP 1: Assess the vital signs. If the patient has no observable blood pressure or pulse, begin cardiopulmonary resuscitation immediately.

STEP 2: Establish an adequate airway.
    a. Straighten the head.
    b. Remove any obstructions from the throat.
    c. Begin artificial respiration, if needed.

d. Perform tracheal intubation, if needed (if possible, use an inflatable cuff tube to permit later gastric lavage).
e. If intubation is not needed and the patient is unconscious, tape a short plastic oropharyngeal airway in the mouth to keep the tongue from obstructing the airway. Place the patient on his side, facing downward, to prevent aspiration of any vomitus.
f. If the patient's jaw is locked from muscle spasm, administer succinylcholine chloride (about 40 mg in adults), except in cases involving phencyclidine, where other muscle relaxants should be used. Anticipate vomiting in response to the succinylcholine.
g. Establish the patient on a respirator, if needed (use 10 to 12 respirations per minute and avoid oxygen, which may decrease spontaneous respiration).

STEP 3: Maintain adequate circulation.
a. If the heart has stopped, use external chest massage and administer intracardiac adrenaline.
b. If there is evidence of cardiac fibrillation, use a defibrillator.
c. If circulation is not adequate, institute an intravenous drip of 50 ml of sodium bicarbonate (3.75 gm) to treat the acidic state.

STEP 4: Perform a rapid physical examination.
a. Observe the condition of the pupils (pinpoint pupils strongly suggest narcotic overdose).
b. Examine the skin for needle marks.
c. Evaluate breath odor.
d. Assess liver size.
e. Listen to breath sounds in the lung.
f. Investigate any evidence of trauma (if head trauma is suspected, examine the tympanic membrane of the ear for blood behind the drum).

STEP 5: Draw blood for chemical analysis.
a. Draw at least 10 cc for a toxicologic screen.
b. Draw 30 to 40 cc for the blood count, electrolytes, blood sugar, BUN and blood gases.

STEP 6: Insert an indwelling Foley catheter to monitor urinary output. Collect 50 ml urine for a toxicologic screen.

STEP 7: Establish an intravenous infusion.
a. Use a large-gauge needle.

        b. Use restraints, if necessary, to keep the needle in place.
        c. Use a slow IV drip until the need for intravenous fluids has been established.
        d. Test for narcotic drugs with slow IV administration of naloxone (0.4 mg in adults; 0.01 mg/kg in children). Prompt improvement of the respiratory rate suggests narcotic overdose. If improvement is not significant, repeat the dose one to two times every two to three minutes. The absence of improvement in respiratory rate and volume implies that factors other than opioids are involved.

STEP 8: If hypoglycemia is suspected, administer 50 cc of 50% glucose immediately.

STEP 9: Start an EKG or rhythm strip to monitor any cardiac irregularities. This is particularly important in antidepressant overdose, because deaths have been reported as a result of arrhythmias. Be prepared to insert a pacemaker, if needed.

STEP 10: If the drug was orally ingested within the preceding four to six hours, consider gastric lavage.
        a. Begin lavage only when the heart rate is stable, to avoid inducing a clinically significant vagal response.
        b. If the patient is not awake, begin lavage only after a tracheal tube with an inflatable cuff is in place, to avoid aspiration.
        c. After evacuating the stomach, administer a saline lavage until the returning fluid looks clear.
        d. Consider administering activated charcoal or castor oil (60 ml) to slow drug absorption.
        e. Measure the fluids lost and replace them with intravenous fluids (plus 20 ml per hour to replace fluids lost through respiration and perspiration).

STEP 11: If the blood pressure is moderately depressed, consider a rapid infusion of one-half normal saline or Ringer's lactate, monitoring the CVP for fluid overload.

STEP 12: If the blood pressure is below 80mm/Hg after correction of volume deficit, consider using plasma expanders or pressors (with care in titrating the needed dose and recognizing the potential for life-threatening drug interactions).

STEP 13: If an anticholinergic drug appears to be involved (as suggested by rapid heart rate, dry skin and mouth, a rash, etc.), consider administering 1.0 to 4.0 mg physostigmine by slow intravenous infusion.

STEP 14: Consider three basic questions:
   a. What is the best supportive care?
   b. Can the absorption rate of an orally ingested drug be slowed?
   c. Would any antidotes by useful?

The immediate objective is to assess and stabilize cardiopulmonary functioning. If the patient is *comatose, apneic* and *hypotensive*, with *absent heart sounds*, emergency cardiopulmonary resuscitation should be started immediately, despite the lack of a diagnosis.[5]

If the patient is in *shock* (characterized by lack of perfusion of vital tissues, rather than low blood pressure alone), treatment depends on identifying the cause. Shock due to an acute allergic reaction should be treated with epinephrine, antihistaminic medications and steroids. Embarrassed heart function requires careful cardiovascular monitoring and treatment to increase perfusion. Blood cultures should be taken to detect systemic infection. In the absence of obvious heart failure, shock should be treated by elevating the patient's legs, lowering the head, and increasing fluid volume as rapidly as possible. Vasopressor agents may be useful, but must be monitored closely.[5]

If the patient is *hyperventilating*, the physician should consider performing a Trousseau and Chvostek test to identify any decrease in calcium ionization. Where intravenous abuse and the resultant complications are suspected, an arterial blood gas determination will indicate whether decreased oxygen is causing the hyperventilation. If medical causes are ruled out, giving verbal reassurance and having the patient count his respirations and breathe into a paper bag usually will correct the hyperventilation. In resistant cases, 10 to 20 mg of oral diazepam usually is helpful (heavy smokers may require two to three times this dose). The hyperventilating patient does best in a quiet, reassuring environment, and should not be left alone.[5]

If the patient is suffering *convulsions*, a quick physical examination is necessary to identify possible metabolic or thermal imbalances. The patient should be protected from aspirating and from self-injury. Tight clothing should be loosened and the patient placed on the floor or in a bed with side rails. A blood sample should be taken for calcium and sugar levels, and intravenous glucose administered. In *status epilepticus* (repeated seizures without a lucid interval between seizures), slow intravenous administration of 10 mg diazepam is the treatment of choice (slow administration is essential to prevent cardiac arrest). Persistent seizures may respond to phenytoin in 600 to 1,000 mg doses given intravenously in 100 mg bolus injections.[5]

After the patient has been stabilized, the physician should evaluate other serious problems by gathering a good history from the patient (or a resource person), performing physical and neurological examinations, and ordering the appropriate laboratory tests.[1,2,3,4] Koumans[6] suggests that this process is facilitated if any friends or relatives who accompany the patient to the treatment facility are asked to stay until all needed information has been collected.

ESTABLISHING A DIFFERENTIAL DIAGNOSIS

Reactions to psychoactive drugs present some of the most complex diagnostic challenges in clinical practice. Diagnosis requires knowledge of the principles of drug action, as well as understanding of the various physical and behavioral reactions that may occur. Rubin and Cluff[7] note that the reaction to a drug depends on a number of variables, including (1) the type of drug used, (2) its purity, (3) its dosage, (4) the presence of contaminants, (5) the time elapsed since the drug was taken, (6) the presence of underlying medical or psychological problems, (7) the degree of tolerance the individual has developed to the drug, (8) the duration of drug use and (9) whether the drug is used alone or in combination with other substances.

Although the physician should make every effort to obtain a history from the patient or resource person, he should recognize that the information he receives may not be complete or accurate. For this reason, knowledge of the various clinical manifestations of drug reactions assumes major importance in establishing a differential diagnosis.

CLINICAL MANIFESTATIONS

GENERAL APPEARANCE: *Restless* or *agitated* behavior most commonly suggests use of amphetamines or LSD, or withdrawal from barbiturates or heroin. Marijuana occasionally produces a similar reaction.[2,7]

Quiet, withdrawn behavior may indicate recent ingestion of barbiturates, heroin or hallucinogens. Withdrawal from stimulants may be characterized by *apathy, somnolence* and *depression,* and be accompanied by distinct *EEG changes.* A state of *detachment* also may follow a panic reaction to hallucinogens or phencyclidines.[4,7]

VITAL SIGNS: *Elevated blood pressure* is most commonly associated with use of amphetamines and other stimulants, but also may suggest use of a hallucinogen. *Orthostatic hypotension* may reflect barbiturate withdrawal or (rarely) use of marijuana. Phenothiazines also can cause this symptom.[2,6]

Pulse irregularities suggest amphetamine use (tachycardia, however, is present in most acute drug reactions).[3,7]

Elevated temperature may indicate ingestion of hallucinogens, an overdose of tricyclic antidepressants, or withdrawal from opioids or barbiturates. (It is important to eliminate the possibility of infection before ascribing such a fever to drug use.)[4,7]

Respiratory depression often indicates ingestion of large amounts of barbiturates or opioids.[2,4,7]

SKIN: *Perspiration* accompanies most acute overdose or withdrawal reactions. *Dry skin* suggests the use of anticholinergic agents, either alone or in combination with a hallucinogen. *Piloerection* ("gooseflesh") is a classic sign of heroin withdrawal and also is seen in acute LSD reactions.[4,7]

Needle tracks most commonly suggest use of opioids (especially heroin), although stimulants and depressants also may be injected intravenously. Opioids, depressants and stimulants sometimes are injected subcutaneously—a practice that can lead to large *abscesses*, *ulcerations* or *draining sinuses* from deeper tissues.[2,4,7]

EYES: Excessive *lacrimation*, as well as *rhinorrhea* and *mydriasis*, are among the earliest manifestations of heroin withdrawal.[4,7]

Lateral *nystagmus* frequently occurs during barbiturate use or withdrawal and occasionally is associated with the use of marijuana. An *exaggerated blink reflex* also is commonly associated with barbiturate withdrawal.[2,4,7]

Heroin use characteristically produces *pinpoint pupils*. Pupillary constriction also may occur with concurrent use of opioids and stimulants such as cocaine or amphetamine.[2,3,7]

Dilated pupils are seen with amphetamines, LSD, cannabinoids and (in some users) meperidine.[4,7] If the pupils do not react to light, use of an anticholinergic agent may be suspected.[7]

NOSE: An *infected, ulcerated* or *perforated nasal septum* may indicate inhalation of cocaine, potent marijuana or volatile substances. *Rhinorrhea* is an early sign of heroin withdrawal.[2,4,7]

CHEST: *Pulmonary edema* and *pulmonary fibrosis* may be precipitated by use of intravenous heroin or some of its contaminants. Heroin use also may precipitate *bronchoconstriction* in the sensitive individual. *Bronchial irritation* may indicate recent heavy smoking of marijuana.[2,4,7]

ABDOMEN: Crampy *abdominal pain* may be a late sign of heroin withdrawal.[2,7]

MENTAL STATUS: *Disorientation* or *overt psychoses* most often are associated with use of hallucinogens and phencyclidines, but also may follow the use of amphetamines, barbiturates, anticholinergics, cocaine or marijuana. Barbiturate withdrawal also may precipitate a psychotic episode. Ampetamine users often are *paranoiac*. In a heroin user, psychosis suggests the use of other drugs or indicates an underlying thought disorder.[7]

MOTOR FUNCTIONS: *Slurred speech* is characteristic of barbiturate intoxication, although any drug of abuse may alter speech patterns in some way.[2,7]

Fine resting *tremors* may indicate amphetamine or hallucinogen use or heroin withdrawal. The tremors induced by barbiturate withdrawal generally are more coarse. *Grand mal seizures* and *ataxia* also may appear during withdrawal from the short-acting barbiturates.[4,7]

Increased *reflex activity* often indicates amphetamine use. During barbiturate intoxication, the deep tendon reflexes are normal, but the *superficial reflexes* may be depressed. On the other hand, barbiturate withdrawal often is characterized by a *rapid blink reflex*.[7]

The most common physical and psychological manifestations of drug reactions are summarized in Table 32, below. In reviewing these signs, however, it is essential to recognize that:

- The patient's condition may result from something other than drug abuse (such as diabetic ketoacidosis or subdural hematoma), even if the patient is a drug abuser.
- There may be coexisting pathology, such as limb fractures, head injuries or other trauma.[5]

SUB-ACUTE MANAGEMENT

After life-threatening problems have been dealt with and a working diagnosis established, it is possible to initiate sub-acute care. At this point, Cherubin,[8] Schuckit,[3] and Senay et al[4] recommend the following general steps:

STEP 1: Check the vital signs every 15 minutes for at least the first four hours, then monitor them every two to four hours over the next two days, even if the patient's condition seems improved. (Many drugs clear from the plasma temporarily and then are released from fat stores, causing severe reintoxication after the patient apparently has improved. Also, most opioid antagonists have a shorter duration of action than the opioids themselves, so intoxication may reemerge.)

STEP 2: Perform a thorough physical examination, giving special emphasis to the status of and any changes in neurological signs.

TABLE 32

Clinical Manifestations of Acute Drug Reactions, by Class of Drug

Signs and Symptoms	Intoxication – Opioids	Intoxication – Depressants	Intoxication – Stimulants	Intoxication – Hallucinogens	Intoxication – Phencyclidine	Intoxication – Cannabinoids	Intoxication – Inhalants	Overdose – Opioids	Overdose – Depressants	Overdose – Stimulants	Overdose – Hallucinogens	Overdose – Phencyclidine	Overdose – Cannabinoids	Overdose – Inhalants	Withdrawal – Opioids	Withdrawal – Depressants	Withdrawal – Stimulants
Abdominal cramps		X									X				X	X	
Aches, muscle															X		
Affect, labile			X	X		X											
Analgesia (pinprick)					X				X			X					
Angina										X							
Anorexia		X	X	X	X			X		X							
Anxiety		X	X	X						X	X	X			X	X	
Arrhythmia			X							X							
Ataxia		X			X				X								
Body image changes				X	X					X	X	X					
Chest pain					X					X		X					
Chills															X		

TABLE 32 *(continued)*

Clinical Manifestations of Acute Drug Reactions, by Class of Drug

Signs and Symptoms	Intoxication							Overdose						Withdrawal		
	Opioids	Depressants	Stimulants	Hallucinogens	Phencyclidine	Cannabinoids	Inhalants	Opioids	Depressants	Stimulants	Hallucinogens	Phencyclidine	Cannabinoids	Inhalants	Opioids	Depressants	Stimulants
Circulatory collapse								X			X					X	
Coma	X	X						X	X								
Comprehension, slow		X			X			X	X	X		X					X
Convulsions												X					X
Coryza															X		X
Delirium		X	X		X			X	X	X	X	X				X	X
Depressed mood		X			X					X							
Diarrhea															X		
Diplopia		X															
Dizziness		X	X	X	X		X				X						
Dysmetria		X		X	X												
Euphoria	X	X	X	X	X												

133

TABLE 32 *(continued)*

Clinical Manifestations of Acute Drug Reactions, by Class of Drug

Signs and Symptoms	Intoxication							Overdose							Withdrawal		
	Opioids	Depressants	Stimulants	Hallucinogens	Phencyclidine	Cannabinoids	Inhalants	Opioids	Depressants	Stimulants	Hallucinogens	Phencyclidine	Cannabinoids	Inhalants	Opioids	Depressants	Stimulants
Facial grimacing					X					X							
Fatigue		X															X
Floating feeling	X	X		X	X												
Flushing	X			X						X	X					X	
Hallucinations			X	X	X	X				X	X	X				X	
Headaches							X			X	X					X	
Hyperphagia															X		
Hypertension			X	X	X					X	X	X					X
Hypotension (orthostatic)		X						X	X							X	
Hyperthermia			X	X						X	X						
Hypotonia	X							X	X		X						X
Irritability		X	X		X				X	X					X	X	

TABLE 32 *(continued)*

Clinical Manifestations of Acute Drug Reactions, by Class of Drug

Signs and Symptoms	Intoxication						Overdose						Withdrawal		
	Opioids	Depressants	Stimulants	Hallucinogens	Phencyclidine	Cannabinoids	Inhalants	Opioids	Depressants	Stimulants	Hallucinogens	Phencyclidine	Cannabinoids	Inhalants	Opioids	Depressants	Stimulants
Lacrimation							X								X		
Memory, poor		X															
Motor seizures (grand mal)					X					X	X	X				X	
Mouth, dry			X							X	X						
Muscle spasm (rigidity)					X							X			X		
Nausea			X	X	X					X	X	X			X	X	
Nystagmus		X			X				X			X					
Paresthesia			X	X						X					X		
Piloerection (gooseflesh)															X		
Psychosis (toxic)		X	X		X					X	X	X				X	
Pupils, dilated			X	X		X				X	X				X		

TABLE 32 *(continued)*

Clinical Manifestations of Acute Drug Reactions, by Class of Drug

Signs and Symptoms	Intoxication						Overdose						Withdrawal		
	Opioids	Depressants	Stimulants	Hallucinogens	Phencyclidine	Cannabinoids	Inhalants	Opioids	Depressants	Stimulants	Hallucinogens	Phencyclidine	Cannabinoids	Inhalants	Opioids	Depressants	Stimulants
Pupils, pinpoint	X							X									
Reflexes, hyperactive			X	X	X				X	X						X	
Respiration, slow and shallow								X	X								
Restlessness			X	X	X										X		X
Rhinorrhea							X								X		
Skin picking	X		X							X							
Sleep disturbance			X	X						X					X	X	X
Sleepiness		X				X	X										X
Speech, slurred		X			X		X					X					
Stare, blank					X							X					
Suspiciousness			X	X	X					X	X	X					

136

TABLE 32 *(continued)*

Clinical Manifestations of Acute Drug Reactions, by Class of Drug

Signs and Symptoms	Intoxication						Overdose						Withdrawal		
	Opioids	Depressants	Stimulants	Hallucinogens	Phencyclidine	Cannabinoids	Inhalants	Opioids	Depressants	Stimulants	Hallucinogens	Phencyclidine	Cannabinoids	Inhalants	Opioids	Depressants	Stimulants
Sweating										X					X		
Tachycardia			X	X	X					X	X				X	X	
Talkativeness			X			X				X							
Tremor			X	X						X	X					X	
Violent behavior		X			X							X					
Vomiting					X					X	X				X		
Yawning		X													X		

Source: Cohen, S. and Gallant, D. M. *Diagnosis of Drug and Alcohol Abusers* Medical Monogragh Series, Vol. II, No. 2 (National Institute on Drug Abuse, Rockville, Md., 1980)
Treatment of the Drug-Abusing Patient for Treatment Staff Physicians Medical Monograph Series, Vol. I, No. 2 (National Institute on Drug Abuse, Rockville, Md., 1977)
Senay, E. C., Becker, C. E. and Schnoll, S. H. *Emergency Treatment of the Drug-Abusing Patient* Medical Monograph Series, Vol. I, No. 4 (National Institute on Drug Abuse, Rockville, Md., 1977)
Schuckit, M. A. *Drug and Alcohol Abuse: A Clinical Guide to Diagnosis and Treatment* (Plenum Medical Book Company, New York City, 1979)

STEP 3: Take a comprehensive history from the patient and, if possible, verify the information with a resource person (always respecting confidentiality).

STEP 4: Establish a flow sheet to record vital signs, medications, fluid intake and output, and other critical data.

STEP 5: Obtain a baseline body weight measurement that can be used to assess fluid balance.

STEP 6: Administer only those medications that are absolutely necessary.

STEP 7: If the patient is comatose, establish careful management of electrolytes and fluids, as well as standard procedures such as eye care, tracheal cleansing and frequent turning.

Dialysis or diuresis are only rarely necessary, but may be indicated for (1) severe intoxication, with markedly abnormal vital signs, (2) report of probable ingestion of a lethal dose of a drug, (3) drug blood levels in the lethal dose range, (4) impaired excretion or metabolism of a drug due to liver or kidney damage, (5) progressive clinical deterioration, (6) prolonged coma, or (7) underlying lung disease. If the physician decides to perform dialysis, Schuckit[3] recommends hemodialysis over peritoneal dialysis because it is more efficient and poses less risk of decreasing respiration. For diuresis, Schuckit[3] suggests regular administration of 40 to 100 mg of furosemide to maintain a urinary output of about 250 ml per hour, or administration of sufficient intravenous fluids to maintain urinary output above 200 ml per hour, using half-normal saline with potassium supplementation.

The major categories of acute drug reaction are described here in terms of the clinical pictures they present, their differential diagnoses, the various etiologic agents for each type of reaction, and the specific symptoms, laboratory tests and treatments suggested for each class of drugs.

ACUTE INTOXICATION/OVERDOSE

CLINICAL PICTURE: The patient has ingested appreciably more than the customary or therapeutic amount of a psychoactive substance and presents with unstable vital signs. The condition may be accompanied by a psychotic reaction or organic brain syndrome.[3,8]

DIFFERENTIAL DIAGNOSIS: There are no major psychiatric syndromes that mimic overdose (with the possible exception of a catatonic-like stupor seen in serious depression), but physiological disorders that can cause coma (such as hypoglycemia or severe electrolyte abnormalities) must be considered.[3]

ETIOLOGIC AGENTS: Life-threatening overdoses are most often seen with drugs that depress the central nervous system, such as opioids, sedatives, phencyclidines and some inhalable solvents.[1,3,4]

LABORATORY TESTS: The physician should rule out all other causes of coma through rapid physical and neurological examinations, skull x-rays, spinal taps, etc. The level of cardiac functioning should be measured with an EKG and, if necessary, the level of brain function with an EEG. Vital signs (particularly blood pressure and body temperature) should be closely monitored. Toxicologic screens of the blood and urine are helpful in identifying the specific drug involved and the amount present in the bloodstream.[3,5,8]

Opioids

Opioid overdose usually is an acute, life-threatening event, involving a semicomatose patient and evidence of recent drug injection.[3] Acute opioid poisoning may result from clinical overdosage, accidental overdosage by drug abusers, or suicide attempts.[8] Also, a delayed reaction sometimes occurs when opioids are injected into chilled skin or by persons who have low blood pressure or are in shock. In these cases, restoration of normal circulation allows sudden absorption of large amounts of the drug.[9]

SIGNS AND SYMPTOMS: By the time he comes to medical attention, the patient overdosed on opioids usually is asleep or stuporous. With a large overdose, the patient cannot be easily aroused and may be in a profound coma.[5,9]

The *respiratory rate* is very low and cyanosis may be present. As the respiratory exchange worsens, blood pressure falls. Early, adequate oxygenation usually restores blood pressure, but untreated hypoxia can lead to capillary damage and shock.[5,9]

The *pupils* usually are symmetrical and pinpoint in size, but may be dilated in severe hypoxia. *Urine formation* is depressed by the antidiuretic effect of the drug and low blood pressure. *Body temperature* falls and the skin becomes cold and clammy. *Skeletal muscles* are flaccid, the jaw is relaxed and the tongue may fall back and block the airway.[8,9]

The triad of *coma, pinpoint pupils* and *depressed respiration* strongly suggests opioid poisoning. The finding of needle marks suggestive of intravenous injection further supports this diagnosis. However, mixed poisonings are not uncommon. In such cases, other agents such as barbiturates or alcohol also may contribute to the clinical picture. Chemical examination of the urine and gastric contents for morphine and other CNS depressants may help to clarify the diagnosis, but the results often become available too late to influence treatment.[7,8,9,10]

If death occurs, it almost always is due to respiratory failure. In some cases, even if respiration is restored, death still may result from complications (such as pneumonia or shock) that develop during the coma.[7,8,9]

PSYCHOLOGICAL STATE: The patient usually is markedly lethargic or comatose.[3]

TREATMENT: The first step is to establish an adequate airway and ventilate the patient. Antagonists such as naloxone can produce dramatic reversal of severe respiratory depression.[10] Extra caution is required in using antagonists such as nalorphine and levallorphan, as their agonistic actions may further depress respiration. Because naloxone has no respiratory depressant action, it is the drug of choice in these cases.[9]

The conservative approach is to administer small intravenous doses of naloxone (0.4 to 0.8 mg) several times over the course of 20 to 30 minutes. The response to such treatment is so predictable that, if no effect is seen after 10 mg of naloxone has been administered, the physician reasonably can question whether opioids caused the toxic reaction.[8,9]

The duration of action of antagonists usually is much shorter than that of the opioids, so the patient must be watched carefully for signs that he is slipping back into coma. This is especially important when the overdose is due to methadone or levo-alpha-acetylmethadol (LAAM) whose depressant effects may persist for 24 to 72 hours. Deaths have resulted from premature discontinuation of treatment with an antagonist drug.[7,8,9]

Antagonists also may precipitate a severe withdrawal syndrome that cannot be readily suppressed during the period of action of the antagonist. In some cases, this withdrawal syndrome can be more life-threatening than the respiratory depression itself. However, it usually is possible to administer a small enough dose of naloxone to antagonize respiratory depression without producing severe withdrawal symptoms.[7,9,11,12,13,14]

Pulmonary edema associated with opioid overdose can be treated with positive-pressure respiration. A Swan-Ganz catheter should be inserted and the patient monitored very carefully. Grand mal seizures (occasionally seen with overdoses of propoxyphene and meperidine) are relieved by administration of naloxone.[7,9]

The same principles are appropriate in treating acute poisoning with codeine, all of the semisynthetic opioids and almost all synthetic opioids.[9,15]

Depressants

Acute depressant intoxication generally develops over several hours, with the patient presenting in an obtunded state. Overdoses may result from (1) combined use of barbiturates and hypnotics or alcohol, (2) a confused state in which the patient takes repeated doses of a drug, (3) ingestion of larger-than-intended doses of an illicitly obtained drug, or (4) a deliberate suicide attempt.[3,16]

The lethal dose of *barbiturates* is variable and cannot be stated with certainty. Severe poisoning is likely to occur when more than 10 times the full hypnotic dose has been ingested at one time. The short-acting barbiturates are more potent and more toxic than the long-lasting compounds.[16,17]

For *benzodiazepines*, the therapeutic index seems to be quite high.[17,18,19] However, hypnotic doses of nitrazepam can cause carbon dioxide narcosis in patients with bronchopulmonary disease.[16]

Mild overdoses of *methaqualone* usually cause central nervous system depression (similar to that of the barbiturates), but a paradoxical reaction involving restlessness and excitation may occur instead. Severe overdoses are marked by delirium, pyramidal signs and frank convulsions. During coma, cardiovascular and respiratory depression is less severe than with the barbiturates. Suicidal intent has been identified in a large proportion of these cases, and most deaths occur in persons who also have ingested alcohol.[16]

Chloral hydrate is a gastric irritant and may cause vomiting when ingested on an empty stomach. Prolonged coma may develop in patients with renal insufficiency or liver disease.[18]

Glutethimide overdose is marked by cyclic variations in CNS depression and a disproportionate fall in blood pressure when compared with barbiturates.[18]

Ethchlorvynol overdose can produce unusually prolonged coma, particularly when the drug is ingested in combination with alcohol or by patients with cirrhosis of the liver.[18]

Bromide salts (available in nonprescription sedatives) intoxication is marked by mental confusion and irrational behavior. Patients also may show alternating periods of stupor and combativeness. Chronic bromide toxicity usually is accompanied by skin lesions.[18]

SIGNS AND SYMPTOMS: While moderate intoxication resembles alcohol inebriation, acute intoxication is marked by coma and loss of superficial reflexes (although deep reflexes may persist for some time). The Babinski sign often is positive.[16,17]

The *EEG* may show the "burst-suppression" pattern, with brief periods of electrical silence. The *pupils* may be constricted and react to light, but late in the course of barbiturate poisoning, they may show hypoxic paralytic dilation.[16]

Respiration is affected almost immediately. Breathing may be slow or rapid and shallow. Respiratory volume is diminished and hypoxia and respiratory acidosis may develop. *Blood pressure* falls as the medullary vasomotor centers become depressed, and in response to the direct action of these drugs on the myocardium, sympathetic ganglia and vascular smooth muscles. Most patients develop a typical shock syndrome, characterized by a weak and rapid pulse, cold and sweaty skin, and a rise in the hematocrit. Hypothermia often is present, as are respiratory complications and renal failure.[16,17]

Patients suffering acute barbiturate poisoning often develop *sweat gland necrosis* and *bullous cutaneous lesions* that heal slowly.[16,17]

PSYCHOLOGICAL STATE: Patients usually are lethargic or comatose, but overdoses of methaqualone can lead to excitation and delirium.[16]

TREATMENT: The general goal of treatment is to support the vital signs until enough of the drug has been metabolized so that the patient is stable.[3] With mild overdoses, simple observation may suffice. However, severe overdoses require more dramatic intervention.[5,16]

A clear airway must be established. The patient may need to be intubated and placed on a respirator, using compressed air at a rate of 10 to 12 breaths per minute.[3,16,17]

Cardiovascular status should be evaluated and any bleeding controlled. If shock is present, it should be treated with plasma expanders, saline, Dextran or other appropriate drugs. External cardiac massage, defibrillation or intracardiac adrenaline should be used as needed.[3,5,17]

Intravenous fluids should be given in an amount equal to all urine output plus 20 ml (for fluids lost through respiration and perspiration) each hour. Urinary output should be measured.[3,5,17]

Gastric lavage may be useful if the drugs were ingested within the preceding four to six hours. If fat-soluble drugs such as glutethimide are involved, 60 ml of castor oil via a stomach tube may reduce absorption.[3,5,16]

Because opioid analgesics sometimes are used in combination with depressants, a naloxone test may prove useful.[5]

Physical and neurological examinations should evaluate pupils, corneal reflexes, tendon reflexes, pathologic reflexes, pain perception and level of awareness.[3,5]

Blood gases, general blood tests to evaluate function, blood counts and toxicologic screens can provide useful information.[3,16]

Hemodialysis, peritoneal dialysis[3] or hemoperfusion[20,21] may be helpful to a patient in deep coma. Such a patient should be turned frequently to prevent decubitous ulcers and the eyes should be protected (by taping the lids shut, if necessary)

With patients who do not respond to immediate treatment, the long-term prognosis can be established by observing the levels and degrees of change in systolic pressure, central venous pressure and acid-base balance (pH). EEGs are not reliable prognostic aids in cases of depressant overdose, because the depressant drugs can produce a temporarily flat EEG, which reverses spontaneously within a matter of days.[3]

Stimulants

Acute intoxication with stimulants is seen most often in members of the "street" drug culture, in persons with highly stressful occupations (such as truck drivers or students at exam time), and in persons with some history of medical use of these drugs. The clinical picture may develop within minutes (as with intravenous use of amphetamines or inhalation of cocaine), or more slowly (as with oral ingestion of amphetamines and other stimulants).[3]

SIGNS AND SYMPTOMS: The most striking sign of stimulant intoxication is *overactivity of the sympathetic nervous system*. Typically, the intoxicated patient presents with a *rapid pulse, increased respiratory rate* and *elevated body temperature*. In severe overdose, patients suffer *grand mal seizures*, markedly elevated blood pressure and significant hyperthermia, which can lead to cardiovascular shock.[3,41]

Patients may show signs of intravenous drug use (needle marks or abscesses) or nasal inhalation (inflammation of the nasal mucous membranes). In chronic cocaine users, all or part of the nasal septum may be destroyed.[3,22,41]

Overdose deaths, although infrequent, can occur as a result of cardiac arrhythmias, high body temperatures or vascular stroke-like phenomena.[41] Schuckit[3] estimates that 100 to 200 mg of dextroamphetamine could cause death in a non-tolerant user, whereas a chronic user could tolerate doses of 1 gm or more.

PSYCHOLOGICAL STATE: Large doses of stimulants produce restlessness, dizziness, loquaciousness, irritability, palpitations, headache and insomnia. As the dose increases, toxic behavioral signs develop, including paranoid thinking, bruxism, repetitive touching of and picking at various objects or parts of the body, and repeated dismantling and reassembly of mechanical objects such as clocks.[3,23,41]

TREATMENT: Patients who have overdosed on stimulants present a variety of clinical pictures. The preferred treatment is directly related to the patient's condition at the time he seeks treatment.

In cases of severe overdose, the first steps are to ensure an adequate airway, provide circulatory stability and treat cardiovascular shock.

Blood and urine should be drawn for baseline studies and toxicologic screens to rule out concomitant use of other substances.[3,5]

Repeated seizures should be countered with intravenous diazepam (5 to 20 mg injected very slowly over 60 seconds, repeated every 15 to 20 minutes, as needed). If diazepam is used, the patient may require intubation, as IV diazepam can produce laryngospasm or apnea.[3,5,23,41]

Diastolic blood pressure above 120 mm for more than 15 minutes requires the usual regimen for malignant hypertension. Failure to treat this problem vigorously could result in hemorrhages of the central nervous system.[3,23,41]

Body temperatures above 102°F. should be treated with cold water, ice packs or a hypothermic blanket. Hyperthermia also can be countered with a dopamine-blocking agent such as haloperidol, as can marked agitation. A suggested initial dose is 5 mg orally per day, but this may have to be adjusted upward for some patients. Alternatively, chlorpromazine can be given in doses of 25 to 50 mg intramuscularly or orally (repeated in 30 to 60 minutes, if needed), but careful monitoring is required to avoid a severe drop in blood pressure or an anticholinergic crisis.[3,5,22,41]

In cases of moderate overdose, or in patients recovering from severe stimulant poisoning, quiet surroundings and avoidance of stimulation are boons to recovery.[3,23]

Hallucinogens

Acute intoxication with hallucinogenic substances is characterized by loss of contact with reality and profoundly disturbed behavior. Symptoms may appear within a few minutes of drug ingestion, or not for several hours.[3,5]

SIGNS AND SYMPTOMS: Although the psychological manifestations of hallucinogen intoxication are the most striking, the attending state of anxiety or panic usually produces abnormalities in the vital signs. These may include *elevated blood pressure and body temperature, perspiration, palpitations* and (occasionally) *blurred vision*. Patients with severe overdose may sustain body temperatures above 103°F., convulsions and shock.[3,5,39]

PSYCHOLOGICAL STATE: Hallucinogen intoxication tends to produce an exaggerated panic reaction. This high anxiety state may be accompanied by frank hallucinations and loss of contact with reality. Depersonalization, confusion and paranoia are frequently noted. These symptoms subside as the drug is metabolized, but may recur for 24 hours or more.[3,5,9,39]

TREATMENT: With moderately intoxicated patients who have relatively stable vital signs, the first step is to gain the patient's confidence with a calm, authoritative manner. Verbal contacts and cues to help the patient reorient himself to reality are especially important in the first 24 hours. (If the clinical signs do not subside within 24 hours, the physician should suspect the use of PCP [phencyclidine] or STP [4-methyl-2, 5-dimethoxyamphetamine].)[3,5]

Infrequently, severe intoxication may be marked by convulsions or hyperthermia. In such cases, the physician should take steps to continuously monitor the vital signs, establish an adequate airway and lower the body temperature through use of ice baths or a hypothermic blanket. Cardiac monitoring and drugs to lower the blood pressure may be required. Convulsions can be treated with a slow injection of diazepam (5 to 20 mg intravenously), if needed. The use of chlorpromazine or any other antipsychotic drug should be avoided.[3]

As in stimulant overdose, a calm, non-stimulating environment hastens recovery.

Phencyclidines

Phencyclidine (PCP) and its analogs have marked medical and psychological effects that vary significantly among individuals, depending on dose size and route of administration.[5] The narrow dose range between the amount that produces the usual intoxication and the dose responsible for a toxic reaction makes it difficult to distinguish between a toxic reaction, a panic reaction and an organic brain syndrome.[3]

SIGNS AND SYMPTOMS: A toxic reaction to phencyclidine is marked by a combination of sympathetic and cholinergic overactivity. With doses as low as 5 mg, symptoms include *vertigo, skin flushing, nausea and vomiting, enhanced reflexes, tremor, pupillary constriction, nystagmus and double vision, drooping eyelids, elevated blood pressure and dry mouth.*[3,5,24]

As the dose increases (in the 10 to 30 mg range), the patient may be *stuporous* or frankly *comatose*. In coma, the patient's *eyes may remain open. Vomiting* and *hypersalivation* may be present.[5]

With large doses (50 to 100 mg), life-threatening symptoms can occur. These include decreased respiration, epileptic seizures, body rigidity and coma.[24] Schuckit[3] observes that the combination of a *coma-like state, open eyes, decreased pain perception, periods of temporary excitation* and *body rigidity* should lead the physician to suspect a toxic reaction to phencyclidine.

Identification of phencyclidine poisoning is complicated by two factors: (1) phencyclidine often is sold as a counterfeit of other drugs, such as tetrahydrocannabinol (THC), so the patient may not know what drug he actually has ingested, and (2) the clandestine nature of phencyclidine manufacture often leads to a high level of impurities. Among these contaminants is a synthetic intermediate (PCC) that contains an organic group that decomposes to yield hydrogen cyanide. Thus, cyanide poisoning may accompany PCP overdose. Senay and Lewis[5] suggest that bloody vomitus may indicate the use of contaminated phencyclidine.

PSYCHOLOGICAL STATE: Psychological changes in response to phencyclidine intoxication include a state of detachment and lack of response to external stimuli, which may be replaced by or alternate with periods of evanescent excitement and hostility.[3,25]

TREATMENT: The optimal treatment of phencyclidine intoxication is still being debated. For example, some investigators recommend treating severe overdoses with diuretics (40 to 120 mg furosemide or sufficient saline water with glucose to maintain urinary output above 250 ml per hour). Other investigators caution against diuresis on the grounds that its effectiveness has not been demonstrated.[3,24,25,26] Senay and Lewis[5] report that acidification of the urine enhances excretion of the drug, thereby shortening the duration of adverse effects. Acidification can be accomplished through use of ammonium chloride via nasogastric tube, or with vitamin C and cranberry juice given orally, to raise the urine pH level to 5. (Candidates for acidification should have adequate renal and hepatic function.)

There is general agreement on the need to support respiration. Because of the high level of muscle rigidity associated with phencyclidine intoxication, anesthetic levels of muscle relaxants may be needed before intubation can be performed.[3,24,25,26] Status epilepticus should be countered with intravenous diazepam in 2 to 3 mg increments.[5]

Severe hypertension should be treated with drugs such as phentolamine. Schuckit[3] recommends an intravenous drip of 2 to 5 mg phentolamine over five to ten minutes, with constant monitoring to ensure that the blood pressure does not fall too far.

Some investigators believe that gastric lavage is helpful with oral doses of phencyclidine.[3,24,25,26]

Senay and Lewis[5] report that back diffusion of phencyclidine into the gastrointestinal tract reduces absorption, as does continuous or intermittent gastric suction.

Reducing sensory stimuli and protecting the patient from self-harm are important adjuncts to treatment. Senay and Lewis,[5] noting that exacerbation of clinical symptoms occurs with even minimal verbal or physical stimulation, suggest placing the patient on a cushioned surface on the floor of a quiet room. They urge constant monitoring of the patient's condition and recommend the use of haloperidol or diazepam to control dramatic fluctuations in behavior. Use of phenothiazines should be avoided because they enhance the anticholinergic effects of phencyclidine.[10]

Cannabinoids

Until recently, the relatively low potency of marijuana grown in the United States—coupled with the almost total absence of the potent imported forms—made acute marijuana intoxication an infrequent problem.[3] The marijuana being smoked today, however, is far more potent than in the past and may bring an increasing number of casualties to medical attention.

SIGNS AND SYMPTOMS: Acute intoxication with cannabinoids is marked by an *increase in heart rate* in the range of 20 to 40 beats per minute, although a tachycardia of 140 beats per minute is not uncommon. Marked *reddening of the conjunctivae* also is frequently seen.[27]

The patient may experience *fine shakes* or *temors*, a slight *increase in body temperature*, *decreased muscle strength* and *impaired balance*, *impaired motor coordination*, *dry mouth* and *bloodshot eyes*. Some individuals experience *nausea*, *headache*, *nystagmus* and *slightly lowered blood pressure*. Tetrahydrocannabinol also can precipitate seizures in epileptics.[3]

PSYCHOLOGICAL STATE: Toxic reactions to marijuana and its more potent derivatives (THC, hash oil, sensimilla, ganja) occasionally are manifested as psychoses or organic brain syndromes.[3,5] Large doses of tetrahydrocannabinol (THC) can induce frank hallucinations, delusions and paranoid feelings. Thinking becomes diffused and disoriented, while depersonalization and altered time sense are accentuated. The typical euphoria may give way to anxiety reaching panic proportions. Use of cannabinoids also has been reported to precipitate acute psychotic episodes in schizophrenics.[27]

TREATMENT: The treatment approach for cannabinoid intoxication involves good general support and reassurance in a calm, nonstimulating environment.[3,5] Schuckit[3] recommends symptomatic treatment that avoids the use of other drugs. The patient should be detained until all symptoms clear, as cannabinoid-induced impairments of psychomotor function make it difficult to safely operate an automobile or other mechanical equipment.[5]

Inhalants

The patient usually experiences abrupt (within minutes) onset of physical distress while inhaling a solvent.[3] Some of these compounds are CNS depressants that may, in high concentrations, produce anesthesia and death. Some have specific toxic effects. For example, chloroform and carbon tetrachloride are toxic to the myocardium, liver and kidneys, and may produce hepatic or renal failure, as well as cardiac arrhythmias with severe hypotension. Mild poisoning with either agent may produce a reversible oliguria of a few days' duration.[10]

Exposure to high concentrations of toluene or benzene may result in acute hepatic failure, bone marrow suppression, and permanent encephalopathy. Cases of fatal aplastic anemia secondary to glue sniffing have been reported.[10]

All of the inhalable solvents are absorbed rapidly in the lungs and have a rapid onset of action. They are excreted either unchanged or as metabolites in the urine and expired air.[10]

SIGNS AND SYMPTOMS: The initial stimulant effects of inhalant intoxication result from cortical disinhibition due to depression of the inhibitory neuronal tracts. This is followed by generalized CNS depression.[28] *Transient ataxia, slurred speech, diplopia,* and *vomiting* have been reported.[10]

There may be an *unpleasant odor* to the patient's breath, *increased salivation, anorexia* and local *irritation to the eyes and mucous membranes.*[10]

A life-threatening toxic picture, characterized by *respiratory depression* and *cardiac arrhythmias,* may follow the inhalation of volatile solvents. The result may be rapid loss of consciousness and sudden death.[3] In the usual reported case, a young person inhales a volatile hydrocarbon and feels an urge to run. After sprinting a short distance, he falls to the ground, dead. The cause of death is assumed to be a cardiac arrhythmia caused by the inhaled agent and intensified by exercise and hypercapnia. Most reported cases have followed inhalation of fluoroalkene gases such as the pressurized propellants contained in many aerosol sprays. This syndrome is popularly known as "Sudden Sniffing Death" or "SSD."[10]

Death also can result from suffocation in individuals who inhale deeply from a plastic bag placed over the head or entire body.[3]

PSYCHOLOGICAL STATE: The psychological effects of volatile inhalants are analogous to those of the early stage of alcohol intoxication or the second stage of anesthesia. Patients may exhibit impulsiveness, excitement, hyperactivity and exhilaration. Feelings of numbness and weightlessness have been described. During the excitation period, feelings of recklessness and omnipotence may be experienced (it is during this stage that the solvent inhaler is dangerous to himself and to others).

As the intoxication deepens, the clinical picture resembles that of a delirium. Mental confusion, psychomotor clumsiness, emotional disinhibition and impairment of perceptual and cognitive skills are observed. Some of the developing symptoms consist of dizziness, slurred speech, staggering gait, drowsiness, drunkenness, and a dreamy, euphoric reverie. As the intoxication continues to develop, illusions, hallucinations and delusional thinking are seen. A further deepening of the state consists of increasing somnolence or stupor, sometimes culminating in coma.[28]

TREATMENT: There are no specific antidotes for the solvent overdose. Treatment consists of good supportive care, including symptomatic control of arrhythmias and respiratory assistance. Thus, therapy is similar to the general life supports used in opioid intoxication and overdose.[3]

WITHDRAWAL

CLINICAL PICTURE: Abrupt cessation or rapidly decreased intake of any psychoactive drug capable of producing dependence can result in a withdrawal state. This syndrome is marked by anxiety, an increased drive to obtain the drug, flu-like symptoms and other effects that usually are the direct opposite of those seen with intoxication.[3,29]

DIFFERENTIAL DIAGNOSIS: Non-drug related physiological disorders that produce flu-like symptoms must be ruled out.[3] (The presence of drug-induced orthostatic hypotension is helpful in making this distinction.) Also, it is important to determine the class (or classes) of drugs on which the patient is dependent, since the specific treatment of withdrawal differs significantly with different drugs.[5]

ETIOLOGIC AGENTS: Withdrawal symptoms serious enough to

warrant medical attention are most common with the opioids, depressants and stimulants.[3,5]

LABORATORY TESTS: Because withdrawal from the depressant drugs is potentially more life-threatening than withdrawal from any other class of drugs, the physician should perform a rapid physical and neurological examination and immediately order all baseline laboratory tests when use of depressants is suspected. Toxicological screens of the blood and urine may disclose the type of drug used, depending on the time elapsed since the last drug dose and the specific substance involved. Patients who use drugs intravenously also should be screened for hepatitis and signs of occult infection.[3,5]

Opioids

Withdrawal from opioids, while seldom fatal, can cause considerable distress and requires medical attention.[5,30] The severity of the abstinence syndrome depends on many factors, including the specific drug used, the total daily dose, the interval between doses, the duration of use, and the health and general personality of the abuser.[10]

As a general rule, opioids with a short duration of action tend to produce a brief, intense withdrawal syndrome, while drugs eliminated from the body at a slower rate produce withdrawal syndromes that are milder but more prolonged.[10]

SIGNS AND SYMPTOMS: The onset of withdrawal symptoms usually begins at the time of the next scheduled drug dose. Among heroin abusers, withdrawal is marked by a relatively benign mixture of emotional, behavioral and physical symptoms. This is the result of the variable potency of heroin obtained on illicit markets. Six to twelve hours after the last dose of heroin, the physically dependent user becomes *restless*, begins to *yawn* and may start to *cough*. Withdrawal soon is accompanied by a cluster of signs and symptoms that resemble a severe case of influenza. These include *anxiety, sialorrhea, rhinorrhea* and *lacrimation*. There also may be profound *diaphoresis*, with *chills* and *pilomotor activity*, resulting in *piloerection* or "gooseflesh" of the skin. Gastrointestinal signs and symptoms include *anorexia, nausea* and *vomiting, diarrhea* and *abdominal cramps*.[3,10,31]

The withdrawal symptoms peak in intensity at 36 to 72 hours after the last drug dose. At this point, the most prominent signs are central nervous system *hyperactivity, restlessness* and *insomnia*. *Muscle spasms* and involuntary *ejaculation*, as well as *kicking movements* and *pains in the back and extremities*, are common.[3,10]

During withdrawal, the *heart rate* and *blood pressure* may be elevated. *Leukocytosis* is common, as are *weight loss, dehydration, ketosis* and *acid-base imbalance*.[3,5,10]

Most withdrawal symptoms subside between the fifth and tenth day after the last drug dose, even without treatment. However, some researchers believe a prolonged abstinence syndrome may follow the acute withdrawal period.[3] The presence of such a syndrome indicates that restoration of complete physiological equilibrium may be complex and protracted.[3,5,10]

Codeine and the *semisynthetic and synthetic opioids* produce withdrawal symptoms that are qualitatively similar to withdrawal from *heroin* and *morphine*. The withdrawal syndrome associated with *methadone* reflects the long-acting qualities of that drug. For example, methadone withdrawal symptoms do not appear until 48 to 72 hours after the last drug dose. Although qualitatively similar to symptoms of withdrawal from heroin and morphine, symptoms of withdrawal from methadone are less severe, reaching their greatest intensity around the sixth day of abstinence. Except for persistent lethargy and anorexia, the symptoms subside by the tenth to fourteenth day of abstinence.[3,10,31]

Meperidine withdrawal symptoms, on the other hand, appear within three hours after the last dose, peak within 8 to 12 hours, and last three to five days. Meperidine withdrawal is reported to produce fewer gastrointestinal effects than heroin or morphine withdrawal, but a greater degree of muscle spasm, anxiety and restlessness.[3,10]

PSYCHOLOGICAL STATE: The predominant psychological symptom of opioid withdrawal—in addition to an increased "craving" for the drug—is emotional irritability.[3,5]

TREATMENT: Treatment of the acute opioid withdrawal syndrome often begins with readministration of an opioid drug to the point at which symptoms are significantly reduced, after which the drug dose can be gradually decreased.[3,5] Although any opioid drug can be used for this purpose, the one most widely recommended is oral methadone.[3,9,10] However, promising results have been reported from initial experiments with clonidine (which has the advantage that it suppresses opioid withdrawal without itself being a narcotic drug) and with drug-free methods such as acupuncture.[3,32]

Senay and Lewis[5] explain that the overall goal in managing withdrawal is to provide the patient with sufficient amounts of a drug substitute to eliminate withdrawal signs, without causing mental clouding or euphoria. Once the patient reaches this stable stage, the dose of the substitute drug is decreased daily until the patient is drug-free. In all withdrawal attempts, constant clinical monitoring is necessary, since patients dependent on opioids often are simultaneously dependent on sedatives or alcohol.[5]

With patients addicted to "street" drugs, for which the actual dose is unknown, Senay and Lewis[5] recommend an initial methadone dose of 10 to 20 mg to suppress withdrawal signs. If 20 mg fails to suppress these signs, they recommend increasing the dose in 5 to 10 mg increments until the symptoms are suppressed. At that point, they reduce the dose by about 5 mg per day until abstinence is achieved. Senay and Lewis[5] believe that, in the absence of coexisting major medical or psychiatric problems, detoxification from heroin can be achieved in seven to ten days, while detoxification from methadone generally requires a longer period of time, especially if high doses have been used. They report that studies of patients detoxifying from methadone show that very slow rates of detoxification are associated with higher retention rates in long-term treatment.[5]

Patients dependent on heroin tend to be manipulative, so the physician should give more weight to objective signs of withdrawal (such as lacrimation, rhinorrhea, pupillary dilation and piloerection) than to subjective reports by the patient.[5,29,33]

Depressants

A depressant withdrawal syndrome should be suspected in any patient who presents with autonomic nervous system dysfunction and agitation. This syndrome may be seen in both the "street" addict, who may be abusing drugs either orally or intravenously, and in the "middle-class" drug abuser, who may obtain his drugs on prescription but takes more than the prescribed amount.[3,5]

Because of the severity and even life-threatening nature of depressant withdrawal, close medical supervision is essential. For this reason, withdrawal from barbiturates and the other sedative/hypnotic drugs normally is accomplished in a hospital setting.[5,37]

SIGNS AND SYMPTOMS: Withdrawal symptoms begin slowly over a period of hours and may not peak for several days. With *barbiturates*, withdrawal generally begins within a half day of stopping or decreasing the medication, peaks in intensity at 24 to 72 hours, and usually subsides before the seventh day.[3,10,34]

With the other *sedative/hypnotic* drugs, the time course of withdrawal depends on the particular drug involved. Symptoms of withdrawal from meprobamate and methaqualone may begin 12 to 24 hours after the last drug dose and peak at 24 to 72 hours. With longer-acting drugs such as phenobarbital, diazepam and chlordiazepoxide, withdrawal symptoms develop more slowly and peak on the fifth to eighth day.[34]

Depressant withdrawal is characterized by a strong mixture of physical and psychological problems.[3] While symptoms do not follow a specific sequence, they can be roughly classified as minor and major. The *minor* signs and symptoms, which appear within 24 hours and may last as long as two weeks, include *insomnia, anxiety, tremor* of the upper extremities, *twitching* movements, *muscle weakness, anorexia, nausea* and *postural hypotension*.[10,35]

The *major* signs and symptoms appear on the second or third day and generally last three to fourteen days. These include *clonic-tonic seizures* of the grand mal type, which may occur as isolated seizures or as status epilepticus. *Hyperthermia* and *agitation* may lead to apparent exhaustion and cardiovascular collapse.[10,36]

PSYCHOLOGICAL STATE: Patients in withdrawal from barbiturates and other sedative/hypnotic drugs may display moderate to high levels of anxiety and a strong drive to obtain the drug.[3] Some patients develop psychoses that resemble the delirium tremens produced by alcohol withdrawal. Such psychotic reactions are marked by disorientation, agitation, delusions and hallucinations.[10]

TREATMENT: Treatment is directed at preventing the major symptoms and minimizing the minor ones.[10] All central nervous system depressants are cross-tolerant and, theoretically, withdrawal from any one of them can be treated with any other drug in this class. However, established practice in many treatment centers is to treat withdrawal from sedative/hypnotics with barbiturates and withdrawal from a minor tranquilizer with another minor tranquilizer, such as diazepam or chlordiazepoxide.[5]

Senay and Lewis[5] observe that the goal is to withdraw the patient slowly from sedative/hypnotic drugs, while carefully monitoring the signs and symptoms to assure a gradual withdrawal and avoid seizures. Treatment may reflect either of two strategies: (1) slow withdrawal of the drug on which the patient is dependent, or (2) substitution of a long-acting barbiturate (such as phenobarbital) for the dependence-producing drug and subsequent gradual withdrawal of the substitute drug.[5,34]

Withdrawal from barbiturates generally is managed by gradually withdrawing the dependence-producing agent at dose levels that induce mild intoxication. Senay and Lewis[5] caution that such withdrawal generally should proceed no faster than reductions of 100 mg of secobarbital or pentobarbital per day. They note that some physicians use a pentobarbital challenge test to establish the degree of barbiturate tolerance before beginning withdrawal treatment. With this technique, 200 mg of a short-acting barbiturate such as pentobarbital is injected intramuscularly and the patient is observed for signs of toxicity to assess the true degree of tolerance.[5,34]

The rationale for managing withdrawal with a substitute drug is much the same as the rationale for substituting methadone for heroin in opioid withdrawal. In both cases, use of a longer-acting substitute permits withdrawal with fewer fluctuations of drug levels in the blood throughout the day, thus allowing the safe use of smaller doses.[5]

For this reason, some clinicians prefer to substitute phenobarbital for the short-acting barbiturates and other sedative/hypnotic drugs, and then to gradually withdraw the phenobarbital. The safety factor for phenobarbital is greater than for the short-acting barbiturates: the fatal dose of phenobarbital is several times larger than the toxic dose, and signs of phenobarbital intoxication (such as sustained nystagmus, slurred speech and ataxia) are easy to observe.[5,34]

In most cases, transferring a patient from short-acting barbiturates to phenobarbital requires two days. The initial dose of phenobarbital is calculated by substituting one sedative dose (30 mg) of phenobarbital for each hypnotic dose (100 mg) of the short-acting barbiturate the patient reports using. Even though many abusers exaggerate the magnitude of their drug use, the patient's report remains the best guide to calculating withdrawal doses, according to Senay and Lewis.[5] They explain that, if the patient grossly exaggerates the extent of his addiction, the physician will be alerted by the appearance of toxic symptoms during the first day or two of treatment. At that point, the physician can omit one or more doses of phenobarbital and recalculate the daily dose.

If *withdrawal* signs such as anxiety, sleep disturbances, orthostatic hypotension, hyperreflexia, muscle twitches or stomach cramps reoccur, the total daily dose of phenobarbital should be *increased* by about 25%. If the patient shows signs of phenobarbital *toxicity* (sustained nystagmus, slurred speech or staggering gait), the total daily dose of phenobarbital should be *reduced* by 25%.[5,34]

The phenobarbital substitution technique can be used with sedative/hypnotic drugs as well as the barbiturates. With the benzodiazepines, however, there is no reason to substitute phenobarbital, since the duration of action of these drugs is similar. For patients dependent on benzodiazepines, detoxification using benzodiazepines is a gradual process, usually requiring several weeks. Abrupt withdrawal can result in seizures but, unlike the seizures seen in barbiturate withdrawal, seizures in benzodiazepine withdrawal can occur several days to several weeks after abstinence is achieved. Therefore, slow withdrawal is especially important.[5,34,37]

Stimulants

It was long thought that stimulant abuse is not associated with a withdrawal syndrome. Current research shows, however, that abrupt cessation of stimulant use is accompanied by changes in brain chemistry and REM sleep patterns that correlate with the clinical depression seen on withdrawal.[10] The stimulant withdrawal syndrome may begin insidiously—with the patient having no idea why he is depressed, lethargic and irritable—or it may have a more dramatic onset.[3,41]

SIGNS AND SYMPTOMS: Stimulant withdrawal usually is not marked by specific physical pathology, other than the medical problems typically seen in drug abusers. Such a withdrawal syndrome can begin *while the patient continues to take drugs*, as tolerance develops. The usual physical signs include a variety of nonspecific muscle aches and pains.[3]

PSYCHOLOGICAL STATE: Patients experiencing withdrawal from stimulants tend to become irritable and often experience depression. The most intense phase of this depression usually ends in four or five days, but the residual effects may persist for months. Some researchers[10,41] maintain that patients are better able to cope with their depression if the physician explains that it is related to transient chemical and electrophysiological changes. Certain patients respond to tricyclic antidepressant therapy for post-amphetamine depression, although this may be difficult to differentiate from the improvement seen with time alone.[10] Feelings of sadness and despair may be so severe as to lead to suicide attempts.[3,41]

Patients undergoing stimulant withdrawal also may experience bad dreams, as the body compensates for the REM sleep deprivation associated with stimulant use.[3]

TREATMENT: Treatment of stimulant withdrawal generally focuses on symptoms, as the major acute syndrome (except for the lethargy and depression) tends to dissipate on its own within one to three days.[3]

Senay and Lewis[5] observe that many cases of stimulant withdrawal are resolved after a single sleep period, which may be 24 to 48 hours long. In other cases, however, depletion of brain catecholamines or other factors cause a withdrawal syndrome that needs additional treatment. This syndrome, which may persist for weeks or months, is characterized by (1) moderate to severe depression, with possible suicidal ideation, (2) sleep disturbances and lethargy, (3) post-psychotic suspiciousness or hostility and (4) mild tremor of the extremities, as well as various aches and pains.[5]

Where these signs are evident, treatment should be designed to restore biologic health. Sedatives that do not produce dependence may be prescribed for night-time use until a normal sleep cycle is restored, an ample diet (including vitamin supplementation) should be followed, and associated pathology (such as hepatitis) should be treated. Major tranquilizers should be used only if a psychosis persists. Similarly, antidepressants should be used cautiously during the first weeks of treatment, as stimulants residual in the blood may cause an undesirable interaction between the two classes of drugs. Antidepressants are useful, however, in treating severe depressive reactions.[5,38]

Hallucinogens

No clinically significant withdrawal syndrome has been associated with abuse of hallucinogens.[3,10,39]

Phencyclidines

The chemical structure of phencyclidines suggests that a withdrawal syndrome may follow chronic abuse. Such a syndrome, however, has not yet been reported in the literature. Treatment would be symptomatic, perhaps involving the use of depressant drugs such as diazepam.[3,5,40]

Cannabinoids

The existence of a clinically significant withdrawal syndrome following use of marijuana or hashish is the subject of some debate. If symptoms develop, the withdrawal picture can be expected to be limited and to clear with time alone.[3,10]

Inhalants

No clinically relevant withdrawal syndrome from the inhalable solvents has been described in the literature.[3,10] Cohen[28] speculates that major symptoms such as delirium or convulsions may not come to medical attention because the time/dose quantity of the absorbed material is insufficient to evoke them. He does note, however, that reports of tremulousness, irritability, loss of appetite and insomnia following abrupt discontinuation of inhalant abuse may represent minor withdrawal symptoms (or nonspecific resurgent anxiety effects).[28]

FLASHBACK REACTIONS

CLINICAL PICTURE: Flashback reactions involve a recurrence of feelings of intoxication some time after the initial drug effects have worn off. For the most part, flashbacks are a benign, self-limiting (if frightening) condition that rarely represents a serious physical threat.[3,10]

DIFFERENTIAL DIAGNOSIS: In establishing a diagnosis, it is important to rule out the possibility of underlying psychiatric disorders, particularly schizophrenia, affective disorder and organic brain syndrome.[3]

ETIOLOGIC AGENTS: Flashbacks occur primarily with the hallucinogens, phencyclidines and, rarely, the cannabinoids.[3,10]

LABORATORY TESTS: Toxicologic screens yield no useful information in diagnosing flashbacks. The usefulness of laboratory tests in this situation is limited to those tests used to rule out coexisting physical disorders.[3]

Opioids

The relatively short half-life of most opioids, coupled with the rapid disappearance of these drugs and most of their metabolites, make flashbacks an extremely rare occurrence in opioid abusers.[3,10]

Depressants

Flashbacks are not known to occur with depressant drugs. If a patient reports them, other diagnoses (such as emotional or neurological diseases) should be considered.[3,34]

Stimulants

The relatively short length of action and the rapid metabolism of the stimulant drugs does not make them conducive to the development of flashbacks.[3,41]

Hallucinogens

Flashbacks develop in a small percentage of hallucinogen users. Typically, these are recurrent "spells" of a few seconds' or minutes' duration, during which the user experiences acute feelings of depersonalization, hallucinations or somatic delusions.[5]

SIGNS AND SYMPTOMS: Flashbacks induced by hallucinogens usually come to medical attention because the patient becomes concerned that the recurrence of drug effects represents permanent brain damage. In the midst of such a state, the patient may experience *sadness, anxiety* or *paranoia*, which can recur periodically for days or weeks after taking the drug. This recurrence of hallucinogenic effects is regarded as at least partially attributable to residual drug metabolites, and may be precipitated by taking a milder drug such as marijuana or by an acutely stressful situation.[3,5,10]

PSYCHOLOGICAL STATE: The patient experiencing a flashback may feel a sense of euphoria and detachment, often accompanied by visual illusions (actual sensory inputs that are misinterpreted by the individual), which last several minutes to several hours. Other types of flashbacks involve isolated feelings of depersonalization or a recurrence of distressing emotional reactions that accompanied the original drug effects.[3,42] Flashbacks must be differentiated from prolonged psychoses, schizophrenic reactions and organic brain syndrome. Whereas flashbacks have a sudden onset and are marked by asymptomatic intervals, psychoses have a more gradual onset and are more prolonged; schizophrenia and organic brain disease present more unremittingly severe symptoms.[42]

TREATMENT: Care of patients experiencing flashbacks is based on reassurance that the syndrome is self-limiting and will gradually decrease in intensity and disappear. The physician should explain the probable cause and course of the flashback and emphasize the need to avoid all other medications, especially marijuana, stimulants and antihistamines.[3,5]

If medication is necessary to relax the patient, diazepam (10 to 30 mg orally, repeated in 5 mg doses if flashbacks recur) or chlordiazepoxide (10 to 25 mg) are preferred.[3,5]

Phencyclidines

Although phencyclidine flashbacks are not well documented in the literature, anecdotal reports indicate that a recurrence of the milder drug effects (such as feelings of unreality or mild sympathomimetic symptoms) probably do occur. Generally, these are not disturbing to the patient and are best treated with reassurance by the physician. In more severe cases, antianxiety drugs may be given and a referral for psychotherapy should be considered.[3,5]

Cannabinoids

Marijuana and hashish have been reported to induce flashbacks in individuals who also have used hallucinogenic substances. In rare cases, flashback symptoms may be chronic or persistent, but this is so unusual that it indicates a need to evaluate the patient for additional neurological or psychiatric disorders.[3,10]

Inhalants

With the exception of possible residual organic brain syndromes, flashbacks are not known to occur with the volatile inhalants.[3,43]

PANIC REACTIONS

CLINICAL PICTURE: Panic reactions are characterized by a high level of anxiety, with the patient expressing fears that he is losing control, "going crazy," having a heart attack or has done some damage to his body. Such a patient may be able to maintain contact with reality in a highly structured environment.[3,5,10]

Most patients who experience panic reactions are novice drug users. Their panic state usually is a benign, self-limited, emotional overreaction to the effects of the psychoactive drug they have used.[3,5,10]

DIFFERENTIAL DIAGNOSIS: It is important to rule out physical disease (such as a genuine heart attack or hyperthyroid state) and to consider possible psychiatric disorders, such as anxiety neurosis, obsessive neurosis or phobic neurosis.[3,5]

ETIOLOGIC AGENTS: Panic reactions most often occur with drugs that stimulate the user and change the level of consciousness, such as hallucinogens, cannabinoids and stimulants.[3]

LABORATORY TESTS: Baseline studies may be useful in ruling out physical causes of the patient's symptoms, and toxicologic screens of blood and urine can help determine the degree of intoxication.[3]

Opioids

As with all sedative drugs, individuals tend to be calmed rather than panicked when they use opioids. Thus, panic reactions rarely, if ever, occur with these drugs.[3,10]

Depressants

Although not a true panic reaction, a state similar to panic is seen in the paradoxical response of some children and elderly persons to depressant drugs. Severe pain also can trigger a paradoxical response. In this state, the patient is frightened and excited, unable to sleep and has excess energy. These symptoms begin in the first hour or so after taking the drug and remain for the time the drug is active. In these cases, the symptoms clear within hours, requiring only general support and reassurance.[3]

Stimulants

SIGNS AND SYMPTOMS: Stimulant drugs can give rise to at least two related forms of panic. In the first type, the patient experiences a *rapid heart rate, palpitations, anxiety, nervousness* and *hyperventilation*. The resulting *chest pains* and *shortness of breath* may lead the individual to believe he is suffering a heart attack.[3,44]

In the second type, use of stimulants results in psychological *anxiety* and *nervousness*. These feelings give way to *panic* and belief that the individual is *losing control* or *"going crazy."*[3,44]

TREATMENT: Treatment of panic reactions associated with use of stimulant drugs involves reassurance that the patient will recover completely and that the distressing feelings will disappear spontaneously within two to four hours. Medications should be used sparingly, if at all. In severe cases, antianxiety drugs such as chlordiazepoxide (10 to 25 mg orally) may be helpful.[3,44]

Hallucinogens and Phencyclidines

SIGNS AND SYMPTOMS: Panic reactions are the most common acute adverse reactions to hallucinogens and phencyclidines.[10] In the panic state, the individual is highly stimulated, frightened, hallucinating and usually fearful of losing his mind. This emotional discomfort generally lasts for the duration of action of the drug.[3]

Panic reactions are most common in individuals who have had little experience with hallucinogens and phencyclidines.[3]

TREATMENT: Treatment should be performed in a nonthreatening fashion. After being examined for any signs of coexisting physiological disorders, the patient should be "talked down" in a quiet, dimly lit room. Low levels of sensory input are desirable because patients suffering panic reaction are highly distractable.[4]

If a friend of the patient is available, it often is helpful to have him or her present, but only a small number of persons should be involved. It is not helpful to directly contradict the patient's fantasies; rather, emphasis should be placed on alleviating the patient's anxiety. Continued reassurance and assistance in orientation to place and time are important. At least one person should remain with the patient until the drug effects have worn off.[4]

Medications usually are not needed to treat this condition. However, if it is impossible to control the patient without medications, antianxiety drugs such as diazepam (10 to 30 mg orally) or chlordiazepoxide (10 to 50 mg orally) are preferred. Chlorpromazine and the other antipsychotic medications should *not* be used because of the possibility of an adverse drug interaction and because the antipsychotics might increase any anticholinergic effects of the ingested drug.[3]

Cannabinoids

SIGNS AND SYMPTOMS: Panic reactions involving cannabinoids are marked by exaggeration of the usual drug effects, which are perceived as threatening, often by a novice user. Feelings of *anxiety, fear of losing control* and *fear of physical illness* are seen in patients who have no preexisting psychopathology, as well as in patients who have a history of erratic or maladaptive behavior.[3,45]

TREATMENT: Treatment is predicated on reassuring the patient that his symptoms will clear within four to eight hours. It helps to place the patient in a quiet room and allow friends to "talk him down."[3,45]

The patient's level of intoxication may fluctuate over the course of five or six hours as active drug is released from the tissues. Given the persistence of tetrahydrocannabinol metabolites in the body, the patient should be warned that mild feelings of drug intoxication could recur over the next two to four days.[3]

If the patient's anxiety cannot be controlled in any other way, antianxiety medications such as chlordiazepoxide (10 to 50 mg orally) may be used. However, the preferred course is to treat the patient without medications.[3,45]

Inhalants

The period of intoxication with inhalants is so brief that panic states usually abate before an individual can seek medical care.[3,46]

PSYCHOTIC REACTIONS

CLINICAL PICTURE: Psychosis represents a loss of contact with reality that occurs in the midst of a clear sensorium. The patient experiencing a drug-induced psychosis usually presents with hallucinations and delusions. Although these symptoms are quite dramatic, they usually are self-limiting and tend to disappear over the course of several days or weeks (with the exception of psychoses induced by phencyclidine and STP).[3,9]

DIFFERENTIAL DIAGNOSIS: Any psychiatric disorder capable of producing a psychotic reaction (schizophrenia, mania, organic brain syndrome or depression) must be considered. If the psychosis is determined to be drug-related, identification of the drug involved is helpful in predicting recovery time.[3]

ETIOLOGIC AGENTS: The drugs most frequently involved in psychoses are the depressants, stimulants, hallucinogens, phencyclidines and cannabinoids.[3,5]

LABORATORY TESTS: Toxicologic screens may help to identify the causative agent. Other laboratory studies should be ordered as needed to rule out coexisting medical problems.

Opioids

The opioids—unlike most other drugs—are not known to produce any type of temporary psychosis.[9,10]

Depressants

SIGNS AND SYMPTOMS: Depressant drugs can produce a temporary psychosis characterized by acute onset of symptoms, a clear sensorium, auditory hallucinations and paranoid delusions.[3]

TREATMENT: Psychotic reactions induced by depressants usually clear within two days to two weeks with supportive care. Medications should not be given unless the paranoia or hallucinations constitute a serious danger to the patient or those around him. In that event, antipsychotic drugs such as haloperidol (1 to 5 mg four times a day) can be used until the symptoms clear.[3]

Stimulants

SIGNS AND SYMPTOMS: Stimulant-induced psychoses are marked by high levels of suspiciousness and paranoid delusions in a clear sensorium. This syndrome usually develops gradually with chronic use, but can appear after one very large dose of amphetamines.[3,44]

The paranoia often is associated with auditory or tactile hallucinations, although visual hallucinations also can occur. Extremely labile mood and repetitive compulsive behavior are frequent accompaniments.[3,41,44]

Upon cessation of stimulant use, the psychosis clears in two to seven days, with the hallucinations disappearing first and the delusions later. This is followed by an increased need for sleep and a depressed state that may last two weeks or more.[3,41]

Stimulant psychosis mimics acute schizophrenia or mania. Distinguishing characteristics of stimulant psychosis are severe *weight loss, excoriations* and *needle marks on the skin*, as well as *elevated body temperature, blood pressure* and *heart rate*. However, these physical findings are quite variable and their absence does not rule out stimulant psychosis.[3,44]

TREATMENT: Treatment of stimulant psychosis should begin with a careful examination for any signs of physical pathology, as psychosis frequently accompanies a stimulant overdose. The physician also should consider the possibility that the patient has been abusing depressants as well as stimulants and is experiencing depressant withdrawal.[3,44]

Vital signs should be carefully recorded and blood pressure above 120 diastolic treated with drugs such as phentolamine (2 to 5 mg over 5 to 10 minutes). Special care must be taken to avoid hypotension.[3]

The patient should be placed in a calm, non-threatening atmosphere and treated with the general precautions one would use with any paranoid patient (such as not performing any procedure without thorough explanation, not touching the patient without permission, and avoiding any rapid movements in the patient's presence). Treatment personnel should project an attitude of self-confidence, but remain alert to the possibility of unprovoked assaultive behavior.[3,41,44]

If the patient cannot be controlled in any other manner, the use of drugs should be considered. Several choices are possible:

Chlorpromazine (50 to 150 mg orally or 25 to 50 mg intramuscularly, repeated up to four times a day, if needed) is recommended by some investigators. However, special care must be taken to avoid anticholinergic problems and hypotension. Another drawback is that chlorpromazine tends to increase the half-life of amphetamines.[3,44]

Haloperidol may be given for three or four days in doses of 5 to 20 mg per day (orally or intramuscularly).[3,41]

Diazepam (10 to 30 mg orally or 10 to 20 mg intramuscularly) can be used to control anxiety and overactivity. However, there is some risk that use of a depressant drug may increase the potential for violent behavior.[3,44]

Hallucinogens

SIGNS AND SYMPTOMS: The psychotic syndrome associated with hallucinogenic drugs is most often marked by *depression, panic, uncontrolled hallucinations* and *intensification of any preexisting paranoid tendencies*.[3,10] The patient's mental state may vary widely, changing quickly from autistic withdrawal, to apparent lucidity, to fearful paranoia. It is in such periods of acute distress, fear and suspiciousness that aggressive or self-destructive acts most often occur.[42]

Hallucinogen-induced psychoses usually clear within a few weeks. If the psychotic state persists beyond that time, the presence of a preexisting psychiatric problem (such as mania, schizophrenia or psychotic depression) is indicated.[3]

TREATMENT: A drug-induced psychosis in an individual with no history of preexisting psychiatric disorders is treated with reassurance, education and general support. Hospitalization may be required if the patient's loss of contact with reality is severe.[3,5]

In a patient with a preexisting affective disorder or obvious schizophrenia, therapy should be aimed at the specific disorder.[3]

If the psychotic state does not clear within 24 hours and no prior psychiatric disorder is apparent, a careful neurological examination should be performed. As with any atypical picture, treatment is symptomatic, involving careful observation, good history-taking and constant reevaluation for possible underlying pathologic diagnoses.[3,5,10]

Phencyclidines

SIGNS AND SYMPTOMS: Prolonged psychotic reactions following phencyclidine ingestion have been reported.[5] The psychotic state may be marked by paranoia or manic behavior (such as grandiosity, hyperactivity, rapid thoughts and speech). The patient may exhibit profound emotional changes, including hostility accompanied by violent outbursts. The degree and persistence of the psychosis seems to be related to the amount of drug ingested. These states have been reported to last from 24 hours to one month.[3]

TREATMENT: Psychoses associated with phencyclidine ingestion should be treated with measures commonly used to treat psychoses from other causes.[5] The patient should be placed in a quiet, sheltered environment and treated symptomatically. If violent outbursts occur, antianxiety drugs such as diazepam or chlordiazepoxide may be used.[3] Phenothiazines should be avoided in acute phencyclidine reactions because they may induce hypotensive crises or hypertensive episodes.[5,40]

To avoid the possibility that the psychotic patient will harm himself or others, placement in a closed psychiatric ward is frequently recommended.[3,40]

Cannabinoids

SIGNS AND SYMPTOMS: A temporary psychotic state, marked by paranoia and hallucinations, may be seen with cannabinoids, but there is no evidence that it leads to permanent mental impairment.[3,45,47] Cannabinoid-induced psychoses resemble other toxic psychoses more than they do a schizophrenic reaction. Generally, the organic nature of the reaction, the fullness of affect, the patient's ability to relate to the physician, and the wild, unpredictable nature of a cannabinoid psychosis distinguish it from schizophrenia.[45]

When such a state is accompanied by visual hallucinations, an excessively large drug dose is indicated. If the state does not clear within several days, a preexisting psychiatric disorder should be suspected.[3,45,47]

TREATMENT: The possibility of an underlying psychiatric disorder is the first factor that should be addressed in treatment.[3,45] If the patient is not in contact with reality, brief hospitalization may be indicated.[3]

Where there seems to be no underlying psychiatric disorder, the patient should be reassured that his problem is temporary. Antipsychotic medications rarely are needed but, if required to control the patient, haloperidol (5 mg per day in divided doses) or chlorpromazine (25 to 50 mg intramuscularly) may be given.[3,45]

Inhalants

Individuals who abuse inhalants are more likely to develop an organic brain syndrome than a psychosis. One possible exception is the occasional violent outburst during intoxication, which can be controlled through reassurance and the use of medications such as diazepam (10 to 30 mg orally) or chlordiazepoxide (25 to 50 mg orally).[3,28,43] Care would follow the general principles for management of an acute delirium: elimination of ambiguous stimuli such as shadows and whispered voices, protection of the patient and others from hostile outbursts, and the provision of a supportive and familiar environment in which the patient can be observed continuously.[46]

ORGANIC BRAIN SYNDROME

CLINICAL PICTURE: Large doses of almost any psychoactive drug can cause an organic state marked by confusion, disorientation and an overall decrease in mental functioning. Such a state may be accompanied by illusions, hallucinations or delusions.[3]

DIFFERENTIAL DIAGNOSIS: The appearance of an organic state should lead the physician to consider the possibility of acute or chronic brain damage, trauma, vitamin deficiency or serious medical problems that could disrupt electrolytes. Any of these disorders might develop into a life-threatening condition.[3]

ETIOLOGIC AGENTS: Although any drug can cause an organic brain syndrome, the drugs most often associated with this condition are the depressants, stimulants, solvents and phencyclidines.[3]

LABORATORY TESTS: Toxicologic screens may help to identify the causative agent. Other laboratory studies should be ordered as needed to rule out coexisting medical problems and establish the differential diagnosis.[3,5]

Opioids

Organic brain syndrome is unusual with opioids, except as part of an obvious toxic overdose.[5,10]

Depressants

A mild, transient organic state may be seen in association with depresant intoxication and overdose, or during withdrawal.[3]

Stimulants

SIGNS AND SYMPTOMS: Organic brain syndrome associated with stimulant abuse is marked by confusion, disorientation, hallucinations, delusions, paranoia, loose association of ideas and behavioral problems such as bruxism and repeated touching or stereotypic behavior. Prolonged use of stimulants may lead to cerebrovascular changes, and investigators have reported cerebral hemorrhages, subarachnoid bleeding, subdural hematomas and vascular lesions resembling periarteritis nodosa.[3] Anecdotal reports also suggest that chronic use of stimulant drugs may lead to permanently reduced levels of mentation and concentration.[5] Thus, Schuckit[3] suggests that abuse of stimulant drugs be considered as part of the differential diagnosis in any patient who presents with signs of central nervous system organicity and, conversely, that levels of neurological functioning be assessed in all stimulant abusers.

TREATMENT: Organic brain syndrome in stimulant abusers tends to be a transient state, so the recommended treatment approach is to give general supportive care, with adequate neurological studies to rule out all other causes of organicity (including a central nervous system focal lesion or intracranial bleeding).[3,44]

Hallucinogens

SIGNS AND SYMPTOMS: Prolonged exposure to hallucinogenic substances may cause a reduction in intellectual functioning. However, it is difficult to establish a cause-and-effect relationship, because persons who tend to use hallucinogens may demonstrate some of the behaviors associated with organicity, even in the absence of drug use. Schuckit[3] suggests that the possibility of brain damage be considered in any chronic abuser of hallucinogens, even though the probability of clinically significant impairment is remote.

TREATMENT: Organic brain damage resulting from hallucinogen use should be treated symptomatically. The patient should be advised to abstain from use of all non-prescribed drugs or alcohol.[3,10]

Phencyclidines

SIGNS AND SYMPTOMS: A state of confusion or decreased intellectual functioning is part of the usual toxic reaction to phencyclidines and is treated as part of the overall response to that clinical picture.[3]

Long-term organic effects of phencyclidine use are suggested in a study by Carlin et al,[48] in which the performance of a group of drug-free former phencyclidine users was compared to that of a control group on certain neuropsychological measures of organicity. In this study, half of the former phencyclidine users showed some degree of impairment, but none of the control group did. The deficits found in the former phencyclidine users involved abstract and perceptuomotor integrative abilities. These results suggest that use of phencyclidines may be associated with neuropsychological disturbances that persist for considerable periods of time after drug use is discontinued.[48]

TREATMENT: Treatment of phencyclidine-induced organic brain syndrome parallels that described previously for phencyclidine panic reactions.[3]

Cannabinoids

SIGNS AND SYMPTOMS: Toxic reactions to marijuana and hashish often include temporary clouding of mental processes, decreased memory and concentration, and dull thinking. This is a temporary condition and usually clears fairly rapidly.[3]

On the other hand, longer-term organic impairments are now being reported by several researchers,[45] although strong clinical evidence of permanent impairment of brain function has not yet been reported.[3]

TREATMENT: The mild, temporary nature of organic states associated with cannabinoids call for careful observation and reassurance, similar to the treatment described for panic reactions.[3]

Inhalants

SIGNS AND SYMPTOMS: Persons who abuse inhalable solvents frequently present in a state of confusion and disorientation. These symptoms, which usually begin immediately after inhalation, may be accompanied by a rash around the patient's nose or mouth, an odor of solvent on the patient's breath, or a semiconscious state.[3,46]

TREATMENT: The organic brain syndrome associated with abuse of inhalable solvents usually is a short-lived phenomenon that clears in several hours. As in any delirium state, treatment should include reassurance, elimination of unnecessary stimuli, protecting the patient from the consequences of any hostile outbursts, and providing a generally supportive environment.[3,46]

SPECIAL PROBLEMS

MULTI-DRUG ABUSE

Patients who abuse more than one psychoactive drug may present with a "bewildering array of medical complications, psychiatric syndromes, and drug-induced reactions," caution Wesson and Smith.[49] Such multi-drug use is growing increasingly common, according to

Senay and Lewis,[5] as abusers administer barbiturates to "smooth out" an amphetamine "trip" or smoke marijuana to heighten the effects of hallucinogens, for example.

Schuckit[3] notes that the effects of any psychoactive drug may be increased or decreased if it is taken in combination with another drug.

The effect is *increased* when two or more drugs with the same actions are taken concurrently, because the drugs must compete for the same enzyme systems in the liver and at the target cells. The result is potentiation, in which (for example) the amount of brain activity that occurs in response to administration of two depressant drugs or a depressant plus an analgesic is more than would be expected from the action of either drug alone. Potentiation can result in unexpected lethal overdoses.[3]

Specific drug interactions are somewhat unpredictable, underscoring the dangers inherent in multi-drug abuse. However, it is possible to make some generalizations about particular drug combinations.

Acute Intoxication/Overdose

Profound reactions typically result from the concomitant use of two depressant-type drugs or of an opioid and a depressant.[3,5]

DEPRESSANT-DEPRESSANT: Multiple-depressant overdose is difficult to manage because the depth of respiratory depression and the length of severe toxicity are not easy to predict. The overall clinical manifestations are the same as those described earlier for depressant drugs.

Treatment includes institution of acute life-preserving measures and the use of general life supports, relying on the body to detoxify the substances. Dialysis or diuresis should be reserved for extremely toxic cases.[3,5,50]

DEPRESSANT-OPIOID: Concomitant use of opioids and depressants results in unpredictable vital signs, reflexes and pupillary reactions, as well as fluctuations between stupor and semi-alertness. The specific symptoms are combinations of those reported for the opioids and depressants separately.

Treatment of combined opioid-depressant overdose requires the life-preserving measures indicated for these drugs separately. Naloxone should be administered in 0.4 mg intravenous or intramuscular doses, repeated every 5 minutes for the first 15 minutes and then every several hours as needed to control stupor and respiratory depression.[3,5,50]

OTHER DRUG COMBINATIONS: The treatment of overdose with other drug combinations is symptomatic in nature. Physostigmine is useful in treating overdoses involving atropine-like drugs (such as over-the-counter hypnotics and antianxiety drugs) or benztropine.[3,5,50]

Withdrawal

The withdrawal pictures most commonly seen in multi-drug abusers occur following the use of multiple depressants, depressants and stimulants, or combined opioid and depressant drugs.[3,29]

DEPRESSANT-DEPRESSANT: The depressant withdrawal syndrome described earlier in this chapter is similar for all central nervous system depressant drugs. The latency of onset and length of the acute withdrawal syndrome roughly parallel the half-life of the drugs, ranging from relatively short periods of time for alcohol to much longer periods of time for drugs such as phenobarbital and chlordiazepoxide.[3]

Treatment follows the steps outlined for withdrawal from a single depressant, except that the time course of the withdrawal syndrome is unpredictable when more than one drug is involved. Thus, it is unwise to decrease the dose of drugs administered faster than 10% a day, taking special care to reinstitute the preceding day's dose at any sign of impending serious withdrawal symptoms. It usually is possible to manage a smooth withdrawal from multiple depressant drugs by administering only one of those drugs to the point where symptoms are abolished.[3,50,51,52]

DEPRESSANT-OPIOID: A patient withdrawing from combined use of depressants and opioids usually demonstrates an opioid withdrawal syndrome, but convulsions and confusion also may occur.[3,5]

In such a case, it may be advisable to administer both an opioid and a depressant until withdrawal is completed. Most authors recommend stabilization with the opioid while the depressant is withdrawn at the rate of 10% a day. After depressant withdrawal is completed, opioid withdrawal can proceed.[3,5,51,52]

DEPRESSANT-STIMULANT: Withdrawal from combined depressants and stimulants closely follows the depressant withdrawal syndrome, but is marked by greater levels of sadness, paranoia and lethargy than would be expected with depressants alone.[3]

Treatment must first address the depressant withdrawal syndrome, since this produces the greatest amount of discomfort and is the most life-threatening. Thus, despite an intensification of some symptoms, it is best to proceed with the standard treatment for depressant withdrawal.[3,5]

OTHER DRUG COMBINATIONS: Withdrawal from combined use

of other classes of drugs generally has a low level of clinical significance and is treated symptomatically.[3]

Flashback Reactions

Flashback reactions are seen with combined use of hallucinogens or marijuana and other drugs. The treatment for flashbacks in multi-drug abusers follows the same steps outlined for flashbacks caused by hallucinogens, phencyclidines or marijuana alone.[3,5]

Panic Reations

The clinical picture, course and treatment of panic reactions in multi-drug abusers follows those seen with the use of stimulants, hallucinogens, phencyclidines or cannabinoids alone.[3]

Psychotic Reactions

The drug-induced psychoses seen with stimulants and depressants are evanescent pictures, disappearing with general supportive care. Little information is available on treatment of the psychoses produced by use of multiple substances.[3,5]

Organic Brain Syndrome

In sufficiently large doses, any drug can cause confusion and disorientation, which are the hallmarks of an organic brain syndrome. With multi-drug abuse, this clinical picture usually is evanescent and treatment should follow the general plans outlined for the drugs separately. However, it should be recognized that with multiple drugs, the course of organic brain syndrome is unpredictable, and the patient probably will be impaired for a longer time than would be expected when a single drug is involved.[3]

THE VIOLENT PATIENT

Management of acute drug reactions in violent patients should be based on two overriding principles, according to Senay et al:[4,5]

- *Do not approach a potentially violent patient alone.* Do so only with a sufficient number of people to control an outbreak of violence. Determining what number of people is "sufficient" requires recognition of the well-documented fact that persons intoxicated with drugs such as phencyclidine often demonstrate physical strength far beyond their customary limits.
- *Avoid offensive actions.* Except where there is an immediate possibility of serious injury, only defensive techniques (such as

holding the patient's legs and arms or rolling the patient in a blanket) should be used.

Members of the treatment team should avoid situations in which they or the patient might be injured. If a member of the team is assaulted, Senay et al[4] believe the most likely cause is ignorance of the many signals of impending loss of control presented by the patient. These include high degrees of agitation, sweating and excessive talking while struggling with violent impulses. Treatment personnel should be taught: (1) to be alert to such signals, (2) to control their fear and (3) to take evasive action (such as leaving the room or calling in help) before the patient's violent impulses are translated into action. Senay et al[4] note that there is nothing wrong with running from a room occupied by a physically threatening patient, armed or unarmed.

The police should be called if a patient is armed or if there are not enough personnel available to control an unarmed but potentially violent patient. Once the police have neutralized the threat, diagnostic and therapeutic activities can be resumed.[4]

THE SUICIDAL PATIENT

Senay et al[4] observe that "drug-abusing patients walk a narrow line between mortgaging today's effect for tomorrow's medical complications." Failure to balance these conflicting needs may precipitate a suicide attempt.

The person who attempts suicide—even if the attempt appears to be minor and innocuous—may be calling for help. Any such attempt should be taken very seriously, because it has great importance to the individual. If possible, the physician should talk with the patient about his emotional state. Treatment staff should try to identify previous depressions or evidence of suicidal intent, as well as determine whether the individual made a careful plan for the attempted suicide.[4,5]

Even while being treated for an acute drug reaction, the potentially suicidal patient must be protected from hazards in the treatment setting. Needles, sharp instruments, drugs and the like should not be left in the patient's immediate proximity, and the patient should be under close observation at all times.[4]

If there is any question about the degree of depression in the suicidal intent, psychiatric consultation should be obtained. Because medications that are useful in treating severe depression require several days to several weeks to take effect, and because the side effects of these medications appear before their therapeutic benefits, patients should be placed in a supportive environment to await the full therapeutic response.[4,5]

ACCIDENTAL POISONING OF CHILDREN AND ADOLESCENTS

Increased use of illicit drugs by adults also results in increased availability of these potential poisons to young children. Psychoactive drugs have been responsible for many acute poisonings and a number of fatalities. In addition, ingestion of drugs by adolescents as the result of practical jokes (such as spiking drinks with LSD) has been reported. Poisonings also occur among naive drug users who unwittingly ingest one drug, believing it to be another. Or the desired drug may be purchased in concentrations that far exceed the amount usually consumed.[53]

The possibility of a suicide attempt must be considered in the differential diagnosis before any case of poisoning is labeled "accidental." This becomes even more crucial when considering drug ingestion by adolescents. Intent is an issue that must be explored in every presumed accidental poisoning of a child or adolescent.[53]

The psychoactive drugs most often involved in accidental poisonings of children and adolescents are the opioids, depressants, stimulants and hallucinogens.

Opioids

Heroin is rarely involved in accidental poisonings of children, probably because it is poorly absorbed from the gastrointestinal tract. In adolescents (as in adults), heroin overdose frequently results from the ever-changing potency of drugs purchased from "street" vendors.[53]

Methadone, on the other hand, is easily absorbed through the intestinal mucosa and, dissolved in fruit juice, is quite attractive to young children. A child suffering from methadone poisoning appears drowsy—if not comatose—within 30 minutes of ingestion. Respirations are depressed or absent, pupils are pinpoint, and blood pressure may be lowered. Although the usual maintenance dose of methadone in adults is 80 to 100 mg, the lethal dose in children may be as small as 10 to 20 mg.[53]

Depressants

A child who has ingested short-acting barbiturates or other sedatives will appear drowsy or comatose, with depressed respiration. Skin bullae may be present over the bony prominences and the body temperature may be subnormal. *Barbiturates* and *glutethimide* differ in that pinpoint pupils that are unresponsive to naloxone may result from an overdose of barbiturates, while glutethimide poisoning produces widely dilated pupils. In addition, the patient intoxicated with glutethimide may have cyclic waxing and waning levels of consciousness, whereas the child in coma from barbiturates usually continues to improve once therapy is initiated.[53]

Stimulants

Although amphetamine overdose deaths in children are rare, toxic reactions to as little as one 30 mg dose may produce hyperactivity, hypertension, tachycardia, cardiac arrhythmias, hyperpyrexia and hyperreflexia.[53]

Hallucinogens

Ingestion of hallucinogenic substances by a child produces symptoms similar to those of an acute schizophrenic reaction in an adult. The major difference is that the hallucinations produced by these drugs usually are visual rather than auditory. Confusion and hyperpyrexia are common. Temperature elevations generally are low grade, but dangerous elevations have been reported.[53]

The lethal dose of LSD in children has not been established. Nutmeg—which is available in most homes—has produced toxic reactions in children in doses of 5 to 15 gm (less than half a can of grated nutmeg).[53]

REFERENCES

1. Dimijian, G. G. Differential diagnosis of emergency drug reactions *in* P. G. Bourne (ed.) *A Treatment Manual for Acute Drug Abuse Emergencies* (National Institute on Drug Abuse, Rockville, Md., 1974)
2. Greenblatt, D. J. and Shader, R. I. Drug abuse and the emergency room physician *American Journal of Psychiatry* 131(5):559 (May 1974)
3. Schuckit, M. A. *Drug and Alcohol Abuse: A Clinical Guide to Diagnosis and Treatment* (Plenum Medical Book Co., New York City, 1979)
4. Senay, E. C., Becker, C. E. and Schnoll, S. H. *Emergency Treatment of the Drug-Abusing Patient for Treatment Staff Physicians* Medical Monograph Series, Vol. I, No. 4 (National Institute on Drug Abuse, Rockville, Md., 1977)
5. Senay, E. C. and Lewis, D. C. *The Primary Physician's Guide to Drug and Alcohol Abuse Treatment* Medical Monograph Series, Vol. I, No. 6 (National Institute on Drug Abuse, Rockville, Md., 1980)
6. Koumans, A. J. R. *Manual for Treatment of Acute Drug Intoxication* (August 1973)

7. Rubin, P. E. and Cluff, L. E. Differential diagnosis of emergency drug reactions in P. G. Bourne (ed.) *A Treatment Manual for Acute Drug Abuse Emergencies* (National Institute on Drug Abuse, Rockville, Md., 1974)
8. Cherubin C. E. Management of acute medical complications resulting from heroin addiction in P. G. Bourne (ed.) *A Treatment Manual for Acute Drug Abuse Emergencies* (National Institute on Drug Abuse, Rockville, Md., 1974)
9. Jaffe, J. H. and Martin, W. R. Opioid analgesics and antagonists in A. G. Gilman, L. S. Goodman and A. Gilman (eds.) *The Pharmacological Basis of Therapeutics* (Macmillan, New York City, 1980)
10. Inaba, D., Way, E. L., Blum, K. and Schnoll, S. H. *Pharmacological and Toxicological Perspectives of Commonly Abused Drugs* Medical Monograph Series, Vol. I, No. 5 (National Institute on Drug Abuse, Rockville, Md., 1978)
11. Gay, G. R., Smith, D. E. and Gutnick, E. I. Treating acute heroin toxicity *Hospital Physician* (May 1971)
12. Todd, J. W. Treatment of narcotic poisoning *The Lancet* 1076 (November 10, 1973)
13. Greene, M. H. and DuPont, R. L. The treatment of acute heroin toxicity in P. G. Bourne (ed.) *A Treatment Manual for Acute Drug Abuse Emergencies* (National Institute on Drug Abuse, Rockville, Md., 1974)
14. Kleber, H. D. The treatment of acute heroin toxicity in P. G. Bourne (ed.) *A Treatment Manual for Acute Drug Abuse Emergencies* (National Institute on Drug Abuse, Rockville, Md., 1974)
15. Nightingale, S. L. The management of methadone intoxication in P. G. Bourne (ed.) *A Treatment Manual for Acute Drug Abuse Emergencies* (National Institute on Drug Abuse, Rockville, Md., 1974)
16. Harvey, S. C. Hypnotics and sedatives in A. G. Gilman, L. S. Goodman and A. Gilman (eds.) *The Pharmacological Basis of Therapeutics* (Macmillan, New York City, 1980)
17. Setter, J. G. Emergency treatment of acute barbiturate intoxication in P. G. Bourne (ed.) *A Treatment Manual for Acute Drug Abuse Emergencies* (National Institute on Drug Abuse, Rockville, Md., 1974)
18. Cronin, R. J., Klingler, E. L., Avasthi, P. S. and Lubash, G. D. The treatment of nonbarbiturate sedative overdosage in P. G. Bourne (ed.) *A Treatment Manual for Acute Drug Abuse Emergencies* (National Institute on Drug Abuse, Rockville, Md., 1974)
19. Finkle, B. S., McCloskey, K. L. and Goodman, L. S. Diazepam and drug-associated deaths *JAMA* 242(5):429 (August 3, 1979)
20. Lorch, J. A. and Garella, S. Hemoperfusion to treat intoxications *Annals of Internal Medicine* 91(2):301 (August 1979)
21. Gelfand, M. C. Hemoperfusion in drug overdose *JAMA* 240(25):2761 (December 15, 1978)
22. Wetli, C. V. and Wright, R. K. Death caused by recreational cocaine use *JAMA* 241(23):2519 (June 8, 1979)
23. *Clinical Aspects of Amphetamine Abuse:* Report of the Council on Scientific Affairs (American Medical Association, Chicago, Ill., 1978)

24. Tong, T. G., Benowitz, N. L., Becker, C. E., Forni, P. J. and Boerner, V. Phencyclidine poisoning *JAMA* 234(5):512 (November 3, 1975)
25. Liden, C. B., Lovejoy, F. H. and Costello, C. E. Phencyclidine: nine cases of poisoning *JAMA* 234(5):513 (November 3, 1975)
26. Corales, R. L., Maull, K. I. and Becker, D. P. Phencyclidine abuse mimicking head injury *JAMA* 243(22):2323 (June 13, 1980)
27. Jaffe, J. H. Drug addiction and drug abuse in A. G. Gilman, L. S. Goodman and A. Gilman (eds.) *The Pharmacological Basis of Therapeutics* (Macmillan, New York City, 1980)
28. Cohen, S. Inhalants and solvents in G. M. Beschner and A. S. Friedman (eds.) *Youth Drug Abuse* (Lexington Books, Lexington, Mass., 1979)
29. Shoemaker, K. E. The acute abstinence syndrome in *Prescription Drugs and Potential for Dependence: A Primer for Physicians* Proceedings of a Symposium, Temple University, New Orleans, La., September 15, 1976 (Excerpta Medica, Princeton, N.J., 1977)
30. Goldstein, A. High on research *U.S. Journal of Drug and Alcohol Dependence* 3(12) (January 1980)
31. Tebrock, H. E. *Drug Abuse and Misuse* (U.S. Department of Justice, Drug Enforcement Administration, Washington, D.C., 1979)
32. Gold, M. S., Pottash, A. C., Sweeney, D. R. and Kleber, H. D. Opiate withdrawal using clonidine: a safe, effective, and rapid nonopiate treatment *JAMA* 243(4):343 (January 25, 1980)
33. Dole, V. P. Management of the opiate abstinence sydrome in P. G. Bourne (ed.) *A Treatment Manual for Acute Drug Abuse Emergencies* (National Institute on Drug Abuse, Rockville, Md., 1974)
34. Smith, D. E., Wesson, D. R. and Seymour, R. B. The abuse of barbiturates and other sedative-hypnotics in R. I. DuPont, A. Goldstein and J. O'Donnell (eds.) *Handbook on Drug Abuse* (National Institute on Drug Abuse, Rockville, Md., 1979)
35. Barbiturate withdrawal (Medical News) *JAMA* 241(14):1447 (April 6, 1979)
36. Preskorn, S. H., Schwin, R. L. and McKnelly, W. V. Analgesic abuse and the barbiturate abstinence syndrome *JAMA* 244(4):369 (July 25, 1980)
37. Wesson, D. R. and Smith, D. E. Managing the barbiturate withdrawal syndrome in P. G. Bourne (ed.) *A Treatment Manual for Acute Drug Abuse Emergencies* (National Institute on Drug Abuse, Rockville, Md., 1974)
38. Wesson, D. R. and Smith, D. E. A clinical approach to diagnosis and treatment of amphetamine abuse *Journal of Psychedelic Drugs* 10(4):343 (October-December 1978)
39. Solursh, L. P. Emergency treatment of acute adverse reactions to hallucinogenic drugs in P. G. Bourne (ed.) *A Treatment Manual for Acute Drug Abuse Emergencies* (National Institute on Drug Abuse, Rockville, Md., 1974)
40. Cohen, S. PCP (Angel Dust): new trends in treatment *Drug Abuse & Alcoholism Newsletter* 7(6):1 (July 1978)

41. Ellinwood, E. H. Emergency treatment of acute adverse reactions to CNS stimulants *in* P. G. Bourne (ed.) *A Treatment Manual for Acute Drug Abuse Emergencies* (National Institute on Drug Abuse, Rockville, Md., 1974)
42. Ungerleider, J. T. and Frank, I. M. Management of acute panic reactions and flashbacks resulting from LSD ingestion *in* P. G. Bourne (ed.) *A Treatment Manual for Acute Drug Abuse Emergencies* (National Institute on Drug Abuse, Rockville, Md., 1974)
43. Swinyard, E. A. Noxious gases and vapors *in* L. S. Goodman and A. Gilman (eds.) *The Pharmacological Basis of Therapeutics* (Macmillan, New York City, 1975)
44. Tinklenberg, J. R. The treatment of acute amphetamine psychosis *in* P. G. Bourne (ed.) *A Treatment Manual for Acute Drug Abuse Emergencies* (National Institute on Drug Abuse, Rockville, Md., 1974)
45. Talbott, J. A. The emergency management of marijuana psychosis *in* P. G. Bourne (ed.) *A Treatment Manual for Acute Drug Abuse Emergencies* (National Institute on Drug Abuse, Rockville, Md., 1974)
46. Glaser, F. B. Inhalation psychosis and related states *in* P. G. Bourne (ed.) *A Treatment Manual for Acute Drug Abuse Emergencies* (National Institute on Drug Abuse, Rockville, Md., 1974)
47. Gersten, S. P. Long-term adverse effects of brief marijuana usage *Journal of Clinical Psychiatry* 41(2):60 (February 1980)
48. Carlin, A. S., Grant, I., Adams, K. M. and Reed, R. Is phencyclidine (PCP) abuse associated with organic mental impairment? *American Journal of Drug and Alcohol Abuse* 6(3):273 (1979)
49. Wesson, D. R. and Smith, D. E. Treatment of the polydrug abuser *in* R. I. DuPont, A. Goldstein and J. O'Donnell (eds.) *Handbook on Drug Abuse* (National Institute on Drug Abuse, Rockville, Md., 1979)
50. Gardner, S. E. Introduction *in* S. E. Gardner (ed.) *National Drug/Alcohol Collaborative Project: Issues in Multiple Substance Abuse* (National Institute on Drug Abuse, Rockville, Md., 1980)
51. Carroll, J. F. X., Malloy, T. E. and Kendrick, F. M. Multiple substance abuse: a review of the literature *in* S. E. Gardner (ed.) *National Drug/Alcohol Collaborative Project: Issues in Multiple Substance Abuse* (National Institute on Drug Abuse, Rockville, Md., 1980)
52. Franken, R. and Seale, F. E. Withdrawal patterns in cross-addicted patients: a report of 100 cases *Texas Medicine* 75:58 (December 1979)
53. Cohen, M. I. and Litt, I. F. Accidental poisonings by drugs of abuse in children and adolescents *in* P. G. Bourne (ed.) *A Treatment Manual for Acute Drug Abuse Emergencies* (National Institute on Drug Abuse, Rockville, Md., 1974)

CHAPTER 7
CLINICAL COMPLICATIONS OF DRUG ABUSE

As drug abuse has come to be accepted as a medical and social problem, rather than solely a legal concern, more and more drug abusers have been turning to the medical profession for care of their health problems. Thus, physicians in primary care settings are seeing an increasing number of patients who, while they take psychoactive drugs for non-medical reasons, also present serious physical and psychological problems that are either directly related to their use of drugs, or at least influenced by such use.

Dimijian[1] cautions that physicians always should suspect a co-existing medical or psychological problem in drug-abusing patients. Such a problem rarely is reported by the patient, who may not even be aware of its usual signs or symptoms. For example, the pain of an acute myocardial infarction or appendicitis may not be felt by a heroin user whose symptoms are masked by the drug's analgesic action. Similarly, a bone injury may not be reported by an LSD user who is too preoccupied with his drug-induced experience to be aware of the trauma he has sustained.

Johnson and Lukash[2] observe that "drug abuse does not protect against other diseases, and physicians must avoid confusing causal and temporal relationships." Postmortem investigations of deaths from drug abuse show that the prevalence of physical abnormalities in drug abusers is similar to that found in non-drug using populations of similar age. In assessing these findings, Johnson and Lukash[2] comment that "the dead are a reminder that we need to treat the whole patient, not just the acute narcosis or the diseased heart or liver. To a large extent, this can be done if the physician, in addition to seeking out and trying to understand the social and psychological dynamics involved, attempts to gain greater sophistication regarding the nature of some of the major complications that can lead to death."

PHYSIOLOGICAL DISORDERS

In acute reaction (overdose) deaths, the most frequent autopsy finding is *severe pulmonary edema*. Foreign material in the lungs is seen almost exclusively in abusers who have intravenously injected pills intended for oral consumption (such as methadone, tripelennamine, pentazocine and barbiturates), as well as the filler material in those pills (such as talc and cellulose). *Cor pulmonae* has been found only in older drug-dependent persons who also had been heavy smokers or who had chronic bronchitis.

Hyperplastic changes in the reticuloendolethial system found at autopsy include prominent hyperplasia of the periportal and peripancreatic lymph nodes, persistence of the thymus gland, splenic enlargement, and mononuclear cell infiltration of the portal triads of the liver (which often has been accepted as secondary to prior hepatitis).[2,3]

Certain *neurological abnormalities*—most strikingly bilateral symmetrical necrosis of the globus pallidium—have been found in a small portion of chronic drug users. These cases may reflect production of hypoxia during earlier episodes of overdose from which the patient recovered, in which event hypoxia could be considered an etiologic mechanism.[2,3]

Death also has occurred as a result of allergic reactions, such as anaphalactic shock in response to cocaine.

Concurrent use of two or more psychoactive drugs over an extended period of time probably increases the risk of developing medical complications, Schuckit[4] believes. He says, however, that the specific problems depend on the particular drugs involved, as well as the individual's age, history of pre-existing medical disorders, nutritional status and experience of stress.

The following clinical complications are those most often identified in drug abusers.

CARDIOVASCULAR COMPLICATIONS

The most important cardiovascular complication of drug abuse is acute infective endocarditis. The valves commonly affected (in order of frequency) are the aortic, mitral and tricuspid. Recent reports have described a few cases of pulmonic valve endocarditis that mimic tricuspid endocarditis. Right-sided endocarditis is frequently found in drug abusers, but left-sided endocarditis occurs twice as often. In addition, 5% to 10% of abusers have mixed right- and left-sided lesions.[5,6,7]

ENDOCARDITIS: Although endocarditis has attracted more attention than the other medical complications of drug abuse, the exact magnitude of this problem is difficult to determine: many drug abusers with cardiovascular complications die outside the hospital or have such short hospital stays that no diagnosis is made. It is known, however, that heroin users have a high incidence of staphylococcal, gram negative bacterial and candidal valve infections, while streptococcal infections are practically non-existent.[2,3,5,6]

Among all patients who develop endocarditis, pre-existing heart disease is found less often in heroin users than in patients who do not use illicit drugs. The unusually high incidence of endocarditis of normal valves in heroin users is the result of the repeated bacteremias associated with heroin use and the virulence of the organisms isolated (especially coagulase-positive *Staphylococcus aureus*). The higher incidence of endocarditis due to *Candida* and to gram-negative bacilli in heroin abusers reflects the use of unsterile equipment and unusual methods of injection. Candidal infections, which affect damaged valves, occur less frequently in abusers with right-sided involvement. Recently, *Pseudomonas* has been isolated in patients with tricuspid endocarditis.[5,6]

The physician should suspect endocarditis in any drug abuser who has a fever of unknown origin, heart murmur, pneumonia, embolic phenomena or positive blood cultures (especially with *Candida*, *Staphylococcus aureus*, enterococci or gram-negative organisms). In some cases, fever is the only indication of endocarditis.[3,5,6] Mortality from endocarditis is related to the promptness with which the condition is diagnosed and treated.

Because endocarditis in drug abusers often is fulminating, producing the frequent embolization and severe valve destruction of acute endocarditis, it is essential that this condition be promptly diagnosed and treated if the patient is to survive. Septic pulmonary emboli may develop in abusers following thrombophlebitis with endocarditis, and tricuspid involvement may occur without heart murmur; it is therefore advisable to suspect that patients with septic pulmonary emboli have endocarditis. Similarly, drug abusers being treated for staphylococcal pneumonia (or acute meningitis) should be observed for seven to ten days following completion of antibiotic therapy to detect the early signs and symptoms of endocarditis.[3,5,6]

OTHER CARDIOVASCULAR COMPLICATIONS: Other cardiac problems frequently found in drug abusers include myocardial disease (possibly due to direct toxic effects of some drugs on the myocardium), blood pressure changes and cardiac arrhythmias. Vascular complications include local changes due to thrombophlebitis, arteritis, arterial occlusion, embolic phenomena, angiothrombotic pulmonary hypotension, and other problems that result from traumatic or myotic aneurysms.[6,7,8,9,10] Tachyarrhythmias also occur with many drugs of abuse. Cannabis, cocaine, hallucinogens, amphetamines and anticholinergic drugs all increase the pulse rate.[3,5,6]

Vascular changes due to polyarteritis (necrotizing angiitis) have been reported in persons who use amphetamines intravenously (principally methamphetamine). These changes frequently result in cerebrovascular occlusion and intracranial hemorrhage.[5,6,8]

Many of the solvents taken by inhalant abusers sensitize the heart to catecholamines, in a manner similar to the volatile anesthetics. This reaction can lead to arrhythmias or to sudden death from ventricular fibrillation.[3,5,6]

Amphetamines and phencyclidine can produce paroxysmal hypertension. When large doses of these drugs have been ingested, the hypertension must be treated vigorously.[3,5,6]

Tricyclic antidepressants (which have been increasingly abused in the past few years) also can cause arrhythmias.[3,5,6]

DERMATOLOGIC COMPLICATIONS

Most dermatologic complications of drug abuse result not from the drug itself, but from the conditions under which the drug is taken. Unsterile and contaminated injections lead to infectious complications. The most common sources of infection are organisms found on the skin and nasopharynx (although other areas of the body also may be involved), as well as viruses, bacteria and fungi present on the injection paraphernalia.[2,3,5,6]

SEPTIC CUTANEOUS COMPLICATIONS: The skin, as the port of entry for contaminated injections, frequently shows the following problems:[2,3,5,6]

Needle track scars caused by unsterile techniques and the injection of fibrogenic particulate matter. Although most common on the arms, tracks can be found almost anywhere on the body, including the penile veins. Also, infections frequently result when abusers attempt to conceal needle tracks with cigaret burns or caustic substances.

Tattooing or *dark pigmentation* at injection sites, resulting from carbon deposited by needles heated with a match for "sterilization." Because the carbon causes a mild inflammatory action and is picked up by macrophages, the tattoo marks become progressively larger.

Abscesses produced by infections around the injection site. These infections (most often caused by skin flora such as staphylococci and streptococci) result from repeated injections without cleaning the skin at the injection site.

Cellulitis (perhaps really a fasciolitis) characterized by a stony or wooden-hard tenseness on an extremity, not necessarily in association with a recent needle puncture or infected site. Subcutaneous injection of sedative/hypnotic drugs causes a form of cellulitis in which the skin becomes reddened, hot, painful and swollen.

Sphaceloderma (gangrene) caused by intra-arterial injections. It usually is accompanied by intense pain distal to the site of injection, and is characterized by swelling, cyanosis and coldness of the extremity.

Camptodactylia from recurrent use of the hand veins for injection. Irreversible contraction of the fingers and lymphedema may result.

PRURITIS AND DERMATITIS: Pruritis, alone or in combination with urticaria, is seen in heroin users. Contact dermatitis results from sensitization to certain exotic fluids that are used to sterilize the skin.[3,5,6]

ENDOCRINOLOGIC COMPLICATIONS

Many drugs of abuse alter endocrine function, but the mechanisms through which these alterations occur are not fully understood. It is known that opioids reduce testosterone levels and that these reductions are associated with decreased libido and, in some cases, impotence.[5] Other alterations of endocrine function in opioid abusers include high resting insulin levels, which result in a delayed and smaller-than-normal rise in insulin levels in a 50 gm oral glucose tolerance test.[6] Elevated levels of growth hormone and thyroxine also have been reported in these patients.[5,6]

GASTROINTESTINAL COMPLICATIONS

Opioid drugs cause a tonic contraction of the bowel, which results in chronic constipation. This problem may even continue while the patient is on methadone maintenance. Withdrawal often is accompanied by diarrhea and abdominal cramps.[5,6]

Opioid-induced spasms of Oddi's sphincter could lead to cholecystitis in abusers, but tolerance apparently develops to this effect.[5,6]

The stimulant drugs and hallucinogens are anorexiants. In large doses, they produce nausea and vomiting that can lead to severe malnutrition in chronic abusers.[5,6]

Persons who abuse both drugs and alcohol may develop pancreatitis, which in early stages can mimic the cramps seen in withdrawal. Differentiation can be made by looking for signs of withdrawal other than abdominal cramps: if these signs are not present, pancreatitis and other abdominal disorders should be considered.[5,6]

GENITOURINARY COMPLICATIONS

Drug abusers have a higher than average incidence of gonorrhea, syphilis, chancroid and lymphogranuloma venerum.[5] Opioid users show high rates of true and false-positive reactions in tests for syphilis (a biological false positive is found in about 25% of all positive reactions).[5,6]

Chronic users of opioids, amphetamines and hallucinogens also have reported hesitancy and, in some cases, prolonged difficulty in initiating micturition. This effect on the bladder and urethra occurs only when the drug is present in the system; when the drug clears, the micturition problem usually is relieved.[6]

HEMATOPOIETIC COMPLICATIONS

Complications involving the hematopoietic system are seen primarily in persons who inject their drugs, although drugs taken orally or by inhalation also can cause problems with the blood and blood-forming cells.[5,6]

Bacteremia is the most common hematopoietic complication of drug abuse. Caused by repeated unsterile injections, it is associated with a high incidence of infections in other organs. Bacteremia usually is caused by normal skin flora, but unusual organisms such as *Serratia marcescens* also have been found. The lymphatic lesions frequently associated with bacteremias usually are found in nodes located proximally to the injection sites, but also may occur in other areas. If lymphadenopathy is found in areas that are not directly draining injection sites, a biopsy should be performed to rule out malignancy.[5,6]

Other findings in intravenous drug users are eosinophilia (which dissipates with cessation of drug use) and microangiopathic hemolytic anemia.[5]

Abuse of drugs containing salicylates can reduce the binding ability of platelets, irritate the gastrointestinal linings, and lead to bleeding problems. (Although salicylates themselves usually are not considered drugs of abuse, they often are taken in large quantities in over-the-counter medications and in combination with other drugs that have abuse potential.)[5,6]

Abuse of solvents—especially high-dose chronic use—has been associated with bone marrow depression and, in some cases, aplastic anemia.[5,6]

Marijuana is implicated in recent reports as the cause of decreased immunocompetence in chronic users. The primary defect is reported to be in cell-mediated immunity. Whether these changes cause any significant clinical problems is currently under investigation.[5]

Chromosomal aberrations from use of LSD have received the most publicity, but similar changes have been reported following the use of many classes of drugs. However, the data on chromosome damage are conflicting and the significance of recent findings is not yet clear.[5]

Most intravenous drug abusers who enter treatment are found to have elevated immunoglobin levels that often are nonspecific, but may lead to false-positive results on many routine serologic tests. The high titers of nonspecific immunoglobin may interfere with specific antibody formation, and contribute to the high incidence of infections seen in intravenous drug users. Once drug use stops, elevated immunoglobin levels usually return to normal.[5,6]

HEPATIC COMPLICATIONS

Hepatitis is the most common medical complication of drug abuse. In some hospitals, as many as 90% of the patients admitted for hepatitis have engaged in parenteral drug use.[5] In one study, fewer than 10% of the drug abusers who inhaled ("snorted") heroin showed SGOT levels above 250, but more than 35% of the users who injected heroin (even once) had SGOT levels above 250. In this group, 66% showed the presence of some liver disease. Among the heroin users who had developed hepatitis, 80% reported that the problem occurred within two years of the time they first injected drugs.[2,3,5,6]

The Australian antigen has become the principal means of detecting serum hepatitis (hepatitis B, long-incubation hepatitis) in drug abusers. This antigen is present in 50% to 70% of drug abusers with overt hepatitis. Whereas the frequency of positive readings is 0.1% to 0.2% in a normal population, it is 2% to 8% in heroin abusers, and as high as 22% in some studies of intravenous heroin users.[5,6] (Increasingly, hepatitis is transmitted to patients by drug-abusing blood donors or to medical personnel who accidentally prick their skin with needles or glassware contaminated by the blood of drug abusers.[5])

In the past, serum hepatitis was thought to be transmitted only by entry of the virus through broken skin; however, it is now recognized that the hepatitis virus also can be transmitted through biting insects such as mosquitoes, through oral intake of the infectious agent, and even through sexual intercourse.[5,6]

Pathological changes frequently are seen in the livers of drug abusers. Histologic changes include acute hepatitis, fibrosis or chronic active disease, and focal inflammation. In fact, the histologic findings of acute liver disease in drug abusers may be more dramatic than the disease itself and, compared to non-abusers with similar histologic changes, the prognosis for abusers is better.[2,3,5,6]

"Junk" hepatitis, which may be the result of contaminated material introduced into a vein along with the drug, is characterized histologically by significant infiltration and inflammation of the portal tract, where eosinophils and various other inflammatory cells may be seen. This form of hepatitis seems to be only a histologic manifestation and has little effect on the outcome of the disease.[2,3,5,6]

Chronic liver disease is a major problem in patients who have liver abnormalities secondary to drug abuse. Among persons with acute reversible hepatitis, the incidence of drug abuse is about 60%; in chronic persistent or chronic progressive hepatitis, the incidence of abuse is 80%; and in post-necrotic cirrhosis associated with viral hepatitis, the incidence is 90%.[3,5,6] Australian antigen-positive drug abusers thus have a high degree of chronicity, characterized by fibrosis or chronic progressive hepatitis. Antigen-negative drug abusers who may have been positive in the past also have some chronicity, as do the 15% to 20% of drug abusers who are antigen-positive and have sporadic or multiple episodes of hepatitis.[2,3,5,6]

Hepatic carcinoma, although rare, has occurred in Australian antigen-positive patients and may prove to be more frequent in drug abusers than in non-abusers. Physicians should be alert to this possibility so that the condition is diagnosed accurately and treated early.[5,6]

Liver necrosis has been reported as a complication of solvent abuse. Recent evidence suggests that this problem is associated with intermittent low-dose use of solvents in combination with alcohol, as well as with chronic exposure such as that found in industrial settings, especially if workers take solvents home to continue the exposure after working hours.[5]

Combined drug and alcohol abuse may lead to cirrhosis. In fact, the drug abuser with hepatitis is three to four times more likely to have hepatic fibrosis if he drinks more than 32 ounces of alcohol a week than if he drinks less than 10 ounces a week.[2,3,5,6]

NEUROMUSCULAR COMPLICATIONS

The exact etiology of the rare neurological complications of drug abuse are difficult to evaluate because of the complexity of the crude, unsterile mixtures ingested and the methods of administration used. For example, transverse myelitis, plexitis and acute rhabdomyolysis may arise after a period of abstinence from heroin, or following a single injection after a drug-free period.[2,3,5,6]

The discovery of immunoglobin and complement in the kidneys of heroin users who develop nephrotic syndrome may implicate heroin as an infectious, toxic or immunologic stimulus that is expressed as a neuritis, vasculitis or nephrotic syndrome.[2,3,5,6]

NON-INFECTIOUS NEUROLOGIC COMPLICATIONS: Overdoses of uncontaminated heroin and other opioids are characterized by coma, depressed respiration, tachycardia and contracted pupils. Such overdoses may be complicated by convulsive seizures and increased intracranial pressure, which often are associated with pulmonary edema and which may be related to hypersensitivity to drug adulterants.[3,5,6]

Convulsive seizures usually are of the grand mal type. Focal seizures and status epilepticus also occur, but usually stop when the patient recovers from the overdose, with no subsequent attacks.[5,6]

Cerebral sequelae may follow an overdose. After a severe overdose reaction, the patient may enter a period of acute delirium, with tremors, agitation and hallucinosis lasting several hours to several days. In rare cases, such delirium may be the forerunner of chronic organic brain dysfunction, probably as the result of anoxia during the overdose.[5,6]

Delayed postanoxic encephalopathy may accompany cardiorespiratory arrest following overdose. Cerebrovascular accidents with embolic phenomena occasionally are seen subsequent to heroin overdose. In these patients, no evidence of vasculitis is found on angiography, but middle cerebral artery occlusion can be demonstrated. Other rare complications include Parkinson syndrome, hemiballistic movements and bilateral deafness (which may be due either to anoxia or toxicity).[2,3,5,6]

Blindness may occur when heroin has been adulterated with quinine. (This toxic adulterant also can affect the central nervous system; the heart, skeletal and smooth muscles; the gastrointestinal tract; the kidneys; the blood; and the auditory system.) Field defect or blindness also may be caused by talc emboli in the retinal arteries.[2,3,5,6]

Acute transverse myelitis is associated with injected heroin. This problem is characterized by sudden (and occasionally persistent) paraplegia and thoracic sensory levels. It may be caused by severe systemic reaction to the heroin, quinine or other adulterants, by transient ischemia, by a hypersensitivity reaction, or by a direct toxic effect of the drug.[3,5,6]

Peripheral nerve lesions may result from direct injection into a nerve or from toxic and allergic reactions. Such lesions also may be the sequelae of chronic infection. Atraumatic neuropathy, which is the most frequent neuropathic complication, is characterized by painless weakness that begins two to three hours after intravenous injection at a site distal to the injection. It usually is caused by compression of the nerve or restriction of its blood supply. Other nerve lesions include brachial and lumbosacral plexitis, traumatic mononeuropathy, and acute and subacute polyneuropathy.[3,5,6]

Acute rhabdomyolysis is the most striking type of muscular involvement in heroin users. Characterized by skeletal muscle pain and tenderness, swelling and weakness, it may occur within a few hours of intravenous injection of the drug. Myoglobinemia and myoglobinuria are present, and acute renal failure may occur.[5,6]

Chronic fibrosing myopathies are relatively common among long-term users of parenteral drugs, probably as a result of chronic myositis due to brawny edema or the toxic effects of direct intramuscular injections. Unilateral myopathies have been observed in patients unconscious from heroin overdose.[5,6]

INFECTIOUS AND POSTINFECTIOUS NEUROLOGIC COMPLICATIONS: Septic states (with or without endocarditis) can lead to bacterial meningitis and central nervous system abscesses. Following fulminating viral hepatitis, there may be rapid onset of hepatic coma, seizures, decerebrate rigidity, and death in two to eight days. The neurologic aspects of tetanus are well known.[3,5,6]

NEUROLOGIC COMPLICATIONS OF NON-OPIOID DRUGS: Seizures are common among drug abusers. They may occur with overdoses of amphetamines, opioids, hallucinogens or phencyclidines. Withdrawal from short-acting sedative/hypnotics also can lead to seizures, which (when they occur) usually appear 24 to 48 hours after the last dose of the drug. However, with longer-acting depressants such as diazepam and other antianxiety agents, seizures can appear five to seven days after the last drug dose.[3,5,6]

It is extremely important to differentiate between drug-induced seizures and those that occur for other reasons: without such a differential diagnosis, the physician may miss a treatable neurologic disease or overtreat a drug-induced seizure. If the patient's history suggests that seizures may be related to drug abuse, a trial without antiseizure medication may be helpful after the drug use has been resolved. The following questions are useful diagnostic considerations:[3,5,6]

- What is the temporal relationship between drug use and seizure activity? Have the seizures followed administration of a drug?
- Is the patient's use of sedative/hynotic drugs sufficient to suggest withdrawal seizures?
- Have seizures occurred at any time when the patient has been drug-free for several months?
- Has the EEG shown spiking at a time when the patient has been drug-free for several months? (The EEG is of limited diagnostic value within two weeks after seizure activity and during drug intoxication or withdrawal.)

Acute intoxication with depressant drugs can produce ataxia which, in some chronic users, does not clear when drug use stops.

This may be due to some residual impairment of cerebellar function.[3,5,6]

Chronic users of amphetamines often engage in purposeless repetitive actions (such as skin-picking), which usually disappear after the drug is withdrawn. However, withdrawal from prolonged amphetamine use may be marked by severe psychomotor retardation and depression that last for several weeks.[3,5,6]

Nystagmus may attend the use of several classes of drugs. For example, almost all depressant drugs can cause nystagmus in horizontal gaze, and chronic users of these drugs also may suffer vertical nystagmus. Horizontal and vertical nystagmus also have been reported in phencyclidine users.[3,]

Sniffing gasoline that contains lead can result in motor neuropathy and encephalopathy. Solvents such as methyl ethyl ketone and hexane can produce motor polyneuropathy.[3,5,6]

In animal studies, cerebral atrophy has been associated with almost all forms of drug abuse. However, it has not been sufficiently studied in humans to allow prediction of a rate of incidence or a precise mechanism of action.[3,5,6]

PULMONARY COMPLICATIONS

The most serious pulmonary effect of drug abuse probably is the respiratory depression, apnea and anoxia associated with depressant and heroin overdose. Acute pulmonary edema also is a frequent concomitant of opioid overdose. In combination with depression of the respiratory center, pulmonary edema often results in death unless appropriate treatment is initiated. A similar pulmonary edema can be produced by overdoses of propoxyphene and methadone.[2,3,5,6]

Pulmonary edema must be differentiated from aspiration pneumonia in heroin overdose patients. Such patients frequently arrive in the emergency department after friends have attempted to revive them with large amounts of milk, coffee or other liquids. Such ineffective efforts to manage the overdose usually do little more than cause the patient to aspirate liquid. Because of the importance of early steroid therapy in treating aspiration pneumonia, a "rule of thumb" in differential diagnosis is that pulmonary edema is accompanied by slowed or normal respirations, while aspiration pneumonia is marked by increased respirations. Pulmonary edema from overdose also may be accompanied by a fever of up to 101°F. and a leukocytosis of 25,000 to 30,000, both of which generally return to normal within 48 hours.[3,5,6] The frequency of pulmonary edema in overdose cases suggests that all such patients be carefully monitored even after the overdose crisis has been resolved.

The lungs are the primary filters of injected drugs. Thus, any insoluble adulterants lodge in the lungs, where they can cause multiple microinfarcts. The most popular adulterants are talc, starch, lactose and bicarbonate of soda. Talc is the least soluble of these materials and thus is the agent most often responsible for microinfarcts.[2,3,5,6]

Microinfarcts are common in long-term users who inject amphetamines and methylphenidate, because those drugs are manufactured in tablet form for oral use. Intravenous injection of dissolved tablets deposits large amounts of insoluble fillers in the lung. The presence of such insoluble particles in the pulmonary vasculature can lead to chronic pulmonary fibrosis and foreign-body granulomas, with resulting poor oxygen diffusion across the alveolar capillary membranes and changes in lung elasticity. Pulmonary hypertension and cardiac failure may result. Chest x-rays may appear normal or show bilateral fine reticular basilar infiltrates, pulmonary artery enlargement or hilar adenopathy. (Pulmonary hypertension also has been reported following high-dose oral amphetamine use, probably due to a direct effect of amphetamine on the pulmonary vasculature.)[3,5,6]

Intravenous administration of illicit drugs also can cause pulmonary parenchymal contamination with a large number of bacteria. These bacteria may be present in the drug itself, in the diluents or paraphernalia, or on the body of the abuser. Whatever the source, this contamination can cause pulmonary infections with bacteria not normally isolated in pneumonitis. Pulmonary abscesses also result from infections of the heart valves, particularly the tricuspid and pulmonic valves. The constant seeding of such bacteria into the pulmonary circulation results in intrapulmonary infections that are difficult to manage.[3,5,6]

Lung infections often are associated with chronic drug abuse. Opioids depress the cough reflex and, in the stuporous and debilitated abuser (who may be vomiting), aspiration pneumonia often results. A similar syndrome is seen in abusers of all forms of depressant drugs, and the resulting pneumonias often involve bacteria that are difficult to manage. Debilitated drug abusers are at increased risk of contracting tuberculosis.[2,3,5,6]

Chronic uvulitis, pharyngitis and bronchitis have been reported in heavy cannabis smokers.[5,6]

RENAL COMPLICATIONS

Intravenous heroin use has been associated with a nephropathy that is not related to bacterial endocarditis. Clinically, this complication presents as a nephrotic syndrome. On renal biopsy, PAS-positive material is seen and, with specific staining, deposits of immunoglobins are found. This disorder is considered to be an immunologic problem, with the deposition of immune complexes in the glomeruli.[5]

Acute renal failure due to crushing injuries or overdoses, glomerulonephritis due to septic emboli, and necrotizing angiitis with focal renal lesions have been associated with parenteral use of the amphetamines and, possibly, heroin.[5]

REPRODUCTIVE COMPLICATIONS

Women who abuse drugs—particularly opioids and cannabinoids—frequently experience irregular menses, at least temporary infertility and a higher than average rate of stillbirths and spontaneous abortions. Recent animal studies suggest that marijuana's effects on fertility are exerted indirectly through the reproductive hormones, rather than directly on the reproductive tissues.[5,11]

Studies of male reproductive processes in human volunteers suggest that marijuana and Δ-9-tetrahydrocannabinol can reduce sperm count, decrease sperm motility and result in sperm of abnormal appearance.[11]

Cytogenic studies of cultured lymphocytes show a greater frequency of chromosome breaks in marijuana and heroin users than in non-users. This incidence appears to return gradually to normal levels during methadone maintenance of heroin abusers or upon cessation of drug use.[5,11]

SEPTIC COMPLICATIONS

Most of the septic complications of drug abuse derive from the conditions under which drugs are taken. The source of organisms usually is the drug abuser's own body, although contaminated drugs and injection paraphernalia also contribute.[2,3,6]

TETANUS: Today, tetanus is seen almost exclusively in heroin users. Since 1955, 70% to 90% of all reported tetanus cases have occurred in drug abusers, in whom the mortality rate for this disease approaches 90%.[5]

More female than male heroin users contract tetanus (a 3:1 ratio usually is cited), because subcutaneous injection ("skin-popping") is more widely practiced by women, who generally have poorer venous development than men and thus eschew intravenous administration. (Injections into the subcutaneous fat, where vascularization is poor, increases the risk of developing an anaerobic infection.) Moreover, fewer women than men have been immunized against tetanus.[5]

The traditionally higher incidence of tetanus among drug abusers on the East Coast and in Chicago is related to the inclusion of 2% to 10% quinine in heroin sold in those areas. Quinine is a protoplasmic poison that reduces the redox potential, thus providing ideal conditions for the germination of *Clostridium tetani* when heroin is injected subcutaneously or intramuscularly.[5,6]

MALARIA: Malaria among drug abusers is closely associated with intravenous drug administration. It was first reported in New Orleans among drug-abusing, needle-sharing sailors who had been exposed to malaria in Africa. When infected World War II veterans returned to the United States, malaria appeared among drug abusers in New York City, but disappeared in that locale in the late 1940's and has not reoccurred, probably because quinine usually is included in heroin sold in that area. Although the amount of quinine used is not sufficient to eradicate malaria, quinine is such a severe protoplasmic poison that it presumably kills the malarial parasites in the syringes used for injection.[5,6]

With the return of veterans from Viet Nam, there was another increase in the incidence of drug-related malaria, but this was confined to the West Coast, where quinine generally is not used to adulterate heroin.[5]

SKELETAL COMPLICATIONS

Drug abusers are at increased risk for septic arthritis and osteomyelitis.[5] Septic arthritis due to *Pseudomonas* has been described in heroin users[12] and polyarteritis as a complication of HA antigenemia has been reported in chronic users of intravenous drugs.[13] These conditions each seem to be related in a different way to the hepatitis-associated or Australian antigen (HAA), that is, they are due to contaminants such as HAA and the immune response such foreign products elicit, rather than to the direct effect of drugs.[12,13] These infections can occur anywhere in the body: low back pain, for example, may be due to an infection of the disc space rather than muscle strain.[5,6]

Crush injuries and fractures also are common in drug abusers. Intoxicated individuals are more likely to have accidents than persons who do not use drugs and (because the analgesic effects of many drugs mask pain) less likely to seek immediate treatment of their injuries. Further, injuries may be accompanied by loss of consciousness, causing the person to rest in an awkward position that cuts off circulation to an extremity. "Frostbite" may result from loss of consciousness outdoors in cold weather.[5,6]

Intra-arterial infections or fasciolitis can cut off circulation to part of an extremity, leading to the development of gangrene or spontaneous amputation of fingers and toes.[5,6,8]

MEDICAL PROBLEMS UNRELATED TO, BUT COMPLICATED BY, DRUG ABUSE

The physician managing a disease that is not *caused* by drug abuse should recognize that any chronic illness may be complicated by the use of illicit drugs.[5,6]

ABDOMINAL PAIN: Opioid users may attribute abdominal pain to withdrawal when, in fact, it is due to appendicitis, pancreatitis, perforated ulcer or some other acute problem.[5,6]

DIABETES: Chronic drug users often neglect diet and hygiene, thus posing serious problems in the management of this metabolic disease. Further, a diabetic patient's insulin requirements may be affected by concurrent use of psychoactive drugs.[5] Recent reports indicate an enhanced frequency of osteomyelitis in diabetics who abuse opioids, especially heroin.[14]

EPILEPSY: The sedative effects of anticonvulsant medications may be intensified by drug abuse, and withdrawal seizures become more likely.[5,6]

HYPERTENSION: Use of psychoactive drugs can alter the patient's requirements for antihypertensive medications, thus impairing the control of elevated blood pressure.[5,6]

SURGICAL PROBLEMS

The higher incidence of crime, disease and violence associated with drug abuse has led to a greater frequency of surgical procedures in drug-dependent persons. Unfortunately, such patients often do not give reliable histories, and the surgeon must exercise great caution if he is to avoid unexpected complications.[3,15]

While the management of surgical patients in the post-addictive stage appears to follow a relatively normal course, the management of acutely intoxicated surgical patients is difficult. The major complications are associated with infection and improper intravenous administration of drugs, as well as the concurrent use of non-narcotic drugs such as salicylates, barbiturates and alcohol.[16]

An important general principle in managing the active drug user is that surgical trauma should not be compounded by an attempt to detoxify the patient. The patient should be maintained on his drug of dependence or an adequate substitute at least until he has recovered from surgery, then—if possible—gradually withdrawn.[3,15]

Awareness of preexisting or current liver disease also is essential to good surgical and anesthetic practice with the drug-dependent patient.[3,15]

ANESTHESIA

A drug abuser's increased tolerance to, and dependence on, narcotic drugs can create a problem with preanesthetic hypotension, making it difficult to achieve the proper level of sedation. Use of the naloxone test may help to determine whether a patient is dependent on opioids. In this test, 0.2 to 0.4 mg of naloxone is administered intravenously, producing pupillary dilation in a patient who has recently ingested narcotics (otherwise, pupillary size is an unreliable guide in determining anesthesia plans).[3,15]

POST-SURGICAL PAIN RELIEF

The analgesia needs of drug-dependent surgical patients are not adequately met by administering methadone. Thus, Senay and Lewis[15] recommend the use of normal doses of dihydromorphinone, meperidine or morphine in addition to the maintenance dose of methadone. Pentazocine should not be used as an analgesic, because it can precipitate withdrawal in a patient who is dependent on opioids.[3]

Tolerance to opioids shortens the time of analgesic effect, so most opioid-dependent and methadone-maintained patients will require more frequent administration of analgesics than a "naive" patient.[15]

Ileus following abdominal surgery on drug-dependent patients has been reported, but its association with drug abuse is not clear. Some patients may complain of inordinate amounts of abdominal pain in an attempt to obtain additional narcotic drugs. When this situation is suspected, interviewing members of the patient's family often elicits the true history. Also, some patients will manage to obtain additional drugs from friends and family and may subsequently behave in a disruptive manner. In such a case, the surgeon should not hesitate to use the full range of his authority to control the patient, including calling hospital guards and seeking psychiatric consultation.[3]

PULMONARY PROBLEMS

Postoperatively, the undetected drug-dependent patient may show signs of congestive heart failure or pulmonary edema without evidence of fluid overload. This relates directly to the pulmonary edema seen in overdose patients and requires careful monitoring and intensive therapy.[3]

The surgeon should consider the possibility of drug abuse in any young surgical patient, but especially a patient admitted with stab or gunshot wounds or any injury suggestive of the drug culture. Such increased awareness also might prevent the occurrence of postoperative withdrawal symptoms.[3]

POSTOPERATIVE MANAGEMENT

An important issue in surgical treatment of the drug abuser is what to do about the patient's dependence after surgery. The patient can be detoxified from drugs once his surgical crisis is past, but management of drug abusers on general hospital services is difficult. Senay et al[3] recommend that, in most circumstances, the surgeon discharge the patient from the hospital with a referral to the nearest drug abuse program or specialist. They maintain that, although this may seem an unpalatable solution, there are few acceptable alternatives. Such a patient usually has sought and obtained illicit drugs for many years, and often can manipulate the non-specialist physician who tries to withdraw him gradually.

MATERNAL AND NEONATAL COMPLICATIONS

Research on the effects of drug abuse on pregnant women and their offspring has produced some contradictory findings. Current evidence does show, however, that pregnancy in the drug-abusing woman carries with it potential health hazards for mother and child, both before and after birth. These problems arise from the pharmacologic impact of drugs on the mother and fetus, as well as from the contaminants and modes of administration associated with illicit drugs.[2,3,5,6]

Other problems arise from the lifestyle of women who abuse drugs—a lifestyle that often includes poor diet and hygiene, higher than average rates of venereal disease and a general lack of prenatal care. Because the majority of all women who abuse drugs are of child-bearing age, and because the incidence of addicted neonates is increasing, attention to these complications is an important aspect of the diagnosis and treatment of drug abuse problems in female patients.[3,5,6]

A less well-documented but widely recognized problem attendant on maternal drug abuse is the apparent frequency with which infants and children of women who abuse drugs die at home. Although the exact relationship between childhood deaths and parental drug use is not clear, the physician should alert both male and female patients to the potential hazards to their offspring, then help the parents identify and deal with such hazards. In many cases, family counseling and other social services should be made part of the patient's treatment plan.[3,5,6]

PROBLEMS DURING PREGNANCY

As with any pregnant patient, the physician should make every effort to ensure the adequacy of pre- and postnatal care of the drug-abusing woman. She is less likely than the average patient to seek such care, but when she does, there is an opportunity for the physician to influence her situation in a positive way.[2,3,5,6]

Diagnosing pregnancy can be difficult in women who abuse drugs. The most common indicators of pregnancy—a history of amenorrhea, a positive pregnancy test and palpation of the gravid uterus—are not reliable indicators in chronic drug users. Amenorrhea is common in such women, and the early signs of pregnancy (fatigue, headaches, nausea and vomiting, hot sweats and pelvic cramps) may be interpreted as withdrawal symptoms by both patient and physician. Diagnostic tests such as Pregnosis and Pregnosticon give a false-positive reaction in about 5% of heroin users and a significant percentage of patients maintained on methadone.[15]

Reluctance to undergo a pelvic examination, coupled with the high incidence of pelvic inflammation among women who abuse drugs, further complicates the diagnosis of pregnancy. Senay and Lewis[15] suggest that the single most reliable method of diagnosing pregnancy and fetal age in these women is ultrasonography at five to six weeks after the last normal menstrual period, or three weeks past the suspected time of conception.

Malnutrition and the other illnesses typically associated with drug abuse present special problems in managing the pregnant drug abuser. The impact of the drugs themselves creates other major complications. For example, a heroin-addicted pregnant woman who is not in treatment is likely to undergo withdrawal because of a lack of drugs or in an attempt to cure her own habit. The fetus of a woman undergoing withdrawal may experience withdrawal symptoms *in utero* and could die as a result.[5,6]

Pregnancy also is an important element in drug abuse treatment. In view of the dangers posed to the fetus, any decision to withdraw a pregnant patient from drugs should be preceded by careful analysis of the relative risks and benefits. In most cases, the preferred treatment is to maintain an opioid-dependent pregnant woman on methadone to avoid the dangers of withdrawal and eliminate the hazards of illicit drug use.[5]

Even methadone maintenance, however, is not without risks to the fetus. Just as the placenta does not act as a barrier to most drugs of abuse, neither does it protect the fetus from medically prescribed drugs, including methadone.[17] Some possibility of creating methadone dependence does exist, although it usually is less of a medical risk than continued use of illicit drugs or sudden withdrawal.[5,6]

PROBLEMS DURING LABOR AND DELIVERY

Bleeding is the most common complication of labor and delivery in women who abuse drugs. This may reflect a very friable cervix, venereal condylotoma, abruptio placentae, uterine atony or toxemia.[12]

Infection is a frequent complication in drug dependent women in labor who have received no prenatal care. Such women may even have prolonged rupture of the membranes for several days prior to admission. Therefore, it is important to obtain cultures from the cervix and any other areas where infection is suspected.[18]

Depending on the type, amount and time of the last drug dose, withdrawal can occur as labor progresses. Pain is a physiologic antagonist to opioid drugs and diminishes the effects of other drugs on which the patient may be dependent. As a result, some drug-abusing women take additional drugs before entering the hospital, in anticipation of labor and delivery pain. If they do not, they may experience withdrawal even though receiving the same amount of drugs that suppressed withdrawal symptoms before labor began.[18,19]

If opioid withdrawal begins, a narcotic should be administered immediately to halt the progression of symptoms. Increased maternal muscle activity during withdrawal can trigger a cycle of reduced availability of maternal oxygen to the fetus and an increased need for oxygen by the fetus. Allowed to progress, maternal withdrawal will result in fetal distress, with the attendant risk of meconium aspiration. Electronic monitoring is useful in the early detection of such distress.[18]

More breech presentations occur in drug-abusing women than in women who do not use drugs, primarily because the rate of premature births is higher in drug abusers. Maternal withdrawal may produce intrauterine irritability and result in the premature onset of labor. If the membranes are intact and the fetus is alive, and if there are no other complications, pharmacological inhibition of labor may be appropriate.[18,20]

As in any labor, the choice and dose of analgesic agent should be determined by the patient's progress and the well-being of the fetus. If the fetus already is dependent on opioid or depressant drugs, it will be less sensitive than non-dependent fetuses to the respiratory depressant effects of analgesics and sedatives given the mother during labor. Methadone or other drugs to control withdrawal symptoms in the mother should be administered *in addition to* the usual analgesics.[18,20]

The choice of anesthetic agent usually is guided by circumstances during labor and delivery. Use of low doses of a parenteral anesthetic, such as thiopental, has been associated with transient arterial hypotension in the mother. Higher doses may induce fetal depression. Therefore, many physicians avoid parenteral anesthetics whenever possible.[18]

For uncomplicated term deliveries, low spinal or epidural anesthesia may be of value. In a multiparous woman experiencing a rapid second stage, a pudendal block or local anesthesia for the episiotomy may suffice. In high-risk patients, it may be advisable to combine very small amounts of inhalation and local anesthesia.[18]

PROBLEMS DURING THE IMMEDIATE POSTPARTUM PERIOD

The need for methadone maintenance of the opioid-dependent woman continues in the postpartum period. In other respects, the postpartum course is monitored as in any other pregnancy. Several areas of management, however, require special attention when maternal drug abuse is involved.[18]

LOW BIRTH WEIGHT: Low birth weight is a frequent occurrence in children of opioid-dependent mothers. Whereas prematurity occurs in only 6% to 7% of all births, it is seen in one of every three births to heroin-addicted mothers (some researchers cite a figure as high as 50%.) Low birth weight is of great importance because of its high correlation with infant mortality and developmental deficits.[5]

NEONATAL WITHDRAWAL SYNDROME: The fetus of a pregnant woman who uses opioid, sedative/hypnotic, psychomimetic or stimulant drugs inevitably is exposed to the potential toxic effects of those drugs. An infant who is introduced to those drugs *in utero* is abruptly removed from the source of drugs at birth. If physical dependence on the drugs has developed, the infant may be expected to experience withdrawal symptoms.[18] Senay and Lewis[15] cite studies placing the frequency of neonatal withdrawal syndrome in offspring of opioid-dependent mothers at 40% to 85%.

The greatest danger is that the withdrawal syndrome may go unrecognized and untreated, resulting at least in the child's suffering and, at worst, the child's death. Thus, the diagnostic role of the physician who treats a potentially opioid-dependent neonate is a critical one. The *early signs* most likely to appear are irritability, hypertonicity, high-pitched shrill cries and tremors. These do not necessarily confirm the existence of dependence and withdrawal, but they do indicate the need for further observation. *Other signs* include vomiting, hyperactivity, poor food intake, diarrhea, fever, sustained Moro's reflex and seizures. *Suggestive signs* include sneezing, respiratory distress, twitching, blueness of skin, yawning, apnea, coryza, tearing and excessive sweating.[5,21]

Treatment of the withdrawal syndrome usually includes administration of paregoric (4 to 8 drops every 6 to 8 hours), phenobarbital (8 to 10 mg/kg/day in four divided oral doses) or chlorpromazine (2.8 mg/kg/day in four divided oral doses). Diazepam also has been effective, but its routine use is not recommended because the parenteral form contains sodium benzoate as a preservative. (Sodium benzoate inhibits albumin binding of indirect bilirubin and may enhance the development of bilirubin encephalopathy in jaundiced infants.)[15]

The physician should be aware that drugs frequently used to treat neonatal withdrawal syndrome (such as phenobarbital and paregoric) also can cause dependence. Therefore, treatment with these drugs should not be prolonged. Otherwise, once the immediate problem has been controlled, the infant might have to be detoxified from the drugs used to treat the original withdrawal.[5]

A neonatal withdrawal syndrome also is seen with depressant drugs, including alcohol. This syndrome is characterized by generalized motor seizures and signs of severe neuromuscular excitability, including hyperactivity, tremor, twitching, shrill cry, poor suck, vomiting, hyperreflexia and opisthotonic posturing. Like the barbiturate withdrawal syndrome in adults, the neonatal withdrawal syndrome in infants can be treated with gradually tapered doses of phenobarbital.[22]

SEXUAL DYSFUNCTION

Psychoactive drugs can have a marked effect on sexual functioning. Patients may not spontaneously report sexual dysfunction to the physician, but diagnosis of such problems is essential to adequate treatment.[6]

Opioids decrease libido and, until tolerance develops, may initially depress pituitary sex hormones. This depression of hormonal function may temporarily decrease fertility in women. When tolerance develops, however, fertility usually is restored.[6,23]

Males complain of delayed ejaculation during high-dose use of *opioids*, but spontaneous ejaculation can occur during irregular use of opioids and drug withdrawal.[6,24]

The effects of *methadone* on sexual function are similar to those of the other opioids. In maintenance doses, however, the primary complaints are decreased libido and delayed ejaculation. (It should be noted that some patients feel delayed ejaculation is a positive effect, as they are able to prolong intercourse.)[6,25]

Chronic use of *depressant* drugs (including alcohol) in high doses may produce inability to achieve an erection or ejaculation. However, potency usually returns to normal when drug use is discontinued.[6,24]

Stimulant drugs usually increase libido, but also may delay ejaculation or orgasm.[6]

Marijuana, although reportedly used to heighten sexual excitation, has been shown to lower testosterone levels in a dose-related curve, and thus may have at least a temporary effect on potency.[6,24]

The social effects of drug use on sexual function are more subtle, but widely reported nonetheless. For example, if drug use begins during adolescence, when sexual functioning is developing and feelings of inadequacy are common, such use may represent an attempt to lower social and sexual inhibitions and repair the user's damaged self-esteem. In such a case, inadequate sexual functioning might be either a cause or an effect of drug abuse.[6]

Some drug users have never had sexual relations except when using drugs. This is an important point of information, since extensive counseling may be required before satisfactory sexual relations can be achieved.[6]

PSYCHIATRIC DISORDERS

Psychiatric problems such as organic and functional psychoses, violence and suicidal behavior are common in drug abuse emergencies. Many of these problems are associated with *acute intoxication* (and are potentially life-threatening), while others are chronic conditions associated with *long-term drug use*.

PROBLEMS OF ACUTE INTOXICATION: Patients under the influence of hallucinogens and other psychoactive substances are likely to present with acute psychiatric decompensation, as well as paranoid and psychotic reactions. In emergency situations, however, it may be difficult to distinguish between acute or chronic mental problems and those that are drug-related. Further, it may be almost impossible to differentiate between organic and functional psychoses. Senay and Lewis[15] offer the following diagnostic guidelines:

Organic psychoses usually are marked by altered levels of consciousness, fluctuating mental status and altered vital signs. Memory and ability to concentrate also may be impaired.

Functional psychoses usually are marked by auditory rather than visual hallucinations. Onset of symptoms is slow and the level of impairment remains relatively constant. The patient usually is oriented as to time, place and person.

Almost all acutely psychotic patients who are suspected of being under the influence of drugs should be handled in a supportive medical setting until a primary thought disorder can be diagnosed or ruled out. The presence of familiar people and objects in a supportive, calm environment should help reduce the patient's level of anxiety.[15]

The mental status examination should include tests of orientation, memory (both recent and remote), level of consciousness, affect, degree of logic, thought content, a description of appearance, and some assessment of judgment and insight.[15]

Senay and Lewis[15] recommend that no tranquilizing drugs be administered unless absolutely necessary. If sedative medications are required, they recommend oral benzodiazepines (10 to 30 mg diazepam), except in patients whose impulse control is poor, since diazepam—like alcohol—tends to lower inhibitions and thus might make control even more difficult. Benzodiazepines are the drugs of choice because they have a wide margin of safety and allow continuation of the mental status examination.

If psychiatric examination indicates the presence of a thought disorder, 25 to 50 mg of a phenothiazine medication such as chlorpromazine may be administered four times a day, preferably orally (intramuscular injection may be indicated in some cases, but intravenous administration should be avoided because of its hypotensive potential).[15]

With initial therapy, there may be atropine-like side effects, hypotension or dystonic reactions. Haloperidol, which has fewer side effects than chlorpromazine, is useful in controlling acute psychotic behavior and can be given in doses of one to 5 mg every two hours until a calming effect is achieved.[15]

PROBLEMS OF LONG-TERM DRUG ABUSE: Several recent studies point to an association between long-term drug abuse and chronic psychiatric and psychological impairments. For example, Grant et al[26] have reported that a group of polydrug abusers showed deficits on both language-related and perceptuomotor neuropsychological tests. Heavy use of depressants and opioids was most strongly related to such impairments, although the authors caution that such an association does not establish a causal link. Alternatively, they propose that previously impaired individuals may prefer the depressants and opioids to help them cope with stresses they feel ill-equipped to manage.

A second major question addressed by Grant and his co-investigators was the reversibility of the observed impairment. They found that, although 25% of the polydrug abusers initially rated as impaired were judged to have improved significantly at three-month follow-up, the overall changes in impairment ratings were not large. Thus, they concluded that the persistence of performance deficits raises the possibility that opioids and CNS depressants may have long-term, slowly reversible or even permanent effects on neuropsychological functioning.[26]

In a study of the relationship between drug abuse and specific psychiatric disorders, McLellan et al[27] found evidence suggesting that abuse of particular drugs has a strong correlation with the development of specific psychiatric illnesses (although the possibility that different preexisting personality disorders led to different kinds of drug abuse could not be excluded). McLellan and his co-investigators studied 51 drug-abusing military veterans treated in the Philadelphia Veterans Administration Medical Center over a six-year period. When the men were first admitted in 1972, they showed low-level symptoms of mental disorders, but there was no significant difference among them. However, six years later, six of the eleven stimulant abusers had developed symptoms of schizophrenia, five of these patients were referred to a psychiatric ward, and four required prolonged inpatient psychiatric treatment. Among the 14 men who continued to abuse depressant drugs, there were extreme increases in symptoms of depression, including suicide attempts by five of eleven group members. (These symptoms of depression did not abate with the completion of detoxification.)[27]

On the other hand, little psychologic change was apparent in the 26 patients who continued to abuse opioids, despite the persistence of heavy drug use that required repeated hospitalizations. The clinical impressions of these subjects continued to be primarily sociopathic and psychopathic character disorders, associated with pervasive problems of family and social relations, criminality and self-support, but with little evidence of psychosis or organic illness. McLellan and his co-investigators[27] attribute the lack of change in this group to the specific pharmacologic effects of opioid drugs. They suggest that heroin, morphine and methadone may have acted as medications for the subjects' underlying psychological problems and helped to reduce their symptoms of anxiety, depression and paranoia.

The authors offer two possible explanations for the increased evidence of psychiatric symptoms in their subjects who abused either stimulant or sedative drugs. One explanation is that these symptoms may have been present at a sub-clinical level at the time of the initial assessment in 1972. If so, the subjects may have required—or responded preferentially to—particular drugs because of the influence of their underlying symptoms. Although the drugs did not prevent the subsequent appearance of symptoms, they may have provided a particular form of relief. This explanation would account for the well-documented tendency of drug abusers to select combinations of drugs with similar physical and psychological effects and to reject other types of available drugs.[27]

A second possible explanation is that the prolonged abuse of specific types of drugs had a direct role in the development and expression of the disorders noted. This view suggests that, although some form of psychiatric illness may have appeared eventually (regardless of drug use), the regular use of specific psychoactive drugs may have hastened its development and determined its nature. The mechanism by which this occurs might include state-dependent learning or biochemical changes in the central nervous system resulting from prolonged alterations of the biogenic amine systems.[27]

Although this study was conducted *post hoc* on a small sample of male opioid, stimulant and sedative drug abusers, its authors believe the results are sufficiently significant and distinct to warrant further investigation.

REFERENCES

1. Dimijian, G. G. Differential diagnosis of emergency drug reactions *in* P. G. Bourne (ed.) *A Treatment Manual for Acute Drug Abuse Emergencies* (National Institute on Drug Abuse, Rockville, Md., 1974)
2. Johnson, R. B. and Lukash, W. M. (eds.) *Medical Complications of Drug Abuse:* Summary of Proceedings of the Washington Conference, Washington, D.C., December 7, 1972 (American Medical Association, Chicago, Ill., 1973)
3. Senay, E. C., Becker, C. E. and Schnoll, S. H. *Emergency Treatment of the Drug Abusing Patient* Medical Monograph Series, Vol. I, No. 4 (National Institute on Drug Abuse, Rockville, Md., 1977)
4. Schuckit, M. A. *Drug and Alcohol Abuse: A Clinical Guide to Diagnosis and Treatment* (Plenum Medical Book Co., New York City, 1979)
5. Cohen, S. and Gallant, D. M. *Diagnosis of Drug and Alcohol Abusers* Medical Monograph Series, Vol. II, No. 2 (National Institute on Drug Abuse, Rockville, Md., 1980)
6. O'Brien, C. P., Wesson, D. R. and Schnoll, S. H. *Diagnosis and Evaluation of the Drug Abusing Patient for Treatment Staff Physicians* Medical Monograph Series, Vol. I, No. 1 (National Institute on Drug Abuse, Rockville, Md., 1976)
7. Tuazon, C. U., Cardella, T. A. and Sheagren, J. N. Staphylococcal endocarditis in drug users *Archives of Internal Medicine* 135:1555 (December 1975)
8. Vascular problems linked to drug abuse (Medical News) *JAMA* 221(4):343 (July 24, 1972)
9. Adams, W. H. Heroin-associated thrombocytopenia *Archives of Internal Medicine* 139:740 (July 1979)
10. Moss, R. A. and Okun, D. B. Heroin-induced thrombocytopenia *Archives of Internal Medicine* 139:753 (July 1979)

11. Russell, G. K. Marijuana: an overview of recent biomedical findings. Testimony submitted to the United States Senate Committee on the Judiciary, January 16-17, 1980 *Health Consequences of Marijuana Use*, Serial No. 96-54 (U.S. Government Printing Office, Washington, D.C., 1980)
12. Gifford, D. B., Patzakis, M., Ivler, D. and Swezey, R. L. Septic arthritis due to pseudomonas in heroin addicts *Journal of Bone and Joint Surgery* 57A(5):631 (July 1975)
13. Healey, L. A. Arthritis and drug abuse *Medical Times* 102(9):99 (September 1974)
14. Whitehouse, F. W. Diabetes and drug abuse *Medical Times* 102(9):99 (September 1974)
15. Senay, E. C. and Lewis, D. C. *The Primary Physician's Guide to Drug and Alcohol Abuse Treatment* Medical Monograph Series, Vol. I, No. 6 (National Institute on Drug Abuse, Rockville, Md., 1980)
16. Friedell, M. T. and Friedell, P. E. Surgery of the narcotic addict (Clinical Seminar D, 1977)
17. Blake, J. P., Collinge, D. A., McNulty, H., Leach, F. N. and Grant, E. J. Drugs in pregnancy: weighing the risks *Patient Care* 21 (May 30, 1980)
18. *Drug Dependence in Pregnancy: Clinical Management of Mother and Child* Services Research Monograph Series (National Institute on Drug Abuse, Rockville, Md., 1979)
19. Glass, L. and Evans, H. Perinatal drug abuse *Pediatric Annals* 8(2):41 (February 1979)
20. Arena, J. M. Drug and chemical effects on mother and child *Pediatric Annals* 8(12):10 (December 1979)
21. Neonatal narcotic dependence *National Clearinghouse for Drug Abuse Information Report Series* 29(1):1 (February 1974)
22. Bleyer, W. A. and Marshall, R. E. Barbiturate withdrawal syndrome in a passively addicted infant *JAMA* 221(2):185 (July 10, 1972)
23. Mirin, S. M., Meyer, R. E., Mendelson, J. H. and Ellingboe, J. Opiate use and sexual function *American Journal of Psychiatry* 137(8):909 (August 1980)
24. Ferguson, P., Lennox, T. and Lettieri, D. J. *Drugs and Sex: The Non-Medical Use of Drugs and Sexual Behavior* Research Issues Series, No. 2 (National Institute on Drug Abuse, Rockville, Md., 1974)
25. Crowley, T. J. and Simpson, R. Methadone dose and human sexual behavior *International Journal of the Addictions* 13(2):285 (1978)
26. Grant, I., Adams, K. M., Carlin, A. S., Rennick, P. M., Judd, L. L. and Schooff, K. The collaborative neuropsychological study of polydrug users *Archives of General Psychiatry* 35:1063 (September 1978)
27. McLellan, A. T., Woody, G. E. and O'Brien, C. P. Development of psychiatric illness in drug abusers: possible role of drug preference *New England Journal of Medicine* 301(24):1310 (December 13, 1979)

CHAPTER 8
POST-ACUTE CARE AND REHABILITATION OF DRUG ABUSERS

The network of drug treatment services available today is influenced by the "complex American perspective about drug use . . . and addiction that has colored this area of human concern for the past 200 years."[1] Services actually reflect a variety of perspectives, which view the problem of illicit drug use as (1) residing essentially within the individual and his attitude toward life, (2) residing in social conditions that create frustrations and deprivations and simultaneously fail to control access to dangerous drugs, and (3) residing in an interaction between the effects of certain drugs and the biological characteristics of the users, some of whom may have a special vulnerability to the effects of those drugs.

Each of these perspectives, as Jaffe[1] observes, leads to a very different approach to the treatment of drug abuse and dependence. Such approaches range from detoxification to maintenance programs, from efforts to alter conditioned behavior to attempts to restructure character, from programs designed to modify mood and self-esteem to classes in vocational skills, and from concerns with the availability of jobs to general attacks on American economic and social institutions and values.

A system that incorporates this diversity of opinion must be understood in terms of its origins as well as judged by its results.

ORIGINS OF MODERN TREATMENT METHODS

There was no medical model for the treatment of substance abuse in colonial days. By the mid-1800's, however, chronic use of opium and morphine came to be viewed as analogous to drunkenness—that is, as simultaneously representing moral weakness and a disease process. Over the next several decades, public concern over widespread use of narcotic drugs continued to mount. The Temperance Movement adopted the position that, since the use of any drug led to enslavement, the only acceptable moral behavior was to avoid drugs entirely. (This view reflected growing acceptance of the idea that opium was an inherently addicting substance.) At the same time, the medical profession was showing greater interest in the problem of drug dependence.[1,2]

By the end of the 19th century, the treatment of drug abusers generally was handled by private physicians. Most often, treatment involved helping the patient through the discomforts of withdrawal.[2] The major areas of medical concern were excessive use of opium, morphine and alcohol, although dependence on cocaine, paraldehyde and chloral hydrate also had been reported. Most of the drugs that now cause concern (barbiturates, amphetamines and benzodiazepines, for example) had not yet been introduced.[1] The psychological element of addiction was largely ignored and, because there was little follow-up of patients after treatment, the problem of relapse was not widely recognized.[2]

Drug abuse became a public health issue in the early years of the 20th century, as the public became increasingly aware of the link between narcotics and organized crime, as well as of the growing incidence of drug addiction among medical professionals. The Harrison Narcotic Act of 1914 permitted the use of opioids and cocaine only by registered physicians and dentists in the course of professional practice. The federal government interpreted this legislation as prohibiting physicians from prescribing maintenance doses of narcotic drugs, and numerous indictments were brought against honest physicians who believed that maintenance was the only useful treatment for drug dependence.[1]

After 1919, when legitimate sources of narcotics were no longer available, thousands of addicts—particularly those in the larger cities—turned to illicit sources of supply. To deal with this new problem, the federal government encouraged large cities to establish temporary clinics for the maintenance of persons dependent on opioids, with the idea of gradually reducing the dosage and withdrawing the drug. Of the 44 clinics established, some claimed success in gradually withdrawing patients, others merely provided maintenance, and a few became notoriously careless in their distribution of drugs.[2] The poor performance of some of the clinics, coinciding with a general shift in public interest away from treatment, led to the closing of the last of the clinics by 1925. Dependence on opium, cocaine and marijuana had come to be viewed as a threat to the fabric of society, and preventing such dependence by controlling the availability of drugs became the highest priority of government drug abuse efforts. Deterrence of drug use through enforcement of criminal penalties became the major strategy. Throughout this period, physicians were discouraged from treating narcotics addiction.[1]

In the following decade, the emphasis on prohibition of illicit use appeared to be meeting with some success, particularly in reducing the number of persons dependent on medically prescribed drugs.

However, a new pattern of drug abuse began to assert itself in the large cities, as the declining population of middle-aged, middle class (and largely female) users of medically prescribed drugs was replaced by a new group of young male users who preferred heroin to morphine.[2,3] From 1925 to 1935, treatment of drug abusers was virtually nonexistent. The medical community had become aware of, and discouraged by, the high relapse rate among chronic users.[2]

Partly in response to the growing number of narcotic addicts in federal prisons, the federal government established hospitals for the treatment of narcotics dependence at Lexington, Kentucky (in 1935) and Fort Worth, Texas (in 1938). Although these facilities were designed primarily for federal prisoners, they also accepted voluntary patients, who soon made up the majority of their population. Treatment of drug dependence also became available in some state and private mental hospitals. Although some of these facilities treated selected patients sporadically with the newly developing techniques of psychoanalysis and psychotherapy, the basis of most treatment was gradual withdrawal of drugs, followed by a period of inpatient treatment that was supposed to last for several months. However, voluntary patients were free to leave whenever they wished, and most did not stay to complete the full treatment period. Follow-up studies showed that a substantial majority of such patients relapsed to drug abuse.[2]

Officially, only persons dependent on drugs controlled by federal statutes (opium, cocaine and marijuana) could be treated in the federal facilities at Lexington and Fort Worth. An individual severely dependent on barbiturates, for example, could not be admitted. In many parts of the country, a reciprocal bias existed at non-federal treatment facilities: persons dependent on narcotics would be turned away, while those who had problems with sedatives or stimulants would be admitted.[2]

Interest in the treatment of drug dependence became more widespread after World War II, with several pilot treatment programs established in the 1950's. Interest grew even more rapidly in the 1960's, apparently in response to the increasing number of heroin users and the seemingly parallel increase in crime rates in the major cities.[1] In 1961 and 1962, New York and California established statewide treatment programs modelled after the federal hospital in Lexington. Treatment in these programs involved withdrawal, psychiatric care and group therapy. It began with a period of mandatory hospitalization and included compulsory aftercare. However, follow-up studies of both the New York and California programs showed disappointingly high relapse rates.[2]

The early 1960's also saw the emergence of self-regulating drug treatment communities. In 1958, Charles Dederich, a recovered alcoholic, established Synanon, a residential facility in Santa Monica, California. Synanon not only admitted heroin abusers, but also demonstrated that they could remain abstinent, productive and self-governing without professional help. Refusing government assistance, Synanon obtained financial support from individuals, from the business community, and from the sale of products and services.[1,2]

Influenced by Synanon, New York State and New York City encouraged a wider range of treatment approaches, including "therapeutic communities" based on the Synanon model.[1]

In 1964, Vincent Dole, M.D. and Marie Nyswander, M.D., began an experimental drug maintenance program in New York. They used the synthetic opioid, methadone, because it could be administered orally in a single daily dose and because tolerance to its effects developed rapidly. In the Dole and Nyswander program, hospitalized patients were gradually stabilized on daily doses of methadone, then released and required to return to the clinic every day for maintenance doses. Patients also received individual counseling and support services. All of the initial group of patients stayed in the program voluntarily, and most showed dramatic improvements in social functioning. Encouraged by this success, Dole and Nyswander expanded their program and enrolled about 4,000 patients over the next three years. An independent evaluation of their program in 1967 found that 80% of the patients had remained in the program and showed significant improvements in social functioning. Based on these results, the federal government permitted the establishment of other experimental methadone maintenance programs. Subsequent experience showed that initial hospitalization was not necessary, which dramatically lowered program costs. Methadone programs proliferated across the country and, by 1972, methadone maintenance had become one of the most widely used methods for treating heroin addicts.[1,2]

At about the same time the methadone experiment was beginning, researchers at Lexington began to experiment with the use of narcotic antagonists. Although these drugs proved useful in counteracting the effects of opioids, their relatively short durations of action, unpleasant side effects (with cyclazocine) and lack of reinforcing effects (with naloxone) discouraged many patients from remaining in treatment.[2]

Expansion of federal support for a variety of treatment programs in the 1960's differed from previous efforts, in that it was aimed not only at heroin and other opioid drugs, but recognized that problems could be associated with many different drugs. Support for treatment reached its apex in June 1971, when the Special Action Office for Drug Abuse Prevention was created within the Executive Office of the President. For the first time in American history, there was an explicit commitment to make treatment available for a variety of drug-related problems. Because heroin use seemed most closely linked to crime, and because a technology was in place to deal with it, the early expansion of treatment programs did focus on heroin dependence. However, there also was a deliberate effort to initiate and expand non-methadone approaches, innovative treatments and special programs for those whose drug dependence problems did not involve opioids.[2]

There were ironic aspects to the drug treatment efforts of the early 1970's. Jaffe[1] notes that, even among medical and psychiatric professionals, no overwhelming satisfaction was expressed. Proponents of therapeutic communities criticized the poor record of detoxification programs, the ineffectiveness of psychotherapy and the importance attached to professional training. Physicians and psychiatrists were critical of the undocumented claims of the therapeutic communities, and pointed out that damage might be done by the harsh confrontation techniques they employed. Professionals in general were critical of the undocumented claims of ambulatory "drug-free" programs, many of which were operated by ex-addicts whose only claim to expertise was their own drug-using experience. Those who advocated methadone maintenance were critical of both short-term detoxification programs and therapeutic communities. There were few who defended simple short-term detoxification programs, and many who doubted the value of compulsory treatment.

What is remarkable about this period in the history of drug treatment, says Jaffe,[1] is that it fostered a network of different approaches committed to self-examination and exploration of new techniques. The fact remains that no single treatment method yet devised has solved, or promises to solve, all of the complex problems involved in drug abuse. There still is confusion and controversy about the nature of drug dependence and how society should deal with it. Ideally, a variety of methods and approaches should be available to help the multitude of people who abuse drugs today.[2]

CONTEMPORARY APPROACHES TO TREATMENT

Today, drug treatment approaches differ not only in the way they conceptualize the problem of drug dependence, but also in the priorities they assign to various treatment goals. No longer do all approaches use total abstinence as the sole criterion of successful treatment. Instead, there is a growing emphasis on achieving productive and socially acceptable behavior and on improving physical health and interpersonal relationships. Sometimes marked changes occur in these areas when drug use is only modified, rather than totally eliminated.[3]

The zeal with which advocates of particular treatment approaches previously sought the exclusive support of funding agencies, communities and patients has given way to a trend toward a "multimodality" approach, which attempts to integrate the features of several treatment methods into an overall plan that is tailored to the needs of individual patients.[4] The types of treatment employed may include detoxification or methadone maintenance, supported by therapeutic communities, outpatient drug-free programs, use of antagonist drugs, and innovative approaches such as behavior modification and acupuncture. Almost always, some amount of individual counseling is required. These treatment methods, or stages, often are employed in the pattern shown in Table 33.

DETOXIFICATION

Detoxification is a process by which an individual who is physically dependent on a drug is withdrawn from that drug, often by administering gradually decreasing doses of the drug of dependence or a drug that is cross-tolerant to it.[5,7,8] The primary objective of detoxification treatment is to provide symptomatic relief from the withdrawal syndrome while the patient adjusts to a drug-free state.[7]

Short-term detoxification *is not*, in itself, a rehabilitative procedure. Without adequate psychological and social rehabilitation, detoxification usually provides only temporary benefits in terms of reduced drug-taking and associated behaviors.[8]

Detoxification treatment of opioid dependence has been widely rejected as a sole treatment modality, with critics focusing on the undeniable limitations of this short-term therapeutic approach.[8] Newman[7] responds to these criticisms by observing that, although detoxification alone is unable to achieve permanent abstinence, decrease unemployment and in other ways rehabilitate a patient, there are important goals that it *can* achieve. For example, the period of detoxification treatment can be used to orient patients to longer term treatment methods and to facilitate referral. Some patients enroll in a detoxification program preparatory to ambulatory or residential drug-free treatment, because many drug-free programs do not provide treatment for withdrawal symptoms. Instead, they encourage (or re-

TABLE 33

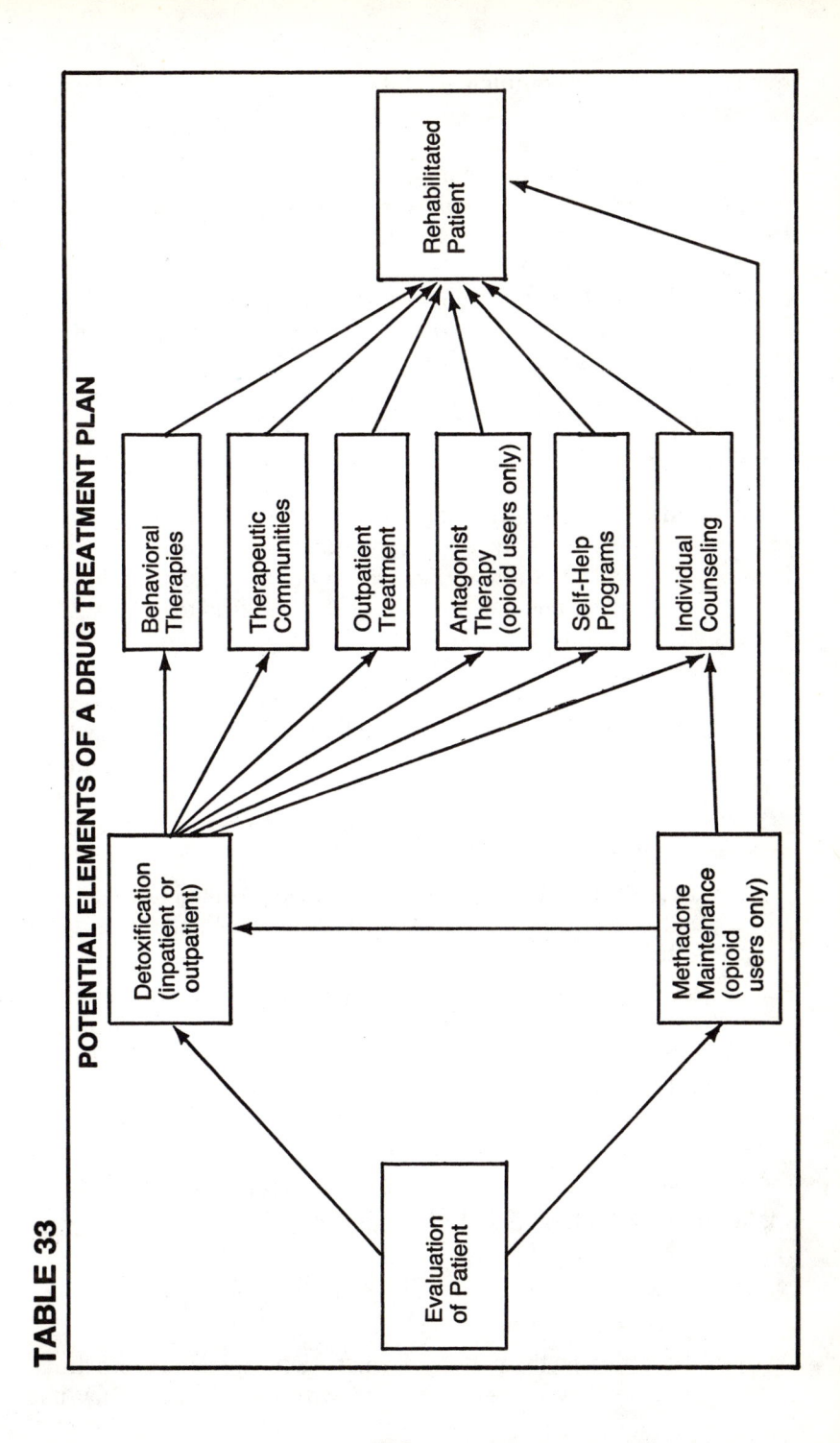

POTENTIAL ELEMENTS OF A DRUG TREATMENT PLAN

- Evaluation of Patient
  - Detoxification (inpatient or outpatient)
  - Methadone Maintenance (opioid users only)
- Behavioral Therapies
- Therapeutic Communities
- Outpatient Treatment
- Antagonist Therapy (opioid users only)
- Self-Help Programs
- Individual Counseling
- Rehabilitated Patient

quire) applicants to complete a brief course of detoxification prior to admission.[7]

More commonly, drug abusers enter a detoxification program because, while they may reject long-term treatment and are unwilling to give up their drug-taking behavior indefinitely, they want temporary relief of the problems associated with drug dependence. Even if such patients frankly admit that their primary goal is to reduce their tolerance to a drug so they can achieve its euphoric effects at lower dose levels, their presence in a detoxification program is an opportunity to encourage them to pursue a drug-free lifestyle[7,8]

Detoxification programs also permit the diagnosis and treatment of many medical problems commonly associated with drug abuse. At a minimum, Newman[7] believes that admission screens should include tests for tuberculosis, venereal disease and other contagious conditions that are common in addict populations. He further recommends Pap smears, pregnancy testing, liver function evaluation, routine hemoglobin determination and microscopic urinalysis as relatively quick, easy and inexpensive procedures that can lead to the detection of medical conditions that require further diagnosis and therapeutic management.

Finally, as part of an ongoing treatment regimen, detoxification can bring a patient through withdrawal and into a drug-free state in which he is more likely to be receptive to aftercare and rehabilitation efforts.

GENERAL PRINCIPLES OF DETOXIFICATION: The following principles of detoxification should be observed regardless of the drug or drugs a patient has been using:

1. Make a preliminary determination of the level of tolerance to, and degree of physical dependence on, each drug the patient has been using. Include any medically prescribed drugs.

2. Assess the patient's physical and emotional status to identify any concurrent illnesses, injuries or severe psychological disturbances that require modification of the usual withdrawal techniques.[5,7,8]

3. If the patient is experiencing a medical or psychiatric crisis, consider stabilizing the patient's drug use pattern and resolving the crisis before initiating withdrawal therapy.[5,7]

4. Wherever possible, substitute a long-acting drug for a short-acting one.[5,7,8]

5. Administer sufficient quantities of the selected drug to suppress severe withdrawal symptoms.[5,7,8]

6. Avoid overdosing the patient. Some patients demand more drugs not because they are experiencing withdrawal symptoms, but

because they miss the disinhibiting effects of intoxication. When in doubt, give no medication, but keep the patient under close observation.[5,7,8]

7. With hospitalized patients, reduce the drug dose by about 10% per day, unless withdrawal symptoms reappear. With ambulatory patients, a slower withdrawal schedule is recommended.[5,7,8]
8. Conform the duration of detoxification to the patient's needs, rather than to a fixed schedule (federal law does, however, limit the administration of methadone for detoxification purposes to 21 days).[5,7,8]
9. Encourage every patient to consider detoxification as the first step in a long-term rehabilitation program.[5,7,8]
10. Develop an aftercare plan that includes follow-up contact to identify the patient's response to treatment and need for further assistance.[5,8]

SELECTING A SETTING FOR DETOXIFICATON: In determining the appropriate environment for detoxification—hospital inpatient, outpatient, or residential facility—the patient's lifestyle, resources, and physical and emotional status should be considered.[5,8]

Inpatient detoxification in a hospital is recommended for (1) a patient dependent on sedative/hypnotic drugs, who may experience life-threatening complications if he is not carefully monitored, and (2) a patient dependent on other drugs, if the patient's medical, surgical, obstetrical or psychiatric status indicates a need for hospital care.

Outpatient detoxification is less costly than inpatient care and thus permits a longer, more gradual withdrawal period. Support services can be provided through referral to community agencies.

Residential detoxification in a facility other than a hospital provides a protective environment, in which needed medical and support services can be made available at lower cost than in a hospital.

Outpatient or *residential* programs also are appropriate for individuals who abuse drugs but are not physically dependent on them. These patients *do not* require withdrawal treatment, but they *do* need help to stop their drug abuse. Treatment for such patients usually involves counseling and support programs that deal with the psychological, social and environmental problems that have contributed to their drug problem.

DETOXIFICATION FROM OPIOIDS, USING METHADONE: Currently, methadone substitution is the preferred and most widely used method for opioid withdrawal.[3,5,7,8] Although it is possible to detoxify a patient with the drug on which he is dependent (such as codeine, meperidine, morphine, etc.), methadone is the only narcotic drug approved by the federal government for use in detoxification and maintenance treatment programs.[8] Propoxyphene hydrochloride (Darvon) and propoxyphene napsylate (Darvon-N) have been used experimentally with good results as substitutes in methadone and heroin detoxification, but their safety and effectiveness for this purpose are not universally accepted. Although they appear to be useful in small analgesic doses to ease withdrawal symptoms, the toxicity of these substances in the relatively large doses needed to completely suppress opioid withdrawal symptoms has made their usefulness as therapeutic agents in opioid detoxification the subject of controversy.[5,8] (Propoxyphene recently was reclassified to narcotic drug status by the Food and Drug Administration.)

Before the detoxification process begins, the patient should be informed that he may experience some mild withdrawal symptoms (often described as "flu-like") during the detoxification process.[3,5,8]

The initial dose of methadone should be large enough to control or mitigate withdrawal symptoms. Commonly, this dose is in the range of 10 to 20 mg of oral methadone. If the withdrawal symptoms are not suppressed, or if they quickly reappear, an additional 5 to 10 mg dose may be given. The total daily methadone dose should not exceed 40 mg, except where there is documented evidence of tolerance to more than 40 mg of methadone per day.[3,8]

The dose level given on the first day should be confirmed by repeating it on the second day, adjusting it as needed. *Patients must be kept under close observation while the optimum dose level is being titrated.*[5,8]

After the patient has been observed for 24 to 36 hours and given methadone as described, a stabilization dose can be calculated. Usually, 1.0 mg of methadone can be substituted for 2.0 mg of heroin, 4.0 mg of morphine or 20 mg of meperidine.[3]

When the patient has been stabilized, detoxification can begin. Because daily dose reductions of 15% generally cause little discomfort, most detoxification schedules call for a reduction of 5 mg per day. At this pace, the majority of patients can be completely withdrawn in seven to ten days, although very mild abstinence symptoms may persist for several days after the last dose of methadone. (Patients detoxified on an outpatient basis may require a slower withdrawal schedule.)[3,5,8]

For patients who experience anxiety or insomnia, a benzodiazepine is preferred to other sedative/hypnotic drugs. Barbiturates should not be prescribed because of their significant abuse potential. Antidepressants of the monoamine oxidase inhibitor type (Marplan, Nardil) have precipitated severe reactions in patients taking meperidine in therapeutic doses, so they should be used cautiously—if at all—in patients receiving methadone.[5,8]

Counseling is an important adjunct to the detoxification process. The patient should be helped to develop coping mechanisms that do not involve drugs, and encouraged to remain in treatment after the detoxification process is completed.[7,8]

Former heroin users who have been stabilized in *high-dose methadone maintenance programs* require special attention during detoxification and a very slow withdrawal schedule. For these patients, the initial detoxification dose should be the *confirmed* daily maintenance dose. This dose can be reduced at the rate of 3 to 5 mg per day.[3,5] When the methadone dose is reduced very slowly, withdrawal symptoms usually do not appear until the daily dose drops below 20 mg. At this point, however, and for months after detoxification has been completed, these patients may experience malaise, fatigue, insomnia, irritability and restlessness, pain, premature ejaculation and gastrointestinal hypermotility. Thus, there is a consensus among researchers[3,5,8] that withdrawal from high-dose methadone maintenance is best achieved through a detoxification process that covers four to six months. Withdrawal schedules shorter than three months are likely to be stressful for these patients, and even for some patients who were maintained on low doses of methadone.

DETOXIFICATION FROM OPIOIDS, USING CLONIDINE: Clonidine hydrochloride, a non-narcotic antihypertensive, is being investigated as a substitute drug for opioid detoxification because single dose studies indicate that .005 mg/kg of clonidine gives substantial relief from the opioid withdrawal syndrome.[5,9]

Development of a non-narcotic substitute for methadone in opioid detoxification is considered desirable for several reasons. First, methadone is a narcotic and patients who are especially eager to "get off" narcotics are sometimes reluctant to use it. Second, post-detoxification treatment with a narcotic antagonist like naltrexone could immediately follow detoxification with clonidine, rather than being delayed while the residual effects of methadone clear the patient's system. Third, maintenance of detoxified patients on small doses of clonidine might eliminate the protracted abstinence syndrome, which persists for months in some methadone patients and which may be the cause of some relapses to opioid use.[9]

Problems associated with the use of clonidine appear to include severe hypotension, sluggishness, drowsiness and dryness of the mouth—all of which occur at high doses—and the possibility of a clonidine withdrawal syndrome when use of the drug is discontinued. Such a syndrome has been identified in patients using clonidine for hypertension who abruptly discontinue their intake of the drug. Withdrawal symptoms in these cases involve a rebound increase in blood pressure, which has been fatal in some hypertensives. However, in studies of opioid detoxification using clonidine, no cases of clinically significant rebound hypertension have been reported.[9]

A final problem with clonidine as an opioid substitute is that it does not suppress all symptoms of withdrawal; however, in most cases, withdrawal symptoms are reduced to a satisfactory level.

Despite these problems, several authorities[5,9,10] consider the early research on clonidine detoxification encouraging and report that its use is now being investigated intensively. Nonetheless, clonidine remains an experimental drug and is not yet approved for general use in detoxification.

DETOXIFICATION FROM PENTAZOCINE: Withdrawal from pentazocine (Talwin) can be accomplished by administering gradually reduced doses of that drug. Pentazocine is a mixed agonist-antagonist, although in clinical practice it is used only for its agonist (analgesic) effects. Because of its antagonist properties, however, it will precipitate immediate withdrawal symptoms in an opioid-dependent person; it never should be given to a patient on methadone maintenance.[5,8]

The use of methadone or other opioids in pentazocine detoxification generally is not recommended because of the possible adverse consequences of substituting a stronger analgesic with greater addictive potential (methadone) for a weaker analgesic with less addictive potential (pentazocine). However, methadone *will* suppress the pentazocine withdrawal syndrome, and there may be certain clinical situations in which methadone is the preferred drug for pentazocine detoxification. For example, in a patient who has been using large doses of parenteral pentazocine or in one who continues to be dependent on pentazocine after several detoxification attempts, use of methadone may be considered.[8]

DETOXIFICATION FROM PROPOXYPHENE: Patients who are physically dependent on either propoxyphene hydrochloride (Darvon) or propoxyphene napsylate (Darvon-N) can be detoxified through use of propoxyphene napsylate. Methadone also will suppress the propoxyphene hydrochloride abstinence syndrome, but, again, many clinicians adhere to the principle that a drug with greater addictive potential should not be substituted for a drug with lower addictive potential.[8]

DETOXIFICATION FROM DEPRESSANTS: Because of the severity and even life-threatening nature of sedative/hypnotic withdrawal, close medical supervision is necessary. Thus, detoxification from barbiturates and other sedative/hypnotic drugs generally should be carried out in a hospital.[11]

The basic principle is to withdraw the patient slowly. Careful monitoring of signs and symptoms is of utmost importance to assure a slow withdrawal and avoid seizures, which may result from too rapid withdrawal. Treatment may follow either of two strategies: (1) slow withdrawal of the drug of dependence, or (2) substitution of a long-acting barbiturate and subsequent withdrawal of the substitute agent.[3,11]

Withdrawal using the drug of dependence is done with an initial, stabilizing dose large enough to produce mild intoxication. Subsequent doses are reduced at the rate of 10% (but no more than 100 mg) per day.[5,11] Even at this rate of withdrawal, recent data from sleep research laboratories suggest that rebound of dreaming intensity (suppressed by doses of hypnotics large enough to produce physical dependence) is sufficient to produce sleep disturbances. Thus, it may be desirable to extend the withdrawal period and reduce the daily dose in smaller increments.[11]

A pentobarbital test does is used by some clinicians to measure the patient's degree of tolerance and dependence and thus help establish the size of the initial, stabilizing dose. Under this method, the patient is given 200 mg of pentobarbital orally. One hour later, the patient is examined for signs of intoxication (such as nystagmus, unsteady gait and slurred speech). If no signs of intoxication are present, an additional dose of 100 mg of pentobarbital is given. Absence of intoxication after this dose is assumed to indicate a significant level of tolerance and physical dependence. (However, some recent studies indicate that this test may not be as discriminating as had previously been believed.)[8,11]

Substitution of a long-acting barbiturate such as phenobarbital follows the same rationale as substituting methadone for heroin. In both cases, substitution of a long-acting drug for a short-acting one permits a withdrawal marked by fewer fluctuations in blood levels throughout the day, thus allowing the safe use of smaller doses.[8,11,12]

Phenobarbital can be used to withdraw patients from all short-acting barbiturates and other sedative/hypnotic drugs. The safety factor for phenobarbital is greater than for the short-acting sedative/hypnotics: fatal doses of phenobarbital are several times larger than toxic doses, and signs of toxicity produced by phenobarbital (such as sustained nystagmus, slurred speech and ataxia) are easy to observe.[3,11,12]

The initial dose of phenobarbital is calculated by substituting one sedative dose (30 mg) of phenobarbital for each hypnotic dose of any sedative/hypnotic the patient reports using. By totalling the number of daily hypnotic doses, the physician can establish the patient's initial requirement for phenobarbital. *In no case should the total daily dose of phenobarbital exceed 500 mg, regardless of the magnitude of dependence claimed by the patient.*[3,8,11,12]

The total daily dose of phenobarbital may be given in a single dose, but divided doses three or four times a day are preferred because they allow more frequent evaluation of the patient for signs of toxicity or withdrawal.[8,12]

If the magnitude of dependence has been overstated by the patient, symptoms of intoxication will occur during the first day or two of treatment. These are managed by omitting one or more doses of phenobarbital and recalculating the daily dose.[8,11,12]

Once the patient is stabilized on phenobarbital, the total daily dose is decreased by 30 mg per day. If signs of *withdrawal* (tremors, muscle weakness, hyperreflexia or postural hypotension) occur, the patient is given a dose of 200 mg of phenobarbital intramuscularly and the total daily dose of phenobarbital is increased by 25%. If signs of *intoxication* occur, the daily dose is reduced by 25% and withdrawal proceeds.[8,12]

Table 34 shows the phenobarbital equivalents for common sedative/hypnotic drugs.

Some researchers[8] prefer to substitute *pentobarbital* rather than phenobarbital in managing barbiturate withdrawal. However, other authorities on the substitution technique prefer phenobarbital as a substitute for barbiturates as well as the other sedative/hypnotic drugs.[5,12]

Detoxification from benzodiazepines is best accomplished by gradually decreasing the daily intake of the drug on which the patient is dependent. There is no need to substitute phenobarbital for the benzodiazepines, since their durations of action and dependence liability are so similar.[8,11]

DETOXIFICATION FROM STIMULANTS: Amphetamine detoxification generally should be accomplished in a controlled environment, where the patient can be kept under close observation, since withdrawal from amphetamines can result in feelings of marked depression and even suicide.[8]

Post-amphetamine depression requires good general psychological support. If tricyclic antidepressants are used, their slow onset of action requires continuation of non-pharmacologic support measures. When the patient is sleeping well and is no longer depressed, the antidepressant should be decreased by 25 mg per week.[8] Caution

TABLE 34

Phenobarbital Withdrawal Equivalents for Common Sedative/Hypnotic Drugs		
Drug	Dose (mg)	Phenobarbital equivalent (mg)
Amobarbital (Amytal)	100	30
Butabarbital (Butisol)	60	30
Chloral hydrate (Noctec, Somnos)	500	30
Ethchlorvynol (Placidyl)	350	30
Glutethimide (Doriden)	250	30
Meprobamate (Equanil, Miltown)	400-600	30
Methaqualone (Quaalude, Sopor)	250-300	30
Methyprylon (Noludar)	300	30
Pentobarbital (Nembutal)	100	30
Secobarbital (Seconal)	100	30

Source: Smith, D. E., Wesson, D. R. and Seymour, R. B. The abuse of barbiturates and other sedative/hypnotics *in* R. I. DuPont, A. Goldstein and J. O'Donnell (eds.) *Handbook on Drug Abuse* (National Institute on Drug Abuse, Rockville, Md., 1979)

is required in administering tricyclic antidepressants to patients who may be schizophrenic or who have paranoid symptomatology, because antidepressants may exacerbate these psychotic symptoms. In such patients, the dose of tricyclic antidepressants may be reduced or a major tranquilizer may be administered concurrently.[8]

If the patient is severely agitated at the time of admission, he may be treated with moderate doses of haloperidol (Haldol), which should be gradually reduced over the first few days of treatment and discontinued as soon as the target symptoms are under control.[8]

The patient may need to sleep more often during the first few weeks of treatment and should be allowed to do so. Additionally, since many high-dose amphetamine users are poorly nourished, adequate protein should be provided in the patient's diet and vitamin supplements may be prescribed.[8]

Following withdrawal, many patients feel an intense desire to return to use of amphetamines and may exert pressure on the physician to prescribe them. *Amphetamines should not be given to such patients.*

DETOXIFICATION FROM MULTIPLE DRUGS: The physician should be alert to the possibility of mixed drug dependence. Appropriate measures for detoxification must be instituted to prevent complications in patients who abuse more than one type of drug.[8,14] Examples of common types of mixed drug dependence follow:

Withdrawal from *opioids and sedative/hypnotics* is marked by some similar symptoms, so the clinical picture is difficult to assess if both drugs are withdrawn at the same time. Therefore, it is preferable to gradually withdraw the sedative/hypnotic first, while preventing opioid withdrawal by administering methadone. When the patient is detoxified from the barbiturate or other sedative/hypnotic, the methadone is withdrawn at the rate of 5 mg per day.[3,8]

When the patient is physically dependent on *opioids and benzodiazepine*, some physicians prefer to forestall opioid withdrawal by administering methadone while partially reducing the dependence on the benzodiazepine. After this partial detoxification is achieved, they gradually withdraw the methadone and then complete detoxification from the benzodiazepine.[3,8]

Management of combined *sedative/hypnotic-alcohol* dependence is similar to that of sedative/hypnotic detoxification. Since alcohol and sedative/hypnotic drugs are cross-tolerant, phenobarbital may be substituted for either. (In establishing the initial dose of phenobarbital, it is important to determine whether the patient used alcohol and sedative/hypnotic drugs simultaneously, as their effects would be additive.) A dose of 15 mg of phenobarbital is substituted for each 30 cc (1 ounce) of 80 to 100 proof alcohol. (One pint of 80 proof alcohol is equivalent to 240 mg of phenobarbital.) The alcohol/phenobarbital equivalent then is added to the amount of phenobarbital calculated to treat withdrawal from the sedative/hypnotic.[3,8]

In detoxifying patients who are physically dependent on both *opioids and alcohol*, the safest method is to withdraw one drug at a time. It is preferable to treat the alcohol dependence first with gradually decreasing doses of chlordiazepoxide or a similar drug, while preventing opioid withdrawal with methadone. The methadone is gradually withdrawn only after alcohol detoxification is completed.[8]

THERAPY WITH ANTAGONIST DRUGS

Treatment with drugs that block the physiological and psychological effects of drugs of abuse is called "antagonist therapy." Such antagonists exert their effects by blocking the access of agonists to the receptor sites at the molecular level. When these sites are occupied by an antagonist, agonists simply have no pharmacologic effect.[14,15]

Because of their greater affinity for the receptors, antagonists displace opioid agonists from the receptor sites. Thus, a patient who is dependent on heroin must be detoxified before he can be treated with antagonists. Once a patient is completely free of opioid drugs, no symptoms are produced by the administration of an antagonist.[3,15]

The rationale for antagonist therapy is based on the concept of extinction, which assumes that euphoriant effects reinforce drug-taking behavior. Thus, if a detoxified patient is given an antagonist and then relapses to drug use, he will experience few (if any) reinforcing effects. This absence of reinforcement is supposed to gradually extinguish the patient's desire to self-administer the agonist drug.[15,16]

Critics of antagonist therapy maintain that antagonist drugs do nothing positive for the individual in treatment, because their only action is to block the effects of an agonist and because there is no pharmacological conseqence (such as withdrawal symptoms) for failing to take the antagonist. In fact, compliance with treatment programs employing antagonist therapy has been quite low.[15,16]

At least three solutions have been proposed to meet these objections. First, antagonists could be administered in forms whose durations of action are a month or more. Second, some form of external coercion might be applied to impel patients to remain in antagonist therapy programs. For example, prisoners released on parole could be subject to reincarceration for lack of compliance. Third, antagonists with some mild agonist euphoriant properties might be developed, so that use of the antagonist is, in itself, reinforcing.[16] These proposals are the subject of widespread discussion among investigators.

The most promising antagonist for the treatment of opioid dependence appears to be *naltrexone*, which is a modification of the naloxone molecule. Naltrexone is essentially a pure antagonist without agonist (euphoriant) effects. Unlike naloxone, it has a long duration of action. Naltrexone has virtually no unpleasant side effects and appears to be safe and effective, although definitive studies are still under way.[5,15,16]

Most heroin-dependent subjects who take naltrexone do so for only a few weeks, but a few have used the drug for as long as a year. Preliminary studies show that it provides significant support for heroin abstinence and is positively correlated with the achievement of social rehabilitation goals. However, only a small proportion of heroin-dependent persons have volunteered to take naltrexone, so it may have a relatively small role in the total treatment effort. Senay and Lewis[5] speculate that naltrexone is likely to become "an important but limited adjunct to treatment during the transition from detoxification to continued abstinence."

Cyclazocine also has been used experimentally to block the effects of opioid drugs, but its widespread use has been hampered by its tendency to produce dysphoria and its unacceptability to many opioid abusers. It is not presently approved for use in antagonist therapy.[14]

Buprenorphine has shown promise as an opioid in early experiments, but its usefulness appears limited to cases involving mild physical dependence.[17]

In rats, *alpha-methyltyrosine* has prevented self-administration of morphine and amphetamines. Other researchers have reported partial blockage of the stimulant effects of amphetamines in rats by use of *fenfluramine*. No true antagonist to the effects of sedative/hypnotic drugs appears to exist.[14]

METHADONE MAINTENANCE

Pioneered by Dole and Nyswander, methadone maintenance currently is the treatment of choice for many chronic abusers of opioid drugs. The consensus of drug treatment experts is that programs using methadone in support of their efforts are useful for 40% to 60% of heroin-dependent patients.[5,6]

Methadone is a synthetic opioid that is subjectively similar to morphine, in that effective analgesia follows the injection of 5 to 10 mg. In non-tolerant individuals, large doses of methadone produce a degree of euphoria comparable to heroin. The duration of euphoric effects from methadone is similar to that for heroin (three to four hours), but the onset of withdrawal symptoms is delayed (12 to 24 hours for methadone, versus six to twelve hours for heroin).[2,5] This extended period of action and the fact that methadone is more effective than heroin when taken orally makes methadone very useful in treating opioid dependence.[2,5,6]

The appropriate methadone dose remains a controversial question. The major difference is the degree of cross-tolerance to other opioids: at high doses (70 to 100 mg) a sufficient degree of cross-tolerance develops so that even large doses of opioids or additional methadone will not produce euphoria or overdose. Dole referred to this effect as "narcotic blockade."[6] It also has been noted that low doses sometimes are associated with the development of withdrawal symptoms in less than 24 hours, and that the accompanying discomfort and anxiety may predispose patients to use alcohol, anxiolytics, sedatives or additional opioids.[6] On the other hand, the ability of a high dose of methadone to block the effects of withdrawal may not be so important as the ability of a relatively low dose (15 to 40 mg) to relieve drug craving. Thus, Senay and Lewis[5] find that patients given a low dose of methadone daily may begin to complain of discomfort at 16 to 18 hours after administration, but seem to adapt readily to the 24-hour interval between doses.

Urinalysis for the detection of methadone, heroin and other drugs has become an integral part of maintenance programs (and is required by federal regulations—see Chapter 9). Heroin addicts often are unreliable in reporting their drug-taking activities, so urinalysis is used to obtain independent data. Urinalysis also may help to deter relapse because the patient may fear that further drug abuse will be detected.[5]

A typical methadone maintenance clinic provides daily administration of oral methadone, as well as support services such as social, legal and vocational counseling. Group therapy also may be offered, but the confrontational nature of group sessions achieves an emotional intensity that can be too anxiety-provoking for some patients.[5]

Provision of chemical support and affiliation with a treatment program seem to be the most important elements of methadone maintenance, but extensive psychotherapy also may be necessary in certain cases. Although the role of antianxiety and antidepressant drugs in methadone maintenance treatment is not yet clear, such agents do appear useful in providing symptomatic relief for some patients.[5,6]

Current federal regulations permit enrollment in methadone maintenance programs only to persons who have been dependent on opioids for more than one year or who meet other specific requirements (see Chapter 9).

FREQUENT CLINICAL PROBLEMS IN METHADONE MAINTENANCE: Methadone often produces side effects, including sedation, constipation, excessive sweating, urinary retention and changes in sex drive. Senay and Lewis[5] cite studies showing that prolonged use of any opioid reduces the elaboration of testosterone, but note that the significance of this effect is not clear. They add that pruritis, urticaria and nausea also are possible side effects of methadone use, as is an increase in appetite that may lead to weight control problems. The most serious complication in patients on methadone maintenance is alcohol abuse.[5] A patient who shows signs of alcohol intoxication should not receive methadone while intoxicated, since methadone and alcohol are synergistic and combined use may be fatal.[5,6]

INDICATIONS FOR METHADONE MAINTENANCE: Methadone maintenance is indicated for heroin-dependent persons who are not strongly motivated to achieve immediate abstinence. While maintenance therapy does not offer the prospect of full social rehabilitation, it does reduce illicit drug use and associated criminal activity, facilitate employment and increase self-esteem, often with attendant improvements in family and community functioning. Thus, methadone maintenance can provide help to a large number of persons who otherwise might return to full-scale criminal activity and illicit drug use.[5,6]

OTHER TYPES OF OPIOID MAINTENANCE: The drug LAAM (levo-alpha-acetylmethadol) is a congener of methadone, but differs from it in that a single dose can suppress opioid abstinence symptoms for two to three days, whereas one dose of methadone suppresses symptoms for 24 hours. Research with LAAM suggests that it is therapeutically similar to methadone, but offers greater flexibility in dispensing schedules.[5]

Although LAAM does offer significant benefits over methadone, it is unlikely to replace methadone on a wide scale, at least partially because it has fewer subjective effects. For example, the patient on methadone does not experience euphoria at maintenance doses, but he *does* feel the sedative effects of having taken a drug. This feeling is less pronounced with LAAM. Thus, the usefulness of LAAM may be limited to patients who do not need the subjective effects of methadone and who prefer the dose scheduling flexibility attainable with LAAM.[5]

At present, LAAM is an investigational drug and has not been approved for general use.[5]

THERAPEUTIC COMMUNITIES

Therapeutic communities are residential treatment programs that attempt to deal with the psychological causes of drug dependence by changing the personality and character of the drug abuser.[2] Synanon, the first therapeutic community for drug abusers, was created in the 1950's by Charles Dederich after the model of Alcoholics Anonymous.[1,2,5]

Treatment in a typical therapeutic community lasts from one to two years, with the goal of enabling the client to reenter the larger community as a successfully functioning, drug-free individual. Some communities patterned after Synanon provide an alternative lifestyle and social milieu for their residents, with the goal of attracting residents to remain in the therapeutic community indefinitely, rather than returning to the larger society.[2,5]

Entry into a therapeutic community usually requires considerable initiative on the part of the prospective resident. In the course of a stressful "intake interview," the applicant must actively commit himself to the program. This method helps screen out candidates with insufficient motivation to benefit from a therapeutic community and provides an explicit and self-defined reason for the applicant to enter treatment.[5,18]

The social status of new residents in a therapeutic community typically is low. Novice members of the community are restricted as to telephone calls, personal possessions, visitors and other privileges. The neophyte may even be given rather poor sleeping quarters and assigned to menial tasks such as washing dishes or sweeping floors. Residents are expected to function well in such tasks, manifest concern about fellow residents, participate in group therapy sessions and obey the "house rules" (no drugs, physical violence or disobeying orders). If these expectations are met, residents are granted increasing degrees of autonomy.[5,18,19]

Reentry into the outside community usually is accomplished in several steps. The patient progresses from being a regular resident with some personal freedom (weekend passes, visitors, etc.) to living outside the therapeutic community while attending occasional group meetings within the community. After a considerable time in outpatient status, a patient "graduates" from the therapeutic community (assuming he has not relapsed to drug use) and is formally considered rehabilitated.[5,18]

Senay and Lewis[5] compare a well-functioning therapeutic community to a very large and tightly run family, and note that the term "family" often is used to describe the entire membership of such a community. They find that therapeutic communities are marked by personal openness and mutual regard on the part of residents, as well as a sense of order and emphasis on cleanliness.

PROBLEMS WITH TREATMENT IN THERAPEUTIC COMMUNITIES: The most serious problem with therapeutic communities is a high rate of premature termination of treatment. Although accurate statistics are elusive, it has been estimated that slightly less than 10% of new members actually complete treatment. Most terminations occur in the first few months of treatment, but they continue at a lower rate up to the time of "graduation."[5,18]

A large proportion of therapeutic community graduates obtain jobs in drug abuse treatment programs, and their continued involvement in the rehabilitation process may help them avoid personal relapses to drug use. However, therapeutic communities tend to produce graduates who are better fitted to this form of employment than any other, which may indicate a lack of breadth in their rehabilitation goals.[5,19]

Some aspects of community life, such as the extreme control over the actions of individual members and the intolerance of minor deviations from the rules, may be disquieting to certain persons. New residents usually are expected to detoxify from heroin without chemotherapeutic supports, which is too difficult for some persons to achieve. However, the expectation that members will continue to participate in community activities while the withdrawal process is under way seems to yield a reduction in the number and severity of subjective withdrawal symptoms.[5]

INDICATIONS FOR THE THERAPEUTIC COMMUNITY APPROACH: A therapeutic community may be the treatment of choice for highly motivated drug abusers who have been deeply involved in drug use. On the other hand, treatment in such a setting might be dangerous for persons who are unable to identify or disclose their feelings. The milieu generally is not supportive of individuals who are unable to function well.[18,19]

Treatment in therapeutic communities generally is more expensive than methadone maintenance; however, such treatment has a greater potential for evoking significant, long-term changes in the lifestyle of the drug abuser. Moreover, it can provide treatment to individuals for whom methadone support is inappropriate.[5,19]

MODIFIED THERAPEUTIC COMMUNITIES: There have been many attempts to modify the therapeutic community approach to reach subgroups of drug abusers who otherwise are unable to benefit from this mode of treatment. Some of these modified approaches offer methadone support during the withdrawal period, for example. Such "mixed" treatment of methadone-supported and abstinent patients allows greater program flexibility, so that treatment can be tailored to the specific needs of individual patients.[5]

OUTPATIENT DRUG-FREE TREATMENT

"Outpatient drug-free treatment" describes several program models that have little in common except that they do not use drugs to treat dependence and they are not residential. The term is defined by the National Institute on Drug Abuse as "a treatment regimen that does not include any chemical agent or medication. However, drugs may be used as an adjunct to treatment or to treat any medical problems the client may have. Temporary use of medication (e.g., tranquilizers) for treating psychiatric problems may occur in drug-free modalities. The primary treatment method is traditional counseling."[20]

Although there are many differences in the scope and level of services offered by outpatient drug-free treatment programs, most provide group or individual psychotherapy, vocational and social counseling, family counseling, vocational training, education and community outreach. Some programs are social or "rap" centers where patients visit occasionally. Others are free clinics that provide a wide range of health services. Still others offer structured methadone detoxification and monitor patient drug use through urinalysis.[2]

The services most commonly offered in outpatient drug-free treatment programs are described below.

CLIENT COUNSELING: Counseling is the backbone of most outpatient drug-free programs. Although the kind of counseling offered, as well as its orientation and frequency, vary with client needs and progress in treatment, most counseling techniques derive from traditional psychotherapy. Individual and group counseling are the most widely used approaches, although some programs also offer family therapy and consultation with individuals who are directly involved with the client, such as school officials, parole and probation officers.[20,21]

FREE CLINICS: More than 500 free clinics nationwide provide direct medical, dental, psychological and rehabilitation services to drug abusers. They also function as a credible source of drug information for young drug users who distrust "establishment" drug education. The staffs of free clinics generally include physicians, nurses, laboratory technicians, counselors, and other trained professional and paraprofessional personnel.[5]

DROP-IN CENTERS: "Rap centers" or "drop-in centers" constitute a broad treatment category that lacks precise programmatic or administrative definitions. The centers represent a range of service delivery systems, from informal (often volunteer) storefront operations to formally funded community-based programs that may be affiliated with larger agencies. The common theme of these centers is to engage and foster peer relationships through various sports, crafts, community or religious activities.[20,21]

FAMILY THERAPY: Engaging families in the treatment process is a concept that is winning wide support among outpatient drug-free programs, which have neither the chemotherapeutic tools of maintenance and antagonist therapy nor the support of a 24-hour residential community as underpinnings of the rehabilitation effort. In fact, some researchers argue that, without family involvement, it is unlikely an outpatient program can be very helpful to its clients.[20,22]

Since many families of drug abusers have a vested psychological interest in having the abuser remain dependent, therapy for the family may be as essential as counseling for the individual.[21,22]

PROBLEMS OF OUTPATIENT DRUG-FREE TREATMENT: Most outpatient drug-free programs have relatively limited resources with which to meet a wide range of patient needs, so the development of referral linkages with other providers of service is essential. Too often, systems to provide these critical support services exist only on paper or are too overwhelmed by demand to be effective.[21,22]

Other areas in whch deficiencies may occur include accurate

assessment of client needs, correct identification of the services offered by the agency to which a referral is made, and careful follow-up and evaluation of the effectiveness of a referral. As Kleber and Slabetz[20] observe, "drug abusers are often not the most appreciative receivers of services, and active involvement of the referring agency may be required at all points in which the client is involved with an outside agency."

INDICATIONS FOR OUTPATIENT DRUG-FREE TREATMENT: Opioid abusers seeking their first long-term treatment experience are appropriate candidates for outpatient drug-free programs for several reasons. First, many such persons do not meet the federal requirements for chemotherapeutic approaches such as methadone maintenance (see Chapter 9). Second, outpatient drug-free treatment is a low intervention approach when compared to methadone maintenance or antagonist therapy. Third, an array of higher interventions is available to patients who need them. Thus, an important function of a low intervention program such as outpatient drug-free treatment is an evaluative one. The client who seeks treatment for the first time often presents little historical information on which to base decisions as to an appropriate level of intervention. In these cases, assignment to an outpatient drug-free program provides an appropriate setting in which to assess a client's strengths, weaknesses and further treatment needs.[20,22]

Outpatient drug-free programs also can provide continuing support to persons who have successfully completed other forms of treatment. The continuation of outpatient therapeutic contact following completion of another treatment regimen often spells the difference between recovery and relapse, and can facilitate reentry into the community. Half-way houses also have an important role in the reentry process.

INNOVATIVE THERAPIES

"Drug abuse is such a frustrating condition," observe O'Brien and Ng,[23] "that, even now, novel treatments for it are continually being tried." Some of these efforts have produced more substantial and more widely accepted results than others. Many are still considered experimental, while others—such as behavior modification and acupuncture—are coming into use in treatment programs across the country.

BEHAVIOR MODIFICATION: Behavioral therapies have proliferated in recent years, as researchers seek to identify the elements of behavior that form the antecedants, concomitants and consequences of substance abuse.[24]

Behaviorists view substance abuse as a learned behavior that is maintained and reinforced by conditioning factors. Thus, the behavioral approach to treatment is two-fold: (1) it attempts to reduce the reinforcing properties of drugs, and (2) it seeks to instill behaviors that are incompatible with drug use. Techniques used to implement this approach include aversive conditioning, relaxation training, systematic desensitization, assertiveness training, and contingent reinforcement methods such as a token economy.[25,26]

Counterconditioning procedures may include electrical and chemical aversion techniques, but more commonly involve "covert conditioning" or "sensitization." Beginning with the initial craving for drugs, a patient is asked to imagine as clearly as possible each link in the chain of events leading to drug-taking. Instead of pleasant drug effects, the patient is asked to imagine becoming severely ill as a consequence of drug use. When a patient imagines avoidance of drugs, on the other hand, he is told to picture pleasant scenes.[23]

Biofeedback relaxation therapy, using electromyographic (EMG) biofeedback to teach muscle relaxation, adds a nonpharmacological coping device to the drug abuser's repertoire of behaviors. When such patients are in situations that usually evoke feelings of anxiety, tension or drug craving, they can attempt to counter those feelings with relaxation rather than drugs.[5,23]

Extinction or desensitization procedures are based on an assumption that conditioned responses help sustain drug-taking behavior. The therapy attempts to extinguish these responses by exposing the patient to situations associated with drug-taking, while depriving the patient of drug effects. As patients are exposed to situations that are increasingly evocative of drug use, hypnosis and relaxation techniques are used to keep the patients from responding to those situations in the usual way: with anxiety and drug ingestion.[23,25,26]

Hypnosis appears to be most valuable when it is used as an adjunct to a comprehensive treatment approach.[5,23] In various treatment programs, hypnosis has been used to link some aspects of drug-taking behavior to negative consequences such as nausea, anxiety and other negative reinforcers (as a type of counterconditioning), as well as to produce a reward response by recreating the imagery of a pleasurable drug experience without the use of a drug (as a substitute gratification).[23]

The usefulness of hypnosis has not yet been tested in controlled studies, despite some promising early reports. The data now available suggest that nonspecific or placebo effects probably are important factors in the success of hypnosis as a treatment technique. It is not yet clear whether hypnosis offers any advantages over other behavior modification methods.[23]

ACUPUNCTURE: The use of acupuncture in the treatment of drug abuse represents a recent application of a very old treatment technique. Its use in the treatment of drug dependence derives from an observation by H. L. Wen of Hong Kong in 1972 that, when acupuncture was used to induce anesthesia for neurosurgery, patients who were withdrawing from opium reported a reduction in withdrawal symptoms during the acupuncture induction. Wen and a colleague subsequently reported on a series of 40 heroin and opium addicts for whom acupuncture, combined with electrical stimulation, was effective in relieving the symptoms of opioid withdrawal.[23]

Since that initial report, several researchers have employed acupuncture to alleviate the opioid withdrawal syndrome and to facilitate opioid detoxification.[27]

Preliminary evidence suggests that manual or electrical needling may activate certain central neurohumoral mechanisms (including the endorphin system).[28] However, it is not yet clear which of the components of acupuncture treatment (needles, stimulation, sites or nature of stimulation) are the critical factors in evoking such responses. It is premature to attribute any causal relationship between the improvement in subjective symptoms reported by some patients and a particular acupuncture technique.[23]

Likewise, while the results of acupuncture treatment published to date seem quite promising, the claims for success of acupuncture in treating drug dependence appear to be based largely on anecdotal reports.[5,23,28]

CONCLUSIONS: The innovative therapies described here reflect the interest of researchers in developing more effective treatments for drug dependence. While the originators of new treatment techniques often are enthusiastic about their results, controlled studies with objective outcome measures are needed to determine efficacy, and even the results of controlled studies may be applicable only to the populations examined.[23,25,26]

ASSESSING PATIENT NEEDS

Indications for treatment vary with the patient's resources and motivation, the drugs being used, and the social and cultural factors that influence the particular pattern of abuse. Although it is likely that changing public and professional attitudes toward drug use will continue to create "grey areas" where the indications for treatment are unclear, there is general agreement that it is appropriate to give treatment for the adverse medical consequences of drug abuse and for the compulsive drug user who voluntarily seeks help.[3]

Drug abusers have a variety of reasons for their drug using behavior, and just as wide a variety of reasons for seeking treatment. Analysis of these reasons helps identify the patient's strengths and weaknesses, while a determination of those strengths and weaknesses serves as an indicator of the patient's potential success or failure in a given treatment program.[11]

The characteristics of the individual patient and of the environment to which he will return have a significant effect on treatment outcome. Influential characteristics, says Jaffe,[1] include age, ethnicity, education, history of drug use, history of criminal or other antisocial activity, family background, and family history of drug use or psychiatric disorder. Recognition that each patient has unique dynamics, characteristics and motivations is critical to effective treatment planning.[3,5,11]

IDENTIFYING PATIENT RESOURCES

For the physician to achieve an understanding of the patient's lifestyle and resources, information must be obtained from the patient in a well organized, focused interview. One useful strategy is to organize the interview format around particular areas of the patient's life history. The information obtained then can be summarized in a case history format, from which an individualized treatment plan may be developed.[11] To obtain a complete history of the patient's drug abuse, the physician should solicit information about the age at onset, types of substances abused (including alcohol), means of use (oral, injection, smoking, etc.) and the number and types of previous treatment episodes.

In interviewing a drug-dependent patient, the physician always should be aware that the patient may be giving false information. This reflects the "conning" behavior that is so important for survival in the street drug culture. The physician should not regard this behavior as a personal affront, but accept it as part of the patient's behavior pattern.[5,11]

The difficulty in obtaining an accurate history means the phyician must place great reliance on observation of the patient and on his own familiarity with the signs and symptoms of chronic drug abuse.[3]

SOCIAL FUNCTIONING: The patient's employment and educational history should be noted, as should information on family life and social activities. The physician should take social functioning into account as he inquires into the patient's readiness for treatment and helps him define specific treatment goals (complete withdrawal, alleviation of medical problems, etc.).

PSYCHOLOGICAL FUNCTIONING: It is not necessary for a primary care physician to make a precise psychiatric diagnosis, but he should be able to determine the existence of psychopathology, so that (if necessary) the patient can be referred for further evaluation and treatment.

The presence of even a severe psychological disturbance does not mean the patient's drug abuse problem is untreatable, but it does indicate that the treatment plan may have to be modified to take the disturbance into account. Therefore, the physician should ask questions to evaluate the presence of disturbances in mood, suicide and violence potential, impulse control, conditioned responses to drug-related stimuli, and thought disorders.[5,11]

SEXUAL FUNCTIONING: After the physician has developed sufficient rapport with the patient, he should take a complete history of the patient's sexual functioning. The current level of sexual functioning should be assessed so that the effects of treatment on this area of behavior can be evaluated. In patients whose drug use began during adolescence, when sexual development is occurring and feelings of inadequacy are common, the use of drugs may represent an attempt to repair the user's damaged self-esteem. For such patients, inadequate sexual functioning may be either a cause or an effect of drug abuse.[5,11]

MEDICAL HISTORY AND EXAMINATION: A medical history should be taken and a physical examination performed to determine whether there are any physical reasons the usual treatment techniques should be modified.[2,3,11] For example, a slower-than-normal withdrawal schedule would be indicated in opioid-dependent patients who also have angina pectoris, ulcerative colitis, pulmonary insufficiency or other debilitating illnesses. In fact, patients who are experiencing severe pain as the result of a medical condition are not appropriate candidates for withdrawal unless alternative means of managing their pain can be found.[3]

In performing the physical examination, the physician should be alert to the more common signs and symptoms of drug abuse (see Chapter 5), as well as to possible medical complications that are either directly or indirectly related to drug abuse (see Chapter 7).

ESTIMATING THE DEGREE OF DEPENDENCE

It is difficult to estimate the degree of dependence on a drug or drugs from the patient history alone, because patients often distort their history of drug use. Their motives for such distortions vary widely, as does the manner in which the history is distorted. For example, heroin users often are unaware of the purity of their drug supply. Many exaggerate their use of heroin or claim to be using large quantities of barbiturates or other sedatives, in hopes that the physician will administer larger quantities of opioids or hypnotics. On the other hand, some persons may completely deny that they are using barbiturates, even when they have been taking amounts sufficient to produce a dangerous degree of physical dependence. Thus, the possibility of physical dependence on a depressant drug always should be considered when a patient who has received enough opioids to suppress withdrawal symptoms continues to demonstrate sleeplessness and excitability.[3]

If a patient is experiencing withdrawal symptoms when he seeks treatment, an experienced clinician usually can identify objective signs that are useful in determining the degree of dependence. For opioids, the Himmelsbach Rating Scale, which rates the severity of withdrawal in an opioid-dependent individual, has been useful.[5] However, objective signs are not always present, particularly if the patient recently injected opioids in amounts sufficient to suppress withdrawal symptoms without causing intoxication.[5,11]

A test with the antagonist naloxone may be used to estimate the patient's degree of dependence on opioid drugs. (This test should not be used on pregnant women, as it may induce abortion.)[11]

Unfortunately, no similar test is available to assess physical dependence on drugs other than opioids. Where non-opioid drug use is suspected, some physicians withhold all drugs and observe the patient for clinical signs of withdrawal (see Chapter 6). Another method is to administer a short-acting drug of the same class as the drug on which the patient is believed to be dependent. Since tolerance to drug effects usually accompanies physical dependence, a physically dependent patient would be able to take a standard dose of the drug (or more) without showing any signs of intoxication.[5,11]

It should be recognized that the severity of physical dependence does not necessarily correlate with the severity of psychological dependence. Thus, a patient may be psychologically dependent but not physically dependent, and vice versa. Also, a positive urine test does not demonstrate dependence; it merely indicates recent drug use.[11]

DEVELOPING A TREATMENT PLAN

Once the patient's needs and resources have been evaluated, it is possible to develop a treatment plan that is designed to do the patient the most good, with the least risk of harm. Because there is no "typical" drug-dependent person, treatment goals and methods must range widely. Tailoring the treatment plan to meet a patient's specific needs can significantly improve the potential for success.

MATCHING PATIENT NEEDS TO TREATMENT RESOURCES

ABUSERS OF OPIOIDS: Persons who abuse opioid drugs—particularly heroin—generally differ from abusers of other classes of drugs in that they tend (1) to be younger, (2) to have engaged in antisocial activities and (3) to abuse ancillary drugs. In view of these special characteristics, treatment of chronic opioid abusers almost always includes individual counseling and support for the patient's family in addition to detoxification or enrollment in a methadone maintenance program. Antagonist therapy may be desirable for specific patients.[14,29]

The middle-class individual who abuses prescription opioids, on the other hand, may be more similar to an alcoholic in lifestyle and history than to the "street" abuser of opioids. Referral to a program that deals primarily with street users generally is not desirable for this type of patient.[29]

ABUSERS OF DEPRESSANTS, STIMULANTS, HALLUCINOGENS AND PHENCYCLIDINES: After determining the need for detoxification and ruling out any major preexisting psychiatric disorder, the physician should determine (1) whether the patient is abusing street drugs or misusing drugs prescribed by a physician, (2) whether the patient is abusing more than one type of drug, (3) under what circumstances the patient misuses drugs and (4) whether the patient is a member of the street drug culture or a middle-class working individual.[29] Therapeutic communities have had notable success in treating chronic members of the street drug culture, whereas outpatient drug-free treatment may be the most appropriate choice for middle-class individuals who are strongly motivated to continue their employment and family lives without interruption.[5]

ABUSERS OF CANNABINOIDS: It usually is not necessary to establish a formal rehabilitation program for persons who are "recreational" users of marijuana.[29] While such casual use is not without hazard and may indicate a need for education and counseling, it does not, in itself, represent a treatable disorder.[3] Regular counseling sessions with the primary care physician or attendance at a "drop-in center" generally will suffice in such cases. Chronic high-dose users of marijuana and other cannabinoids, however, may require extensive medical and psychological support.

ABUSERS OF INHALANTS: The pharmacological properties of inhalable substances generally make detoxification treatment unnecessary, although more than experimental use of such substances may indicate a need for counseling, as well as careful medical examination to detect physical sequelae.

ABUSERS OF MULTIPLE DRUGS: The multi-drug abusing population is highly diverse in age, socioeconomic status and reasons for using drugs. Abusers whose primary motives for drug-taking are social and recreational should be treated differently than persons who are abusing multiple drugs in an effort to alleviate pain, anxiety or other psychological discomfort. Adolescents who are using drugs for social and recreational purposes often are best served by day treatment centers, while persons who abuse multiple drugs to meet physical and psychiatric needs generally require a more structured treatment setting.[14,29]

SPECIAL CONSIDERATIONS: The drug-dependent patient who also has *serious medical problems* usually is best treated on a general medical ward. In such cases, the primary treatment is medical, but support personnel can be enlisted to help carry out detoxification (if needed) and enhance the patient's receptiveness to long-term treatment.[5,29]

Patients with serious *primary affective disorders* should be referred to a psychiatrist. If these patients have *active suicidal ideation*, they should be treated in a psychiatric facility where appropriate patient safeguards can be provided. After detoxification, any indicated pharmacologic treatment of the affective disorder can be initiated.[11,29]

SELECTING A TREATMENT SETTING: In the absence of overriding medical or psychological considerations, selection of an inpatient or outpatient treatment setting should be based on the preferences of the patient and his family. Although there are no absolute indications for hospitalization after detoxification, patients who have major medical or emotional problems, or who face severe crises, usually function best in a structured environment. Also, time away from life stresses is an important part of treatment for many drug abusers.[29]

It is important for the physician to recognize certain hazards associated with prolonged inpatient treatment, including loss of income or employment, loss of contact with peers, or family dissolution through separation. In addition, the inpatient environment is largely an artificial one, and the lessons learned there may not be readily transferable to everyday living. Although inpatient care is an important treatment option, the decision as to whether to use such care and for how long should reflect careful consideration of its negative and positive aspects.[3,14,29]

TABLE 35

PHASES OF DRUG ABUSE TREATMENT

Categories of service	Phase 1 Crisis service (1-2 days)	Phase 2 Short-term stabilization (0-4 weeks)	Phase 3 Long-term stabilization (4-24 weeks)	Phase 4 Rehabilitation (6 months-2 years)
Medical	Treat— Overdose Acute withdrawal symptoms Acute medical problems	Detoxify patient	Evaluate and treat chronic medical problems	Arrange for ongoing medical/psychiatric care
Psychological	Provide crisis intervention Deal with— Suicidal and homicidal thoughts Acute anxiety reactions Acute psychotic reactions	Provide— Psychological support during detoxification Group and individual psychotherapy	Continue short-term psychotherapy Initiate biofeedback relaxation therapy	Provide analytical psychotherapy for depression, anxiety
Residential	Arrange— Emergency housing Hospitalization	Arrange supportive environment for detoxification	Arrange halfway house placement Investigate alternative residential placements	Initiate long-term living situation
Economic	Arrange emergency social service funds	Initiate disability claim	Assess feasibility of return to work	Assist in return to employment, if possible
Work/educational	Assist in arranging leave of absence from work/school		Evaluate potential for— Vocational rehabilitation Return to school	Refer for vocational rehabilitation Assist in return to school
Legal	Assist in diversion from criminal justice system		Assist in resolving pending legal charges	Develop follow-through plan for conditions of probation or necessary court appearances

Source: Wesson, D. R. and Smith, D. E. Treatment of the polydrug abuser *in* R. I. DuPont, A. Goldstein and J. O'Donnell (eds.) *Handbook on Drug Abuse* (National Institute on Drug Abuse, Rockville, Md., 1979)

INTEGRATING TREATMENT APPROACHES

Wesson and Smith[14] suggest that, while drug abuse treatment often is conceptualized in terms of specific treatment methods for particular drugs of abuse (such as methadone maintenance for heroin abuse), it may be more useful to conceptualize treatment as a series of strategic interventions that can be adapted to various individuals and settings. The timing of such interventions is critical, as a treatment method that may be highly effective at one point in a patient's efforts to move away from drug use may be entirely inappropriate at a different point. For this reason, they suggest that comprehensive treatment (especially of persons who abuse multiple drugs), be separated into clinically useful phases (see Table 35).

While many of the larger drug treatment programs offer access to most or all of these services through a single source, the individual physician also can obtain many of the same services for his patients through judicious referral to community-based service agencies. Of course, not all patients require assistance in every phase depicted in Table 35. For example, while many patients who enter treatment need crisis intervention for acute overdose or withdrawal symptoms (Phase 1), others may be ready for detoxification (Phase 2). At times, a patient's treatment may revert to a previously completed phase, as when a detoxified patient resumes drug use and overdoses.[14]

The importance of the model proposed by Wesson and Smith is that it provides a logical framework for treatment planning. Most treatment plans thus constructed involve the coordinated use of several approaches whose effects are complementary and often mutually reinforcing.[14]

GENERAL CONSIDERATIONS IN
DEVELOPING A TREATMENT PLAN

In selecting a treatment modality, the physician should recognize that the recovery rate for any form of intervention sometimes is surprisingly high.[3] In fact, Jaffe[1] finds the evidence "overwhelming that, while in treatment in a variety of programs, and for varying periods thereafter, a significant proportion of drug users exhibit substantial improvement in a number of areas: more job stability, less illicit drug use, and less antisocial behavior." He suggests that the question is not whether these patients improved, but to what degree their improvement is attributable to the treatment intervention.

Because patients who seek medical assistance for a drug-related crisis may be prepared to "do almost anything" to make matters improve, Schuckit[29] offers the following guidelines for the physician who must develop a treatment plan:

1. *Justify your actions.* Because drug abuse problems tend to fluctuate naturally in intensity, regardless of the mode of intervention, the physician must constantly justify his actions in terms of benefits versus financial costs, patient and staff time, physical and emotional hazards to the patient, and the trauma of separation from job and family.
2. *Know the natural course of the disorder.* Development of an adequate treatment plan is possible only if the physician understands the probable course of various patterns of drug abuse.
3. *Guard against overzealous acceptance of new treatments.* Most patients in treatment show some degree of improvement, no matter what method of treatment is used. Therefore, controlled investigations are needed to assess the validity of new treatment methods.
4. *Keep it simple.* Select the least costly, least potentially harmful and simplest treatment approach, unless there are good data to justify more complex procedures.
5. *Apply objective diagnostic criteria.* Standard diagnostic criteria should be applied to each patient in order to understand the natural course of his drug dependence and predict future problems. An individual may be labelled "ill but undiagnosed" or assigned a working diagnosis, but care must be taken to reevaluate these labels at a later date. In addition, all patients should be evaluated for major preexisting physical or psychiatric disorders that require treatment or affect the prognosis.
6. *Establish realistic goals.* The physician's objectives should be to maximize the patient's chances for recovery, to encourage abstinence in a shorter time than might have been achieved without intervention, to offer good medical care, to help the people close to the patient understand the course of the patient's illness and treatment, and to educate the patient so that he can make informed decisions about treatment methods and goals.
7. *Understand the patient's motivations.* It is important to understand the patient's reasons for entering treatment: does he seek long-term abstinence, or is his actual goal detoxification or help in meeting a crisis?
8. *Make a long-term commitment.* Recovery from drug-related problems usually is a long-term process, requiring some counseling and continuation of a therapeutic relationship for at least a year.

9. *Use interpersonal resources.* Part of the treatment effort should be directed to encouraging the patient's family (and, in some cases, his employer) to understand the patient's problem. With such understanding, these important resources can help the patient achieve recovery and, to some extent, function as "ancillary therapists" in helping to carry out the treatment plan in the home or workplace.
10. *Do not take final responsibility for the patient's actions.* In the final analysis, the decision to achieve and maintain abstinence is the patient's responsibility. If the patient initially stops using drugs only to please the physician, he will soon find an excuse to become angry with the physician and resume his drug abuse.

INITIATING THERAPY

The first major task for the physician who chooses to treat a drug-dependent patient is to win the patient's trust and confidence. This requires that the physician accept the patient as a person and relate to him in a non-judgmental way. It also is important for the physician to demonstrate that he is actively interested in the patient and will support him in his struggle. Until the patient becomes convinced of this, little progress can be made. Most drug-dependent persons have been criticized for years by parents, spouses, friends, employers and probation officers; they are hypersensitive to criticism, which they perceive as rejection. Many also are poorly motivated or at least ambivalent about treatment. Drug-dependent persons typically are extremely skeptical of their ability to function without drugs, and so will deny that they have any physical or emotional problems or that they need assistance, even though they have asked for help. Attempts to motivate such patients through fear do not work; rather, such an approach carries a strong risk of stimulating severe anxiety in the patient, who may respond by fleeing from treatment and back to the protection of a drug.

To develop a truly therapeutic relationship with a physician, the patient must feel safe in expressing his true feelings, without fear of how the physician will react. Frykman[30] suggests steps the physician can take to foster such a climate of trust.

1. Make it clear that all confidences will be respected.
2. Offer help in such a way that it can as easily be refused as accepted.
3. Concentrate on the problems presented by the patient, even when deeper ones are detected.
4. Try to understand the patient's problems from the patient's point of view.

5. Demonstrate positive support for the patient's struggle and interest in what he has to say.
6. Rather than solving problems for the patient, help the patient understand how he can solve his problems for himself.
7. Gently steer the conversation toward what the patient is leaving out.
8. Understand that the patient probably has a preconceived notion of what the physician's reactions will be, based on his previous experiences with physicians and other treatment personnel.

The physician should attempt to establish a relationship that is consistent and continuing, no matter what course of treatment is selected.

Direct provision of services usually involves general medical care, with some counseling. A supportive social service contact for the patient's family may be available at public and voluntary agencies, which also can help the patient who is seeking employment and job placement; vocational guidance and training; education; financial support, housing, clothing and food; child care; marital and family counseling; recreational and social outlets; and opportunities to exercise personal and community responsibility.

REFERRING A PATIENT FOR CARE

The physician who does not feel comfortable in the role of therapist to a drug-abusing patient, or who detects physical or psychological problems that require higher-level intervention (such as methadone maintenance or long-term psychotherapy) will want to refer the patient to an appropriate source of care.

To locate possible sources for referral, the physician may consult peers, school guidance departments, mental health clinics, community health centers, hospitals, state and local medical societies, and single state agencies.[31] An excellent source of information on treatment resources is the *National Directory of Drug Abuse and Alcoholism Treatment Programs*,* which lists approximately 9,100 government and private agencies throughout the United States that provide such services.

State agencies that have information on treatment resources in their local jurisdictions are listed in Table 36.

The American Medical Association has urged its members to become acquainted with local drug abuse programs so they can promptly refer patients when such assistance is required.[32]

---

*Available from the Clearinghouse of the National Institute on Drug Abuse, 5600 Fishers Lane, Rockville, Md. 20857.

TABLE 36

Sources of Information on Drug Abuse Treatment Programs: State Agencies

State	Agency	Address	Telephone
ALABAMA	Div. of Alcoholism and Drug Abuse Dept. of Mental Health	135 S. Union St., Montgomery 36130	(205) 265-2301
ALASKA	Dept. of Health & Social Services Office of Alcoholism and Drug Abuse	Pouch H-05-F, Juneau 99811	(907) 586-6201
ARIZONA	Drug Abuse Section Dept. of Health Sciences	2500 E. Van Buren, Phoenix 85008	(602) 255-1239
ARKANSAS	Office on Alcohol and Drug Abuse Prevention	1515 W. 7th Ave., Little Rock 72205	(501) 371-2604
CALIFORNIA	Dept. of Alcohol and Drug Abuse	111 Capital Mall, Sacramento 95814	(916) 445-1940
COLORADO	Alcoholism and Drug Abuse Div. Dept. of Health	4210 E. 11th Ave., Denver 80220	(303) 320-8333
CONNECTICUT	Alcohol and Drug Abuse Council	90 Washington St., Hartford 06115	(203) 566-4145
DELAWARE	Bureau of Substance Abuse	1901 N. DuPont Hwy., Newcastle 19720	(302) 421-6101
DISTRICT OF COLUMBIA	Mental Health, Alcohol and Addiction Services Branch	1329 E St., N.W., Washington, D.C. 20004	(202) 724-5641
FLORIDA	Drug Abuse Program	1309 Winewood Blvd., Tallahassee 32301	(904) 488-0900
GEORGIA	Alcohol and Drug Section Div. of Mental Health	618 Ponce de Leon Ave., N.E., Atlanta 30308	(404) 894-4785
HAWAII	Alcohol and Drug Abuse Branch	1270 Queen Emma St., Honolulu 96813	(808) 548-7655
IDAHO	Bureau of Substance Abuse Dept. of Health & Welfare	700 W. State, Boise 83720	(208) 384-7706
ILLINOIS	Dangerous Drugs Commission	300 N. State St., Chicago 60610	(312) 822-9860

TABLE 36 *(continued)*

State	Agency	Address	Telephone
INDIANA	Div. of Addiction Services Dept. of Mental Health	5 Indiana Sq., Indianapolis 46204	(317) 633-4477
IOWA	Dept. of Substance Abuse	418 Sixth Ave., Des Moines 50319	(515) 281-3641
KANSAS	Alcoholism & Drug Abuse Section	2700 W. Sixth St., Topeka 66606	(913) 296-3925
KENTUCKY	Alcohol and Drug Branch Bureau of Health Sciences	275 E. Main St., Frankfort 40621	(502) 564-7450
LOUISIANA	Bureau of Substance Abuse Dept. of Health & Human Resources	200 Lafayette St., Baton Rouge 70801	(504) 342-2575
MAINE	Office of Alcoholism and Drug Abuse Prevention, Bureau of Rehabilitation	32 Winthrop St., Augusta 04330	(207) 289-2781
MARYLAND	State Drug Abuse Administration	201 W. Preston St., Baltimore 21201	(301) 383-7404
MASSACHUSETTS	Div. of Drug Rehabilitation	160 N. Washington St., Boston 02114	(617) 727-8614
MICHIGAN	Office of Substance Abuse Services Dept. of Public Health	3500 N. Logan St., Lansing 48914	(517) 373-8600
MINNESOTA	Chemical Dependency Program Div. Dept. of Public Welfare	658 Cedar, St. Paul 55155	(612) 296-4610
MISSISSIPPI	Div. of Alcohol & Drug Abuse Dept. of Mental Health	619 Robert E. Lee State Office Bldg., Jackson 32901	(601) 354-7031
MISSOURI	Div. of Alcoholism and Drug Abuse Div. of Mental Health	2002 Missouri Blvd., Jefferson City 65101	(314) 751-4942
MONTANA	Alcohol & Drug Abuse Div. Dept. of Institutions	Helena 59601	(406) 449-2827
NEBRASKA	Commission on Drugs	P.O. Box 94726, Lincoln 68509	(402) 471-2691
NEVADA	Bureau of Alcohol & Drug Abuse	505 E. King St., Carson City 89710	(702) 885-4790

TABLE 36 (continued)

State	Agency	Address	Telephone
NEW HAMPSHIRE	Program on Alcohol & Drug Abuse	61 S. Spring St., Concord 03301	(603) 271-3531
NEW JERSEY	Div. of Narcotic & Drug Abuse Control	129 E. Hanover St., Trenton 08625	(609) 292-5760
NEW MEXICO	Substance Abuse Bureau Behavioral Services Div.	P.O. Box 968, Santa Fe 87503	(505) 827-5271
NEW YORK	Div. of Substance Abuse Services	Executive Park S., Box 8200, Albany 12203	(518) 457-7629
NORTH CAROLINA	Alcohol and Drug Abuse Section Dept. of Human Resources	325 N. Salisbury St., Raleigh 27611	(919) 733-6650
NORTH DAKOTA	Div. of Alcoholism & Drug Abuse	909 Basin Ave., Bismarck 58505	(701) 224-2767
OHIO	Bureau of Drug Abuse	65 S. Front St., Columbus 43215	(614) 466-9023
OKLAHOMA	Drug Abuse Services Dept. of Mental Health	P.O. Box 53277, Capitol Station, Oklahoma City 73152	(405) 521-2811
OREGON	Drug Abuse Program Mental Health Div.	2575 Bittern St., N.E., Salem 97310	(503) 378-2163
PENNSYLVANIA	Governor's Council on Drug & Alcohol Abuse	2101 N. Front St., Harrisburg 17120	(717) 787-9857
RHODE ISLAND	Div. of Substance Abuse Rhode Island Medical Center	303 General Hospital, Cranston 02920	(401) 464-2091
SOUTH CAROLINA	Commission on Alcohol & Drug Abuse	3700 Forest Dr., Columbia 29204	(803) 758-2521
SOUTH DAKOTA	Div. of Drugs & Substance Control	Joe Foss Bldg., Pierre 57501	(605) 773-3123
TENNESSEE	Alcohol & Drug Abuse Services	501 Union Bldg., Nashville 37219	(615) 741-1921
TEXAS	Drug Abuse Prevention Div. Dept. of Community Affairs	P.O. Box 13166, Austin 78711	(512) 475-6351

TABLE 36 *(continued)*

State	Agency	Address	Telephone
UTAH	Div. of Alcoholism & Drugs	P.O. Box 2500, Salt Lake City 84110	(801) 533-6532
VERMONT	Alcohol & Drug Abuse Div. Dept. of Social & Rehabilitation Services	State Office Bldg., Montpelier 05602	(802) 241-2170
VIRGINIA	Div. of Substance Abuse State Dept. of Mental Health	P.O. Box 1797, Richmond 23214	(804) 786-5313
WASHINGTON	Bureau of Alcoholism & Substance Abuse Dept. of Social & Health Services	Dept. of Social & Health Services Office Bldg., Olympia 98504	(206) 753-3073
WEST VIRGINIA	Div. of Alcohol and Drug Abuse State Capitol	1800 Kanawha Blvd. E, Charleston 25305	(304) 348-3616
WISCONSIN	Bureau of Alcohol & Other Drug Abuse	One W. Wilson St., Madison 53702	(608) 266-2717
WYOMING	Substance Abuse Programs	Hathaway Bldg., Cheyenne 82002	(307) 777-7118
PUERTO RICO	Dept. of Addiction Control Services	Box B-Y, Rio Piedras Station, Rio Piedras 00928	(809) 763-5014
AMERICAN SAMOA	Mental Health Clinic	Govt. of American Samoa, Pago Pago 96799	—
GUAM	Mental Health & Substance Abuse Agency	P.O. Box 20999, Guam 96921	—
VIRGIN ISLANDS	Div. of Mental Health, Alcoholism & Drug Dependency	P.O. Box 520, Christiansted, St. Croix 00820	(809) 774-4888
TRUST TERRITORIES	Health Services Office of the High Commissioner	Saipan 96950	FTS 8-556-0220

Source: *National Directory of Drug Abuse and Alcoholism Treatment Programs* (National Institute on Drug Abuse, Rockville, Md., 1979)

When a referral is made, several items of information should be given to the patient:
- The name, address and telephone number of the referred agency.
- The agency's hours of operation.
- Cost of services and possible sources of financial assistance.
- Range of services available.
- Eligibility requirements.
- Preparations for the first visit (fasting, urine specimen, etc.).

In some cases, the physician may wish to suggest more than one referral possibility, but should not confuse the patient by offering too many choices.

With the patient's approval, the physician may initiate contact with the agency. This step can ease the patient's apprehension and facilitate completion of the referral.

If the patient accepts the referral, the physician may offer to remain available for consultation about general medical care. By doing so, he indicates a continuing interest in the patient's well-being and also facilitates evaluation of treatment effectiveness.

If the patient refuses the referral, the physician may arrange to see the patient weekly for four to six weeks. If the patient makes progress during this time, such visits can be scheduled monthly until, by mutual agreement, the patient no longer requires medical counseling. If, however, there is no progress after four to six weeks, the physician should insist even more firmly that a referral is necessary. At this point, the patient's refusal indicates a lack of commitment to treatment, and his motives for seeking assistance should be reassessed. If it appears that the patient merely wishes help with medical problems while continuing his drug use, the physician may continue to treat him on this basis, using treatment visits as an opportunity to educate the patient about the probable health consequences of continued drug abuse.[31]

PROVIDING LONG-TERM FOLLOW-UP

Long-term care is an important element of the treatment process because it helps recovering drug abusers make use of newly acquired coping skills in adapting to life in the community. Whether the patient has been treated by a primary care physician or enrolled in an inpatient or outpatient treatment program, efforts to change his perceptions and behaviors will have been strongly tied to the treatment milieu. Community resources that support the patient's changed lifestyle must be found to sustain these treatment-induced changes outside the treatment locale. There is little reason to assume that the patient will make the transition to stable employee, responsible family member or attentive student either rapidly or with ease. It is in this area of continued support that aftercare efforts may be not only useful, but essential.[33]

Aftercare also can serve as a first line of defense against relapse to drug use. A physician's continuing interest in his patient's activities in the community and continuing support for prosocial activities after discharge from treatment can help that patient remain drug-free.[33]

The primary care physician is in an excellent position to contribute to aftercare of the recovering drug abuser, whether he conducted the treatment himself or referred the patient to a treatment program. In the course of routine office visits, the physician can express continuing support of the patient's efforts toward recovery and be alert for early signs of any relapse to drug abuse.

CONCLUSIONS

Long-term efforts to treat drug abusers have, as Newman[4] notes, too often been viewed as an "all or none proposition: either the treatment is 'successful' and clients remain permanently abstinent, or clients return to drug abuse, and therapy is deemed a failure." This "simplistic dichotomy," he says, ignores the fact that drug dependence represents a chronic, relapsing condition similar to epilepsy, for which the reasonable and attainable objective is to control or reduce the frequency of seizures, rather than to eliminate the disease itself.

The therapeutic techniques necessary to treat a drug abuser involve much more than simply treating the drug dependence as a medical problem. A reasonably accurate assessment of the patient's rationality, along with the use of appropriate therapeutic measures (including psychotherapy and pharmacotherapy) should be included in the overall treatment plan that is developed for each patient. The population of drug abusers is a heterogeneous one, and more than one treatment approach may be needed.[11] Treatment of drug abusers, like treatment of other patients who suffer from chronic conditions, requires that the physician make a long-term commitment to provide psychological support and medical care.

Understanding what current treatment methods can and cannot do may be a major challenge for decades to come. Jaffe[1] finds it "entirely conceivable that a 20-year follow-up of heroin addicts ... would reveal little difference in status between a cohort who had participated in current treatments and a comparable group which, for some reason, had not been given access to treatment." Should the long-term data show such similar outcomes, he says, it will be tempting to infer that treatment has been without effect. However, it is the quality of the intervening years that must be judged, rather than the status of a given patient at a fixed point in time.

REFERENCES

1. Jaffe, J. H. The swinging pendulum: the treatment of drug users in America in R. I. DuPont, A. Goldstein and J. O'Donnell (eds.) *Handbook on Drug Abuse* (National Institute on Drug Abuse, Rockville, Md., 1979)
2. *Treatment of Drug Abuse: An Overview* Report Series 34, No. 1 (National Clearinghouse for Drug Abuse Information, Rockville, Md., 1975)
3. Jaffe, J. H. Drug addiction and drug abuse in A. G. Gilman, L. S. Goodman and A. Gilman (eds.) *The Pharmacological Basis of Therapeutics* (Macmillan, New York City, 1980)
4. Newman, R. G. Planning drug abuse treatment: critical decisions *Bulletin on Narcotics* 30(2):41 (April-June 1978)
5. Senay, E. C. and Lewis, D. C. *The Primary Physician's Guide to Drug and Alcohol Abuse Treatment* Medical Monograph Series, Vol. I, No. 6 (National Institute on Drug Abuse, Rockville, Md., 1979)
6. Lowinson, J. H. and Millman, R. B. Clinical aspects of methadone maintenance treatment in R. I. DuPont, A. Goldstein and J. O'Donnell (eds.) *Handbook on Drug Abuse* (National Institute on Drug Abuse, Rockville, Md., 1979)
7. Newman, R. G. Detoxification treatment of narcotic addicts in R. I. DuPont, A. Goldstein and J. O'Donnell (eds.) *Handbook on Drug Abuse* (National Institute on Drug Abuse, Rockville, Md., 1979)
8. Czechowicz, D. *Detoxification Treatment Manual* (National Institute on Drug Abuse, Rockville, Md., 1979)
9. Cohen, S. Clonidine (Catapress): nonopiate detoxification *Drug Abuse & Alcoholism Newsletter* 9(6):1 (July 1980)
10. Gold, M. S., Pottash, A. L. C., Sweeney, D. R. and Kleber, H. D. Clonidine detoxification: a fourteen-day protocol for rapid opiate withdrawal in L. S. Harris (ed.) *Problems of Drug Dependence, 1979* Research Monograph 27 (National Institute on Drug Abuse, Rockville, Md., 1979)
11. Senay, E. C. and Raynes, A. E. *Treatment of the Drug Abusing Patient for Treatment Staff Physicians* Medical Monograph Series, Vol. I, No. 2 (National Institute on Drug Abuse, Rockville, Md., 1977)
12. Smith, D. E., Wesson, D. R. and Seymour, R. B. The abuse of barbiturates and other sedative-hypnotics in R. I. DuPont, A. Goldstein and J. O'Donnell (eds.) *Handbook on Drug Abuse* (National Institute on Drug Abuse, Rockville, Md., 1979)
13. Wesson, D. R. and Smith, D. E. A conceptual approach to detoxification *Journal of Psychedelic Drugs* 6(2) (1974)
14. Wesson, D. R. and Smith, D. E. Treatment of the polydrug abuser in R. I. DuPont, A. Goldstein and J. O'Donnell (eds.) *Handbook on Drug Abuse* (National Institute on Drug Abuse, Rockville, Md., 1979)

15. Resnick, R. B., Washton, A. M. and Schuyten-Resnick, E. Treatment of opioid dependence with narcotic antagonists: a review and commentary *in* R. I. DuPont, A. Goldstein and J. O'Donnell (eds.) *Handbook on Drug Abuse* (National Institute on Drug Abuse, Rockville, Md., 1979)
16. Renault, P. F. Treatment of heroin-dependent persons with antagonists: current status *Bulletin on Narcotics* 30(2):21 (April-June 1978)
17. The scene *Addiction and Substance Abuse Report* 11(3):1 (March 1980)
18. DeLeon, G. and Rosenthal, M. S. Therapeutic communities *in* R. I. DuPont, A. Goldstein and J. O'Donnell (eds.) *Handbook on Drug Abuse* (National Institute on Drug Abuse, Rockville, Md., 1979)
19. Jones, M. Therapeutic communities, old and new *American Journal of Drug and Alcohol Abuse* 6(2):137 (1979)
20. Kleber, H. D. and Slabetz, F. Outpatient drug-free treatment *in* R. I. DuPont, A. Goldstein and J. O'Donnell (eds.) *Handbook on Drug Abuse* (National Institute on Drug Abuse, Rockville, Md., 1979)
21. Tennant, F. S. Jr. Outpatient treatment and outcome of prescription drug abuse *in* L. S. Harris (ed.) *Problems of Drug Dependence, 1979* Research Monograph 27 (National Institute on Drug Abuse, Rockville, Md., 1979)
22. Stanton, M. D., Todd, T. C. and Steier, F. Outcome for structural family therapy with drug addicts *in* L. S. Harris (ed.) *Problems of Drug Dependence, 1979* Research Monograph 27 (National Institute on Drug Abuse, Rockville, Md., 1979)
23. O'Brien, C. P. and Ng, L. K. Y. Innovative treatments for drug addiction *in* R. I. DuPont, A. Goldstein and J. O'Donnell (eds.) *Handbook on Drug Abuse* (National Institute on Drug Abuse, Rockville, Md., 1979)
24. Rawson, R. A., Glazer, M., Callahan, E. J. and Liberman, R. P. Naltrexone and behavior therapy for heroin addiction *in* N. Krasnegor (ed.) *Behavioral Analysis and Treatment of Substance Abuse* Research Monograph 25 (National Institute on Drug Abuse, Rockville, Md., 1979)
25. Pickens, R. A behavioral program for treatment of drug dependence *in* N. Krasnegor (ed.) *Behavioral Analysis and Treatment of Substance Abuse* Research Monograph 25 (National Institute on Drug Abuse, Rockville, Md., 1979)
26. Stitzer, M. L., Bigelow, G. E. and Liebson, I. Reinforcement of drug abstinence: a behavioral approach to drug abuse treatment *in* N. Krasnegor (ed.) *Behavioral Analysis and Treatment of Substance Abuse* Research Monograph 25 (National Institute on Drug Abuse, Rockville, Md., 1979)
27. *Heroin Detoxification* (Haight Ashbury Free Medical Clinic, San Francisco, Cal., n.d.)
28. Blum, K., Newmeyer, J. A. and Whitehead, C. Acupuncture as a common mode of treatment for drug dependence: possible neurochemical mechanisms *Journal of Psychedelic Drugs* 10(2):105 (April-June 1978)
29. Schuckit, M. A. *Drug and Alcohol Abuse: A Clinical Guide to Diagnosis and Treatment* (Plenum Medical Book Co., New York City, 1979)
30. Frykman, J. H. *A New Connection: An Approach to Persons Involved in Compulsive Drug Use* (The Scrimshaw Press, San Francisco, Cal., 1971)

31. Masland, R. P. Jr. Adolescent drug and alcohol use: how to deal with it *Consultant* 190 (June 1980)
32. *Referral of Patients to Chemical Dependency Programs*, House of Delegates Resolution 31, I-79 (American Medical Association, Chicago, Ill., 1979)
33. Brown, B. S. and Ashery, R. S. Aftercare in drug abuse programming *in* R. I. DuPont, A. Goldstein and J. O'Donnell (eds.) *Handbook on Drug Abuse* (National Institute on Drug Abuse, Rockville, Md., 1979)

Section III
Legal and Social Issues

CHAPTER 9
LEGAL CONSIDERATIONS IN TREATING DRUG ABUSERS

The relationship between government policies restricting the availability of a given drug and government policies on the treatment of persons who abuse such a drug is not fixed;[1] however, the history of drug abuse legislation in the United States shows certain clear parallels between the severity of prohibitions on access to a drug and the stringency of legal limitations on the treatment of persons who abuse that drug.[2]

Several major pieces of drug legislation and Presidential initiatives have shaped public policy in the drug field. One of the first pertinent measures passed by Congress was the District of Columbia Pharmacy Act of 1906. Although this law applied only to the District of Columbia, it set a precedent for future Congressional action on drug-related issues. The act permitted physicians to prescribe narcotic drugs to addicts only for the cure of addiction; it prohibited the prescription of narcotic drugs to non-addicted persons except in the treatment of illness or injury. These provisions were intended to prevent the spread of addictive drug abuse. In fact, they represented the first involvement of federal regulations with the prescribing practices of private physicians.[3]

Since 1914, the federal government has enacted numerous laws and administrative regulations on the distribution of narcotics and other drugs. The thrust of these rules and regulations has been to ensure an adequate supply of psychoactive drugs to meet medical and scientific needs, while restricting the use of such drugs outside the medical-scientific community. The most significant of the federal drug laws are summarized below in chronological order:

HARRISON NARCOTIC ACT (1914): The Harrison Act established a mechanism for distribution of narcotic drugs and initiated a policy that remains the basis of most contemporary drug control programs. It required that all persons who imported, manufactured, produced, compounded, sold, dealt in, disposed of, or transferred narcotic drugs must register annually with the Treasury Department and pay a graduated occupational fee of $1 to $24 per year. Registrants were required to keep records of the drugs they handled, make those records available to law officers, and file returns specified by the Secretary of the Treasury. The act also imposed a tax on opium, isonipecaine, coca leaves and opioids, as well as compounds, manufactures, salts, derivatives, preparations and substances chemically identical to those drugs.[2] However, numerous patent medicines containing small amounts of morphine, cocaine, opium and heroin were still permitted to be sold by mail order or in general stores.[3]

Through regulations issued by the Treasury Department pursuant to the Harrison Narcotic Act, the federal government restricted the medical treatment of heroin and morphine addiction by private practitioners.[3]

NARCOTIC DRUGS IMPORT AND EXPORT ACT (1922): This act widened the prohibition against opium imports (established in 1909) to other drugs, including morphine, coca leaves and their derivatives. The amount of narcotics that could be legally imported was limited to an amount determined by the Commissioner of Narcotics to be necessary for medical and scientific uses. Manufactured drugs and preparations could be exported only under a rigid system of controls to ensure that the drugs were needed for medical purposes in the country of destination.[3]

PORTER ACT (1929): This act called for the construction of two federal facilities (one at Lexington, Kentucky, opened in 1935, and one at Fort Worth, Texas, opened in 1938) for the compulsory treatment of persons convicted in criminal courts of narcotics abuse.[3]

MARIJUANA TAX ACT (1937): This revenue act required all persons who imported, manufactured, produced, compounded, sold, dealt in, dispensed, prescribed, administered or gave away marijuana to register with the Treasury Department and pay an occupational tax. It also limited the transfer of marijuana to those transactions made on the authority of official order forms. In 1969, the Supreme Court found the Marijuana Tax Act unenforceable when an accused claims the Fifth Amendment privilege against self-incrimination. The Court also declared unreasonable the act's presumption that a person who possesses a quantity of marijuana knows that it was imported illegally. This ruling removed the Marijuana Tax Act as a major government weapon against marijuana traffic.[2]

FEDERAL FOOD, DRUG, AND COSMETIC ACT (1938): The Food, Drug, and Cosmetic Act gave the federal government broad authority to regulate the manufacture, distribution and labeling of drugs. Amendments in 1962 and 1965 widened the scope of this authority, established new record-keeping and inspection requirements, and imposed—for the first time—standards for the handling of certain types of drugs by persons who register.[1]

OPIUM POPPY CONTROL ACT (1942): This statute prohibited the

production of opium poppies in the United States, except under license granted by the Secretary of the Treasury. No license has ever been issued under this statute.[2]

HARRISON NARCOTIC ACT AMENDMENT (1946): This amendment extended the provisions of the Harrison Narcotic Act to include synthetic substances that have dependence producing or sustaining qualities similar to those of morphine or cocaine.[2]

BOGGS AMENDMENT (1951): This legislation increased the penalties for violations of federal narcotic and marijuana laws.[2] For the first time, penalties for violations of the marijuana laws became as severe as those for misuse of narcotic drugs.[3]

NARCOTIC CONTROL ACT (1956): This act banned the possession of heroin and imposed inflexible penalties for narcotics offenses.[2]

NARCOTIC MANUFACTURING ACT (1960): This legislation established a system for licensing manufacturers to produce narcotic drugs and set manufacturing quotas for the basic classes of such drugs.[2]

DRUG ABUSE CONTROL AMENDMENTS (1965): These amendments reflect the recommendations of a Presidential Commission that stronger restrictions be imposed on three classes of drugs—depressants, hallucinogens and stimulants—included in the 1965 Amendments to the Food, Drug and Cosmetic Act. The Drug Abuse Control Amendments also extend the federal government's regulatory authority to drugs in intrastate commerce, on the grounds that difficulties in determining place of origin and consumption made it impossible to regulate commerce in drugs solely through interstate transactions.[2,3]

NARCOTIC ADDICT REHABILITATION ACT (1966): This legislation provided for civil commitment and treatment of persons dependent on narcotic drugs, in lieu of criminal prosecution.[2,3]

COMPREHENSIVE DRUG ABUSE PREVENTION AND CONTROL ACT (1970): This act consolidated more than 50 federal drug-related laws into one comprehensive act designed to control the legitimate drug industry and curtail the importation and distribution of illicit drugs.[2,3]

CONTROLLED SUBSTANCES ACT (1971): Passage of this legislation marked the transfer of control over narcotics and dangerous drugs from the Treasury Department to the Department of Justice. Under the act, many drugs not previously restricted were included in the list of controlled substances, and stricter requirements for obtaining and handling these drugs were established.[2,4] (See Chapter 10 for the specific provisions of this act as they relate to prescribing practices.)

RESTRICTIONS ON THE TREATMENT OF DRUG ABUSERS

For reasons that are not entirely clear, legal restrictions on (and public attitudes toward) the treatment of "narcotics addiction" came to be differentiated from restrictions on the treatment of non-narcotic dependence in the years after World War I. Thus, even when the dependence liability of the barbiturates became widely recognized in the 1920's, the treatment of such dependence remained within the purview of medicine. Barbiturate-dependent patients were free to obtain maintenance doses of the drug from physicians or to undergo detoxification, as they and their physicians saw fit. Similarly, amphetamine dependence, although recognized in the 1940's, remained for many years a medical problem rather than a legal concern. Private physicians were free to treat chronic amphetamine users through outpatient maintenance or inpatient withdrawal.[5] Although most contemporary authorities agree that few patients benefit from maintenance programs involving stimulant and depressant drugs, even today there are no specific federal regulations that prohibit the use of stimulants or general CNS depressants in the treatment of compulsive users of nonopioid drugs.[6]

The modes of treatment open to narcotics addicts, on the other hand, have been severely limited by federal legislation since enactment of the Harrison Narcotic Act in 1914. Nowhere is this more evident than in federal regulations governing the use of methadone. Methadone and similar drugs are used in the detoxification and maintenance treatment of heroin addiction at several hundred separate programs throughout the United States. While such treatment has many advantages, it also poses certain problems and public health risks. For example, patients who participate in these programs can be sources of illicit diversion of drugs (especially if they are permitted to take home substantial amounts), thus creating a potential for primary methadone addiction in others. In addition, some primary heroin users may develop severe physical dependence if they are inappropriately admitted to methadone programs. To minimize these risks, the federal government has enacted regulations that legitimize the use of methadone, but limit the amount of methadone patients may take home from treatment centers and make it difficult for patients to obtain methadone from more than one source.[6] Until very recently, federal regulations severely restricted the type of patient who could be enrolled in a methadone maintenance program, as well as the actual conduct and management of such a program.[3]

Although private physicians still are not allowed to maintain heroin-dependent patients on methadone (unless they register and are approved as treatment programs), regulations announced late in 1980[7] give considerably more latitude than those imposed under the Comprehensive Drug Abuse Treatment and Control Act of 1970 and the Narcotic Addict Treatment Act of 1974. For example, the 1980 criteria for admission to methadone maintenance programs are more flexible than the earlier standards, requiring that patients demonstrate only a one-year history of addiction, rather than the previously required two-year history. In addition, persons with prior histories of addiction who have resided in penal or chronic care insitutions for one month or more now have up to six months after release to decide whether to enroll in a methadone program (in the past, such enrollment was allowed only within the first seven days after release). The effect of this change is to allow such persons sufficient time to determine whether they can remain drug-free after their release, while retaining the option of enrolling in a treatment program if they cannot.[7]

Because methadone must be taken daily to alleviate heroin withdrawal symptoms and because it usually is dispensed only in the treatment setting, it has caused serious disruptions in family, school and work schedules. To meet this problem, the new regulations allow certain patients who have been in maintenance for three years and who meet very stringent criteria to take home up to a six-day dose.[7]

Urine testing is required in methadone maintenance programs to determine if clients are using other drugs of abuse and thus violating their treatment agreement. However, rather than requiring weekly screening as before, the new regulations require an initial screening at the time of admission and at least eight additional urinalyses during the first year of treatment. At least four more urinalyses must be performed on patients who remain in treatment for a second year.[7]

The 1980 regulations represent greater flexibility than the federal laws they amend, but they still exert considerable control over the conditions under which drug abusers (especially heroin abusers) may receive treatment. Other federal regulations impose very specific criteria for all facets of drug treatment programs. These criteria govern the types of services offered, admissions procedures and diagnostic studies, the size of therapy groups, the amount of active treatment delivered and even the programs' hours of operation. Adjunct services such as vocational and educational counseling, job development and placement, and legal support services are required. Each program must have a licensed medical director, maintain patient records to document the care delivered, and perform follow-up studies of discharged clients.[8]

Even the private physician who wishes to treat drug dependent persons on an individual basis is subject to a variety of legal restrictions, record-keeping and reporting requirements. Although certain of these requirements are based on federal laws and regulations, many are imposed at the state level and thus vary widely from one jurisdiction to the next. Therefore, every physician who contemplates treating a drug dependent patient for his drug-related or other medical problems is advised to consult local authorities for information on legal limitations and requirements. In many areas, state and local medical societies can provide this information. Physicians also may consult their state licensing boards or state drug abuse agencies (the names, addresses and telephone numbers of these agencies are listed in Chapter 8).

Maclean and Feurig[9] suggest that clarification of several legal questions be obtained. In all cases, the physician should check with his own counsel or local medical society. Pertinent issues include:

- *What constitutes treatment of drug dependence?*
  Generally, the law distinguishes between treatment of drug *reactions*, which require short-term care of physical and psychological complications of drug use, and treatment of drug *dependence*, which may involve long-term maintenance or other therapeutic regimens. Local regulations should be consulted on this point.

- *In an emergency situation involving drugs, is a physician obligated to obtain consent before initiating treatment?*
  The law may not require a physician to obtain consent before initiating emergency treatment, drug-related or otherwise.

- *What are the requirements for informed consent in a non-emergency situation?*
  In the treatment of drug dependence, as in the treatment of other medical problems, the physician should explain in advance those reasonably foreseeable risks and hazards of treatment, as well as of non-treatment.

- *If a situation involving drugs is not life-threatening, must a physician obtain consent from a parent or guardian before treating a minor?*
  In many states, a minor who is (or professes to be) dependent on drugs of abuse may give a valid consent to treatment; the consent of a parent or guardian is not required.

- *When parents demand that a minor receive treatment for drug abuse but the minor refuses, what is the physician's role?*
  The governing principle here is that, without a patient, there is no treatment. The physician can make his services available to the

minor, who has the option of accepting or rejecting them (although parents may have the right to insist that treatment be provided, even if the child objects).

- *Does the physician have a legal obligation to report that he is treating (or about to treat) a patient who is dependent on drugs?* Whether reporting is appropriate in a particular case may depend on whether the physician treats a patient for drug dependence or treats a drug dependent patient for a separate medical condition.[10] Local legislation and regulations must be consulted on this point.

CONFIDENTIALITY ISSUES IN THE TREATMENT OF DRUG ABUSERS

If drug dependent persons are to seek medical help for their problems, the treating physician or program must be able to give reasonable assurance that the treatment will not cause some unforeseen harm in the future. Inappropriate disclosure of the patient's drug problem could cause such harm. Of course, medical ethics always have bound physicians to uphold the principle of privileged communication, but the increasing interest of third parties such as government agencies, employers and insurers in the course and outcome of treatment may threaten to violate such confidences in fact, if not in principle.

In response to the special problems associated with drug and alcohol abuse patients' records, the federal government promulgated new regulations on this subject in 1975.[11] Whether an individual physician is subject to the federal requirements depends on the nature and purpose of the records in question, not on the status or primary function of the physician. The regulations apply to records of the identity, diagnosis, prognosis or treatment of any patient, maintained in connection with the performance of any "drug abuse prevention function" (defined as any program or activity relating to education, training, treatment, rehabilitation or research), if that "function" is (1) conducted by a United States government department or agency, (2) required to be licensed or authorized by the federal government, (3) assisted by federal funds, either directly through grants and contracts, or indirectly by funds supplied to state and local governments by the federal government, or (4) assisted by the Internal Revenue Service through tax deductions for contributions made to the program or a grant of tax-exempt status to the program.

In view of these regulatory provisions, the answer as to whether the regulations would apply to a particular physician would depend on at least two facts in each case:

1. Are the records maintained as part of a drug abuse program?
2. Does that program receive federal assistance in one or more of the forms described above?

If the answer to both questions is "yes," then a private practitioner who is in possession of such records probably would be subject to the regulations. On the other hand, if the physician has no involvement with records generated by such federally assisted programs, then presumably he or she would not be subject to the regulations.

Briefly, the 1975 regulations supply guidelines to answer the following questions:

- *What kinds of communication are not considered disclosure of confidential information?*
  Communication between staff members within a program, and communications between staff of a program and a "qualified service organization" (a provider of service that has agreed in writing to be bound by the federal confidentiality regulations) are not considered disclosures. Also, information that contains no patient identifying data is not considered a disclosure of confidential information.[11,12]

- *What information can be disclosed in an emergency?*
  In a medical emergency situation in which the patient is incapacitated, information needed for diagnosis and emergency treatment may be released without consent. Family members or others personally related to the patient may be notified of the patient's condition without his consent *only* if the patient is so incapacitated as to be incapable of rational communication.[11,12]

- *When is written informed consent required?*
  Except in a few special cases, *all* other instances of information disclosure require written consent, signed by the patient. Blanket consent forms are not acceptable for this purpose.

  The federal regulations make it the responsibility of the party who releases the information to check the consent form and refuse to disclose information if the consent is incomplete or false.[11,12]

- *What information may be disclosed, with proper consent?*
  Disclosure should be limited to information actually needed for the purpose stated on the consent form. For example, personal and family histories might legitimately be sent to a treating physician, but should *not* be sent to an insurance company or state employment

agency. General guidelines provided in the regulations cover the following situations:

—TREATMENT PROGRAMS: Information necessary to the diagnosis, treatment and rehabilitation of the patient may be disclosed.

—LEGAL COUNSEL: With the proper consent, information may be released to a patient's attorney upon written application by the patient, endorsed by the attorney. The attorney may not further disclose this information.

—FAMILY AND FRIENDS: With proper consent, family and friends may receive information about the patient's status if, in the judgment of the treating professional, such disclosure will not harm the patient.

—EMPLOYERS AND EMPLOYMENT AGENCIES: Information may be released with proper consent if, in the view of the treating professional, the employer or agency will use the information to assist in the patient's rehabilitation and not against the interests of the patient. Information should be limited to verification of status in treatment or a general evaluation of progress.

—THIRD-PARTY PAYERS OR FUNDING SOURCES: With proper consent, only such information as is reasonably needed to process the patient's claim may be released.

—CRIMINAL JUSTICE SYSTEM: In specific cases where participation in a treatment program is a condition of the patient's release from confinement, or has a bearing on the disposition of any criminal proceedings, special rules on disclosure to the court, parole or probation departments apply.

—OTHER RELEASES OF INFORMATION: With proper consent, information may be released to any other party for any valid purpose, if disclosing the information will not be harmful to the patient, the patient-program relationship, or the program's capacity to provide services.

Under the regulations, even the statement that a person is (or is not) a patient in a particular program represents disclosure of confidential information. Therefore, a facility that treats a variety of conditions may acknowledge the presence of a particular patient in the facility, but may not acknowledge that patient's presence in a drug treatment unit without specific consent.[11,12]

• *How may the recipient treat the information disclosed?*
Under the federal regulations, no person or organization that re-

ceives confidential information may redisclose such information without proper consent. Even *with* consent, the recipient can reveal information only if it is no longer available from the primary source (unless the information was expressly given for redisclosure).[11,12]

- Under what circumstances may courts order disclosure?
The courts may authorize disclosure of confidential information where there is good cause to do so. The federal regulations contain specific procedures and criteria for this process. In general, the scope of a court order is limited to objective data from primary sources, and only *removes the prohibition against* disclosure, rather than *requiring disclosure.*[11,12]

- Under what circumstances can confidential information be used for research, audit and evaluation purposes?
The federal regulations contain specific guidelines on the use of confidential information for the purposes of scientific research, management and financial audits, and program evaluation. Although disclosure for these purposes does not require written consent from each patient, it does entail a variety of written assurances from the recipient of such information.[11,12]

- What safeguards are required in keeping patient records?
The regulations require that every person or program maintaining records on drug abuse treatment take proper precautions to protect those records and keep them in a locked place when not in use. Each program is required to develop written policies for handling and controlling access to such records. The federal regulations also govern such actions as disposing of records when a program is discontinued, the use of identification cards, use of undercover agents, use of central registries to prevent enrollment in multiple drug programs, and regulation of methadone programs.[11,12]

Although these regulations were drafted specifically to govern the conduct of federally assisted drug abuse programs, they provide sound guidance for the conduct of individual physicians (who should, however, consult local authorities and their own legal counsel for requirements that may exceed those of the federal law).[13,14]

REFERENCES

1. Jaffe, J. H. The swinging pendulum: the treatment of drug users in America in R. I. DuPont, A. Goldstein and J. O'Donnell (eds.) *Handbook on Drug Abuse* (National Institute on Drug Abuse, Rockville, Md., 1979)
2. Cornacchia, H. J., Smith, D. E. and Bentel, D. J. *Drugs in the Classroom: A Conceptual Model for School Programs* (C. V. Mosby Company, St. Louis, Mo., 1978)
3. Drug Abuse Council *The Facts About "Drug Abuse"* (The Free Press, New York City, 1980)
4. Drugs of abuse *Drug Enforcement* 6(2):2 (July 1979)
5. *Treatment of Drug Abuse: An Overview* Report Series 34, No. 1 (National Clearinghouse for Drug Abuse Information, Rockville, Md., April 1975)
6. Jaffe, J. H. Drug addiction and drug abuse in A. G. Gilman, L. S. Goodman and A. Gilman (eds.) *The Pharmacological Basis of Therapeutics* (Macmillan, New York City, 1980)
7. Methadone for treating narcotic addicts; joint revision of conditions for use *Federal Register* 45(185):62693 (September 19, 1980)
8. *National Drug Abuse Treatment: Insight and Perspectives* (National Institute on Drug Abuse, Rockville, Md., 1979)
9. Maclean, C. B. and Feurig, J. S. The physician and the law: legal implications of treating drug reactions (unpublished manuscript) 1973
10. *Controlled Substances Regulations Reference* (California Department of Justice, Division of Law Enforcement, Sacramento, Calif., 1979)
11. Confidentiality of alcohol and drug abuse patient records: general provisions *Federal Register* 40(127): Part IV (July 1, 1975)
12. Blume, S. B. *Confidentiality of Medical Records in Alcohol-Related Problems* (National Council on Alcoholism, New York City, n.d.)
13. Schuchman, H. Confidentiality: practice issues in new legislation *American Journal of Orthopsychiatry* 50(4):641 (October 1980)
14. Nye, S. G. Patient confidentiality and privacy: the federal initiative *American Journal of Orthopsychiatry* 50(4):649 (October 1980)

CHAPTER 10
PRESCRIBING PRACTICES
AND DRUG ABUSE

The subject of psychoactive drug use and misuse is highly complex, for several reasons. First, the term "psychoactive drugs" refers to a wide variety of drugs with various medical uses, including uses apart from their psychoactive effects. Psychoactive drugs have widely diverse actions; thus, it is not proper scientifically to generalize about them as a group. Such drugs are appropriately used in a variety of medical conditions, ranging from transient situational anxiety or insomnia, to physical pain, to the major psychoses. The specific indications, benefits and risks for each class of psychoactive drugs are quite distinct.[1]

Second, there are no reliable data to indicate the precise way these drugs are used in medical practice. Statistics on the total annual number of prescriptions written for a particular drug cannot, of themselves, answer questions as to whether that drug is overprescribed or misprescribed. For example, the medical need for a certain antianxiety agent may have been underestimated, particularly in the absence of data as to the number of persons whose anxiety symptoms are severe enough to warrant a physician's attention. Higher than expected use of such a drug also could be attributed to increased access to health care under federal programs such as Medicare and Medicaid, or to the trend toward treating mental illness in the community rather than in state institutions, or to factors beyond the control of medicine, such as inflation, unemployment, strained family relationships or shifting social values.[1]

Nonetheless, in view of the recent proliferation of psychoactive substances, physicians should guard against contributing to drug abuse through injudicious prescribing practices or by acquiescing to the demands of certain patients for instant chemical solutions to all their problems. Through his own attitude, each physician should convey to patients the concept that all drugs—no matter how helpful—are only part of an overall plan of treatment and management. He also can play a major role in reducing the abuse of prescription drugs by exercising good judgment in administering and prescribing psychoactive drugs, so that diversion to illicit use is avoided and the development of drug dependence is prevented or minimized.[2]

Underprescribing psychoactive drugs is a practice as unsound as overprescribing, since the patient is not optimally treated in either circumstance. For example, in managing terminally ill patients in pain, some physicians hesitate to provide sufficient analgesia for fear of addicting the patient,[3] despite clinical evidence that more than 90% of severe pain can be controlled through the appropriate use of narcotic analgesics.[4,5] "When it is clear that a patient is terminal," says Cohen,[3] "concerns about addiction become irrelevant. The primary goal is the comfort of the individual."

The greatest concern today, however, centers on the issue of overprescribing. Raskin[6] described overprescribing as "ordering medication which is not useful to meet the needs of the patient or, if it is useful, ordering an amount that is excessive in relation to the anticipated time-course of treatment." He suggested that overprescribing of psychoactive drugs occurs in response to two dominant influences:

LACK OF KNOWLEDGE: Asserting that physicians are not always as cognizant as they should be of the adverse consequences of excessive drug use, Raskin pointed to the fact that "most of the medically useful psychoactive drugs which are now extensively used were introduced after the majority of those physicians now practicing had completed their formal medical education." Other studies[7] cite the tendency of physicians to rely on pharmaceutical advertisements and package inserts for prescribing information.

PATIENT PRESSURE: Fed by articles in the popular press that report (often prematurely and inaccurately) the alleged benefits of a variety of drugs, some patients demand those drugs almost as a right. Raskin noted that such pressures can be powerful and are not always successfully resisted. Also, as Cohen[3] observes, "the symbolic meaning of the prescription ... to some patients cannot be denied." A prescription may be the only tangible item a patient takes away from a visit to the physician and, to some patients, it comes to signify that a caring relationship exists.

In addition to lack of knowledge and patient pressure, Cohen[3] enumerates several other factors that contribute to misuse or abuse of prescription drugs:

EXCESSIVE USE OF PRESCRIBED DRUGS: Patients may use psychoactive drugs in amounts larger than those prescribed to achieve intoxication or other desired mood changes, or intentionally or inadvertently increase the dose as tolerance develops.

PATIENTS WITH COMPLEX PROBLEMS: Patients with long histories of physical and emotional disorders that have not responded to treatment are highly vulnerable to drug dependence because of drug availability, the symptomatic relief obtained, and personality factors.

DIVERSION OF LEFTOVER DRUGS: Leftover prescription drugs in the family medicine cabinet can be a source of supply in initiating or maintaining drug dependence in family members other than those for whom the drugs were prescribed.

PATIENTS WITH MULTIPLE PHYSICIANS: Some patients with multiple complaints visit several physicians and receive prescriptions from all of them. Even if the drugs prescribed have a low abuse potential individually, combining them may potentiate their effects. For example, abusers have been known to dissolve tablets of Talwin (pentazocine) and Pyribenzamine (tripelennamine) and inject the combined solution—popularly known as "T's and Blues"—to achieve a heroin-like rush.[8,9] Other patients intentionally or inadvertently increase the mood-altering effects of prescription compounds by combining them with over-the-counter drugs.

CARELESS PRESCRIPTION WRITING: A prescription can be altered easily (as from 10 dosage units to 100) unless the physician takes specific steps to prevent this practice. Entering the quantity in Roman numerals or written form, as well as in Arabic numerals, is a widely advocated measure, as is careful completion of the refill information.[3,10,11] Stamping the prescription with a request to "please phone physician before filling" also is gaining popularity.

POOR PRESCRIPTION SECURITY: The prescription pad, Cohen maintains, is "worth more than its weight in gold to the drug-dependent person." A stolen pad of blank prescriptions can be used to obtain thousands of doses of prescription drugs for illicit purposes.

POOR SAFEGUARDING OF PHYSICIAN SUPPLIES: Repeated office break-ins occur when drug abusers discover that a physician keeps large quantities of drugs and syringes in his office or that security is poor. Similarly, a physician's bag left in plain view in an automobile invites break-ins.

DECEPTION OF PHYSICIANS BY DRUG ABUSERS: Because the addict's ability to deceive usually is greater than the physician's ability to cope with deception, Cohen asserts that any physician, no matter how ethical and alert, occasionally can be duped by "an addict whose waking hours are totally absorbed in generating ideas for obtaining drugs."

THE IMPAIRED PHYSICIAN: An impaired physician (especially one who is dependent on drugs or alcohol) can become a source of illicit drugs in several ways: by prescribing larger than necessary amounts of drugs as a reflection of his own substance abuse, in response to blackmail by someone who knows of his problem, or by becoming a "script doc" to generate sufficient income to support his own dependence.

THE SCRIPT DOC: Current estimates are that about one percent of all physicians deliberately overprescribe or misprescribe psychoactive drugs for profit.[3,12] This practice, says Cohen, can range from a deliberate operation in which a prescription is written for a fee every few minutes, to an easily duped physician who is "conned" repeatedly by drug abusers after he develops a reputation for gullibility.

REIMBURSEMENT REGULATIONS: Regulations and limitations imposed by third-party payers can impede sound prescribing practices. For example, if reimbursement rules allow only one office visit per month for patients suffering chronic pain, depression or anxiety, the physician may prescribe a larger amount of drugs than he otherwise would to maintain therapy until the patient's next visit.

INAPPROPRIATE ACTIONS BY SUPERVISORY BOARDS: Whereas, in the past, county and state medical ethics boards often were ineffective in correcting serious diversions of abusable drugs by medical professionals, current public concern has led some of these agencies to overzealousness. For example, some compliance authorities are using package inserts and the *Physicians' Desk Reference* as prescribing rules rather than guidelines. Observers have described situations in which conscientious physicians were arraigned for prescribing amounts in excess of the *PDR* dosage recommendation or for indications not mentioned in the *PDR*, while more serious forms of diversion were left unchecked.[3]

At a time when the deliberate alteration of mood states by chemicals is spreading, Cohen[3] says, a reevaluation of prescribing practices is warranted. Although heroin, marijuana, hallucinogens and inhalants do not reach illicit markets through medical channels, a certain amount of depressants, sedatives, analgesics and stimulants do. "Anything that can be done to reduce the availability of abused drugs should be done," he adds, "because increasing the difficulty of procurement tends to reduce the demand."

GUIDELINES FOR PRESCRIBING PSYCHOACTIVE DRUGS

Measures to counteract overprescribing and overutilization can take several approaches, including education, persuasion and legal control. Recognizing that physicians must be permitted the greatest latitude feasible in their use of drugs, the American Medical Association has initiated and participated in activities designed to influence physicians' prescribing practices through education and persuasion. For example, in 1971 the AMA House of Delegates adopted a resolution[13] urging all physicians to "limit their use of amphetamines and other stimulant drugs to specific, well-recognized medical indications." Extensive information on prescribing indications for the psychoactive drugs are published in the *AMA Drug Evaluations*.[2] Recently, the AMA collaborated with other professional organizations and federal agencies* in the development of guidelines for prescribers of controlled substances. These guidelines, issued by the federal Drug Enforcement Administration and endorsed by the AMA, provide "acceptable professional responses to the demands of the Controlled Substances Act."[14] Formulated to encourage voluntary compliance by physicians, the guidelines are neither a pronouncement of law nor a code of ethics. Rather, they are designed to supplement and support the ethical principles endorsed by the prescribing professions.[10]

The six general guidelines state that:

- Controlled substances have legitimate clinical usefulness and the prescriber should not hesitate to consider prescribing them when they are indicated for the comfort and well-being of patients.
- Prescribing controlled substances for legitimate medical uses requires special caution because of their potential for abuse and dependence.
- Good judgment should be exercised in administering and prescribing controlled substances so that diversion to illicit uses is avoided and the development of drug dependence is minimized or prevented.
- Physicians should guard against contributing to drug abuse through injudicious prescription writing practices, or by acquiescing to unwarranted demands by some patients.
- Each prescriber should examine his or her individual prescribing practices to ensure that all prescription orders for controlled substances are written with caution.
- Physicians should make a specific effort to ensure that patients are not obtaining multiple prescription orders from different prescribers.[10]

The eight specific guidelines for writing prescription orders state that:

- The prescription order must be signed by the prescriber when it is written. The prescriber's name, address, and DEA registration num-

---

*American Dental Association, American Nurses Association, American Osteopathic Association, American Podiatry Association, American Veterinary Medical Association, National Institute on Drug Abuse, Drug Enforcement Administration

ber, as well as the full name and address of the patient, must be shown on prescriptions for controlled substances.
- The written prescription order should be precise and distinctly legible to enhance exact and effective communications between prescriber and dispenser.
- The prescription order should indicate whether or not it may be renewed and, if so, the number of times or the duration for which renewal is authorized. Prescription orders for drugs in Schedules III, IV and V may be issued either orally or in writing and may be renewed if so authorized on the prescription order. However, the prescription order may only be renewed up to five times within six months after the date of issue. A written prescription order is required for drugs in Schedule II. The renewing of Schedule II prescription orders is prohibited. A dispenser may accept an oral order for Schedule II drugs only in an emergency, and such an oral order must be followed up by a written order within 72 hours. Controlled substances that are prescribed without an indication for renewal cannot be renewed without authorization by the prescriber.
- Physicians should prescribe no greater quantity of a controlled substance than is needed until the next check-up.
- Prescription orders should be made alteration-proof. When prescribing a controlled substance, the actual amount should be written out as well as given in Arabic numbers or Roman numerals to discourage alterations. Prescribers should consider placing a number of check-off boxes on their prescription blanks to show amounts within which the prescribed amount falls, such as 1-25, 26-50, 51-100, and over 100.
- A separate prescription blank should be used for each controlled substance prescribed.
- Physicians should avoid using prescription blanks that are pre-printed with the name of a proprietary preparation.
- When institutional prescription blanks are used, the prescriber should print his/her name, address, and DEA registration number on such blanks.

The guidelines conclude with a reminder that the prescriber has "a responsibility to inform patients of the effects of the prescribed drugs, consistent with good medical practice and professional judgment. The patient has a corresponding duty to comply with the prescriber's directions for use of the prescribed medication."[10]

RESTRICTIONS ON PRESCRIBING PSYCHOACTIVE DRUGS

The federal Comprehensive Drug Abuse Prevention and Control Act was passed in 1970 to regulate the manufacture, distribution and dispensing of controlled substances by providing a "closed" system for legitimate handlers of drugs. The act established five schedules of controlled drugs, with varying degrees of control for each schedule. Each drug subject to control is assigned to a schedule according to the following criteria:[16]

1. Scientific knowledge of the drug's pharmacological effects.
2. The state of current scientific knowledge regarding the substance.
3. The drug's history and current pattern of abuse.
4. The scope, duration and significance of abuse.
5. What, if any, risk the drug poses to the public health.
6. The drug's psychic or physiological dependence liability.
7. Whether the drug is an immediate precursor of a substance already controlled.

The schedules established by the Controlled Substances Act are as follows:[16]

SCHEDULE I: The drug or other substance has a high potential for abuse.
The drug or other substance has no currently accepted medical use in treatment in the United States.
There is a lack of accepted safety for use of the drug or other substance under medical supervision.

SCHEDULE II: The drug or other substance has a high potential for abuse.
The drug or other substance has a currently accepted medical use in treatment in the United States or a currently accepted medical use with severe restrictions.
Abuse of the drug or other substance may lead to severe psychological or physical dependence.

SCHEDULE III: The drug or other substance has a potential for abuse less than the drugs or other substances in Schedules I and II.

> The drug or other substance has a currently accepted medical use in treatment in the United States.
>
> Abuse of the drug or other substance may lead to moderate or low physical dependence or high psychological dependence.

SCHEDULE IV:
> The drug or other substance has a low potential for abuse relative to the drugs or other substances in Schedule III.
>
> The drug or other substance has a currently accepted medical use in treatment in the United States.
>
> Abuse of the drug or other substance may lead to limited physical dependence or psychological dependence relative to the drugs or other substances in Schedule III.

SCHEDULE V:
> The drug or other substance has a low potential for abuse relative to the drugs or other substances in Schedule IV.
>
> The drug or other substance has a currently accepted medical use in treatment in the United States.
>
> Abuse of the drug or other substance may lead to limited physical dependence or psychological dependence relative to the drugs or other substances in Schedule IV.

The major drugs classified under each schedule are shown in Table 37, below.

Responsibility for administration of the federal Comprehensive Drug Abuse Prevention and Control Act is assigned to the Drug Enforcement Administration (DEA). *A Manual for the Medical Practitioner*, which explains the provisions of the Controlled Substances Act, may be obtained from the DEA.* The *United States Pharmacopeia* includes the latest DEA regulations on prescribing controlled substances.[2]

Separate laws governing the prescribing of controlled substances have been enacted by most states. Although most of these are patterned after the federal law, some state requirements are more stringent than federal law and do not allow certain practices that may be authorized under federal law. Moreover, drugs may be classified differently by the states than by the federal government. Thus, physicians are urged to acquaint themselves with the exact provisions of the statutes and regulations in their local jurisdictions.[2,11]

---

*Drug Enforcement Administration, U.S. Department of Justice, Attention: Voluntary Compliance Programs, Washington, D.C. 20537

TABLE 37

Abbreviated Schedule of Controlled Substances: Federal Classification*

Schedule I	Schedule II	Schedule III	Schedule IV	Schedule V
NARCOTIC ANALGESICS Acetylmethadol (LAAM) Heroin STIMULANTS Amphetamine variants HALLUCINOGENS Analogs of phencyclidine Ibogaine Lysergic acid-25 (LSD) Marijuana, Hashish Mescaline Peyote Psilocybin, Psilocyn Tetrahydro-cannabinols	NARCOTIC ANALGESICS Alphaprodine Anileridine Codeine Dihydrocodeine Ethylmorphine Etorphine (M99) Fentanyl Hydrocodone Hydromorphone Levorphanol Meperidine (Pethidine) Methadone Morphine Opium Oxycodone Oxymorphone Phenazocine DEPRESSANTS Amobarbital Methaqualone Secobarbital Pentobarbital STIMULANTS Amphetamine Cocaine Methamphetamine Methylphenidate Phenmetrazine HALLUCINOGENS Phencyclidine	NARCOTIC ANALGESICS Acetaminophen + codeine APC + codeine Aspirin + codeine Nalorphine Paregoric DEPRESSANTS Any compound containing an unscheduled drug and: Amobarbital Secobarbital Pentobarbital Glutethimide Methyprylon STIMULANTS Benzphetamine Clortermine Mazindol Phendimetrazine	DEPRESSANTS Barbital Chloral betaine Chloral hydrate Chlordiazepoxide Clonazepam Clorazepate Diazepam Ethchlorvynol Ethinamate Fenfluramine Flurazepam Meprobamate Mephobarbital Oxazepam Paraldehyde Pentazocine Phenobarbital Propoxyphene Prazepam STIMULANTS Diethylpropion Phentermine Pemoline	Mixtures containing limited quantities of narcotic drugs, with non-narcotic active medicinal ingredients. Less abuse potential than Schedule IV. Generally for antitussive and antidiarrheal purposes. May be distributed without a prescription order.

*This table is based on federal regulations. State regulations may result in different classifications.

INDICATIONS FOR PRESCRIBING PSYCHOACTIVE DRUGS

Despite the widespread use of psychoactive drugs in medical practice, the number of patients who become dependent on drugs through medical treatment is relatively small. Hollister[18] observes that "millions of doses of opiates, sedatives and, until recently, stimulants, are administered to patients each day throughout the world. Yet cases of medically induced abuse of these drugs are rare. It would be a great pity if, because of exaggerated fears about using drugs, patients would be deprived of the real benefits that can be derived from their proper medical use."

OPIOIDS/NARCOTIC ANALGESICS

INDICATIONS: The problem of opioid dependence and the potential for non-medical use have caused physicians concern about prescribing narcotic analgesics.[4] Yet morphine and the other opioids have legitimate clinical usefulness in providing analgesia and other symptomatic relief. These drugs remain the primary agents for the relief of moderate to severe pain that cannot be alleviated by non-narcotic analgesics.[2,4]

For patients with chronic or intractable pain, it is legitimate practice to administer morphine-like drugs for prolonged periods when all reasonable alternatives (including the administration of other analgesics) have failed.[2] In such cases, patient comfort should be the physician's primary concern.[4] Long-term administration of morphine-like drugs most often is indicated in the treatment of terminal disorders, but—under certain circumstances—such treatment also may be indicated in non-fatal illnesses. However, the physician should keep in mind that long-term use (especially with parenteral administration) may result in tolerance to the therapeutic effects of the drug and some degree of dependence.[2]

The more potent narcotic analgesics generally are not indicated in the treatment of mild to moderate pain, particularly when such pain is caused by benign conditions, or in the treatment of pain that can be alleviated by non-narcotic analgesics. However, narcotics should not be withheld for short-term therapy of moderate to severe pain if the patient's needs warrant the use of such drugs. *Morphine* or its potent congeners is the drug of choice to relieve severe pain, such as that associated with biliary, renal or ureteral colic or acute myocardial infarction.[2,4]

Other indications for morphine-like drugs include preoperative sedation in anesthesia, control of cough or diarrhea, relief of certain forms of dyspnea, and relief of insomnia due to pain or cough.[2]

Although less potent that morphine on a milligram basis, *codeine* has a higher oral/parenteral potency ratio. Thus, it is commonly used in oral form to alleviate mild to moderate pain and as an antitussive. Codeine is classified as a Schedule II drug under the Controlled Substances Act because it is an opium derivative. However, products that contain codeine in combination with other drugs (such as acetominophen or APC) are classified as Schedule III drugs.[2,4]

ABUSE POTENTIAL: Morphine and morphine-like drugs usually are prescribed in the smallest effective dose and as infrequently as possible to minimize the development of physical dependence and tolerance. This is especially true in the treatment of chronic conditions or problems that might lead to drug abuse. With prolonged use of morphine-like drugs, the development of tolerance varies from patient to patient: some persons appear to develop little tolerance to the effects of these drugs, while others require increasing doses to achieve the same effect. Therefore, a patient who requests an increased dose of a morphine-like drug should be evaluated to determine if the patient's request is motivated by an increase in the severity of pain, an increased level of anxiety in the patient, or development of tolerance to the effects of the drug.[2]

The fact that morphine-like drugs relieve anxiety and tend to promote a feeling of well-being, in addition to producing analgesia, increases the potential for abuse by some patients. Such responses should be identified and those patients' use of the drugs monitored to prevent abuse and dependence. Most patients who are given a morphine-like drug for analgesia are able to discontinue its use without difficulty, even when they have developed mild degrees of dependence. A careful history is useful in determining which patients are at the greatest risk of developing a serious dependence problem and thus need to be monitored most closely.[2,4]

The dependence liability of codeine is less than that of morphine, and physical dependence seldom results from the use of codeine as an oral analgesic. However, abuse of codeine (especially in the form of cough syrup) is not uncommon.[2]

Patients who are already dependent on a morphine-like drug or who have a history of such dependence require special attention when they present with other medical or surgical problems. If adequate diagnostic evaluation indicates a genuine symptomatic need, the physician should prescribe analgesic medication in the same way he would for any other patient. However, several special considerations also require the physician's attention in such situations: (1) the effective dose level of morphine-like drugs will depend on the degree of tolerance already established, (2) abrupt withdrawal of such drugs can increase morbidity or result in death if a patient with an established dependence on morphine-like drugs undergoes major medical or surgical trauma, and (3) the patient may be simulating a disease condition in an effort to obtain the drug on which he is dependent. In managing a patient with such a problem, the physician may administer sufficient amounts of the drug to maintain the patient until he has recovered from his concurrent medical problem, then begin a regimen of gradual withdrawal from the dependence-producing drug.[2,4]

SEDATIVE/HYPNOTICS

INDICATIONS: All sedative and hypnotic drugs produce a degree of central nervous system depression. The principal purpose of therapy with these drugs is the relief of anxiety or insomnia without producing dependence.[2] In recent years, the *benzodiazepines* have virtually superseded other drugs for the treatment of anxiety or tension in medicine and surgery, as well as in psychiatry.[19] Although some patients may respond as well to carefully selected doses of non-benzodiazepine drugs, the more favorable benefit/risk ratio of the benzodiazepines has made them the drugs of choice when an antianxiety, sedative or hypnotic action is required. The development of tolerance, dependence, adverse drug interactions and overdose deaths is lower with the benzodiazepines than with many other sedative/hypnotic drugs.[2]

Clorazepate, chlordiazepoxide, diazepam, lorazepam, oxazepam, and *prazepam* (all of which are benzodiazepine derivatives) are used primarily to control moderate to severe anxiety and insomnia.[2] Another benzodiazepine, *flurazepam,* although seldom used for anxiety, is the most widely prescribed drug for insomnia. *Lorazepam* is used for insomnia associated with anxiety. (Some investigators[7] question the effectiveness of all hypnotic drugs in the long-term treatment of insomnia.) Other benzodiazepines are used to treat skeletal muscle hyperactivity, such as spasticity or localized spasm caused by trauma.[2,20]

Indications for prescribing *barbiturates* vary considerably among the agents available. *Phenobarbital* is used to manage certain convulsive disorders, as well as for insomnia and daytime sedation to reduce awareness, spontaneous activity and mild anxiety. *Butabarbital* also is used for insomnia and mild anxiety. *Amobarbital, secobarbital* and *pentobarbital* are used primarily in the treatment of insomnia. These drugs are not analgesics: when given to patients in pain without concurrent use of analgesics, they may produce paradoxical excitement.[2,21]

In selected patients, *chloral hydrate* is used as a hypnotic instead of the benzodiazepines or barbiturates. *Ethchlorvynol, ethinamate, glutethimide, methaqualone,* and *methyprylon* are no more effective hypnotics than the benzodiazepines or barbiturates and have the disadvantage of producing a degree of toxicity more serious than that of the benzodiazepines and often as severe as that seen with the barbiturates.[2,20] *Meprobamate* is used only to treat mild to moderate anxiety or localized muscle spasm. It is not as effective as the benzodiazepines for severe anxiety and has a greater potential for producing physical dependence. *Hydroxyzine* also is used to treat mild to moderate anxiety and apprehension, especially if antihistaminic and antiemetic actions also are desired. The potential for physical dependence is not as great with hydroxyzine as with meprobamate.[2,21]

The sedative and hypnotic drugs are not recommended for use with patients who have minor distress or discomfort. With such patients, the physician first should attempt to diagnose and treat the underlying disorders, rather than relying on these drugs exclusively for symptomatic relief.[2,21]

ABUSE POTENTIAL: Prolonged, uninterrupted use of barbiturates may result in tolerance and physical or psychological dependence, or both. Therapeutic doses of barbiturates and other sedative/hypnotics seldom induce physical dependence, but psychological dependence can result from therapeutic doses. Such psychological dependence may lead to continued use of increased doses, even when the clinical indications for drug therapy no longer prevail. Self-medication with large doses may constitute a chronic abuse problem and eventually produce physical dependence.[2]

Non-barbiturate hypnotics other than the benzodiazepines also have a high abuse potential, so substituting one of these drugs for a barbiturate does not necessarily reduce the risk of developing dependence.[2]

Intermediate- and short-acting barbiturates have a greater abuse potential than the long-acting barbiturates because of their more rapid onset of action and the relatively high intensity of their psychoactive effects. These barbiturates are classified in Schedule II of the Controlled Substances Act, as is methaqualone (which is widely popular as a drug of abuse). Phenobarbital and other long-acting barbiturates penetrate the brain gradually, so they do not produce the rapid euphoria sought by drug abusers; thus, their abuse potential is comparatively low.[2,19]

Barbiturate dependence does not follow a typical dose-response curve. Moderate doses (less than 300 mg per day) do not produce detectable physical dependence, although such doses may lead to psychological dependence. Physical dependence usually develops at doses in excess of 600 mg per day over a period of six to seven weeks. Tolerance becomes important as the individual increases the self-administered dose.[2,19]

In a patient with strong physical dependence on barbiturates, abrupt cessation of the drug is followed in two or three days by a severe withdrawal syndrome that usually is more serious than the opioid withdrawal syndrome. Convulsions, delirium, fever, coma and even death may result. When the physician suspects physical dependence on a sedative/hypnotic other than a benzodiazepine, substitution of phenobarbital is recommended for withdrawal through gradual reduction of dosage. Using benzodiazepines to withdraw patients from barbiturate dependence is not recommended.[2]

Prolonged administration of benzodiazepines or meprobamate (even within the therapeutic range) also may result in physical dependence. The symptoms are similar to those of chronic intoxication with alcohol or barbiturates. If the drug is abruptly discontinued, withdrawal reactions similar to those seen with barbiturates may appear within 36 hours to one week, depending on the drug's half-life and whether it is converted to an active metabolite.[2] This withdrawal reaction can be avoided by reducing the drug dosage gradually.[2,20,21]

Wesson[21] and Smith[22] suggest that the risk of developing tolerance to or dependence on sedative/hypnotic drugs can be reduced by encouraging patients to take "therapeutic holidays" from their drug regimens. With the longer-acting benzodiazepines, Wesson[21] believes these drug-free periods should be a week or more to allow the benzodiazepine metabolites to clear from the body. During this "holiday," symptoms suppressed by the drug may return, but the patient should be encouraged to tolerate the symptoms for the designated period of time to decrease tolerance and permit the physician to assess the continued need for the medication. Again, Wesson[21] and Smith[22] recommend gradually reducing drug dosage before each holiday to minimize physiological rebound and avoid a withdrawal reaction.

Hollister[23] summarizes the guidelines for prescribing anxiolytic drugs with Mies van der Rohe's dictum that "less is more," suggesting that using these drugs less may give better results. He recommends that the clinical use of antianxiety drugs be predicated on the assumption that they are an adjunct to other treatment, on the fluctuating natural course of anxiety, on the individualization of dosage to meet different patients' needs, and on a dosage schedule that maximizes symptomatic relief and minimizes daytime oversedation.

In recognition of the dependence liability of the sedative/hypnotic drugs, they are included in Schedule IV of the Controlled Substances Act. In addition, the Food and Drug Administration has asked the manufacturers of benzodiazepines to include labels warning that "anxiety or tension associated with the stress of everday life usually does not require treatment with an anxiolytic drug."[24]

STIMULANTS

INDICATIONS: Amphetamines and several chemically related drugs are central nervous system stimulants. Small doses of these drugs give the user a feeling of increased mental alertness and well-being. As dose size or frequency of administration increase, apprehension, decreased appetite, volubility, tremor and excitation occur. Because tolerance and dependence can develop quickly at high doses, the physician should prescribe amphetamines and other stimulants only for a specified purpose and length of time.[2]

Smith and Seymour[25] note that the medical use of stimulants for indications other than narcolepsy and hyperkinetic behavioral disorders of children—and, in short courses, for the initial treatment of obesity—is diminishing. In fact, abuse problems with these drugs have caused many physicians to stop prescribing them altogether. In the past, *amphetamines* were widely used as anorexiants to help patients limit their food intake and facilitate weight loss. However, the long-term efficacy of amphetamines as anorexiants has not been demonstrated, so the use of other drugs and non-drug programs for the treatment of obesity is preferred.[2]

Amphetamines also have been suggested for the diagnosis and treatment of depression, but these suggested indications are not supported by the results of controlled studies. They have been reported useful in combination with scopolamine to prevent very severe motion sickness, in conjunction with morphine to potentiate analgesic action, and (rarely) in conjunction with some anticonvulsants to counteract the sedative effects of those drugs.[2]

It is generally accepted that the use of amphetamines to allay fatigue is not justified except under the most extraordinary circumstances, since such use only impels the individual to a greater expenditure of his physical resources, sometimes to a hazardous point of fatigue whose symptoms are masked by the drug effects.[2,25]

Prolonged administration of stimulants to individuals who are dependent on barbiturates or alcohol is not appropriate therapy because such use can induce the patient to take increasing amounts of depressant drugs. Amphetamine-type drugs also are contraindicated in the treatment of other dependence-prone individuals, and their regular use to counteract the "hangover" effect of alcohol or barbiturates is hazardous.[2]

Cocaine's stimulant action accounts for its popularity among drug abusers, but its medical use is limited to topical anesthesia and, under certain surgical circumstances, nasal decongestion. However, prolonged use for the latter indication may result in ischemic damage to the nasal mucosa.[2]

Methylphenidate, a mild central nervous system stimulant, is useful in the management of hyperkinetic children and in the treatment of narcolepsy. Like the amphetamines, however, it has a potential for abuse and should be prescribed with caution. *Pemoline* is another stimulant used to treat hyperkinesis in children.[2,25]

ABUSE POTENTIAL: In prescribing stimulants for any medical purpose, the physician should be alert to signs of developing dependence and recognize that some patients may seek additional sources of supply, either on the illicit drug market or from another physician. There also is a danger that the efficacy of stimulants in helping a patient reach a time-limited goal might lead that person to regard amphetamine-type drugs as desirable rather than dangerous, thus encouraging future abuse.[2]

Amphetamine abuse can cause three types of medical problems: (1) chronic medical complications associated with drug effects (such as exacerbation of hypertension and development of arrhythmias or self-induced strokes and retinal damage due to vasospasm) or with drug administration (such as septicemia and endocarditis from contaminated needles), (2) emergency problems, including hyperthermia and convulsions resulting from toxic doses and acute amphetamine psychosis, and (3) signs and symptoms during the abstinence period following regular use that indicate drug dependence.[2,25]

Abuse of multiple drugs, especially concomitant use of amphetamines with sedative/hypnotics (including alcohol), is common. The use of stimulants in the morning and depressants at night is an exceedingly common pattern of abuse. In fact, problems associated with the secondary drug may mask the signs of amphetamine abuse.[2]

To reduce the potential for abuse, Smith and Seymour[25] recommend that physicians who prescribe stimulants supervise the patient carefully, review the drug program periodically, and—as with the sedative/hypnotics—introduce regular drug-free "holidays" into the medication regimen.

Amphetamines, methylphenidate and phenmetrazine are included in Schedule II of the Controlled Substances Act; other stimulants and anorexiants are classed as Schedule III and IV drugs.

ADDITIONAL FACTORS IN THE PRESCRIBING DECISION

Even when sound medical indications have been established for using a psychoactive drug, three additional factors should be weighed in deciding on the dosage and duration of drug therapy.[2]

1. *The severity of symptoms, in terms of the patient's ability to accommodate them.* Symptomatic relief is a legitimate goal of medical practice, but the use of many psychoactive drugs to achieve complete symptomatic relief requires caution because of the abuse potential and dependence liability of these drugs.
2. *The patient's reliability in taking medication, noted through observation and careful history-taking.* The physician should assess the patient's susceptibility to drug abuse before prescribing any psychoactive drug and weigh the benefits against the risks. The possible development of dependence in patients on long-term therapy should be monitored through periodic check-ups and family consultations.
3. *The dependence-producing capability of the drug.* Patients should be warned about possible adverse effects caused by interactions with other drugs, including alcohol.

IMPROVING PATIENT COMPLIANCE

The question of patient compliance with a prescribed drug regimen becomes especially pertinent when the drug in question has abuse potential. Surveys of patient compliance are not reassuring: as many as half of all patients sampled have deviated from the physician's directions in the following ways:[3]

- Never obtaining the prescribed drug.
- Never taking the prescribed drug.
- Taking the prescribed drug improperly (this involved taking an incorrect quantity per dose or an incorrect number of dosage units per day, omitting or "doubling up" doses, or discontinuing the drug prematurely).
- Taking non-prescribed drugs or discontinued medications in addition to or in place of the prescribed drug (the use of alcohol is frequently mentioned in this category).

Patient compliance is enhanced if the flow of information between physician and patient is open and reciprocal. Especially in prescribing psychoactive medications, the physician should carefully describe the purpose and use of the drug, as well as important adverse effects that might be experienced. Patients should be encouraged to report any untoward symptoms or significant deviations from the therapeutic regimen.[3,7]

Cohen[3] suggests that patient compliance can be improved if physicians take the following steps:

1. Inform the patient (or the person who will administer the medication) of the nature of the condition being treated.
2. Explain the effects of the prescribed drug in relation to the condition being treated. If the drug effects will be delayed, make this clear, to prevent the drug being abandoned before it can become effective.
3. Describe the exact amount of medication to be taken, how and when it should be taken, and for how long it should be taken. Specify the time of day and whether the drug should be taken before, with or after meals.
4. Mention any other drugs, foods or beverages that should be avoided while taking the prescribed drug.
5. Describe the side effects most likely to occur and explain what should be done about them (such as discontinuing the drug and/or calling the physician).
6. Review the drug program at each office visit. Ask the patient if he is using any other medications.

Cohen[3] advises that the drug program be kept as simple as possible, especially if the patient shows signs of difficulty in understanding it. For such patients, the physician might suggest the use of a drug diary, in which the patient records every dose of every drug immediately after it is ingested. Such a diary should be reviewed by the physician at the time of office visits.

IDENTIFYING THE "PATIENT HUSTLER"

Aside from patients who fail to comply with a prescribed drug regimen through lack of information or insufficient motivation, prescription drug misuse has another face: chronic drug abusers who approach physicians for the specific purpose of securing drugs to support their dependence. In the drug culture, such an approach is known as "working" or "making a doctor."[11] Almost every physician will encounter these "patient hustlers," whether in private practice, a clinic setting, a neighborhood health center, a busy emergency room, a rural area or a large metropolitan hospital.[26]

Chappel[12] cites four types of manipulative approaches used by "patient hustlers":

FEIGNING PHYSICAL PROBLEMS: A variety of physical problems can be convincingly portrayed by drug-seeking patients. These run the gamut from bleeding (often stimulated by the use of anticoagulants) and self-inflicted skin lesions, to gastrointestinal and musculoskeletal disorders.[12] Three of the most common presenting ailments among patients who seek narcotic drugs are renal colic, toothache and tic douloureux.

The patient feigning *renal colic* complains of pain on the left side of the body (to avoid a diagnosis of appendicitis) and a burning sensation on urination. If the physician asks for a urine sample, the patient might even prick his finger and drop a little blood into the urine.[11]

The patient presenting with *toothache* often claims to be from another town and to have left at home the medications prescribed by his own dentist. Should the physician wish to verify this claim, the telephone number supplied for the home-town dentist often is that of an accomplice. If the person actually has an abscessed tooth, he or she usually makes full use of it by visiting a series of physicians and dentists to ask for pain medication.[11]

Tic douloureux is a favorite approach among patient hustlers because it has no clinical or pathological signs. Patients complain of recurring, intense episodes of facial pain lasting several seconds to several minutes. Some patients are able to contort their faces to simulate an attack of pain.[11]

FEIGNING PSYCHOLOGICAL PROBLEMS: Most drug seekers who feign psychological problems are attempting to obtain stimulants or depressants rather than analgesics. The psychological complaints most often presented by these "patient hustlers" include anxiety, insomnia, fatigue and depression.[12]

DECEPTION: Manipulative techniques employed to deceive physicians include prescription theft, forgery and alterations, concealing or pretending to take medications, and requesting refills in a shorter period of time than originally prescribed (often with the excuse that the medication was "lost" or "stolen").[11,12]

PRESSURING THE PHYSICIAN: Coercive tactics include eliciting sympathy or guilt (as by suggesting that medical treatment caused the patient's drug dependence), direct threats of physical or financial harm, the offer of bribes, or using the names of influential family members or friends.[12,26]

Although these tactics seem obvious when described, they can be employed very convincingly, especially in the midst of a busy medical office or emergency department. However, the physician can protect himself if he is alert to certain behaviors that are common among drug seekers:

- The patient who presents a dramatic and compelling, but vague, complaint.[12,26]
- The patient whose subjective complaints are not accompanied by the usual objective signs.[12]
- The patient who makes a self-diagnosis and specifically requests a certain drug.[12]
- The patient who has no interest in a diagnosis, fails to keep appointments for x-rays or laboratory tests, or refuses to see another physician for a consulting opinion.[11,12]
- The patient who rejects all forms of treatment that do not include psychoactive drugs.[12]

The pressure drug seekers can bring to bear on a physician are considerable. However, the physician who is alert to the tactics employed by these individuals usually can avoid being deceived or manipulated. Wilson and Gilmore[26] suggest that, in the face of such tactics, the physician (1) maintain control of the doctor-patient relationship, (2) remain professional in the face of ploys for sympathy or guilt and (3) regard the drug seeker as a patient with a serious illness.

In situations where the patient's motives are not clear and the patient history or physical examination indicates that the complaint may be real, Chappel[12] suggests that the physician prescribe the smallest possible amount of an appropriate drug pending the results of confirming diagnostic procedures.

A THEORETICAL FRAMEWORK FOR RATIONAL PRESCRIBING

As Cohen[3] observes, "the relationship between the doctor, the patient and the prescription medication merits reexamination to improve information exchange and compliance." Such reexamination can help physicians and patients achieve the optimal therapeutic use of drugs and avoid the unintentional sustenance of drug dependence. To achieve an optimal level of prescribing practice, Cohen,[3] Anylan[7] and Chappel[12] suggest that thorough training in pharmacology and therapeutics be provided at the medical school, internship and residency levels, as well as in continuing education programs. They also encourage physicians to:

- Stay abreast of the current literature on therapeutic advances.
- Provide patients with relevant information about all drugs prescribed, including refill instructions and what to do with any unused amounts.

- Keep adequate records of the effects and side effects of every drug prescribed.
- Continue to learn about clinical therapeutics from personal experience in treating patients and through exchange of information with peers.

REFERENCES

1. Boyle, J. F. and Freedman, D. X. *Statement of the American Medical Association Before the Select Committee on Narcotics Abuse and Control on the Use of Psychotropic Drugs in Medical Practice* (United States House of Representatives, September 19, 1978)
2. *AMA Drug Evaluations* (American Medical Association, Chicago, Ill., 1980)
3. Cohen, S. Drug abuse and the prescribing physician in C. Buchwald, S. Cohen, D. Katz and J. Solomon (eds.) *Frequently Prescribed and Abused Drugs: Their Indications, Efficacy and Rational Prescribing* Medical Monograph Series, Vol. II, No. 1 (National Institute on Drug Abuse, Rockville, Md., 1980)
4. Schnoll, S. H. Pain in C. Buchwald, S. Cohen, D. Katz and J. Solomon (eds.) *Frequently Prescribed and Abused Drugs: Their Indications, Efficacy and Rational Prescribing* Medical Monograph Series, Vol. II, No. 1 (National Institute on Drug Abuse, Rockville, Md., 1980)
5. Kotulak, R. Cancer pain improperly treated, expert says *Chicago Tribune* (April 4, 1978)
6. Raskin, H. A. The problem of drug misuse and overmedication *Federation Bulletin* 59(11):383 (November 1972)
7. Elliott, J. Physician prescribing practices criticized; solutions in question *JAMA* 241(22):2353 (June 1, 1979)
8. Pentazocine reclassified in Illinois *JAMA* 240(21):2234 (November 17, 1978)
9. Hecht, A. The saga of T's and Blues *FDA Consumer* 10 (March 1979)
10. *Guidelines for Prescribers of Controlled Substances* (U.S. Department of Justice, Drug Enforcement Administration, Washington, D.C., December 1979)
11. *Controlled Substances Regulations Reference* (California Department of Justice, Division of Law Enforcement, Sacramento, Cal. 1979)
12. Chappel, J. N. *Patient Manipulation of the Physician* (Workshop on the Ethics & Practice of Prescribing Psychoactive Drugs, Haight Ashbury Training and Education Project, San Francisco, Cal., July 18, 1980)
13. *Proceedings of the House of Delegates 269* (American Medical Association, Chicago, Ill., 1971)
14. DEA guidelines endorsed *American Medical News* (December 12, 1979)
15. Buzzeo, R. W. DEA investigations, DAWN, and prescription guidelines for practitioners *Federation Bulletin* 66:325 (November 1979)
16. Criteria by which drugs are scheduled *Drug Enforcement* 6:8 (July 1979)

17. *Controlled Substances Act of 1970* (U.S. Department of Justice, Drug Enforcement Administration, Washington, D.C., 1970)
18. Hollister, L. Psychotropic drug interactions *in* C. Buchwald, S. Cohen, D. Katz and J. Solomon (eds.) *Frequently Prescribed and Abused Drugs: Their Indications, Efficacy and Rational Prescribing* Medical Monograph Series, Vol. II, No. 1 (National Institute on Drug Abuse, Rockville, Md., 1980)
19. Rees, W. L. Psychotropic drugs: uses in medical and psychosomatic disorders *Psychosomatics* 20(12):837 (December 1979)
20. Kales, A., Kales, J. D. Scharf, M. B. and Soldatos, C. R. The prescription of hypnotic drugs *in* C. Buchwald, S. Cohen, D. Katz and J. Solomon (eds.) *Frequently Prescribed and Abused Drugs: Their Indications, Efficacy and Rational Prescribing* Medical Monograph Series, Vol. II, No. 1 (National Institute on Drug Abuse, Rockville, Md., 1980)
21. Wesson, D. R. Anxiety: its meaning and psychotropic drug treatment *in* C. Buchwald, S. Cohen, D. Katz and J. Solomon (eds.) *Frequently Prescribed and Abused Drugs: Their Indications, Efficacy and Rational Prescribing* Medical Monograph Series, Vol. II, No. 1 (National Institute on Drug Abuse, Rockville, Md., 1980)
22. Smith, D. E. *Benzodiazepines* (Workshop on the Ethics & Practice of Prescribing Psychoactive Drugs, Haight Ashbury Training and Education Project, San Francisco, Cal., July 18, 1980)
23. Hollister, L. E. Uses of psychotherapeutic drugs *Annals of Internal Medicine* 79(1):88 (July 1973)
24. FDA acts to clamp down on tranquilizers *Chicago Tribune* (July 11, 1980)
25. Smith, D. E. and Seymour, R. B. The prescription of stimulants and anorectics *in* C. Buchwald, S. Cohen, D. Katz and J. Solomon (eds.) *Frequently Prescribed and Abused Drugs: Their Indications, Efficacy and Rational Prescribing* Medical Monograph Series, Vol. II, No. 1 (National Institute on Drug Abuse, Rockville, Md., 1980)
26. Wilson, S. J. and Gilmore, R. Manipulative tactics of narcotics addicts *Medical Times* 102(9):81 (September 1974)

CHAPTER 11
THE DRUG-ABUSING PHYSICIAN

Physicians whose health is impaired usually are not able to give optimal medical care to their patients.

The physician who has a physical illness or disability may be reluctant to recognize that fact, but the signs and symptoms of the illness generally are fairly apparent, both to himself and to others. Likewise, the degree of his impairment and the limitations it places on his professional activities can be determined without too much difficulty.[1]

Not so with the physician who has a problem with drug abuse. Yet, as Shortt[2] observes, drug abuse is "an illness to which physicians are inordinately susceptible." Citing statistical evidence that drug abuse was the primary diagnosis in approximately one in five cases of physicians receiving inpatient psychiatric treatment, Shortt concludes that physicians seem twice as likely to misuse mood-altering drugs as their social peers.

Until recently, however, neither the public nor the medical profession had responded significantly to this situation. State licensing laws and regulatory agencies typically had restricted practice privileges only upon proof of fault or of injury to patients. Also, most states failed to grant civil immunity to persons who reported instances of questionable professional conduct associated with drug abuse or other disorders. This lack of protection against possible litigation reinforced the reluctance of colleagues to bring an impaired physician to the attention of licensing authorities, medical societies and hospital committees. An uneasy feeling that "next, it could be me" also contributed to inaction, as did the mistaken notion that a physician would be sufficiently astute to recognize his own disability and seek help in overcoming it.[1]

However, the impaired physician who was that "astute" seldom received encouragement. More often than not, he felt isolated and was unwilling to turn to colleagues out of fear of notoriety and loss of self-esteem and professional standing. Such a physician was confronted by a series of difficult questions. Would seeking out treatment mean a loss of status in the community? Would it necessitate suspension of practice for an extended period of time, with a consequent sacrifice of income? Would recovery fail to restore the confidence of fellow physicians and the trust of patients? And, if the answers to all these questions appeared to be "yes," would seeking help really be the best alternative?

It is only within the past 10 years that this dilemma has attracted the interest of legislators and consumers of health care and stimulated the medical profession to develop programs for the identification and treatment of impaired physicians. While the mechanics of these programs vary considerably, most rely heavily on the general physician population for the initial identification of colleagues suspected of abusing alcohol or other drugs, or suffering emotional disorders.[3]

On a national level, the American Medical Association provided early leadership in the area of physician impairment. In 1972, the AMA House of Delegates adopted a policy statement[4] declaring that any physician who became aware of an apparent problem in a colleague had an ethical responsibility to take affirmative action—to seek treatment or rehabilitation for his fellow physician. In 1974, the AMA Council on Legislation drafted model legislation[5] that state legislatures could use in modifying individual medical practice acts to provide for the treatment and rehabilitation of impaired physicians.

The response of state medical societies to these initiatives has been dramatic. Whereas an AMA survey in the early 1970's showed that only seven state medical societies had identifiable committees on the problems of impaired physicians, today such committees have been established in nearly every state.[6]

STATE MEDICAL SOCIETY PROGRAMS

A state medical society is in a particularly advantageous position to act as the impaired physician's advocate. The society can give such physicians an opportunity to seek help while maintaining their dignity, preserving their anonymity and sparing them embarrassment. A structured medical society program encourages coordination of efforts and gives the impaired physician a charted course to follow. Also, programs at the state level generally assure confidentiality and privacy, while simultaneously providing opportunities for constructive persuasion.[7] (Up-to-date information on state medical society programs is available from the Department of Mental Health, American Medical Association.)

Generally speaking, all medical society programs can be characterized as coercive or non-coercive. Coercive programs typically offer the impaired physician confidential and non-punitive assistance, but report such a physician to the state's board of medical examiners if he refuses to cooperate in his own rehabilitation and if his continued practice is not deemed to be in his patients' best interests. Non-coercive programs will not take this second step, although they may suggest such action to the persons who originally expressed concern about a physician.

Medical society programs usually have a mechanism that allows for confidential reporting of perceived distress or impairment. Reports may come from colleagues, hospital administrators, nurses, patients or the physician's family. In states where there is close cooperation between the licensing board and the medical society, referrals may come from the board.

Clear channels of contact, accessible to all physicians, aid greatly in encouraging reporting. The use of "hot lines," in which the medical society sets up a central telephone number to receive allegations of impairment, has been found to be useful in soliciting reports. Other programs, preferring that reporters contact a committee member, publish the names and telephone numbers of committee members in society journals or distribute such a listing to all member physicians.

Once it is determined that a report is correct, significant and warrants further action, the information typically is given to the committee member or members who are responsible for confronting the physician with evidence of his impairment and persuading him to seek treatment. Some societies have a separate committee or group to handle the confrontation process.

Treatment is best carried out beyond the confines of the medical society program. To discourage overlapping of roles, it generally is recommended that a physician who serves on an impaired physician program and who has been directly involved in confronting a particular physician should not serve as that physician's therapist.

It also is recommended that the medical society monitor only the fact that treatment has occurred, not the actual course of treatment, to preserve the confidentiality of the physician-patient relationship. If the impaired physician is aware that his therapist reports treatment details to the medical society, he may withhold information that is necessary for successful treatment.

Although some states have laws that prohibit medical society involvement in treatment and rehabilitation, the medical society can prepare a list of treatment facilities that accept physicians as patients, both in the state and out of state. The society also can prepare a list of resources available for aftercare and act as the physician's advocate during reentry and, if necessary, before a licensing body.

Cooperative efforts among residents' house staff organizations and medical society programs can be beneficial to all involved. The medical society can help sponsor educational programs aimed at preventing impairment, train residents in confrontation techniques and fund facilitators to work with support groups.

HOSPITAL-BASED PROGRAMS

A hospital is legally responsible for everything that occurs within its confines. A lawsuit resulting from the negligence of an impaired physician, for example, may be brought against not only the individual physician, but also the hospital where he has staff privileges. In addition, an impaired physician may bring suit against a hospital for allowing him to practice while impaired.[8]

Consequently, several hospitals have established programs to ensure adequate monitoring of staff physicians and other practitioners to detect emerging impairment and encourage early treatment. Ideally, these programs are coordinated with those of local and state medical societies.

Recommended features of effective hospital-based programs include:

1. Incorporating a formal policy on impairment in the hospital's by-laws. A defined, sanctioned mechanism can encourage physicians to seek help early.
2. Establishing a special group or committee of the medical staff to receive and verify allegations of impairment.
3. Training selected members of the medical staff in intervention techniques, if confrontation is to be handled within the hospital program. It generally is recommended that a confrontation team include the physician's department head, plus one or two other well-liked and respected staff members. Staff officers who have disciplinary authority ordinarily should not be included because their presence might discourage reporting.
4. Adopting a non-punitive approach in which the hospital serves as advocate for the physician who agrees to undergo treatment. A physician who refuses to cooperate, however, might be warned that his staff privileges could be suspended or revoked.
5. Publicizing the existence of the hospital's policy on impairment to staff members and their spouses.
6. Initiating an educational program for medical staff, hospital workers and administrative staff to increase their awareness, change negative attitudes and provide cognitive information on drug abuse and other forms of impairment. Enlisting a recovered physician to discuss his impairment and rehabilitation often is helpful.
7. Developing educational programs for medical spouses to encourage early reporting by the physician's family.

STATE MEDICAL BOARD PROGRAMS

Medical boards, by their very nature, owe primary allegiance to the public, but many are sympathetic to the problems of impaired physicians and devote much time, patience and thought to treating and rehabilitating physicians who come before them. A licensing board that espouses such an approach can be a valuable resource to a medical society program for impaired physicians. In the case of an uncooperative physician, for example, the board can protect the public while simultaneously providing significant motivation for the impaired physician to complete treatment.

The AMA Model Disabled Doctor Act[5] urges close cooperation between medical societies and licensing boards. In states where this level of cooperation exists, boards refer impaired physicians to medical society programs so that the physicians can be persuaded to undergo treatment. If these persuasive efforts are unsuccessful, the medical society often refers the physicians back to the medical board for disciplinary action.[9]

CONFRONTING THE DRUG-ABUSING PHYSICIAN

Confrontation is tantamount to motivation. For this reason, it is recognized as a valuable technique for assessing the nature and seriousness of a physician's drug problem and helping him (or her) to seek appropriate treatment, while protecting his dignity, preserving his anonymity and sparing him embarrassment.

Confrontation is not synonymous with provocation: it can be a supportive and informative experience. The fact remains, however, that it is not an easy or pleasant task, or one that should be lightly undertaken.

THE CONFRONTATION TEAM

Confrontation should be a team effort by at least two persons. It takes courage to confront a colleague, and the team concept allows the confronters to give one another emotional support and monitor each other's progress.

At least one of the confronters should be someone with whom the physician can identify: someone in the same specialty, of the same sex, or recovered from the same impairment. It is recommended that there be no prior social or personal connection between the confronters and the impaired physician; thus, it often is advisable to use confronters from a different geographic area.

Confronters must possess certain attributes: compassion, empathy and sincerity; a non-judgmental and supportive attitude; cognitive knowledge or expertise in treating impairment; training in intervention strategies; and tolerance and patience.

PREPARING FOR THE CONFRONTATION

Before a confrontation is undertaken, allegations of impairment must be carefully verified, although this does not necessarily have to be done by the confronters.

The confronters should have access to all information about the physician's impairment. Before they contact the impaired physician, the confronters should become thoroughly familiar with this information, develop a specific confrontation plan and define an appropriate goal for the confrontation. A psychiatrist may be consulted to help the confrontation team anticipate and handle the impaired physician's reaction.

Once the confronters are prepared attitudinally and informationally, the confrontation should take place without delay. One of the reasons impairment so often is severe is that it has long gone undetected and untreated. The earlier the physician can be persuaded to seek treatment, the better his prognosis for recovery.

THE CONFRONTATION PROCESS

The confrontation team should make an appointment to meet with the impaired physician as soon as possible. The physician should be told that the appointment is to discuss an urgent professional matter that requires prompt attention.

The location of the confrontation meeting should be one that is comfortable for the physician being confronted. Because confrontation often is an emotionally charged and volatile episode, it is best to avoid public places.

The following outline describes the process used by many confrontation teams:

1. Introduce yourself and your colleague(s) to the physician and explain that you represent the medical society or hospital staff.
2. Explain the medical society's or hospital's program for impaired physicians and stress its advocacy role.
3. Present information on the physician's drug-abusing behavior in a factual, non-judgmental manner. Be specific.
4. Anticipate the physician's responses, such as denial, anger or rationalization. (Often, a person who rationalizes his behavior is

beginning to acknowledge that there is a problem.) Never argue with him, express anger or become defensive about your actions as a confronter, even in the face of a personal or professional attack.

5. Don't allow the physician to sidetrack the discussion with demands that you divulge your sources of information. Maintain the anonymity of the reporter.
6. Ask specific questions to reinforce the consequences of the physician's drug-abusing behavior, but don't harp on his indiscretions.
7. Ask the physician what the term "drug abuse" means to him. (Generally, he will portray a drug abuser in terms far removed from his own circumstances.)
8. Tell him how you define drug abuse. Advise him as to the nature of this behavior and its prognosis, treated and untreated. Bring printed information on drug abuse that you can leave with the physician.
9. Give the physician your assessment of the seriousness of his problem, based on the reports received and your own observations. Point out that he is responsible for his own recovery.
10. Explain what may happen if the physician does not seek treatment, mentioning any coercive aspects of the medical society's program.
11. Discuss possible treatment resources, both local and out of state. Emphasize again that rehabilitation is available and usually effective. Give the physician hope for recovery.
12. Once a mutually acceptable treatment source is agreed upon, give the physician information on how to contact that resource. If necessary, have him make the call while you are with him.

The preceding outline assumes that the initial confrontation will motivate the impaired physician to seek treatment. However, this is the exception rather than the rule: further confrontation usually is required.[10]

TREATING THE DRUG-ABUSING PHYSICIAN

The drug-abusing physician often is seriously ill by the time he enters treatment. Typically, he is more deteriorated and adaptively impoverished in every sense—physical, psychological, social and spiritual—than the non-physician patient. He is likely to have been so completely absorbed in his practice that he has become isolated from other people and unable to articulate his feelings. Because elaborate defense and denial mechanisms are part of his illness, he will go to great lengths to deny that a problem exists and to maintain the illusion that his life is under complete control. These are formidable obstacles to treatment.

One of the key problems in treating an impaired physician is that he often vehemently rejects the role of patient.

TREATMENT CONSIDERATIONS

Differential diagnosis of drug dependence always must consider the possibility that a major psychiatric syndrome is associated with the chemical dependence. Among drug-dependent physicians, however, there is a relatively low incidence of thought disorder. Rather, most psychopathology involves depression related to the dependency state.[11]

Taking the initial history and making treatment plans for detoxifying the drug-abusing physician is complicated by two important factors: the usual presence of a higher level of physical dependence than is encountered with non-physician patients, and the frequency with which physicians attempt to minimize the severity of their problem.

While physicians who abuse drugs are a heterogeneous group, they do have several characteristics in common, and these commonalities help to determine treatment techniques. For example, whereas "street" addicts tend to congregate in a drug culture, physician addicts do not. Addiction is a private and isolated part of the physician's life and he usually avoids contact with others for fear that his drug abuse will be discovered.

INPATIENT TREATMENT

Most drug-dependent physicians cannot be treated initially as outpatients. Typically, they have been taking extremely high doses of drugs in relatively pure form. Because of this fact, most opioid-dependent physicians cannot be detoxified with non-narcotic medications: methadone usually is needed. Often detoxification must be done in a private facility rather than a public hospital because of the physician's reluctance to be treated in a public setting.

Inpatient treatment is almost always indicated if there are medical complications or if the physician's denial is considerable. An inpatient setting gives therapists continual opportunities to confront the physician with the realities of his illness and to break through his denial mechanisms. In such an environment, moreover, a higher degree of directive therapy is possible and the risk of suicide is minimized. Inpatient treatment centers also provide close-knit groups to help the physician overcome his sense of loss in giving up the use of drugs. Such treatment underscores the serious nature and reality of the illness and establishes a basis for continued therapy in subsequent outpatient care.

OUTPATIENT TREATMENT

General guidelines for treating drug-dependent physicians on an outpatient basis include: (1) don't moralize, but give the physician every encouragement that recovery will occur, (2) be firm, yet kind and compassionate, (3) be honest and develop trust, (4) be extremely cautious in the use of any mood-altering drugs that can provide a new outlet for the physician's drug dependence, (5) be certain that the physician remains in the role of patient and does not take over management of his own treatment, and (6) do not ignore continued drug-taking and continue treatment as if this behavior were not present. In such cases, consider the possibility of hospitalizing the physician. If treatment is instituted in the early stages of drug dependence, outpatient care may allow some physicians to remain in practice while being treated (however, their practice may have to be curtailed or restricted in some ways).

TREATMENT PROGNOSIS

Although there are few controlled studies of treatment outcome for impaired physicians, the existing data seem to show that physicians have a better than average chance of making a good recovery. Experience at the Hazeldon Foundation indicates that poor outcome generally is related to use of multiple mood-altering substances, in combination or sequentially, and to the number of prior treatment efforts: recovery chances diminish for the physician who has been treated repeatedly. Data on patients treated at the Mayo Clinic show that physicians are twice as likely as non-physicians to complete the prescribed course of treatment.[11]

Experience at the Haight Ashbury Free Medical Clinic and the San Francisco Polydrug Research Project indicate that, if certain key steps are accomplished (overcoming denial, getting the physician to admit he needs help, developing a treatment program tailored to the physician's needs, and persuading the drug-abusing physician to enter treatment), the prognosis is better for physicians than for "street" addicts. The physician's professionalism often gives him the sense of self-worth necessary to complete the treatment process.[11]

AFTERCARE AND REENTRY

The drug-abusing physician needs effective aftercare and counseling to modify the lifestyle and attitudes that caused his problem in the first place. Since most physicians want to return to practice as soon as possible and feasible, aftercare often is provided on an outpatient basis. Residential programs and group processes used in the treatment of non-physicians generally are not as effective with physician-patients. Group therapy has varied success, as physicians tend not to remain in groups that include a significant number of non-physicians. Thus, aftercare for the drug-dependent physician can be very difficult to develop.

Vocational rehabilitation and re-education of the impaired physician can be effective if they are tailored to meet individual needs. Of course, physicians who are substantially impaired need more assistance than those who are not. On the other hand, most social and vocational reentry problems can be avoided if the physician's ability to practice remains intact throughout the treatment process.

Wherever possible, the therapist should serve as an advocate for the recovering physician with colleagues and the public. If the physician is unable to resume his previous practice, he should be helped to develop an alternative career consonant with his abilities.

OPPORTUNITIES FOR PREVENTION

The critical time for prevention efforts is during medical student and residency training, for that is the time behavioral patterns are established. Teaching students and residents how to cope with the stresses of medical education, as well as how to support and accept each other, may decrease the incidence of impairment in the future.

For any prevention effort to succeed, medical schools must accept responsibility for reducing impairment potential by actively supporting the concepts of personal development and well-being, ensuring that adequate attention is given to the humanistic dimensions of education, and—where possible—eliminating unnecessary sources of stress. The continuum of medical education should be structured in a way that allows medical students and residents to develop a lifestyle compatible with the demands of education. Students also should be encouraged to develop stabilizing outside interests.

During orientation, students and residents should be given a realistic description of medicine that highlights the stresses and strengths of the profession, including its high vulnerability to psychiatric disorders, alcoholism and drug dependence. Predictable areas of stress should be identified and the availability of resources to help students and residents through their training should be publicized.

The value of appropriate role models cannot be overemphasized. Healthy identification with faculty members helps students and residents develop attitudes about themselves and their careers that may serve as buffers against future impairment. It is essential, therefore, that faculty members understand the value of role models, the necessity of caring human relations, and the need for positive interaction with students. Faculty members also can help foster the development of a social network among their students by focusing on common tasks.

Cognitive information on drug dependence and alcoholism should be included in the curriculum, with an opportunity to discuss stereotypical perceptions and any ingrained attitudes the students may have. Such education alerts students and residents to the true nature and prognosis of addiction, increases the likelihood that they will recognize substance abuse in peers, teachers and patients, and promotes understanding and compassion for those so impaired. Interested students should be given an opportunity to acquire further skills in diagnosis and treatment.

Support groups can be most valuable by giving students and residents an opportunity to get to know their peers outside the classroom, as well as to identify and express personal problems, fears and doubts. Students also learn to take risks—to confront, to share, to receive and give support, and to adapt to stress. Fostering such exchanges during medical education increases the likelihood that they will continue in the practice years.

A program for early detection and intervention can be successful only with the active support of medical school administration, but also requires clear separation from the administration if it is to be viewed as constructive rather than punitive. Students need to understand that if they develop a problem, they will be given help. They need to know that asking for help and/or seeking treatment will not jeopardize their careers and that, if long-term treatment is needed, they will be able to resume their education, consonant with their abilities.

A successful intervention program must allow for early and confidential identification of developing impairment. The moral and ethical responsibility of the faculty, administrators and peers in identifying troubled students should be stressed to encourage such reporting. A highly visible contact person, assurance of strict confidentiality, and a manifest attitude of respect and compassion facilitate early identification.

Although confrontation should be undertaken when necessary, it is a process that requires an experienced staff. While peer confrontation can be beneficial, few students or residents are comfortable in making such an approach. The use of intervenors from outside the program has the advantage of assuring the necessary impartiality and confidentiality.

Once impairment is identified, access to treatment resources should be rapid. Counseling should be available through the university or through a private group outside the university structure. Support groups also can be used effectively in rehabilitation. The administration should be involved only if intervention techniques fail or if the impairment is so severe as to warrant immediate action.

Rehabilitation is always preferable to removal, but if impairment is profound or a student refuses to seek help after repeated confrontations, removal may be necessary.

Successful programs of identification, confrontation and rehabilitation, as well as innovative programs aimed at preventing impairment, are functioning in several medical schools and residency programs, and can serve as models for other institutions.[12]

REFERENCES

1. Steindler, E. M. (ed.) *The Impaired Physician: An Interpretive Summary of the AMA Conference on "The Disabled Doctor: Challenge to the Profession"* (American Medical Association, Chicago, Ill., 1976)
2. Shortt, S. E. D. Psychiatric illness in physicians *Canadian Medical Association Journal* 121:283 (August 4, 1979)
3. Niven, R. G. Physicians' perceptions and attitudes toward disabled colleagues in J. J. Robertson (ed.) *The Impaired Physician: Proceedings of the Third AMA Conference* (American Medical Association, Chicago, Ill., 1979)
4. Policy Statement on Physician Impairment (American Medical Association, Chicago, Ill., 1972)
5. Model Bill for an Act Concerning the Practice of Medicine (American Medical Association, Chicago, Ill., 1974)
6. Smith, R. J. Overview of impaired physician programs in J. J. Robertson (ed.) *The Impaired Physician: Proceedings of the Third AMA Conference* (American Medical Association, Chicago, Ill., 1979)
7. State medical society programs—organization and operation in J. J. Robertson (ed.) *The Impaired Physician: Proceedings of the Third AMA Conference* (American Medical Association, Chicago, Ill., 1979)
8. Hospital programs for impaired medical staff in J. J. Robertson (ed.) *The Impaired Physician: Proceedings of the Third AMA Conference* (American Medical Association, Chicago, Ill., 1979)

9. State medical boards and impaired physicians in J. J. Robertson (ed.) *The Impaired Physician: Proceedings of the Third AMA Conference* (American Medical Association, Chicago, Ill., 1979)
10. Confrontation techniques in J. J. Robertson (ed.) *The Impaired Physician: Proceedings of the Third AMA Conference* (American Medical Association, Chicago, Ill., 1979)
11. Inpatient and outpatient treatment techniques in J. J. Robertson (ed.) *The Impaired Physician: Proceedings of the Third AMA Conference* (American Medical Association, Chicago, Ill., 1979)
12. *Beyond Survival* (Resident Physicians Section, American Medical Association, Chicago, Ill., 1980)

CHAPTER 12
APPROACHES TO
DRUG ABUSE PREVENTION
AND EARLY INTERVENTION

Prevention of drug abuse has been fraught with controversy since the late 1960's,[1] when a public alarmed by reports of dramatic increases in illicit drug use demanded government programs to reverse the trend.[2] Since that time, a multitude of techniques and approaches have been proposed. Those now in use include:

- Programs to enhance individual self-esteem, including school-based approaches to affective development.
- Approaches aimed at improving communication skills at both the individual and group levels, including skill-building exercises for teachers and other adults who work with youth.
- Development of conflict resolution and problem-solving techniques.
- Approaches that involve improving school climate and classroom discipline.
- Recreational and job-oriented programs.
- Peer tutoring and peer counseling programs.
- Individual and group-oriented counseling programs.[3]

Most of the early prevention approaches focused on two principal targets: *individuals,* and *small groups* in which individuals have significant interaction, particularly family and peer groups. More recently, prevention programs that facilitate constructive, mutually agreed upon change within schools, youth service agencies and places of employment, for example, have had an impact on *organizations* as well, adding a third dimension to program planning. Many of the newest prevention and education programs are designed to affect an entire *community.* The goals of these programs may range from linking families with community services, to improving neighborhoods, to influencing public policy and legislation.[3]

However, the value of many of these programs has been questioned by legislators, community leaders and parents; even prevention professionals disagree about the effectiveness of the various strategies.[1] Much of the confusion stems from the lack of adequate differentiation among prevention, intervention and treatment activities. The term "prevention" generally has been applied to efforts to persuade individuals either to *abstain* from drug use or to *moderate* such use, depending on the substance in question. Failure to differentiate the goal of preventing any drug use at all from that of preventing the harmful aspects of misuse makes the concept of prevention ambiguous, and makes it difficult to separate the good programs from those that do not work.[2]

Current concepts of prevention emphasize stimulating an individual to reach a high level of functioning, which—when achieved—presumably will prevent problems associated with drug use. These concepts are based on an assumption that enriched personal and social development will "immunize" against the problems and negative consequences associated with drug use.[1] This positive view of prevention recently was endorsed by approximately 20 prevention professionals, representing a range of views, in a policy review session at the White House Office of Drug Abuse Policy.[4] These professionals also agreed that prevention programs are most likely to be successful if they:

- Result from the combined efforts of schools, families and community projects.
- Combine personal and social growth (affective education) with drug information.
- Are integrated into the ongoing activities of schools, families, employers and community organizations.
- Synthesize and extract the basic themes from a variety of educational materials and integrate them into existing programs.[4]

Swisher[1] maintains that, to be effective, prevention programs must carefully coordinate the use of resources in the government and the community, draw upon the perspectives of several disciplines (such as medicine, education and the law), use a range of promising techniques, and monitor outcomes to develop accountability and a knowledge base as to what types of programs achieve the best results.

THE PHYSICIAN'S ROLE IN PREVENTION AND EARLY INTERVENTION

Primary care physicians have significant opportunities to reduce the impact and limit the spread of drug abuse among their patients and in their communities. Such opportunities for prevention and early intervention present in many forms. For example, physicians have an opportunity to prevent drug abuse by carefully considering the abuse potential of the drugs they prescribe and by closely monitoring their patients' use of such drugs (see Chapter 10). Adolescent patients or their parents may ask the physician for information and guidance on drug-related issues. Schools, employers and community organizations may seek the physician's counsel in developing programs of drug abuse education, as well as assistance in implementing such programs. And, of course, physicians who treat children and adolescents have an excellent opportunity for primary education and early intervention in the problems associated with youth drug abuse.

ANSWERING PARENTS' QUESTIONS

Perhaps the most frequently encountered situation—aside from patients identified as actual or potential drug abusers through the physician's own screening efforts (see Chapter 5)—involves parents who turn to a physician for advice when they know or suspect that their child is using illicit drugs. Masland[5] suggests the following responses to questions parents frequently ask physicians about their children's use of drugs:

Question: *Why do young people use drugs?*

Response: Probably for the same reasons adults drink alcohol or take tranquilizers, sleeping pills or appetite suppressants: pleasure, mood change and social intercourse. Adolescents are not people who delay gratification. Curiosity, experimentation—call it what you will—young people on the way to becoming adults will try adult behavior patterns.

Question: *Isn't my son (or daughter) very young to have this problem?*

Response: There is no special age of vulnerability to drug abuse. Some nine and ten year olds use marijuana and alcohol. During early adolescence, there is a large amount of experimentation, followed in mid-adolescence by a natural separation into groups who use drugs socially, regularly, or not at all. By late adolescence and the early adult years, an individual's pattern of drug use is fairly well established.

Question: *Should we, as parents, try the drug in question and share this experience with our children?*

Response: No! There is absolutely no reason for parents to feel compelled to try a drug in order to understand how to talk about that drug with their children.

Senay and Lewis[6] believe that, in responding to parents' questions, it is essential to clarify what questions are really being asked and to determine the significance of drugs in the child's overall behavior. They note that parents often are not clear about what information they are seeking because they are expressing a concern or fear that is not explicit. For example, a parent who says, "My daughter is using marijuana. Will she become a drug addict?," is expressing a fear rather than asking a direct question. A physician who responds with comments and questions that help to clarify the fear is providing much greater assistance than one who merely answers, "Yes (no), your child probably will (won't) become an addict." Such an answer implies closure of the discussion and does not help the parents develop an understanding of what information they really want and need.

Instead of quickly closing off this line of discussion, Senay and Lewis suggest that the physician ask questions to elicit information. For example:

How do you know that your daughter (or son) is using marijuana?
Who does she (or he) use it with?
Where does she (or he) use it?
How often does she (or he) use it?

Through questions such as these, the physician can gain an understanding of the relative importance of drug-using behavior in the adolescent's life. If a young person is doing well in school, participating in age-appropriate activities such as band, sports and clubs, and generally is adapting satisfactorily, the physician may conclude that the parent has a normal young person who is experimenting with marijuana in response to the pressures of modern youth culture.[5,6]

If, on the other hand, the physician elicits information that suggests a seriously disturbed young person who has a major drug problem, the physician can proceed with appropriate diagnostic and treatment (or referral) steps.

In either event, Senay and Lewis[6] recommend that the physician communicate to the parents his intention to follow the situation. Creating a feeling of support and continuity, they observe, can be of great importance to both the family and the youth with the problem.

COUNSELING ADOLESCENT PATIENTS

An adolescent may approach a physician directly for advice on drug-related concerns. Frequently, young patients are not able to ask for help in a straightforward way, but will talk in generalities about the subject. For example, an adolescent might ask, "What can a 'bad trip' do to you?" The physician should recognize the adolescent's reticence in such discussions and respond with the information requested until the adolescent feels sufficiently comfortable to disclose the true nature of his problem.[6]

In answering adolescents' questions about drug abuse, Lantner et al[7] emphasize the importance of supplying honest information that is based on valid, up-to-date research. Even if accurate information does not change the patient's behavior, they suggest it is important to make the patient aware of the possible medical and social consequences of that behavior. They believe that physicians should clearly express their intention to *inform*, rather than *reform*, and thus should encourage their young patients to discuss, question and even challenge the physician's information.

In any conversation with adolescents about illicit drugs, the physician should stress that such discussions are confidential and that no information will be shared with others (including parents) except by mutual agreement of the patient and physician. Because the adolescent may be consulting the physician about a confidential matter for the first time, some initial reticence is to be expected.[5,6] Masland recommends that, in addition to providing the medical information requested, the physician should demonstrate a willingness to listen and respond to the social implications of drug abuse. "School problems, antisocial behavior, and depression are real problems for chronic drug users," he observes, "particularly for adolescents struggling to become adults in a society that sets increasingly high standards of performance for young people."[5]

SCREENING ADOLESCENTS FOR DRUG USE

Primary medical care of children and adolescents can provide a superb opportunity for discussions directed at early intervention as well as prevention. A physician who treats pre-adolescent and adolescent patients in an office, clinic or hospital should let those patients know that he is interested in the subject of substance abuse and open to discussions of such abuse. This is a signal to the patient that the physician will talk about a subject that too often is avoided by adults.[5]

The physician also should ask questions about substance abuse of any youngster over age 10 who presents with a medical condition that might be related to such abuse. For example, a youngster with a persistent cough might be asked if he or she smokes, one with diarrhea might be questioned about alcohol use, and a young patient with chronic rhinitis might be asked if he or she uses marijuana. Similarly, signs of depression in an adolescent indicate the possibility of drug use. (See Chapter 5 for other signs and symptoms of drug use.) Where such use is suspected, Masland[5] suggests questions such as the following:

Question: *Have you ever used marijuana?*

If the patient answers affirmatively, additional questions are in order:

How often do you smoke? Do you smoke alone or with other people? Are you a frequent (daily) user or an occasional (social) one? In response to these questions, the patient should be allowed to elaborate on his or her usage. This may involve terms that are not familiar to the physician, who should ask the patient for clarification.

Question: *Do you think marijuana is harmful?*

Whether the patient's reply is affirmative or negative, the physician should reinforce the point that marijuana *can* be harmful by citing information based on objective clinical evidence. On the other hand, the physician's credibility may be enhanced if he also notes that marijuana and THC are being investigated for their potential usefulness in medical treatment.

If a patient expresses some concern about the harmful effects of drug use, the physician should probe those feelings with questions such as, *Why do you use drugs? How did you get started? Do you feel you have a problem? Do you want to stop?*

Lantner et al[7] suggest that the physician will be most effective by keeping discussions of drug abuse at a factual level and avoiding counterproductive emotional debates. "Issues like the dangers of marijuana relative to tobacco or alcohol," they caution, "are less germane than which drugs [the patient] is using, how often, and why." In this regard, Masland[5] observes that "it is far better for a discussion to take place that can be buttressed with facts and information, supplied by [the physician's] responses to direct questions and by reading material." (Suggested sources of patient information on drug abuse are listed at the end of this chapter.)

If the information supplied by the patient suggests that his or her drug use is of an infrequent, experimental nature, the physician might schedule a follow-up visit for further discussion of the medical and social implications of drug abuse. Parents, schools and adolescents themselves generally are receptive to this approach in the case of a novice drug user.[5,6]

If the information obtained during the first one or two patient visits is not sufficient to allow a determination of the extent of the patient's drug use, a visit with the parents and then with the patient and parents together may be helpful. In such a case, the physician may wish to recommend additional counseling visits on a monthly basis for three or four months.[5]

If, however, the history given by either the patient or the parents indicates a variety of school, family and peer problems, the physician may wish to obtain a psychiatric evaluation. Such an evaluation might involve the services of a social worker, a psychiatrist or a psychologist, working with the primary physician. Following a psychiatric evaluation, the physician should have sufficient information to offer specific recommendations to the patient and family.[5]

When it is clear that a patient's problems extend beyond early, experimental use of drugs, early intervention should be thorough and professionally precise. The physician should approach the diagnostic work-up in the same way he would for a patient with disabling headaches or gastrointestinal disease, calling on appropriate consultants as needed.[5]

DRUG ABUSE PROGRAMS IN THE SCHOOLS

In a recent statement,[8] the American Academy of Pediatrics Committee on Drugs concluded that:

> The pediatrician's best recourse, at present, is to become active in efforts at prevention. Before they reach the age of greatest risk, school-age children should be well informed about physiological and psychological effects of marijuana, alcohol, and other psychoactive agents. The physician's role is to provide such information; his caveats must be accurate and not overstated if the child is to continue to look to the practitioner as a source of truthful information.

While there is general agreement that some form of drug education is desirable, the beneficial effects of programs now being used in the schools have not been documented; however, adverse effects have been found to attend certain approaches. Kearney and Hines[9] observe that "scare tactics have been widely used and have resulted in mistrust, cynicism and an increased desire by some to experiment with drugs." They add that "another major educational approach was that of providing students with a wealth of drug factual information. Researchers have found that students taught extensive drug factual information later used more illicit drugs than did students not taught all those facts."

Chng[10] notes that "with the recognition that the mere dissemination of information about drugs is grossly inadequate to influence drug-using behavior, values clarification has gained increasing acceptance among drug educators." Simon and deSherbinin[11] describe "values clarification" as a method of "reaching students by examining their values. Instead of focusing exclusively on drugs, [this method] involves young people in looking at their total lives. The young discover what they prize and cherish and begin to think about the consequences of their actions. Eventually, they learn techniques for examining the harder issues of their lives, such as whether or not to use drugs."

Values clarification has numerous critics, however, who argue that (1) the emphasis on the *process* of reaching a decision ignores the *content* of that decision, (2) values clarification is based on "ethical relativism," which holds that all values are equally valid and morally defensible, (3) group approaches tend to encourage conformity to group values at the expense of personal development, and (4) there is a strong risk of indoctrination. Perhaps the most basic objection to this approach is framed by Chng,[10] who observes that "the available literature has not established conclusively that drug users or abstainers can be differentiated on the basis of clarity of their values."

In the face of these conflicting opinions, what kind of drug education program *can* a physician reasonably recommend? In what framework would a physician's participation be most valuable and effective? Cornacchia et al[12] suggest a multidimensional program to meet the needs of both drug users and non-users. In addition to drug abuse, such a program would give attention to the increasing alcoholism problem among school age children, as well as to their overall mental health. It would involve parents and community organizations, because, the authors contend, "school programs should not be developed in isolation from community programs, since drugs affect and are used by all people in varying ways and degrees. The greatest impact on students will undoubtedly be achieved through coordinated efforts of the school and the community."

Briefly, the type of program recommended by Cornacchia et al involves (1) formal and informal drug education, using a variety of print and audiovisual materials and including attention to values clarification, decision-making skills and overall mental health, (2) services to identify drug abusers and procedures for helping such students, (3) development of a school atmosphere that is conducive to understanding student unrest, and to meeting the physical and emotional needs of students, and (4) coordination of administrative policies and procedures regarding the sale, use and possession of drugs in school.[12]

Sources of information on designing a school drug program, as well as examples of the types of instructional materials that might be used in such a program, are listed at the end of this chapter.

DRUG ABUSE PROGRAMS IN THE WORKPLACE

Primary care physicians can make a positive contribution to drug abuse prevention and early intervention through their roles as medical consultants to government units, business and industry, and labor unions. Employer and union programs to help employees with health, health-related and personal problems have a long history. Occupational alcoholism programs, for example, have been in existence for at least 35 years, and the increasing number of these programs indicates employer recognition that the provision of such services can achieve cost savings and retention of valued employees.[13]

Although industrial awareness of the problems of drug abuse (other than alcoholism) in the workplace occurred only in the late 1960's and early 1970's, the National Institute on Drug Abuse has identified more than 100 major companies that had drug abuse programs in place by 1978.[13] The growth of these programs was spurred by the realization that the economic costs associated with drug abuse (absenteeism, turnover, lowered productivity, etc.) often outweigh the potential costs of providing assistance to employees who have drug abuse problems. It also became increasingly apparent that the successful rehabilitation of persons with drug abuse problems is significantly influenced by their ability to secure and maintain employment. Thus, the coordination of intervention and treatment efforts with the business community appears to be critical to attempts to deal with the drug problem on a community or national basis.[13]

In companies that do not yet have drug abuse programs, a recent survey[14] by the National Institute on Drug Abuse found that the reason most often cited was an insufficient number of drug-using employees. However, data developed in the NIDA survey show that most business officials are unaware of the true incidence of employee drug use.

Surveys of management[14] indicate that early punitive reactions to cases of suspected drug abuse have shifted in recent years toward more humane treatment of such persons. Similarly, recent research indicates a serious commitment on the part of organized labor to the development of drug abuse education, referral and counseling programs in industry.[13] At the same time, rehabilitation agencies have developed "a better understanding of the problems of industry and the need to help the business sector define its position more effectively.[15]

A program to assist employees and their families with drug abuse problems may take one of several forms: it may be designed to deal specifically with drug abuse, it may focus on both alcohol and drug problems, or it may use the broader "employee assistance program" approach, in which drug abuse problems are handled in the context of services provided for a wide range of employee problems.[13]

While the decision on which approach to take depends to a large extent on the types of problems that exist and the resources that are available, other factors also must be considered. For example, there has been a recent trend in occupational programs away from explicit references to specific problems (such as "alcoholism" or "drug abuse") and toward a more general "troubled employee" approach. This broader concept implies assistance for employees no matter what their problem may be. As it specifically relates to drug abuse, the "troubled employee" concept has two distinct advantages: (1) employees with drug abuse problems are less likely to avoid contact with the program out of fear of being labeled "addicts" or "drug abusers," and (2) the penetration rate of the program may increase as employees with drug abuse problems contact the program for help with related difficulties.[13]

Regardless of the program approach used, research by the National Institute on Drug Abuse shows that five basic components are common to almost all successful employee drug abuse programs:[13]

1. *Identification and outreach.* There should be a mechanism through which employees with drug abuse problems can be brought to the attention of program staff or responsible management. At the same time, the confidentiality of the worker needs to be protected. Two approaches (preferably used together) appear to be the most productive:
   a. Training supervisors and/or union stewards to recognize and document job performance problems and to refer troubled employees to the medical department or an appropriate staff member, while maintaining confidentiality.
   b. Providing a climate—including strict protection of confidentiality—that encourages employees to seek assistance on their own.
2. *Diagnosis and referral.* Once employees in need of assistance have been identified or self-referred, the nature of the employee's problem should be determined and a referral made to a counseling or treatment resource.
3. *Counseling and treatment.* Counseling and treatment services should be provided. This often involves coordination of company and community resources and usually is the point at which the primary care physician has the most direct involvement in such a program.
4. *Follow-up.* Follow-up services should be provided to employees who no longer are receiving counseling or treatment.
5. *Record system.* A system should be in place to retain and safeguard the records of individual employee problems and the types of assistance provided. Although such records are necessary to eval-

uate the effectiveness of the overall program, the privacy of employees should be protected by limiting access to the records.

These five basic components may be structured in different ways to reflect the needs and resources of individual employers or labor unions.

Programs in the workplace also have preventive potential, even though their early intervention and treatment aspects have received primary emphasis. Trice[16] observes that such programs may well produce a double "payoff": confrontation may act to blunt the progression of one experimental drug user into chronic abuse, as well as provide an avenue for another employee to reach treatment.

A growing body of literature is available to guide organizations and medical consultants interested in establishing drug abuse prevention and intervention programs in the workplace. Some of these information resources are listed at the end of this chapter.

CONCLUSIONS

One ubiquitous observation about drug abuse prevention holds that there is little research to show that prevention and education programs work—that they prevent drug abuse.[17] Plant[18] concurs that the real effects of drug education probably are intangible and may require a very long time to become apparent. Yet, despite the "nagging possibility" that individual patterns of drug use "follow a natural course that is little influenced by conventional social policies or controls," he contends that "it does not logically follow that health education in relation to drug misuse is either doomed or fruitless." Citing the "symbolic value" of drug education and prevention activities to the general public, to specific target groups such as schoolchildren, and to policymaking bodies, Plant[18] suggests that educational activities do promote awareness of the problem of drug abuse and probably enhance the possibility that public policies in this area will be "tempered with humanity and restraint."

At an individual level, Brill[19] maintains that physicians "can and do influence the lifestyles of some individuals." This contention is supported by Sheppard's[20] review of 16 separate attitudinal surveys of youth and adults, including both drug users and non-users. These surveys found that professionals, and especially physicians, were perceived as good sources of drug information.

Of course, the better informed the physician is on matters pertaining to drug abuse, the more effective will be his or her efforts at drug abuse prevention and early intervention. There are numerous excellent sources of up-to-date information on drug abuse, and many consultations with parents, adolescents and other troubled patients can be conducted satisfactorily by referring to those sources.

Physicians also are urged to become familiar with drug abuse prevention and treatment programs in their communities (see Chapter 8 for sources of this information).

Finally, Senay and Lewis[6] observe that, although the stereotypical attitude among drug abusers is that one does not ask doctors questions about drug abuse or anything else, "the physician who is willing and able to assist . . . [with] drug-related problems will be able to serve."

SOURCES OF ADDITIONAL INFORMATION

INFORMATION FOR PATIENTS

Hancock, D. C. *Points for Parents Perplexed About Drugs,* 1978 (Hazeldon Books, Box 176, Center City, Minn. 55012)
 Suggests guidelines to help parents recognize, evaluate and deal with drug abuse problems in their children.

Marin, P. and Cohen, A. Y. *Understanding Drug Use: An Adult's Guide to Drugs and the Young,* 1971 (Harper & Row, New York City)
 Designed to help parents and other adults understand the reasons for youthful drug experimentation and to develop appropriate attitudes and approaches to help young people deal with "pro-drug" pressures.

Fornacieri, S. *How to Talk to Kids About Drugs,* 1980 (Prevention Materials Institute, P.O. Box 152, Lafayette, Cal. 94549)
 A guide for parents on how to discuss drug-related issues with children in an open, constructive way.

The following publications are available from the National Clearinghouse for Drug Abuse Information (an agency of the United States government), P.O. Box 1909, Rockville, Md. 20850 (single copies are free).

A Family Response to the Drug Problem: FIND (Families Involved in Nurture and Development), 1976
 Presents six sessions employing various types of learning experiences, with emphasis on sharing ideas, attitudes and feelings in group discussions.

Come Closer Around the Fire, 1979
 Uses Native American tribal legends, myths and stories as drug abuse education aids.

Communicating with Our Sons and Daughters, 1979
 Examines the role of Mexican-American parents in helping their children avoid drug use.

Parents, the Real Teachers, 1979
 Addresses problems unique to Pacific Islands/Asian parents in the United States and describes how such parents can help their children develop a "natural resistance" to drug use.

PCP Flyer, 1979 (English and Spanish language editions)
 Describes what PCP is, how it is used and the dangers of abuse.

Inhalants Flyer, 1979 (English and Spanish language editions)
Describes what inhalants are, the general effects and long-term dangers of their use, and the warning signals of abuse.

Health Consequences of Marijuana Use, 1980 (Hearings before the Subcommittee on Criminal Justice of the Committee on the Judiciary, United States Senate; U.S. Govenment Printing Office, Washington, D.C.)
Presents the latest research findings on the health effects of marijuana use.

The following publications are available from the Addiction Research Foundation (an agency of the Province of Ontario), 33 Russell St., Toronto, Ontario, Canada M5S 2S1.

Facts About Drugs (English and French language editions)
Presents information on the history, appearance, short- and long-term effects and safety of the major drugs of abuse.

My Kid on Drugs?, 1980
Suggests approaches parents can use in dealing with their children's use of drugs.

Drug Knowledge Survey, 1980
Clarifies popular misconceptions about drugs of abuse. Can be used as a self-teaching device or to guide group discussions.

Substance Abuse Among the Elderly
Explains how substance abuse among elderly persons differs from that in other age groups. Discusses the effects of increased leisure time, loneliness, changes in body metabolism, and the stress of aging as contributors to substance abuse. Designed for use by professional and lay audiences.

Psychoactive Drugs and Pregnancy, 1978
Consolidates existing information concerning the effects of psychoactive drugs on pregnancy.

Psychoactive Drugs (OP 455, American Medical Association, P.O. Box 821, Monroe, Wis. 53566)
Explores the effects and risks associated with five categories of drugs: narcotics, sedatives, stimulants, hallucinogens and marijuana.

What You Should Know About PCP: A Scriptographic Booklet, 1980 (Channing L. Bete, Inc., South Deerfield, Mass.)
Uses simple language and line drawings to explain the hazards of PCP to school age children.

The following booklets are available from Citizens for Informed Choices on Marijuana, Inc., 300 Broad St., Stamford, Conn. 06901.

Marijuana in Junior and Senior High . . . A Parent's Introduction, 1979
Describes the health effects of marijuana and current use trends among school age children.

What Every Parent Can Do About Marijuana, 1979
Discusses the effects of parental attitudes and actions on youth drug use.

The Parent Peer Group, 1979
Explains the steps involved in forming parents' organizations to oppose youth drug abuse.

Parents Talk to their Children About Marijuana, 1979
Describes the experiences of an Atlanta, Ga., parents' group in discussing marijuana's use and dangers with their children.

Helping Your Child Resist the Marijuana Culture, 1979
   Outlines a drug education program that can be employed by parents.
Information on the formation and location of parents' anti-drug groups is available from the National Federation of Parents for Drug Free Youth, P.O. Box 57217, Washington, D.C. 20037.

INFORMATION ON DRUG ABUSE PROGRAMS IN THE SCHOOLS

Cornacchia, H. J., Smith, D. E. and Bentel, D. J. *Drugs in the Classroom: A Conceptual Model for School Programs,* 1978 (C. V. Mosby, St. Louis, Mo.)
   Describes a multidimensional, differential school drug program designed to meet the needs of student drug users and non-users. Focuses on preventive efforts aimed at students in kindergarten through grade 12 and includes behavioral objectives for drug education. Presents guidelines for identifying, educating and assisting student drug abusers.

Woodcock, J. "Action in the Schools" in R. Blum et al (ed.) *Drug Dealers — Taking Action,* 1973 (Jossey-Bass, San Francisco, Cal.)
   A theoretical/critical study of drug education models, including a discussion of how to evaluate drug education programs.

Evaluating Drug Information Programs, 1973 (National Research Council, Washington, D.C.)
   Describes methods of evaluating drug education programs, methodological factors in the success of such programs, and sources of information on drug use and abuse.

Curriculum Guides: Drug education curriculum guides are available from many state departments of education and local school districts.

Textbooks: Drug education texts are available from many publishing houses, including:

   Allyn & Bacon, Inc.
   American Education Publications
   Book-Lab
   Children's
   Fearon Publishers
   Fell
   Ginn and Company
   Harcourt Brace Jovanovich, Inc.
   J. B. Lippincott Co.
   Laidlaw Bros.
   Macmillan
   McGraw Hill Book Co.
   Oxford Book Co.
   Pendulum Press
   Pergamon
   Prentice-Hall
   Ramapo House
   Reader's Digest Services, Inc.
   Scholastic Book Services
   Science Research Associates, Inc.
   Scott, Foresman & Company
   U.S. Government Printing Office
   William Morrow

Films: Drug education films for classroom use are available from a number of sources, including the Drug Abuse Film Collection of the National Audiovisual Center, Washington, D.C. 20409. A selective guide to currently available drug education films is *The Drug Abuse Films Directory,* published by the National Coordinating Council on Drug Education (NCCDE), 1346 Connecticut Ave., N.W., Washington, D.C. 20036.

INFORMATION ON DRUG ABUSE PROGRAMS IN THE WORKPLACE

Developing an Occupational Drug Abuse Program, 1978 (National Institute on Drug Abuse, Rockville, Md.)
    Presents some practical considerations and conceptual guidelines for the establishment of drug abuse programs in the workplace. Information is based on a review of the relevant business and professional literature, consultations with experts in occupational programming, and on-site interviews with officials and program staff at 15 companies and two unions that operate drug abuse programs. The book is divided into four sections: (1) a brief summary of studies on the extent and costs of employee drug use, (2) practical and conceptual issues in assessing the basis of a drug abuse program, (3) suggestions on implementing such a program, and (4) basic program models. Appendices provide sample policy statements and descriptions of in-place programs.

Drug Use in Industry, 1979 (National Institute on Drug Abuse, Rockville, Md.)
    Summarizes the results of a three-part research study consisting of (1) a survey and analysis of management-level employees in 197 companies as to management's perception of the extent and nature of drug use in industry, (2) an indepth survey and analysis of 2,500 employees in 20 companies, and (3) case studies of drug use in a unit of a federal agency, a local industry community and a firm with a community-based treatment program.

Trice, H. and Roman, P. *Spirits and Demons at Work: Alcohol and Other Drugs on the Job*, 1972 (Cornell University, New York State School of Industrial and Labor Relations, Ithaca, N.Y.)
    Examines the effects of employee use of alcohol, marijuana, amphetamines and opioids on work performance and industrial accidents. Discusses occupational drug use as it relates to employer policies, drug availability, employee problems and stress.

Ward, H. *Employment and Addiction: Overview of Issues*, 1973 (Drug Abuse Council, Washington, D.C.)
    Discusses issues surrounding employer policies on addict employment, employee drug programs and rehabilitation of drug-abusing employees.

Kieffer, S. "Summation of Conference—Drug Abuse in Industry" in P. Carone and S. Krinsky (eds.) *Drug Abuse in Industry*, 1973 (Charles C. Thomas, Springfield, Ill.)
    Summarizes a conference on drug-related deaths in industry, screening for and detection of drug abuse, and employer policies on dismissals for drug use and drug education programs.

Malinowski, F. "Employee Drug Abuse in Municipal Government" *Public Personnel Management* 4(1):59 (1975)
    Reports the results of a survey of 32 units of municipal government as to attitudes toward drug use and drug education, use of screening and detection programs, and employer policies on employee drug use.

Hilker, R. R. J., Asma, F. E., Daghestani, A. N. and Ross, R. L. "A Drug Abuse Rehabilitation Program" *Journal of Occupational Medicine* 17(6):351 (1975)
   Describes a drug abuse rehabilitation program at Illinois Bell Telephone Company. The in-plant program consists of individual counseling and group therapy, with referral to community resources for other forms of treatment. This study is unique in that it contains follow-up data on individuals who have received treatment and returned to their jobs.

Drugs and Employment, Research Issues Series (National Institute on Drug Abuse, Rockville, Md.)
   Presents 31 abstracts on attitudes toward drug use by employers and employees, the effects of drug use on work performance, hiring and firing practices, and employer rehabilitation programs. Includes specific studies on drug use in medicine, sports and aviation.

REFERENCES

1. Swisher, J. D. Prevention issues *in* R. I. DuPont, A. Goldstein and J. O'Donnell (eds.) *Handbook on Drug Abuse* (National Institute on Drug Abuse, Rockville, Md., 1979)
2. Drug Abuse Council, *The Facts About "Drug Abuse"* (The Free Press, New York City, 1980)
3. Resnik, H. S. *Drug Abuse Prevention for Low-Income Communities: Manual for Program Planning* (National Institute on Drug Abuse, Rockville, Md., 1980)
4. Policy Review Seminar on Primary Prevention, The White House, Washington, D.C., December 1977.
5. Masland, R. R. Jr. Adolescent drug and alcohol use: how to deal with it *Consultant* 190 (June 1980)
6. Senay, E. C. and Lewis, D. C. *The Primary Physician's Guide to Drug and Alcohol Abuse Treatment*, Medical Monograph Series, Vol. I, No. 6 (National Institute on Drug Abuse, Rockville, Md., 1980)
7. Lantner, I. L., O'Brien, J. E. and Voth, H. M. Answering questions about marijuana use *Patient Care* 112 (May 30, 1980)
8. *Statement on Drug Abuse* (American Academy of Pediatrics, Evanston, Ill., October 1979)
9. Kearney, A. L. and Hines, M. H. Evaluation of the effectiveness of a drug prevention education program *Journal of Drug Education* 10(2):127 (1980)
10. Chng, C. L. A critique of values clarification in drug education *Journal of Drug Education* 10(2):119 (1980)
11. Simon, S. and deSherbinin, P. Values clarification: it can start gently and grow deep *Phi Delta Kappan* 55:679 (June 1975)
12. Cornacchia, H. J., Smith, D. E. and Bentel, D. J. *Drugs in the Classroom: A Conceptual Model for School Programs* (C. V. Mosby Company, St. Louis, Mo., 1978)
13. *Developing an Occupational Drug Abuse Program* (National Institute on Drug Abuse, Rockville, Md., 1978)

14. *Drug Use in Industry,* Services Research Report (National Institute on Drug Abuse, Rockville, Md., 1979)
15. Meiselas, H. and Brill, L. Drug abuse in industry—issues and comments *Industrial Medicine* 41(8):10 (August 1972)
16. Trice, H. M. Job-based alcohol and drug abuse programs: recent program developments and research *in* R. I. DuPont, A. Goldstein and J. O'Donnell (eds.) *Handbook on Drug Abuse* (National Institute on Drug Abuse, Rockville, Md., 1979)
17. Schaps, E., Churgin, S., Palley, C. S., Takata, B. and Cohen, A. Y. Primary prevention research: a preliminary review of program outcome studies *International Journal of the Addictions* 15(5):657 (1980)
18. Plant, M. A. Drug taking and prevention: the implications of research for social policy *British Journal of Addiction* 75:245 (1980)
19. Brill, H. Can physicians influence life style? *New York State Journal of Medicine* 1414 (August 1980)
20. Sheppard, M. A. Sources of information about "drugs" *Journal of Drug Education* 10(3):257 (1980)

INDEX

Abdominal pain 130, 132, 181, 191
Abortions, spontaneous 189
Abscesses 118, 130, 180
Abuse of multiple drugs 168
Abuse potential of commonly prescribed drugs 273, 275, 278
Acapulco Gold (also see Cannabinoids) 67
Ace (also see Cannabinoids) 67
Acetaminophen 98
Acetone (also see Inhalants) 75
Aches, muscle 132
Acid (also see Hallucinogens) 53
Acidification 146
Acne excoriee 118
Acupuncture 151, 228
Adhesives (also see Inhalants) 75
Adipex (also see Stimulants) 42
Adrenaline 126
Aerosol sprays (also see Inhalants) 75
Affect, labile 132
African Yohimba bark (also see Hallucinogens) 50
Agitation 129
Alcohols (also see Inhalants) 75
Aliphatic hydrocarbons (also see Inhalants) 75
Aliphatic nitrite (also see Inhalants) 75
Allergic reactions 128, 178
Alpha-methyltyrosine 220
Alphaprodine (also see Opioids) 27
Amenorrhea 194
Amobarbital (also see Depressants) 33, 35, 274
Amphetamines (also see Stimulants) 41, 42, 277
Amphetamine sulfate (also see Stimulants) 42
Amputation, spontaneous 191
Amyl nitrite (also see Inhalants) 73
Amytal (also see Depressants) 35
Amytal + Seconal (also see Depressants) 35
Analgesia, obstetric 196
Analgesia, pinprick 132
Anaphalactic shock 178
Anemia 182
Anesthesia, obstetric 195
Anesthesia, surgical 192
Anesthetics (also see Inhalants) 73

Aneurysms 179
Angel Dust (also see Phencyclidines) 60
Angina 132
Anileridine (also see Opioids) 27
Anorexia 132
Anoxia 187
Antagonist drugs 26, 218
Antidotes 128
Anti-freeze (also see Inhalants) 75
Anti-histamines 97
Anti-social behavior 6
Anti-social personality 10
Anxiety 132
Apathy 129
Apnea 128, 187
Appendicitis 191
Aromatic hydrocarbons (also see Inhalants) 75
Arrhythmia 132, 180
Artane (also see Hallucinogens) 53
Arteriograms 119
Arteritis 179
Arthritis, septic 190
Ataxia 131, 132, 186
Ativan (also see Depressants) 35
Atropy, cerebral 187
Autopsy findings in drug abusers 177
Azene (also see Depressants) 35

Babinski sign 142
Bacarate (also see Stimulants) 42
Bacteremia 182
Banapple gas (also see Inhalants) 74
Bang (also see Cannabinoids) 67
Barbiturates (also see Depressants) 33, 35, 274
Barbs (also see Depressants) 35
Barrels (also see Hallucinogens) 53
Beans (also see Depressants) 35
Beans (also see Stimulants) 42
Behavior modification 226
Bennies (also see Stimulants) 42
Benzedrine (also see Stimulants) 42
Benzene (also see Inhalants) 75
Benzodiazepines (also see Depressants) 34, 35, 274
Benztropine mesylate (also see Hallucinogens) 53
Berkeley Boo (also see Cannabinoids) 67

Bhang (also see Cannabinoids) 67
Big H (also see Opioids) 27
Biofeedback relaxation therapy 227
Biphetamine (also see Stimulants) 42
Black Beauties (also see Stimulants) 42
Black Cadillacs (also see Stimulants) 42
Black Mollies (also see Stimulants) 42
Blindness 185
Blink reflex, exaggerated 130
Blockbusters (also see Depressants) 35
Blood pressure 127
Blood tests 119, 126
Blotter Acid (also see Hallucinogens) 53
Blow (also see Stimulants) 42
Bluebirds (also see Depressants) 35
Blue Cap (also see Hallucinogens) 53
Blue Devils (also see Depressants) 35
Blue Dragon (also see Hallucinogens) 53
Blue Heavens (also see Depressants) 35
Blues (also see Depressants) 35
Bo (also see Cannabinoids) 67
Body image changes 132
Body weight 138
Boggs Amendment 253
Boo (also see Cannabinoids) 67
Boy (also see Opioids) 27
Breech presentation 195
Bromides 98
4-bromo-2, 5-dimethoxy-amphetamine (also see Hallucinogens) 53
Bronchial constriction 130
Bronchial irritation 130
Bronchitis 188
Broom (also see Hallucinogens) 50
Brown (also see Opioids) 27
Brown & Clears (also see Stimulants) 42
Brown Sugar (also see Opioids) 27
Bufotenine (also see Hallucinogens) 53
Bullae 118
Bullous impetigo 118
Buprenorphine 220

Businessman's Special (also see Hallucinogens) 53
Butabarbital (also see Depressants) 34, 35, 274
Butisol (also see Depressants) 35
Butyl nitrite (also see Inhalants) 74
Buzz bombs (also see Inhalants) 73

C (also see Stimulants) 42
Caballo (also see Opioids) 27
California Poppy (also see Hallucinogens) 50
California Sunshine (also see Hallucinogens) 53
Camel (also see Hallucinogens) 53
Camptodactylia 181
Candles (also see Hallucinogens) 53
CANNABINOIDS 64
　Characteristics of 23, 64, 71
　Dependence on 70, 71
　Dose range 65, 72
　Drugs in the class 65
　Duration of effects 71, 72
　Effects of 67, 68, 71, 72
　Flashback reactions with 158
　In combination with other drugs 170
　Intoxication, acute, with 147
　Mode of administration 71, 72
　Organic brain syndrome with 167
　Overdose with 147
　Panic reactions with 160
　Pattern of abuse 66
　Prevalence of abuse 66, 95
　Psychoactive properties of 71, 72
　Psychotic reactions with 164
　Street names for 67
　Therapeutic potential of 70
　Tolerance to 70, 71
　Toxicity of 70
　Treatment, long-term 207, 232
　Treatment of acute reactions 125
　Treatment of sub-acute problems 147, 156, 158, 160, 164, 167
　Withdrawal from 156
Cannabis indica (also see Cannabinoids) 67
Cannabis sativa (see also Cannabinoids) 67
Carbamates (also see Depressants) 35
Carcinoma, hepatic 184

Cardiac fibrillation 126
Cardiac irregularities 127
Cardiovascular problems related to drug abuse 68, 178
Catheterization 126
Catnip (also see Hallucinogens) 50
Causes of drug abuse 8
Cellulitis 180
Cerebral atrophy 187
Cervix, friable 195
Chancroid 181
Charas (see also Cannabinoids) 67
Cheilitis 118
Chest pain 132
Chest x-rays 119
Chills 132
China white (also see Opioids) 27
Chiva (also see Opioids) 27
Chloral hydrate (also see Depressants) 35, 36, 275
Chlordiazepoxide (also see Depressants) 34, 35, 274
Christmas Trees (also see Depressants) 35
Chromosome breaks 189
Cinnamon (also see Hallucinogens) 50
Circulatory collapse 133
Cirrhosis 184
CLINICAL MANIFESTATIONS OF DRUG REACTIONS 129, 130, 131
 Flashback reactions 156
 Intoxication, acute (overdose) 138
 Organic brain syndrome 165
 Panic reactions 158
 Psychotic reactions 161
 Withdrawal 149
Clonazepam (also see Depressants) 35
Clonidine 151
Clonopin (also see Depressants) 35
Clorazepate (also see Depressants) 34, 35, 274
Coca (also see Stimulants) 42
Cocaine (also see Stimulants) 41, 42, 278
Cocaine hydrochloride (also see Stimulants) 42, 92
Cocaine freebase, prevalence 92
Cocaine, N.F. (also see Stimulants) 42
Codeine (also see Opioids) 24, 27, 273
Codeine cough compounds 97

Cogentin (also see Hallucinogens) 53
Coke (also see Stimulants) 42
Cola (also see Stimulants) 42
Colombian (also see Cannabinoids) 67
Coma 128, 133, 138
COMPLICATIONS OF DRUG ABUSE (also see specific conditions)
 Cardiovascular 178
 Dermatologic 180
 Endocrinologic 181
 Gastrointestinal 181
 Genitourinary 181
 Hematopoietic 182
 Hepatic 183
 Neonatal 196
 Neuromuscular 184
 Obstetric 193
 Psychiatric 198
 Pulmonary 187
 Renal 188
 Reproductive 68, 189
 Septic 189
 Sexual 197
 Skeletal 190
 Surgical 191
Comprehension, slow 133
Comprehensive Drug Abuse Prevention and Control Act 253
Confidentiality of records 257
Confronting drug abusers 119
Confronting drug-abusing physicians 289
Congestive heart failure 192
Consent to treatment 256
Contact dermatitis 118
Controlled Substances Act 253, 269
Convulsions 128, 133, 185
Copilots (also see Stimulants) 42
Coryza 133
Counseling, individual 121, 225
Counterconditioning 227
Crank (also see Stimulants) 42
Crap (also see Opioids) 27
Cross-dependence 8
Crosses (also see Stimulants) 42
Crossroads (also see Stimulants) 42
Cross-tolerance 7
Crush injuries 190
Crystal (also see Phencyclidines) 60
Crystal (also see Stimulants) 42
Cube (also see Opioids) 27

319

Cultures of wounds or
  drainage 119
Cupcake (also see
  Hallucinogens) 53
Cutaneous signs of drug
  abuse 117
Cyanide poisoning 146
Cyclazocine 219
Cyclone (also see
  Phencyclidines) 60
Cylert (also see Stimulants) 42

Dalmane (also see Depressants) 35
Damiana (also see
  Hallucinogens) 50
Darvon (also see Opioids) 27
Dava (also see Opioids) 27
Dead on Arrival (also see
  Phencyclidines) 60
Decompensation 198
Degreasers (also see Inhalants) 75
Delirium 133
Delta-9-tetrahydrocannabinol (also
  see Cannabinoids) 67
Delysid (also see
  Hallucinogens) 53
Demerol (also see Opioids) 27
Dental disorders 118
DEPENDENCE, PHYSICAL OR
  PSYCHOLOGICAL
  Cannabinoids 70, 71
  Depressants 38, 39
  Hallucinogens 55, 57
  Inhalants 78, 79
  Opioids 30, 31
  Phencyclidines 63, 64
  Stimulants 44, 46
DEPRESSANTS 33
  Abuse potential of 275
  Antagonist drugs 218
  Characteristics of 22, 33, 39
  Dependence on 38, 39
  Detoxification from 215
  Dose range 38
  Drugs in the class 33
  Duration of effects 38, 39
  Effects of 37, 39
  Flashback reactions with 157
  In combination with other
    drugs 168, 169
  Intoxication, acute, with 141
  Mode of administration 38, 39
  Organic brain syndrome
    with 165
  Overdose with 141
  Panic reactions with 159
  Pattern of abuse 36
  Prescribing indications for 274
  Prevalence of abuse 36, 91
  Psychoactive properties of 38,
    39, 40
  Psychotic reactions with 162
  Street names for 35
  Tolerance to 38, 39
  Toxicity of 37
  Treatment, long-term 207, 232
  Treatment of acute
    reactions 125
  Treatment of sub-acute
    problems 141, 152, 157, 159,
    162, 165
  Withdrawal from 152
Depressed mood 129, 133, 200
Dermatitis 181
Dermatologic problems related to
  drug abuse 180
Desbutal (also see Stimulants) 42
Desensitization procedures 227
Desoxyn (also see Stimulants) 42
DET (also see Hallucinogens) 53
Detachment 129
DETOXIFICATION 208
  Before surgery 191
  From depressants 215
  From multiple drugs 217
  From opioids, using
    clonidine 213
  From opioids, using
    methadone 211
  From pentazocine 214
  From propoxyphene 215
  From stimulants 216
  General principles 210
  Phenobarbital substitution
    technique 215
  Settings for 211
Dexedrine (also see
  Stimulants) 42
Dexies (also see Stimulants) 42
Dextroamphetamine (also see
  Stimulants) 42
Dextroamphetamine +
  amphetamine (also see
  Stimulants) 42
Dextroamphetamine +
  prochlorperazine (also see
  Stimulants) 42
Dextropropoxyphene (also see
  Opioids) 27
Diabetes 191
Diacetylmorphine (also see
  Opioids) 27
DIAGNOSIS OF ACUTE DRUG
  REACTIONS 129

Differential diagnosis 129-137
  Flashback reactions 156
  Intoxication, acute
    (overdose) 138
  Multiple drugs 168
  Organic brain syndrome 165
  Panic reactions 159
  Psychotic reactions 161
  Withdrawal 149
Diagnostic tests for drug use 119
Dialysis 138
Diarrhea 133, 181
Diazepam (also see
  Depressants) 34, 35, 274
Didrex (also see Stimulants) 42
Diethyltryptamine (also see
  Hallucinogens) 53
Dilaudid (also see Opioids) 27
2,5-dimethoxy-4-ethyl-
  amphetamine (also see
  Hallucinogens) 53
2,5-dimethoxy-4-methyl-
  amphetamine (also see
  Hallucinogens) 53
Dimethyltryptamine (also see
  Hallucinogens) 53
Diphenoxylate + atropine (also see
  Opioids) 27
Diphentamine (also see
  Stimulants) 42
Diplopia 133
District of Columbia Pharmacy
  Act 251
Diuresis 138
Diversion of drugs from licit
  medical channels 265
Dizziness 133
d-lysergic acid diethylamide (also
  see Hallucinogens) 53
DMT (also see Hallucinogens) 53
DOA (also see Phencyclidines) 60
DOB (also see Hallucinogens) 53
DOE (also see Hallucinogens) 53
DOM (also see Hallucinogens) 53
Do-Jee (also see Opioids) 27
Dolophine (also see Opioids) 27
Doriden (also see Depressants) 35
DOSES, PSYCHOACTIVE
  Cannabinoids 65, 72
  Depressants 38
  Hallucinogens 52, 56
  Inhalants 74, 76
  Opioids 31
  Phencyclidines 61, 62, 64
  Stimulants 45
Double cross (also see
  Stimulants) 42

Downers (also see Depressants) 35
Drop-in centers 225
DRUG ABUSE
  Alcoholism and 3
  Anti-social behavior and 6
  Anti-social personality and 10
  Attitudes of abusers 8
  Attitudes of physicians 103
  Attitudes of society 3
  By physicians 285
  Causes of 8
  Complications (also see
    Complications of drug
    abuse) 177
  Confrontation techniques
    119, 289
  Counseling 121
  Defined 5
  Diagnostic tests 119
  Diversion of drugs 265
  Drug Abuse Warning Network
    (DAWN) 86
  Early intervention 299
  Economic costs 307
  Emergency room visits 89
  Euphoria and 21
  Genetic factors in 15
  Historical patterns 85
  In U.S. population 88
  Legal restrictions 251
  Medical problems (also see
    Complications of drug
    abuse) 177
  Monitoring systems 86
  Patient education on 310
  Physiological factors in 14
  Predictors of 9
  Prevalence (also see Prevalence
    of drug abuse) 88
  Prevalence in alcoholics 115
  Prevalence in general patient
    population 113
  Prevalence in physician
    population 285
  Prevention (also see Prevention
    of drug abuse) 299
  Psychological factors in 10
  Psychological problems of
    abusers 198
  Referring a patient for
    treatment 238
  Risk factors for 10
  Selection of abused drug 21, 85
  Screening for 113
  Signs, cutaneous 117
  Signs, systemic 117
  Sociological factors in 11

Surgical problems   191
Surveys of   86
Symptoms of   115
Treatment, acute   125, 138, 149, 156, 158, 161, 165
Treatment, long-term   207
Trends (also see Prevalence of drug abuse)   85
DRUG ABUSE BY PHYSICIANS   285
   Aftercare   294
   Confrontation   289
   Hospital-based programs for   288
   Incidence   285
   Intervention, early   295
   Legal status   285
   Medical board programs for   289
   Medical school programs for   294
   Medical society programs for   286
   Prescribing practices of   265
   Prevention of   294
   Prognosis for   293
   Re-entry   294
   Support groups   295
   Treatment, inpatient   292
   Treatment, outpatient   293
   Treatment planning   291
Drug Abuse Control Amendments   253
Drug Abuse Warning Network (DAWN)   86
DRUG DEPENDENCE   7
   Cross-dependence   8
   DSM-III definition of   8
   ICD-9 definition of   8
   WHO definition of   7
DRUG ENFORCEMENT ADMINISTRATION   270
   Authority   253
   Prescribing guidelines   267
Drug experimentation   4
Drug "hustlers"   280
Drug paraphernalia sales   93
Drug reactions, acute   123, 124, 129
Drugs of abuse (see Cannabinoids, Depressants, Hallucinogens, Inhalants, Opioids, Phencyclidines, Stimulants)
Drug use   5
Dry skin   130
Dummy dust (also see Phencyclidines)   60
DURATION OF EFFECTS
   Cannabinoids   71, 72

Depressants   38, 39
Hallucinogens   56, 57, 58
Inhalants   78, 79
Opioids   31, 32
Phencyclidines   61, 63
Stimulants   45, 46, 47
Dust of angels (also see Phencyclidines)   60
Dysmetria   133

Edema of the eyelids   118
Edema of the hand   118
Edema, pulmonary   130, 187
Effects, duration of (see Duration of drug effects)
Effects, physical (see Physical effects of drug abuse)
Effects, psychological (see Psychological effects of drug abuse)
Ejaculation, delayed   197
Ejaculation, spontaneous   197
Electrolytes   126
Embalming fluid (also see Phencyclidines)   60
Embolism   179
Emergency care (also see Treatment, acute drug reactions)   125-128
Empirin with codeine (also see Opioids)   27
Encephalopathy   185, 187
Endocarditis   178
Endocrinologic problems related to drug abuse   68, 181
Endogenous opiates   15
Enkephalins   15
Eosinophilia   182
Ephedrine   97
Epilepsy   191
Equanil (also see Depressants)   35
Eskatrol (also see Stimulants)   42
Esters (also see Inhalants)   75
Estuffa (also see Opioids)   27
Ethanol (also see Inhalants)   75
Ethchlorvynol (also see Depressants)   34, 35, 275
Ether frolics (also see Inhalants)   73
Ethinamate (also see Depressants)   35, 275
Ethyl acetate (also see Inhalants)   75
Euphoria   133
Excoriations   118
Exogenous opiates   15
Experimental drug use   4
Extinction of drug-abusing behavior   227

Facial grimacing 134
Family therapy 225
Fasciolitis 191
Fatigue 134
Fenfluramine 220
Fentanyl (also see Opioids) 27
Fertility 197, 258
Fever of unknown origin 179
Fibrosis 183
First line (also see Opioids) 27
Fixed drug eruption 118
Flake (also see Stimulants) 42
FLASHBACK REACTIONS 156
    Clinical manifestations of 129, 130, 131, 156
    Defined 123
    Diagnosis, differential 156
    Drug reactions 123, 124, 129
    Etiologic agents 157
    Laboratory tests 157
    Psychological state 157, 158
    Symptoms of 157, 158
    Treatment, acute 125
    Treatment, sub-acute 131, 138, 157, 158
    With cannabinoids 158, 170
    With depressants 157
    With hallucinogens 157, 170
    With inhalants 158
    With multiple drugs 170
    With opioids 157
    With phencyclidines 158, 170
    With stimulants 157
Floating feeling 134
Flurazepam (also see Depressants) 34, 35, 274
Flushing 134
Foam dispensers (also see Inhalants) 75
Food, Drug and Cosmetic Act 252
Foolpills (also see Depressants) 35
Footballs (also see Stimulants) 42
Four-way (also see Hallucinogens) 53
Fractures 131, 190
Freebase (also see Stimulants) 42
Freebase (cocaine), prevalence 92
Free drug treatment clinics 225
Freon (also see Inhalants) 75
Frostbite 190

Ganga (also see Cannabinoids) 67
Gasoline (also see Inhalants) 75
Gastric lavage 126, 127
Gastrointestinal problems related to drug abuse 181
Genetic factors in drug abuse 15

Genitourinary problems related to drug abuse 181
Girl (also see Stimulants) 42
Glutethimide (also see Depressants) 34, 35, 275
Gold (also see Cannabinoids) 67
Golden Crescent 90
Golden Triangle 90
Goofballs (also see Depressants) 35
Goma (also see Opioids) 27
Goma de Mota (also see Cannabinoids) 67
Gonorrhea 181
Goon (also see Phencyclidines) 60
Gotu kola (also see Hallucinogens) 50
Grass (also see Cannabinoids) 67
Griffa (also see Cannabinoids) 67
Green Dragon (also see Hallucinogens) 53
Green Dragons (also see Depressants) 35

H (also see Opioids) 27
Hallucinations 43, 47, 56, 62, 64, 134
HALLUCINOGENS 47
    Characteristics of 23, 47, 57
    Dependence on 55, 57
    Dose range 52, 56
    Drugs in the class 48
    Duration of effects 56, 57, 58
    Effects of 52, 54, 55, 57
    Flashback reactions with 157
    In combination with other drugs 170
    Intoxication, acute, with 144
    Mode of administration 52, 57
    Organic brain syndrome with 166
    Overdose with 144
    Panic reactions with 160
    Pattern of abuse 52
    Prevalence of abuse 52, 94
    Psychoactive properties of 56, 57
    Psychotic reactions with 163
    Street names for 53
    Tolerance to 55, 57
    Toxicity of 55
    Treatment, long-term 207, 232
    Treatment of acute reactions 125
    Treatment of sub-acute problems 144, 156, 157, 160, 163, 166
    Withdrawal from 156

Harrison Narcotic Act   251
Harrison Narcotic Act
  Amendment   253
Hash (also see Cannabinoids)   67
Hashish (also see
  Cannabinoids)   67
Hashish oil (also see
  Cannabinoids)   67
Hash oil (also see
  Cannabinoids)   67
Hawaiian (also see
  Cannabinoids)   67
Hay (also see Cannabinoids)   67
Haze (also see Hallucinogens)   53
Headaches   134
Heart murmur   179
Hearts (also see Stimulants)   42
Heaven dust (also see
  Stimulants)   42
Hematoma, subdural   131
Hematopoietic problems related to
  drug abuse   182
Hemodialysis   143
Hemoperfusion   143
Hemorrhage, intracranial   180
Hemp (also see Cannabinoids)   67
Hepatic enzyme studies   119
Hepatic problems related to drug
  abuse   183
Hepatitis   183, 186
Herb (also see Cannabinoids)   67
Herbal preparations (also see
  Hallucinogens)   50, 53
Heroin (also see Opioids)   27
Heroina (also see Opioids)   27
Himmelsbach rating scale   231
History of treatment methods   203
Hog (also see Phencyclidines)   60
Hombre (also see Opioids)   27
Hops (also see Hallucinogens)   50
Horse (also see Opioids)   27
Hydrangea (also see
  Hallucinogens)   50
Hyperphagia   134
Hypertension   129, 134, 180,
  188, 191
Hyperthermia   134
Hyperventilation   128
Hypnosis   227
Hypoglycemia   127
Hypotension   128, 134, 179, 192
Hypotonia   134

Ibogaine (also see
  Hallucinogens)   53
Ileus following abdominal
  surgery   192

Impaired physicians (also see Drug
  abuse by physicians)   285
Incidence of drug abuse (also see
  Prevalence of drug abuse)   88
Indolealkylamines (also see
  Hallucinogens)   53
INFECTIONS   118
  Bacterial   179
  Candidal   179
  Gynecologic   195
  Nasal   130
  Skin   118
  Staphylococcal   178
  Streptococcal   179
  Systemic   128
Infestations, skin   118
INHALANTS   73
  Characteristics of   23, 73, 79
  Dependence on   78, 79
  Drugs in the class   73
  Duration of effects   78, 79
  Effects of   76, 79
  Flashback reactions with   158
  Intoxication, acute, with   148
  Mode of administration   78, 79
  Organic brain syndrome
    with   165
  Overdose with   148
  Panic reactions with   161
  Pattern of abuse   74
  Prevalence of abuse   74, 96
  Psychoactive properties of   78,
    79, 80
  Psychotic reactions with   165
  Street names for   75
  Tolerance to   77, 79
  Toxicity of   78
  Treatment, long-term   207, 232
  Treatment of acute
    reactions   125
  Treatment of sub-acute
    problems   148, 156, 158, 161,
    165, 167
  Withdrawal from   156
International trends in drug
  abuse   99
INTERVENTION, EARLY   299
  Employer programs for   306
  Physician's role in   113,
    300, 303
  School programs for   305
INTOXICATION, ACUTE
  (OVERDOSE)   138
  Clinical manifestations of
    129, 130, 131, 138
  Defined   123
  Diagnosis, differential   129-
    137, 138

324

Drug reactions   123, 124, 129
Etiologic agents   139
Laboratory tests   139
Psychological state   140, 142, 144, 145, 146, 147, 149
Symptoms   132-137, 139, 142, 143, 145, 147, 148
Treatment, acute   125-128
Treatment, sub-acute   131, 138, 140, 142, 144, 145, 148, 149
With cannabinoids   147
With depressants   141, 168
With hallucinogens   144
With inhalants   148
With multiple drugs   168
With opioids   139, 168
With phencyclidines   145
With stimulants   143
Ionamin (also see Stimulants)   42
Irritability   134
Isopropanol (also see Inhalants)   75

J (also see Cannabinoids)   67
Jac Aroma (also see Inhalants)   74
Jamaican (also see Cannabinoids)   67
Jaundice   118
Jay (also see Cannabinoids)   67
Jive (also see Opioids)   27
Joint (also see Cannabinoids)   67
Juniper (also see Hallucinogens)   50
Junk (also see Opioids)   27

Kavakava (also see Hallucinogens)   50
Ketamine (also see Phencyclidines)   60
Ketoacidosis   131
Ketones (also see Inhalants)   75
Kiff (also see Cannabinoids)   67
Killer weed (also see Phencyclidines)   60
King Tut (also see Hallucinogens)   53
Kola nut (also see Hallucinogens)   50
Krystal (also see Phencyclidines)   60

LAAM   222
LABORATORY TESTS
For drug use   119
In flashback reactions   157
In intoxication, acute (overdose)   139

In organic brain syndrome   165
In panic reactions   159
In psychotic reactions   161
In withdrawal   150
Lacrimation   135
Lady (also see Stimulants)   42
Laughing gas (also see Inhalants)   73
LAWS, FEDERAL   251
Boggs Amendment   253
Comprehensive Drug Abuse Prevention and Control Act   253
Controlled Substances Act   253, 269
District of Columbia Pharmacy Act   251
Drug Abuse Control Amendments   253
Food, Drug and Cosmetic Act   252
Harrison Narcotic Act   251
Harrison Narcotic Act Amendment   253
Marijuana Tax Act   252
Methadone regulations   254
Narcotic Addict Rehabilitation Act   253
Narcotic Control Act   253
Narcotic Drugs Import and Export Act   252
Narcotic Manufacturing Act   253
Opium Poppy Control Act   252
Porter Act   252
Prescribing guidelines   267
Prescribing restrictions   269
Schedule of controlled substances   269, 271
Laws, state   256
Legal restrictions on drug abuse treatment   251
Leritine (also see Opioids)   27
Levo-Dromoran (also see Opioids)   27
Levorphanol (also see Opioids)   27
Libido, decreased   197
Librium (also see Depressants)   35
Life support measures (also see Treatment of acute drug reactions)   125-128
Line (also see Stimulants)   42
Liquid incense (also see Inhalants)   74
Lobelia (also see Hallucinogens)   50
Locker Popper (also see Inhalants)   74

325

Locker Room (also see
    Inhalants) 74
Lomotil (also see Opioids) 27
Lorazepam (also see
    Depressants) 34, 35, 274
Love pill (also see
    Hallucinogens) 53
Low birth weight 196
LSD (also see Hallucinogens) 53
Ludes (also see Depressants) 35
Luminal (also see Depressants) 35
Lymphadenopathy 182
Lymphogranuloma venerum 181

Magic Mexican mushroom (also see
    Hallucinogens) 53
Malaria 190
Malnutrition 181
Mandrake (also see
    Hallucinogens) 50
Mappine (also see
    Hallucinogens) 53
Marijuana (also see
    Cannabinoids) 67
Marijuana Tax Act 252
Mary Jane (also see
    Cannabinoids) 67
Material (also see Opioids) 27
Mate (also see Hallucinogens) 50
MDA (also see Hallucinogens) 53
Medical history, as a screening
    device 114
Medical problems in drug abusers
    (see Complications of
    drug abuse)
Memory, poor 135
Meningitis 179, 186
Menses, irregular 189
Meperidine (also see Opioids) 27
Meprobamate (also see
    Depressants) 35, 275
Mescaline (also see
    Hallucinogens) 53
Meth (also see Stimulants) 42
Methadone (also see Opioids) 27
METHADONE
    MAINTENANCE 220
    Clinical problems 221
    Dosage 220
    History 220
    Indications for 221
    LAAM 222
    Legal restrictions on 221, 255
    Urinalysis 221, 255
Methadone, use in
    detoxification 211
Methamphetamine (also see
    Stimulants) 42

Methamphetamine + pentobarbital
    (also see Stimulants) 42
Methanol (also see Inhalants) 75
Methaqualone (also see
    Depressants) 34, 35, 275
Methedrine (also see
    Stimulants) 42
3-methoxy-4,5-methylene-
    dioxyamphetamine (also see
    Hallucinogens) 53
Methyl butyl ketone (also see
    Inhalants) 75
Methylene chloride (also see
    Inhalants) 75
Methylenedioxyamphetamine (also
    see Hallucinogens) 53
Methyl ethyl ketone (also see
    Inhalants) 75
Methylmorphine (also see
    Opioids) 27
Methylphenidate (also see
    Stimulants) 41, 42, 278
Methyprylon (also see
    Depressants) 35, 275
Mexican mud (also see
    Opioids) 27
Mexican reds (also see
    Depressants) 35
Microdots (also see
    Hallucinogens) 53
Microinfarcts 188
Micturition 182
Miltown (also see Depressants) 35
Minibennies (also see
    Stimulants) 42
Mintweed (also see
    Phencyclidines) 60
MMDA (also see
    Hallucinogens) 53
Model cement (also see
    Inhalants) 75
MODES OF ADMINISTRATION
    Cannabinoids 71, 72
    Depressants 38, 39
    Hallucinogens 52, 57
    Inhalants 78, 79
    Opioids 30, 31
    Phencyclidines 61, 64
    Stimulants 45, 46
Monkey dust (also see
    Phencyclidines) 60
Morf (also see Opioids) 27
Morfina (also see Opioids) 27
Mormon tea (also see
    Hallucinogens) 50
Morning glory seeds (also see
    Hallucinogens) 53

Morphine (also see Opioids) 24, 27, 272
Morpho (also see Opioids) 27
Morphy (also see Opioids) 27
Mota (also see Cannabinoids) 67
Mouth, dry 135
Mr. *Natural* (also see Hallucinogens) 53
Mud (also see Opioids) 27
Mujer (also see Stimulants) 42
MULTI-DRUG ABUSE
   Detoxification 217
   Prevalence 98
   Treatment, acute 168
   Treatment, long-term 207, 233
Muscle spasm 126, 135
Mushroom (also see Hallucinogens) 53
Mutah (also see Cannabinoids) 67
Myelitis, transverse 185
Myocardial disease 179
Myopathies, chronic fibrosing 186
Myristica (also see Hallucinogens) 53

Naloxone 219
Naloxone test 140, 143, 231
Naltrexone 219
Naphazoline 97
Naphthalene (also see Inhalants) 75
Narcotic Addict Rehabilitation Act 253
Narcotic Control Act 253
Narcotic Drugs Import and Export Act 252
Narcotic Manufacturing Act 253
Narcotics (see Opioids)
National Prescription Audit 92
National Surveys on Drug Abuse 87
Nausea 130
n-Butyl acetate (also see Inhalants) 75
Nebbies (also see Depressants) 35
Necrosis, liver 184
Needle tracks 118, 130, 180
Nembutal (also see Depressants) 35
Neonatal withdrawal syndrome 196
Nephropathy 188
Nerve lesions, peripheral 185
n-Ethyl-1-phenylcyclohexylamine (also see Phencyclidines) 60
Neuromuscular problems related to drug abuse 184
Neuropathy, motor 187

n-Heptane (also see Inhalants) 75
n-Hexane (also see Inhalants) 75
Nimbies (also see Depressants) 35
Nisentil (also see Opioids) 27
Nitrous oxide (also see Inhalants) 73, 75
Noctec (also see Depressants) 35
Noludar (also see Depressants) 35
Nomenclature, drug 23
Non-prescription drugs 97
Nose candy (also see Stimulants) 42
n-Propyl acetate (also see Inhalants) 75
Number (also see Cannabinoids) 67
Numorphan (also see Opioids) 27
Nutmeg (also see Hallucinogens) 53
Nystagmus 135, 187

Obstetrical management of drug abusers 193
Occasional drug use 5
Occlusion, arterial 179
Occlusion, cerebrovascular 180
Op (also see Opioids) 27
Opiate binding sites 15
OPIOIDS 23
   Abuse potential of 273
   Antagonist drugs 26, 218
   Characteristics of 22, 23, 31
   Dependence on 30, 31
   Detoxification from 211
   Dose range 31
   Drugs in the class 24
   Duration of effects 31, 32
   Effects of 28, 29, 31
   Flashback reactions with 157
   In combination with other drugs 168, 169
   Intoxification, acute, with 139
   Methadone maintenance 220
   Mode of administration 30, 31
   Organic brain syndrome with 165
   Overdose with 139
   Panic reactions with 159
   Pattern of abuse 28
   Prescribing indications for 272
   Prevalence of abuse 28, 90
   Psychoactive properties of 31
   Psychotic reactions with 161
   Receptor sites for 15
   Street names for 27
   Tolerance to 29, 31
   Toxicity of 29
   Treatment, long-term 207, 232

Treatment of acute
  reactions 125-128
Treatment of sub-acute
  problems 139, 168
Withdrawal from 150
Opium (also see Opioids) 27
Opium Poppy Control Act 252
Orange sunshine (also see
  Hallucinogens) 53
Oranges (also see Stimulants) 42
ORGANIC BRAIN
  SYNDROME 165
  Clinical manifestations of 129,
    130, 131, 165
  Defined 123
  Diagnosis, differential 165
  Drug reactions 123, 124, 129
  Etiologic agents 165
  Laboratory tests 165
  Psychological state 167
  Symptoms of 165, 166, 167
  Treatment, acute 125-128
  Treatment, sub-acute 131, 138,
    165, 166
  With cannabinoids 167
  With depressants 165
  With hallucinogens 166
  With inhalants 167
  With multiple drugs 170
  With opioids 165
  With phencyclidines 166
  With stimulants 166
Osteomyelitis 190
Outpatient drug-free
  treatment 224
Overdose (see Intoxication, acute)
Overprescribing (also see
  Prescribing practices) 6, 264
Over-the-counter drugs 97
Oxazepam (also see
  Depressants) 34, 35, 274
Oxycodone (also see Opioids) 27
Oxymorphone (also see
  Opioids) 27
Ozone (also see
  Phencyclidines) 60

Paint thinner (also see
  Inhalants) 75
Pajao rojo (also see
  Depressants) 35
Panama red (also see
  Cannabinoids) 67
Pancreatitis 181, 191
PANIC REACTIONS 158
  Clinical manifestations of 158
  Defined 123
  Diagnosis, differential 159
  Drug reactions 123, 124, 129
  Etiologic agents 159
  Laboratory tests 159
  Psychological state 159,
    160, 161
  Symptoms of 159, 160
  Treatment, acute 125
  Treatment, sub-acute 131, 138,
    159, 160, 161
  With cannabinoids 160
  With depressants 159
  With hallucinogens 160
  With inhalants 161
  With multiple drugs 170
  With opioids 159
  With phencyclidines 160
  With stimulants 159
Paper acid (also see
  Hallucinogens) 53
Paradise (also see Stimulants) 42
Paradoxical drug effect 159
Paraldehyde (also see
  Depressants) 35
Paranoia 130, 198
Paregoric (also see Opioids) 27
Parepectolin (also see Opioids) 27
Paresthesias 135
Parkinson syndrome 185
Passion flower (also see
  Hallucinogens) 50
Patient behavior, as a screening
  device 116
Patient compliance with drug
  regimens 279
Patient history 129, 138
Patient "hustlers" 280
Patient interview, as a screening
  device 115
Patient questionnaire, as a
  screening device 114
PATTERNS OF ABUSE
  Cannabinoids 66
  Depressants 36
  Hallucinogens 52
  Inhalants 74
  Opioids 28
  Phencyclidines 61
  Stimulants 43
PCE (also see
  Phencyclidines) 60
PCP (also see
  Phencyclidines) 60
PCPy (also see
  Phencyclidines) 60
Peace (also see
  Phencyclidines) 60

PeaCe pill (also see Phencyclidines) 60
Peaches (also see Stimulants) 42
Pentazocine (also see Opioids) 27
Pentazocine, detoxification from 214
Pentobarbital (also see Depressants) 33, 35, 274
Pep pills (also see Stimulants) 42
Percodan (also see Opioids) 27
Perforated septum 118
Perico (also see Stimulants) 42
Peritoneal dialysis 143
Periwinkle (also see Hallucinogens) 50
Persian (also see Opioids) 27
Persian brown (also see Opioids) 27
Peruvian flake (also see Stimulants) 42
Pethadol (also see Opioids) 27
Peyote (also see Hallucinogens) 53
Pharmaceutical powder (also see Stimulants) 42
Pharyngitis 188
Phenargan with codeine (also see Opioids) 27
PHENCYCLIDINES 58
  Analogs of 60
  Characteristics of 23, 58, 63
  Dependence on 63, 64
  Dose range 61, 62, 64
  Drugs in the class 58
  Duration of effects 61, 63
  Effects of 61, 63
  Flashback reactions with 158
  In combination with other drugs 170
  Intoxication, acute, with 145
  Mode of administration 61, 63
  Organic brain syndrome with 166
  Overdose with 145
  Panic reactions with 160
  Pattern of abuse 61
  Prevalence of abuse 59, 94
  Psychoactive properties of 63, 64
  Psychotic reactions with 164
  Street names for 60
  Tolerance to 62, 63
  Toxicity of 62
  Treatment, long-term 207, 232
  Treatment of acute reactions 125-128
  Treatment of sub-acute problems 145, 156, 158, 160, 164, 166
  Withdrawal from 156
Phenmetrazine (also see Stimulants) 41, 42, 278
Phenobarbital (also see Depressants) 34, 35, 274
Phenobarbital substitution technique 143, 144, 215
1-(1-phenylcyclohexyl)pyrrolidine (also see Phencyclidines) 60
Phenylephrine 97
Phenylethylamines (also see Hallucinogens) 53
Phenylisopropylamines (also see Hallucinogens) 53
Phenylpropanolamine 97
PHP (also see Phencyclidines) 60
Physical abnormalities in drug abusers 177
Physical dependence on drugs (see Dependence, physical)
PHYSICAL EFFECTS OF DRUG ABUSE
  Cannabinoids 66, 68, 71
  Depressants 37, 39
  Hallucinogens 52, 55, 57
  Inhalants 76, 79
  Opioids 28, 31
  Phencyclidines 61, 63
  Stimulants 43, 46
Physical examination 116, 129, 131
Physician attitudes toward drug abuse 113
Physicians who abuse drugs (see Drug abuse by physicians)
Physiological factors in drug abuse 14
Pigmentary problems 118
Pigmentation, dark 180
Piloerection 118, 130
Pink Ladies (also see Depressants) 35
Pinks (also see Depressants) 35
Placentae abruptio 195
Placidyl (also see Depressants) 35
Planograms 119
Plegine (also see Stimulants) 42
Plexitis 184
Pneumonia 179, 187
Poisoning of children/ adolescents 172
Polvo (also see Opioids) 27
Polvo blanco (also see Stimulants) 42

Polyarteritis 179, 190
Poppers (also see Inhalants) 74
Poppy (also see Opioids) 27
Pop scars 118
Porter Act 252
Postoperative analgesia 192
Postoperative withdrawal 193
Pot (also see Cannabinoids) 67
Potentiation of drug effects 168
Prazepam (also see
    Depressants) 34, 35, 274
Predictors of drug abuse 9
Pregnancy 194
Preludin (also see Stimulants) 42
Premature labor 195
Pre-Sate (also see Stimulants) 42
PRESCRIBING PRACTICES 263
    Abuse potential,
        depressants 275
    Abuse potential, opioids 273
    Abuse potential, stimulants 278
    Compliance problems 279
    Controlled substances
        schedule 271
    Deceptions employed by drug
        abusers 281
    Diversion of drugs 265
    Drug-abusing patient,
        identifying 280
    Drug-abusing physicians as poor
        prescribers 265
    Federal restrictions 269
    Guidelines for prescribing 267,
        279, 282
    Indications for depressants 274
    Indications for opioids 272
    Indications for stimulants 277
    Overprescribing 264
    Prescription alteration, forgery,
        theft 265, 281
    Prescription writing
        safeguards 265, 267
    Preventing misuse of prescribed
        drugs 267, 280, 282
    Script docs 266
    State restrictions 270
    Underprescribing 264
PREVALENCE OF
    DRUG ABUSE 88
    Alcohol in combination with 89
    Cannabinoids 66, 95
    Deaths from drug abuse 89
    Depressants 36, 91
    Drug Abuse Warning Network
        (DAWN) 86
    Emergency room visits 89
    Hallucinogens 52, 93

    In adolescents 90, 91, 92, 94,
        95, 96
    In general patient
        population 113
    Inhalants 74, 96
    In older adults 90, 91, 92, 94,
        95, 96
    In physician population 285
    International data 99
    In U.S. population 88
    In young adults 90, 91, 92, 94,
        95, 96
    Multi-drug abuse 98
    National Surveys on Drug
        Abuse 87
    Opioids 28, 90
    Over-the-counter drugs 97
    Phencyclidines 59, 94
    Stimulants 41, 92
PREVENTION 299
    Abstention vs. moderation 300
    Counseling adolescents 302
    Employer programs 306
    Of physician drug abuse 294
    Patient information 310
    Physician's role in 300, 309
    Preventing abuse of prescribed
        drugs 267, 280, 282
    School programs 305
Prickly poppy (also see
    Hallucinogens) 50
Product (also see Opioids) 27
Propoxyphene (also see
    Opioids) 27
Propoxyphene, detoxification
    from 215
Pruritis 118, 181
Pseudo acanthosis nigricans 118
Pseudocaine 97
Psilocybin (also see
    Hallucinogens) 53
Psilocyn (also see
    Hallucinogens) 53
Psychiatric disorders in drug
    abusers 198
PSYCHOACTIVE PROPERTIES
    OF ABUSED DRUGS
    Cannabinoids 71, 72
    Depressants 38, 39, 40
    Hallucinogens 56, 57
    Inhalants 78, 79, 80
    Opioids 31
    Phencyclidines 63, 64
    Stimulants 44, 46
Psychological dependence on drugs
    (see Dependence, psychological)

PSYCHOLOGICAL EFFECTS
OF DRUG ABUSE
  Cannabinoids   66, 67, 71, 72
  Depressants   37, 39
  Hallucinogens   54, 55, 57
  Inhalants   76, 79
  Opioids   29, 31
  Phencyclidines   61, 63
  Stimulants   43, 46
Psychological factors in drug abuse   10
Psychological history, as a screening device   116
PSYCHOLOGICAL MANIFESTATIONS OF ACUTE DRUG REACTIONS
  Flashback reactions   157, 158
  Intoxication, acute (overdose)   140, 142, 144, 145, 146, 147, 149
  Organic brain syndrome   167
  Panic reactions   159, 160, 161
  Psychotic reactions   161, 162, 163
  Withdrawal   151, 153, 155, 156
Psychological problems, feigned   281
Psychological problems related to drug abuse   69, 198
Psychosis, toxic   130, 131, 135
PSYCHOTIC REACTIONS   161
  Clinical manifestations of   129, 130, 131, 161
  Defined   123
  Diagnosis, differential   161
  Drug reactions   123, 124, 129
  Etiologic agents   161
  Laboratory tests   161
  Symptoms of   161, 162, 163, 164, 165
  Treatment, acute   125-128
  Treatment, sub-acute   131, 138, 161, 162, 163
  With cannabinoids   164
  With depressants   162
  With hallucinogens   163
  With inhalants   165
  With multiple drugs   170
  With opioids   161
  With phencyclidines   164
  With stimulants   162
Pulmonary edema   187, 192
Pulmonary embolism   179
Pulmonary fibrosis   130
Pulmonary hypertension   188
Pulmonary problems, postoperative   192

Pupils, dilated   135
Pupils, pinpoint   130, 136
Purple hearts (also see Depressants)   35
Purple haze (also see Hallucinogens)   53
Purpura   118
Pyelograms   119

Quaalude (also see Depressants)   35
Quads (also see Depressants)   35
Quas (also see Depressants)   35

Rainbows (also see Depressants)   35
Reality base   125
Receptor sites   15, 16, 218
Redbirds (also see Depressants)   35
Red devils (also see Depressants)   35
Red dragon (also see Hallucinogens)   53
Reds (also see Depressants)   35
Reds & blues (also see Depressants)   35
Reefer (also see Cannabinoids)   67
Referring a patient for treatment   238
Reflexes, hyperactive   131, 136
Regular drug use   5
Rehabilitation (see Treatment, long-term)
REM sleep   155
Renal colic, feigned   281
Renal problems related to drug abuse   188
Reproductive problems related to drug abuse   68, 189
Respirator   126
Respiratory depression   130, 136, 187
Respiratory problems related to drug abuse   68, 187
Restlessness   129
Rhabdomyolysis, acute   185
Rhinorrhea   130, 136
Ritalin (also see Stimulants)   42
Roach (also see Cannabinoids)   67
Robitussin A-C (also see Opioids)   27
Rocket fuel (also see Phencyclidines)   60
Rocks (also see Stimulants)   42
Room odorants (also see Inhalants)   75

Rosas (also see Stimulants)   42
Roses (also see Stimulants)   42
Rubber cement (also see
   Inhalants)   75
Rufus (also see Opioids)   27
Rush (also see Inhalants)   74
Salacen (also see Depressants)   35
Salicylates   98
Sanorex (also see Stimulants)   42
Satan's Scent (also see
   Inhalants)   74
Sativa (also see Cannabinoids)   67
Scag (also see Opioids)   27
Schedule of controlled drugs
   269, 271
Schizophrenia   148, 200
Scotch broom (also see
   Hallucinogens)   50
SCREENING FOR
   DRUG ABUSE   113
   Cutaneous signs   117
   Diagnostic tests   119
   Medical history   114
   Patient behavior   116
   Patient interview   115
   Patient questionnaire   114
   Physical examination   116
   Psychological history   116
   Social history   116
   Symptoms   115
Script docs   266
Scuffle (also see
   Phencyclidines)   60
Secobarbital (also see
   Depressants)   33, 35, 274
Seconal (also see Depressants)   35
Seizures   128, 135, 185, 186
Self-induced tattoos   118
Septic problems related to drug
   abuse   179, 189
Serax (also see Depressants)   35
Serenity-tranquility-peace pill
   (also see Hallucinogens)   53
Sernyl (also see
   Phencyclidines)   60
Sernylan (also see
   Phencyclidines)   60
Sexual disorders of drug
   abusers   197
Sherman (also see
   Phencyclidines)   60
Shock   128
Shooting tattoos   118
Silly putty (also see
   Hallucinogens)   53
Sinsemilla (also see
   Cannabinoids)   67

Sinuses, draining   130
Skeletal problems related to
   drug abuse   190
Skin infections   118
Skin infestations   118
Skin picking   136
Skin tracks   118
Sleep aids   97
Sleep disturbances   136
Sleepiness   129, 136
Sleeping pills (also see
   Depressants)   35
Smack (also see Opioids)   27
Smash (also see Cannabinoids)   67
Smoke (also see Cannabinoids)   67
Snakeroot (also see
   Hallucinogens)   50
Snow (also see Stimulants)   42
Soapers (also see Depressants)   35
Social history, as a screening
   device   116
Sociological factors in drug
   abuse   11
Soles (also see Cannabinoids)   67
Somnos (also see Depressants)   35
Sopes (also see Depressants)   35
Sopor (also see Depressants)   35
Speed (also see Stimulants)   42
Speech, slurred   131, 136
Sperm, abnormal   69, 189
Sperm count, low   189
Sperm motility   69, 189
Sphaceloderma   118, 180
Splash (also see Stimulants)   42
Spray shoe polish (also see
   Inhalants)   75
Stare, blank   136
Status epilepticus   185
Stick (also see Cannabinoids)   67
Stillbirth   189
STIMULANTS   40
   Abuse potential of   278
   Characteristics of   23, 40, 46
   Dependence on   44, 46
   Detoxification from   216
   Dose range of   45
   Drugs in the class   40
   Duration of effects   45, 46, 47
   Effects of   43, 46
   Flashback reactions with   157
   In combination with other
      drugs   169
   Intoxication, acute, with   143
   Mode of administration   45, 46
   Organic brain syndrome
      with   166
   Overdose with   143

Panic reactions with 159
Pattern of abuse 43
Prescribing indications for 277
Prevalence of abuse 41, 92
Psychoactive properties of 44, 46
Psychotic reactions with 162
Street names for 42
Tolerance to 43, 46
Toxicity of 44
Treatment, long-term 207, 232
Treatment of acute reactions 125-128
Treatment of sub-acute problems 143, 154, 157, 159, 162, 166
Withdrawal from 154
Stofa (also see Opioids) 27
STP (also see Hallucinogens) 53
STREET NAMES FOR DRUGS 23
  Cannabinoids 67
  Depressants 35
  Hallucinogens 53
  Inhalants 75
  Opioids 27
  Phencyclidines 60
  Stimulants 42
Stuff (also see Opioids) 27
Stumblers (also see Depressants) 35
Styrene (also see Inhalants) 75
Sudden Sniffing Death (SSD) 149
Suicidal patients 141, 155, 171, 198, 233
Sunshine (also see Hallucinogens) 53
Supergrass (also see Phencyclidines) 60
Supportive care 128
Surfer (also see Phencyclidines) 60
Surgical management of drug abusers 191
Suspiciousness 130, 136
Sweating 130, 137
SYMPTOMS OF ACUTE DRUG REACTIONS 132
  Flashback reactions 157, 158
  Intoxication, acute (overdose) 139, 142, 143, 145, 147, 148
  Organic brain syndrome 165, 166, 167
  Panic reactions 159, 160
  Psychotic reactions 161, 162, 163, 164, 165
  Withdrawal 150, 152, 155, 156
Symptoms of drug abuse 115

Synalar (also see Phencyclidines) 60
Synanon 222
Syphilis 181

T (also see Phencyclidines) 60
Tachyarrhythmias 179
Tachycardia 129, 137
Talkativeness 137
Talwin (also see Opioids) 27
Tattoos 118, 180
TCP (also see Phencyclidines) 60
Tea (also see Cannabinoids) 67
Tenuate (also see Stimulants) 42
Tepanil (also see Stimulants) 42
Tetanus 189
Tetrachloroethylene (also see Inhalants) 75
THC (also see Cannabinoids) 67
The Force (also see Hallucinogens) 53
Therapeutic communities 222
1-(1/-2-thienyl/-cyclohexyl) piperidine (also see Phencyclidines) 60
Thing (also see Opioids) 27
Thorn apple (also see Hallucinogens) 50
Thrombophlebitis 118, 179
Thrusters (also see Stimulants) 42
Tic douloureux, feigned 281
Tic tac (also see Phencyclidines) 60
Tincture of opium (also see Opioids) 27
Tobacco (also see Hallucinogens) 50
Tolerance, mechanism of 7
TOLERANCE, POTENTIAL FOR
  Cannabinoids 70, 71
  Depressants 38, 39
  Hallucinogens 55, 57
  Inhalants 77, 79
  Opioids 29, 31
  Phencyclidines 62, 63
  Stimulants 43, 46
Toluene (also see Inhalants) 75
Tooies (also see Depressants) 35
Toot (also see Stimulants) 42
Toothache, feigned 281
Tourniquet pigmentation 118
Toxemia 195
TOXICITY OF DRUGS OF ABUSE
  Cannabinoids 70
  Depressants 37
  Hallucinogens 55
  Inhalants 78

Opioids 29
Phencyclidines 62
Stimulants 44
Toxicologic screens 126
TPCP (also see
  Phencyclidines) 60
Tracheal intubation 126
Tranq (also see
  Phencyclidines) 60
Tranxene (also see
  Depressants) 35
Trauma 126, 131
TREATMENT, LONG-TERM 207
  Acupuncture 228
  Aftercare 243
  Behavior modification 226
  Biofeedback relaxation
    therapy 227
  Counseling, individual 225
  Counterconditioning 227
  Crisis service 234
  Current methods 207
  Dependence, estimating degree
    of 230
  Desensitization techniques 227
  Detoxification 208
  Drop-in centers 225
  Extinction techniques 227
  Family therapy 225
  Free clinics 225
  Follow-up care 243
  Himmelsbach rating scale 231
  History of 203
  Hypnosis 227
  Indications for 226
  Initiating therapy 237
  Medical problems,
    coexisting 233
  Methadone maintenance 220
  Multimodality approach 208
  Naloxone test 231
  Needs, assessing 228
  Of cannabinoid abusers 232
  Of depressant abusers 232
  Of hallucinogen abusers 232
  Of inhalant abusers 232
  Of multi-drug abusers 233
  Of opioid abusers 232
  Of phencyclidine abusers 232
  Of stimulant abusers 232
  Outpatient drug-free
    treatment 224
  Patient history, obtaining a 229
  Problems of 225
  Psychiatric disorders,
    coexisting 233
  Referring a patient 238

Rehabilitation 234
Resources, identifying 229
Stabilization 234
Suicidal patients 233
Therapeutic communities 222
Treatment method, selecting
  a 234, 235
Treatment plan, developing
  a 232, 235
Treatment programs, information
  on 238, 239
Treatment setting, selecting
  a 233
TREATMENT OF ACUTE
  DRUG REACTIONS 125, 129
  Flashback reactions 156
  Intoxication, acute 138
  Organic brain syndrome 165
  Overdose 138
  Panic reactions 158
  Poisoning of children/
    adolescents 172
  Psychotic reactions 161
  Suicidal patients 171
  To cannabinoids 147, 156, 158,
    160, 164, 167
  To depressants 141, 152, 157,
    159, 162, 165
  To hallucinogens 144, 156, 157,
    160, 163, 166
  To inhalants 148, 156, 158, 161,
    165, 167
  To multiple drugs 168
  To opioids 139, 150, 157, 159,
    161, 165
  To phencyclidines 145, 156,
    158, 160, 164, 166
  To stimulants 143, 154, 157,
    159, 162, 166
  Violent patients 171
  Withdrawal 149
Treatment of physicians who
  abuse drugs 291
TREATMENT RESTRICTIONS
  Confidentiality regulations 257
  Disclosure of information 257
  Informed consent 256
  Legal requirements 256
  Parental consent 256
  Record-keeping
    requirements 256
  Reporting requirements 257
Trees (also see Depressants) 35
Tremor 131, 137
Trench mouth 118
Trends in drug abuse (also see
  Prevalence of drug abuse) 85

Trichloroethylene (also see Inhalants) 75
Trihexyphenidyl (also see Hallucinogens) 53
Truck drivers (also see Stimulants) 42
Tubercular skin tests 119
Tuberculosis 188
Tuinal (also see Depressants) 35
Tybatran (also see Depressants) 35
Tybamate (also see Depressants) 35
Tylenol with codeine (also see Opioids) 27

Ulcerations, nasal septum 130
Ulcerations, skin 118, 130
Ulcer, perforated 191
Underprescribing (also see Prescribing practices) 264
Uppers (also see Stimulants) 42
Urinalysis 119, 126, 221, 255
Urticaria 118, 181
Uterine atony 195
Uvulitis 188

Valerian (also see Hallucinogens) 50
Valium (also see Depressants) 35
Valmid (also see Depressants) 35
Vascular changes 179
Venereal condylotoma 195
Ventricular fibrillation 180
Verstran (also see Depressants) 35
Violent patients 137, 171, 198
Vital signs 125, 130, 131
Volatile substances (also see Inhalants) 75
Vomiting 137
Voranil (also see Stimulants) 42

Wake-ups (also see Stimulants) 42
Water (also see Stimulants) 42
Wedges (also see Hallucinogens) 53
Weed (also see Cannabinoids) 67
Whippets (also see Inhalants) 73
White (also see Stimulants) 42

White Lightning (also see Hallucinogens) 53
Wild lettuce (also see Hallucinogens) 50
Windowpanes (also see Hallucinogens) 53
Windshield washing fluids (also see Inhalants) 75
WITHDRAWAL 149
 Clinical manifestations 129, 130, 131, 149
 Defined 123
 Diagnosis, differential 129, 149
 Drug reactions 123, 124, 129
 Etiologic agents 149
 From cannabinoids 156
 From depressants 152, 169
 From hallucinogens 156
 From inhalants 156
 From multiple drugs 168, 169
 From opioids 150, 169
 From phencyclidines 156
 From stimulants 154, 169
 Laboratory tests 150
 Neonatal 196
 Psychological state 151, 153, 155, 156
 Symptoms 132, 150, 152, 155, 156
 Treatment, acute 125-128
 Treatment, sub-acute 131, 138, 151, 153, 155, 156
Wormwood (also see Hallucinogens) 50
Wrist scars 118

Xylene (also see Inhalants) 75

Yawning 137
Yellow jackets (also see Depressants) 35
Yellows (also see Depressants) 35
Yerba (also see Cannabinoids) 67
Yohimba (also see Hallucinogens) 50

Zig-zag man (also see Hallucinogens) 53